CONTINENTAL DIVIDE

CONTINENTAL

DIVIDE

A HISTORY OF AMERICAN MOUNTAINEERING

MAURICE ISSERMAN

W. W. NORTON & COMPANY
Independent Publishers Since 1923
NEW YORK · LONDON

Manufacturing by RRDonnelley Harrisonburg
Book design by Daniel Lagin
Production manager: Julia Druskin

ISBN 978-0-393-06850-4

W. W. Norton & Company, Inc.
500 Fifth Avenue, New York, N.Y. 10110
www.wwnorton.com

W. W. Norton & Company Ltd.
Castle House, 75/76 Wells Street, London W1T 3QT

1 2 3 4 5 6 7 8 9 0

Continental Divide *is dedicated to those Oregon friends in whose company, in younger days, I first encountered mountains.*

I keep a mountain anchored off eastward a little way, which I ascend in my dreams both awake and asleep.

—HENRY DAVID THOREAU,
NOVEMBER 16, 1857

What we call a mountain is . . . in fact a collaboration of the physical forms of the world with the imagination of humans—a mountain of the mind. . . . Mountains—like deserts, polar tundra, deep oceans, jungles and all the other wild landscapes that we have romanticized into being—are simply there, and there they remain, their physical structures rearranged gradually over time by the forces of geology and weather, but continuing to exist over and beyond human perceptions of them. But they are also the products of human perception; they have been imagined into existence down the centuries.

—ROBERT McFARLANE,
MOUNTAINS OF THE MIND, 2003

CONTENTS

CONTINENTAL DIVIDE

PREFACE AND ACKNOWLEDGMENTS

This is a book about mountains, and what they have meant to Americans over nearly four centuries, especially to that minority of Americans who climb them. At the dawn of American mountaineering, in New England in 1642, the population of the British colonies in North America included exactly one mountaineer, and he was deemed mad by his contemporaries. Three hundred and seventy-two years later, in 2014, approximately six and a half million Americans went climbing (either outdoors or in a climbing gym)—which sounds like a lot, except when compared to the fifty-one-plus million Americans who went fishing that year, or the nearly forty-one million who went running or jogging. And while climbers are no longer condemned as insane (for the most part) by their fellow Americans, neither are they considered quite as respectable as joggers and fishing enthusiasts.[1]

And yet, if Americans remain ambivalent about mountaineers, mountains themselves are regarded as sacred places in the American landscape, second only to battlefields, part of the "mystic chords of memory" that Abraham Lincoln referred to in his first inaugural address, and that bind together the nation. The experience of touring a Gettysburg battlefield is expected to leave the visitor improved and even exalted. A visit to a mountain summit is supposed to offer a similar (if less sanguinary) sense of uplift, even if accomplished by mechanical transport (Americans may be the only people on earth who brag about *driving* to a mountaintop, as the ubiquitous "This Car Climbed Mount Washington" bumper stickers in the Northeast attest). The present American veneration of mountains did not always exist, and this book is an attempt to account for how it came to be.

This is my second book devoted to the history of mountaineering. The first, coauthored with fellow historian and occasional climbing partner Stewart Weaver, was *Fallen Giants: A History of Himalayan Mountaineering from the Age of Empire to the Age of Extremes*, published in 2008. That book began with a disclaimer that I feel honor-bound to repeat here: I am not (alas) a climber of the caliber of those whose exploits I will be chronicling in this book. Many of the climbs I describe in these pages have been recounted before by the actual participants, and some of those (among them Henry David Thoreau, John Muir, Charlie Houston, Bob Bates, Bradford Washburn, and Tom Hornbein) were writers who brought grace and insight to the task.

What I bring to this project is a historian's perspective. Which is to say that I start from the assumption that American climbers, from 1642 to the present, were and are the products of their own eras, and the reasons why they climb, as well as the ways that they climb, can help map a larger cultural, political, and social terrain. *Continental Divide* is thus a book about American history, as seen through the prism of mountaineering.

Although I have tried to provide as comprehensive an account as possible, I have not attempted to write the "Encyclopedia of American Mountaineering." Inevitably, in weighing the contractual limits of the space available to me, the likely limits of readers' patience, and the brevity of our allotted time on earth, I had some difficult choices to make about which climbs and climbers to include or—alas, all too often—to omit. I also felt that with the establishment of mountaineering as a mass participation sport in the United States in the mid-1960s, I had reached the logical outcome of the story I was attempting to tell. I thus offer only the briefest glance at the half century that followed, a time of first-rate mountaineering achievements including, as I was putting the finishing touches on this book, Tommy Caldwell and Kevin Jorgeson's first free ascent of the Dawn Wall of Yosemite's El Capitan in January 2015.

In the seven years that I have been at work on this book, I have accumulated a small mountain of debt to those who have assisted along the way. Two institutions, one in the East and one in the West, were critical to my research: the Appalachian Mountain Club Library and Archives in Boston, Massachusetts; and the Henry S. Hall Jr. Library of the American Alpine Club in Golden, Colorado. I spent many hours of research in their pleasant reading rooms, and bombarded their patient and ever-helpful staff members with literally hundreds of follow-up e-mails requesting additional information. In particular, I am indebted to Becky Fullerton, director of the AMC library, as well as Dana Gerschel, director, and Katie Sauter, manager, of the AAC library, and their assistants, Allison Bailey and Dan Cohen. Reid S. Larson, reference librarian at Hamilton College, was also invaluable, as were Rare Book Room director Christian Goodwillie and photographer Marianita Peaslee. So, too, have been librarians at the Bancroft Library of UC Berkeley, the Department of Special Collections at Stanford University, and the Howard Gotlieb Archival Research Center at Boston University.

I am also grateful to the following individuals (climbers, climbing historians, climber friends, and relations) for their assistance: Kathy Bedayn, Walter R. Borneman, Nick Clinch, Gretchen Daiber, Greg Glade, Sallie Greenwood, Tom Hornbein, Katie Ives, Steve Jervis, Bruce Johnson, Russell Lawson, David Mazel, Jim McCarthy, Bernadette McDonald, John Middendorf, Pat Morrow, Phil Powers, Bill Putnam, Todd Rayne, Zac Robinson, Steve Roper, Martha A. Sandweiss, Jay Taylor, and Stewart Weaver. Doubtless there are others I'm forgetting, for which I apologize. Any errors that have crept into the pages that follow are, of course, solely my own responsibility.

CHAPTER ONE

PIONEERS, 1642–1842

Well could I curse away a winter's night,
Though standing naked on a mountain top,
Where biting cold would never let grass grow,
And think it but a minute spent in sport.

—WILLIAM SHAKESPEARE,
HENRY VI, ACT 3, SCENE 2

And it shall come to pass in the last days, that the mountain of the LORD's house shall be established in the top of the mountains, and shall be exalted above the hills; and all nations shall flow unto it.

—ISAIAH 2:2, AUTHORIZED
(KING JAMES) VERSION

In the spring of 1642, in what was then the Upper Plantation of Massachusetts Bay Colony—later the colony, and still later the state, of New Hampshire—Darby Field, a thirty-two-year-old Englishman of Irish descent, was doing something unprecedented in England's newly established North American colonies: climbing a mountain.

Field, a resident of the community of Pascataquack (present-day Durham, New Hampshire), left no written record of his climb or indication of its purpose. But others, including John Winthrop, governor of Massachusetts Bay Colony, took note of this odd endeavor.[1] Mountain-climbing was something few people anywhere did in the seventeenth century, and Field seems to have been regarded by his contemporaries as a bit eccentric, if harmless. Following his death in 1649, it was remarked that his was a life of "merriness marred by insanity."[2]

Whatever his state of mind, on a cloudy spring day in 1642, Field picked his way through the stony debris on the upper slopes of what he called the "White Hill." One or two Native Americans from the local Abenaki tribe, the Pigwacket, reluctantly accompanied him; several others had accompanied him up the Saco River as far as the mountain's base and then refused to proceed, fearing evil consequences.[3]

The Pigwacket knew Field's White Hill as Agiocochook; today it is called Mount Washington, at 6,288 feet the highest peak in the northeastern United States.[4] Europeans had spotted the mountain soon after the discovery of the New World. Italian navigator John Cabot, sailing on behalf of the English, may have glimpsed it in 1497, and Italian navigator Giovanni da Verrazzano, sailing on behalf of France, definitely did in 1524. Frenchman Samuel de Champlain saw it in 1605, as did Englishman John Smith in 1614. In Smith's 1616 *Description of New England*, he noted that the rivers of the New England coast "are most pure, proceeding from the intrals [entrails] of rockie mountains."[5] By 1672, the range, which runs 70 miles across present-day central and northern New Hampshire into western Maine, acquired its enduring name, the White Mountains. Seventeenth-century travelers described the mountains as covered in snow year-round; this is no longer true, but it was possible in the "Little Ice Age" that prevailed in the Northern Hemisphere in the seventeenth and eighteenth centuries.[6]

The White Mountains are part of a chain of ranges known as the Appalachians that stretches more than 1,600 miles from near the southern bank of Canada's Saint Lawrence River to Alabama's Gulf Coastal Plain. In addition to the White Mountains, the Appalachians include the Acadian highlands, Green Mountains, Taconic Mountains, Berkshire

Hills, Allegheny Mountains, and Blue Ridge Mountains. (The Adirondacks, often thought of as part of the Appalachians, are actually part of the Laurentian mountain range that stretches from upper New York State into southern Quebec.) These ranges together represent the Eastern Continental Divide, separating the Atlantic Seaboard watershed from the Gulf of Mexico watershed. (The name "Appalachian" derived from a tribe of Indians, the Apalachee, encountered by Spanish explorer Álvar Núñez

This 1562 map of the New World, by Diego Gutiérrez, shows North American mountains.

Cabeza de Vaca in northern Florida in 1528. The Apalachee actually lived nowhere near the range that commemorates the tribe.)[7]

When Europeans caught their first glimpses of the Appalachians, it was a reunion of sorts. Beginning about 480 million years ago, a series of collisions between what geologists call the North American craton (the stable interior of the continent) and multiple oceanic and continental plates started the formation of the supercontinent Pangaea. By about 300 million years ago, the African Plate approached North America, and the resulting collision of continental crust pushed bedrock upward, creating a range of mountains that reached Himalayan altitudes near the middle of the supercontinent. When Pangaea began to break up about 220 million years ago, the formation of the Atlantic Ocean divided the western and eastern branches of the complex. In North America, what remained was the core of the Appalachians, while in Europe and Africa, a series of ranges stretched from the uplands of Norway and the Scottish Highlands to the Atlas Mountains of Morocco, Algeria, and Tunisia.[8]

As Darby Field and his two native companions neared the summit of the White Hill in 1642, the clouds lifted. From the flat top of the mountain, they could peer over the edge to the east and see a broad glacial cirque with a steep headwall (Tuckerman Ravine). Down the west side they could see a rocky slope descending to two alpine lakes (Lakes of the Clouds). Immediately to the north, the mountain fell away, as Winthrop recorded, "into such a precipice, as they could scarce discern to the bottom" (the Great Gulf); the climbers also saw, to the north, nearby summits "rising above the rest, but far beneath them."[9] Those peaks, later known as part of the White Mountains' Presidential Range, include 5,712-foot Mount Jefferson, 5,774-foot Mount Adams, and 5,367-foot Mount Madison—three of the seven peaks in the Whites that top the 5,000-foot mark, and of the forty-eight that top 4,000 feet.

Field made a return trip and second ascent of Mount Washington about a month later, with five or six others "of his company"; whether his companions on that climb were native or European-born is unclear from Governor Winthrop's account. That time, he brought back some stones from the mountaintop, which, Winthrop recorded, Field "supposed had been diamonds." Early reports of Field's climb prompted "divers others" to follow in his footsteps, Winthrop noted, "but they found nothing worth their pains."[10]

Diamonds do not lie around for the picking atop Mount Washington. All that Darby Field had to show for his efforts were some worthless pieces of quartzite or mica schist. That, and a summit altitude record in North American mountaineering that would last for nearly a century and a half.[11] As for Mount Washington and the surrounding summits, once the excitement of 1642 had passed, no more than a handful of climbers visited them until the early nineteenth century.[12]

THE CITY ON A HILL

John Winthrop famously compared Massachusetts Bay Colony to a "city on a hill," a godly community that less well-situated souls would look up to. But it was a modest hill, not a high peak, he had in mind. In the King James Bible, English Puritans like Winthrop could find some wonderful evocations of mountain splendor, as in Isaiah 2:2, where the Lord's house is "exalted above the hills." Noah's Ark found landfall from the flood atop Mount Ararat, Moses received the Ten Commandments from God on Mount Sinai, and he climbed Mount Pisgah to peer over into the Promised Land, so mountains had some positive associations for God's Chosen People. On the other hand, in the book of Genesis, where God's creations are listed, mountains go unmentioned, leading medieval theologians to conclude that in its earliest days, the earth's surface was uniform, flat, and fertile. It was Adam and Eve's expulsion from paradise, or perhaps the deluge sent in Noah's time to punish the wickedness of men, that had thrown up the mountains—cold, dark, dangerous places where men and women could not live and crops could not be sown. As Protestant theologian Martin Luther wrote in a commentary on the Old Testament, "Even the earth is compelled to bear sin's curse," as revealed in its mountainscapes.[13]

Christian ambiguity regarding mountains was manifest in the New Testament. Jesus rose to heaven from Jerusalem's Mount of Olives—a good thing indeed. On the other hand, according to the Gospel of Matthew, when Satan wished to tempt Jesus, he took him "to an exceedingly high mountain" to view the glories of the kingdoms of the earth, the better to distract him from fulfilling his divine mission. As late as the seventeenth century, it was still commonly believed in Europe that mountains were the abodes of witches and dragons.[14]

Most of the Protestant dissenters (Pilgrims and Puritans) who came to New England in the early years of the seventeenth century had been raised in the flat, open country of eastern England. Few, if any, had seen a mountain even as high as Scotland's Ben Nevis, at 4,409 feet the highest in Britain (which would go unclimbed until 1771).[15] Mountains were outside of the British colonists' experience, and when they employed mountains as literary devices in sermons and histories, they usually linked the image with something unpleasant. In his *History of Plymouth Plantation*, William Bradford, governor of Plymouth Colony, complained that his fellow pilgrims were unable to "go up to the top of Pisgah, to view from this wilderness and more goodly country to feed their hopes," for they were surrounded on all sides by "a hideous and desolate wilderness, full of wild beasts and wild men."[16] A half century later, Nathaniel Saltonstall, historian of the bloody Indian uprising in New England of 1672 known as King Philip's War, complained that the native combatants hid themselves away in "Boggs, rocky Mountains, and Thickets," from which they launched devilish attacks on white settlers.[17]

Native Americans in the New England region shared the negative perspective on high places that was characteristic of the European newcomers. No archaeological evidence from the precolonial era suggests that they ever climbed any of the region's loftier mountains, though they may have hunted on or crossed some of the lower slopes. The tales they told of encounters with mountain spirits were not the sort that would encourage exploration of high places. John Giles of Pemaquid, Maine, captured at age twelve by Abenaki Indians in 1689 during King William's War, later recorded stories he had heard during his captivity, including one about three Indians who violated the taboo against climbing to the summit of 5,268-foot Mount Katahdin. On the fourth day of the attempted climb, they became "strangely disordered with delirium," and the next thing they knew found themselves returned to a spot near the base of the mountain. "How they came to be thus transported they could not conjecture," Giles reported, "unless the genii of the place had conveyed them."[18]

These unfavorable sentiments regarding mountains dominated the New England mind well into the eighteenth century. The revivalist Jonathan Edwards, best remembered for preaching hellfire and damnation in his "Sinners in the Hands of an Angry God" sermon, was known on other occasions to evoke the beauty of "flowery meadows and gentle breezes of the wind" to celebrate "the sweet benevolence of Jesus Christ."[19] But mountains remained for Edwards and his contemporaries, as for the original Puritan settlers of New England, an impediment to holiness. In a funeral sermon in 1733, Edwards compared the individual sinner's path into heaven to a wilderness journey: "There are many mountains, rocks and rough places that we must go over in the way."[20] In early New England, mountains were obstacles to be avoided, sanctuaries for bloodthirsty enemies, and certainly not places to be appreciated for either natural beauty or spiritual inspiration.

SOUTHEASTERN MOUNTAIN EXPLORATION

Unlike Darby Field's quixotic search for diamonds on Mount Washington, mountaineering pioneers to the south had more attainable ends in mind: the pelts of beavers and other fur-bearing mammals. Fur traders, in the vanguard of explorers of the southern Appalachians, unfortunately left few records of their visits to high places. Abraham Wood, one of Virginia's earliest settlers and a prominent landowner, built a fur-trading post at the falls of the Appomattox River. From there he dispatched several exploring parties westward between 1650 and 1675 to probe the upper reaches of the James and Roanoke Rivers and the surrounding mountains.[21]

The first officially sponsored expedition to explore America's mountains took place in 1669 when Sir William Berkeley, colonial governor of Virginia, sent John Lederer, a twenty-five-year-old German adventurer, on a mission to explore the as-yet-unnamed Blue Ridge Mountains (seen from a distance, the heavily timbered slopes of the ridge appear through a bluish haze). Considered in its entirety, the Blue Ridge begins with South Mountain in southern Pennsylvania and stretches southward through Maryland, Virginia, North and South Carolina, and into northern Georgia.

Much of the range is below 4,000 feet, but in western North Carolina, where the Blue Ridge stretches for 200 miles, it encompasses forty-three peaks exceeding 6,000 feet, including the highest mountain east of the Mississippi, 6,684-foot Mount Mitchell.[22] To early generations of white settlers, they seemed a nearly impenetrable barrier to westward expansion. Thomas Jefferson, who could view the range from his Virginia plantation, wrote that the "mountains of the Blue Ridge . . . are thought to be of a greater height, measured from their base, than any others in our country, and perhaps in North America."[23]

Governor Berkeley was first in a distinguished line of Virginian gentry, ending with Jefferson himself, who sought to find a "Northwest Passage" across the North American continent to the Pacific. As he wrote in 1669, Berkeley hoped "to do his Majestie" King Charles II, "a memorable service, which was to goe to find out the East India Sea."[24] At Berkeley's behest, Lederer made three trips in search of the Northwest Passage (and, of more immediate concern, in search of an easy passage over the Blue Ridge Range). On his first trip, in March 1669, Lederer traveled northwest up the Pamunkey River from his starting point in Chickahominy.

In an account published a year later, Lederer reported that on March 17, 1669, he reached the foothills of "the *Apalataei*," where he found the air "very thick and chill." What followed amounted to the first climbing narrative in American literature (and almost certainly the only one originally composed in Latin):

> The eighteenth of *March* . . . I alighted, and left my horse with one of the Indians, whilst with the other two I climbed up the Rocks, which were so incumbred with bushes and brambles, that the ascent proved very difficult: besides, the first precipice was so steep, that

if I lookt down, I was immediately taken with a swimming in my head; though afterwards the way was more easie. The height of this Mountain was very extraordinary: for notwithstanding I set out with the first appearance of light, it was late in the evening before I gained the top, from whence the next morning I had a beautiful prospect of the *Atlantick*-Ocean washing the *Virginian*-shore; but to the North and West, my sight was suddenly bounded by Mountains higher than that I stood upon. Here did I wander in Snow, for the most part, till the Four and twentieth day of March, hoping to finde some passage through the Mountains; but the coldness of the Air and Earth together, seizing my Hands and Feet with numbness, put me to a *ne plus ultra*; and therefore having found my Indian at the foot of the Mountain with my Horse, I returned back by the same way that I went.[25]

Although he misinterpreted some of what he saw (the Atlantic is not visible from the Blue Ridge), Lederer was the first white man to catch a glimpse of the Shenandoah Valley and the long line of mountains beyond to the west. It is not possible from his narrative to reconstruct exactly where he stood that day in March, but it was somewhere along the ridge of the Southwest Mountains, to the northwest of present-day Charlottesville, Virginia. Failing to find a pass over the mountain that would allow him to continue westward, he determined to seek another route.

Lederer's second trip, in May and June 1670, took him southward along the eastern slopes of the Blue Ridge, into the Carolinas, where again no easy passage across the mountain presented itself, and where, moreover, he feared capture by Spanish marauders ranging north from Florida. On the final trip, in August 1670, Lederer climbed the Blue Ridge near present-day Front Royal, and spotted North Mountain, part of the main body of the Appalachians across the Shenandoah Valley. Atop the summit, Lederer's party "drank the Kings Health in Brandy" and "gave the mountain his name."[26] (The mountain in question, which no longer bears the name of the English king, has been variously identified as 2,909-foot Compton Peak, 3,368-foot Mount Marshall, or 2,365-foot

High Knob.) Lederer concluded that there was "no possibility of passing through the Mountains" to the western frontier from the point he had reached.[27] It was nearly another half century before white settlers began to move into the Shenandoah Valley beyond the line of the Blue Ridge that Lederer had explored in 1669–70.[28]

THE CLASH OF EMPIRES, THE BIRTH OF A NATION

In 1755, Lewis Evans, a Welsh-born surveyor living in Philadelphia, published a "General Map of the Middle British Colonies in America" depicting the region from northern Virginia to New York. In both the colonies and the mother country, Evans's map was widely circulated and considered an indispensable guide to future British settlement in North America. Among other innovations, it was the first to depict the as-yet-unnamed Cumberland Gap—a thousand-foot-deep cleft in the Appalachians, discovered in 1750 by explorer Thomas Walker (a business partner of Thomas Jefferson's father, Peter Jefferson)—a landscape feature destined to be the key to settlement of the trans-Appalachian region of Kentucky and Tennessee. But to the modern eye, what is most striking about Evans's map is the lack of geographical detail of the lands to the west of the front range of the Appalachians. Those spaces carried notations like "Endless Mountains" and "Impenetrable Mountains."[29] Evans's map also left a blank space where the Adirondacks lay in northern New York, noting, "This Country by Reason of Mountains Swamps and drowned land is impassable and uninhabited."[30]

The century following John Lederer's exploration of the Blue Ridge in 1669–70 represented a long fallow period in the history of American mountaineering. The only significant mountain exploration in North America during the first three-quarters of the eighteenth century was taking place far to the west, where Spanish soldiers and French traders were becoming aware of a chain of mountains variously described as the Shining or Stony or Rocky Mountains.[31]

In the East, exploration took second place to imperial conflict through much of the eighteenth century, with the British and French fighting four wars between 1689 and 1763 for control of North America. The decisive battles in these wars were fought over strategic waterways like the Saint Lawrence, Richelieu, Hudson, and Mohawk Rivers, as well as Lake George, Lake Champlain, and Lake Ontario. Apart from minor skirmishes, there were no battles fought atop or to control mountains.[32]

However, with the final defeat of France in the French and Indian War of 1754–63, mountains took on a new importance in Britain's North American empire. In a royal proclamation issued October 7, 1763, King George III forbade his American subjects to settle anywhere "beyond the Heads or Sources of any of the Rivers which fall into the Atlantic Ocean from the West and North West"—that is, the eastern slopes of the Appalachians. British authorities hoped the proclamation would serve to avert clashes with the Indian tribes that inhabited lands to the west of the mountains. But white settlers already had pushed beyond the crown of the Appalachians, and with the coming of peace, many more were contemplating doing the same. Among those with significant financial interests tied up in trans-Appalachian land speculation was one George Washington of Virginia. The attempt to hem in colonial settlement by means of a mountain barrier became one more irritant in the deteriorating relations between the British and Americans, along with the better-remembered issues of taxation, representation, liberty, and self-government.[33]

Armed conflict began in April 1775, and in September of that year, as the British lay besieged within Boston by General Washington's army, Kentucky hunter and explorer Daniel Boone was leading a party of settlers, including his own family, through the Cumberland Gap to Boonesborough, Kentucky.[34] Other settlers in those years of revolutionary war found their way into the White Mountains, on the primitive roads being constructed through Crawford Notch to the west and Pinkham Notch to the east of Mount Washington. They opened up a pathway from the mountainous interior of New Hampshire and the upper Connecticut Valley to the Maine and New Hampshire coastlines.[35]

The Patriot victory in 1783 closed the era of mountains as barriers to settlement in eastern North America. Vast new areas of land were soon being explored and laid claim to by whites in upstate New York and the Ohio Valley, as well as Kentucky and Tennessee, with very little regard for the earlier and competing claims of Native Americans. In June 1783, even before the last British soldiers had withdrawn from the United States, General Washington wrote to Congress from the military encampment of Newburgh, New York, to support a petition from Continental Army officers and soldiers asking to be rewarded for their military service with western land grants. These ex-soldiers, Washington believed, would prove themselves "superior to any common class of Emigrants . . . who have heretofore extended themselves beyond the Apalachian Mountains," both in their ability to achieve a *"Competence and Independence* for themselves," and to stand as a bulwark against the depredations of hostile Indians.[36]

ENLIGHTENMENT MOUNTAINEERING

The years following the Revolution brought vast changes to the newly independent United States. The most visible and celebrated, of course, consisted of the institution of republican government and the constitutional guarantees of fundamental liberties. Less momentous politically, but important nonetheless in the nation's future, was an evolution in American attitudes toward mountains, expressed alternately (although sometimes simultaneously) in terms of scientific interest and aesthetic enjoyment.

The founding fathers were heirs to European Enlightenment thought, as propounded by such figures as Francis Bacon, Isaac Newton, and John Locke (in an 1811 letter, Jefferson described the trinity as "the three greatest men the world had ever produced").[37] Locke taught that all knowledge was gained directly through the senses, rather than being innate in humans. His disciples were devoted to the gathering of facts that they were certain would reveal the rational system of order that governed the natural world (including human society). Locke's *Essay Concerning Human Understanding* thus gave birth to the scientific method and to rationalism. In the ensuing Age of Enlightenment, which spread from Europe to the American colonies, it was assumed that pursuit of knowledge was key to social progress and human happiness.

The center of the American Enlightenment, the American Philosophical Society, which was founded in Philadelphia in 1743 by Benjamin Franklin and later recruited Thomas Jefferson to its leading circle, was known for a while as "The American Philosophical Society for Promoting Useful Knowledge," with "useful" broadly defined. Jefferson, who was elected president of the society in 1796, and who held that position for eighteen years (including the time he spent as president of the United States), sought to increase his own knowledge, and that of his countrymen, in fields ranging from astronomy to zoology. He took particular interest in the geography of North America, and he collected many books on the subject (later part of the broader collection he sold to the Library of Congress). Jefferson was not alone in his geographical curiosity. Eighteenth-century American newspapers often carried advertisements for maps of every known quarter of the world; subscription libraries, like the Library Company of Philadelphia, devoted more of their collections to works of geography than to politics.[38]

Scientifically minded Americans in the eighteenth century considered themselves students of "natural history," a field of study that their more formally trained successors would divide into a number of disciplines, including meteorology, geology, botany, zoology, and ethnology. The methods used by these early natural historians included collecting objects (rocks, fossils, shells, seeds, plants, insects, animals), as well as closely observing and recording natural phenomena.[39] Several members of this community of natural historians would play important roles in eighteenth- and early-nineteenth-century mountaineering, either as explorers or as sponsors of exploration. This was the age of Enlightenment mountaineering.

In the mid-eighteenth century, a vogue for establishing botanical gardens spread from Britain to its colonies in North America. Mountain slopes in the Southeast, abounding in rare plant specimens, lured scientifically minded explorers like William Bartram to the Appalachians. Bartram, born in 1739, was the son of John Bartram, a cofounder with

Franklin of the American Philosophical Society. In 1773, on the eve of the American Revolution, the younger Bartram set off on a four-year quest to acquire rare plants and birds in the Southeast, a journey that took him from Florida to the banks of the Mississippi, through the Carolinas and Georgia, and to a number of southern Appalachian mountaintops.

Traveling in northern Georgia in 1775, Bartram climbed a peak that he named "Mount Magnolia," for "a new and beautiful species of that celebrated family of flowering trees" that he found growing on its slopes (thought to be 4,696-foot Rabun Bald, the second-highest peak in Georgia). Although he was interested primarily in the plants growing at higher elevations rather than in mountains for their own

President Thomas Jefferson.

sake, Bartram found Mount Magnolia "magnificent," "exalted," and "sublime." The lyrical description of landscapes and native peoples in a 1791 book chronicling his travels would influence the English Romantic poets, especially Samuel Taylor Coleridge and William Wordsworth, as well as American transcendentalists, including Henry David Thoreau.[40]

Thomas Jefferson once proudly described himself in a letter to a correspondent as "a savage of the mountains," which seems the least likely epitaph for this most worldly and well-bred of men.[41] While his friend and correspondent William Bartram clambered up southern mountain slopes, Jefferson learned his natural history from a comfortable distance, usually in his study on his plantation at Monticello, near Charlottesville, Virginia.[42] Nonetheless, Jefferson's writings and correspondence contain scores of references to mountains. He wondered why, for example, fossils of seashells were sometimes to be found on high summits. The conventional explanation of the time was that they had been left there by the same flood that, according to the Bible, deposited Noah's Ark atop Mount Ararat. Jefferson was inclined to seek natural rather than miraculous reasons to account for such mysteries. Tectonic uplift was not part of the scientific vocabulary of his day, but he made a plausible if mistaken guess in the original edition of *Notes on the State of Virginia*, his one published book, when he posited that the fossils had been extruded onto the mountaintops "through the pores of calcareous earths and stones."[43]

Further geological speculation can be found in a passage in *Notes* in which Jefferson described the view of the water gap at Harper's Ferry from "a very high point of land," known subsequently as Jefferson Rock. That view of the Potomac cutting through the Blue Ridge inspired Jefferson's admiration for "one of the most stupendous scenes in Nature." It led him to consider the origins of mountains. Unlike the medieval view of a perfect globe that only later acquired mountains through some sudden God-created catastrophic event like the biblical flood, Jefferson intuited a much longer process, in which natural and ongoing forces shaped the mountainscape over long duration (an interpretation that was considered heretical not just by churchmen, but by geologists for some decades to come):

The first glance of this scene hurries our senses into the opinion that this earth has been created in time, that the mountains were formed first, that the rivers began to flow afterwards, that in this place particularly they have been so dammed up by the Blue Ridge of mountains as to have formed an ocean which filled the whole valley; that, continuing to rise, they have at last broken over at this spot and have torn the mountain down from its summit to its base.[44]

Jefferson would later reason that just as, he supposed, the Potomac River breached the Blue Ridge at Harper's Ferry, so the Missouri River might breach the Rocky Mountains.[45]

While Jefferson was putting the finishing touches on *Notes of the State of Virginia*, a scientific expedition was setting off for a return engagement with what had been the site of the first recorded American mountain climb, Mount Washington in New Hampshire. The leaders of this venture were the Reverend Jeremy Belknap of Dover, New Hampshire, and the Reverend Manasseh Cutler of Ipswich, Massachusetts, who both combined their religious vocation with a keen amateur interest in natural science. Several other ministers, scientists, and local dignitaries joined them en route, including Captain John Evans, a local settler who had built the road through Pinkham Notch and who was veteran of two previous climbs of the mountain. Because of the prominence of the climbers and the detailed accounts they left of their adventure, the Belknap-Cutler expedition attracted considerable public attention. It has been credited by some historians with being "as much the starting point of modern mountain climbing in the United States as any single event."[46]

Departing Dover by horseback on July 21, 1784, the Belknap-Cutler party reached the head of the Ellis River, near present-day Pinkham Notch, two days later. Starting out early the following morning, they climbed the mountain's eastern flank, beginning near the trailhead of the present-day Tuckerman Ravine Trail, but veering off northward. The heavy-set Reverend Belknap turned back before the party reached timberline. But the others persevered, arriving at the summit in early afternoon (how precisely they got there is a matter of some controversy among climbing historians—although it may have been via the as-yet-unnamed Boott Spur or Lion Head or Nelson Crag). To mark their achievement, they chiseled the initials "NH" (presumably for "New Hampshire") on a summit rock and left behind a lead plate bearing their names.

Throughout the climb they had taken careful notes detailing the plant life as it adapted to higher elevation, and the plunging temperatures from base to summit—the first such observations recorded in the White Mountains. Their findings, while scientifically inclined, were not particularly accurate. From barometric observations, Cutler calculated the height of the mountain at 10,001 feet above sea level, which he believed placed it "among the highest mountains on the globe."[47]

Descending at midafternoon, with clouds obscuring visibility, the climbers lost their way, finding their descent blocked by a steep precipice that was likely the headwall of one of the mountain's two great glacial cirques on its eastern flank (later known as Tuckerman and Huntington Ravines). Captain Evans went ahead to find their route but suffered a fall of several hundred feet before being able to self-arrest with an ax he was carrying—the first recorded climbing accident in North America, thankfully not fatal. By retracing their steps, they found their original route and made their way to tree line, where they bivouacked for the night, re-joining Reverend Belknap the following day.

Subsequent to their climb, Belknap and Cutler decided that such a splendid mountain should be named for the general who had commanded the Continental Army in the Revolutionary War, and it was thereafter known as Mount Washington. Although he failed to reach the summit, Belknap was nonetheless pleased with the prospect from its base. "Everything . . . sublime and beautiful is here realized," he noted. "Stupendous mountains, hanging rocks, chrystal streams, verdant woods . . . fill the mind with such ideas as every lover of nature and every devout worshipper of its Author would wish to have."[48]

THE AMERICAN MOUNTAIN SUBLIME

In the seventeenth and through much of the eighteenth centuries, mountains were regarded by most Americans as hideous and desolate. Suddenly, at the end of the eighteenth century, America's rocky features had become "sublime and beautiful." In the decades to follow, it would be hard to find an educated American who did not agree that nature in general, and mountains in particular, were "sublime."

Consider the use of the term by the Reverend Timothy Dwight, eighth president of Yale College and the grandson of Jonathan Edwards. An inveterate traveler, and occasional mountain-climber, he was en route from his home in New Haven to Vermont in September 1798, when he spotted on the horizon what he called "Taghconic" mountain (later in the nineteenth century renamed Mount Everett, at 2,602 feet the highest mountain in the Taconic Range that stretches from western Massachusetts and Connecticut into eastern New York). Dwight was pleased to see the familiar landmark, having first climbed it in 1781. The mountain, he recorded, was "clad at this time in misty grandeur." Although "its sides are not precipitous, nor its summits angular," the attributes of a truly magnificent mountain, still "it is a highly sublime object."[49]

It would never have occurred to Dwight's grandfather, the Reverend Jonathan Edwards, to rate a mountain's appeal by the steepness of its slope or the angularity of its summit. This aestheticization of mountains, which accompanied the rise of scientific interest in them, was something new in American writings about landscape and wilderness. At just the moment they had achieved independence from the British Crown, Americans were learning to see their mountains, as it were, through others' eyes, by means of a cultural borrowing from their former mother country.

In the eighteenth century, the English gentry developed a rite of passage that involved taking a "grand tour" of European sites, and a broader swath of literate Englishmen acquired a taste for reading travel accounts. Essayist and playwright Joseph Addison anticipated these trends in a description of his grand tour of 1699 in *Remarks on Several Parts of Italy*. That work included the seemingly disconcerting observation that "the Alps . . . fill the mind with an agreeable kind of horror."[50]

How could "horror" be agreeable? In Addison's usage, a sight that inspired horror stirred deep emotions, a sense of awe, and an awareness of the divine presence—all good things to experience. Mountains, with their great and towering bulk, precipitous slopes, and storm-encircled summits, were ideal for evoking this sort of agreeable horror, a psychological tonic for the jaded sensibilities of men of wealth and education.[51]

A generation later, a youthful Edmund Burke penned a short work, exploring similar ideas, entitled *A Philosophical Enquiry into the Origins of Our Ideas of the Sublime and Beautiful*. Published in 1756, it was widely read on both sides of the Atlantic. The "beautiful" in Burke's aesthetic theory suggested order and symmetry, usually brought about by the application of the human hand, as in classical architecture or a formal garden. The beautiful was fully in accordance with the Enlightenment preference for civilized landscapes. But "sublime" was something quite different—and out of step with the rationalism dominating European intellectual discourse at the time.

Mountains were inherently resistant to the rationalist impulse, because no human hand had groomed them; there the disorderly mass of rocks that met the eye was the work of God or nature or accident alone. Burke argued that the chaos of the wild provided observers with a spiritually bracing touch of "the passions which concern self-preservation."[52] And there was the added advantage that these passions were available without any need to put oneself in actual danger (say, by climbing a mountain). The terrors of the sublime could be experienced vicariously and at a safe distance. By the late eighteenth century, British tourists were traveling in a steadily increasing stream to the Continent for the express purpose of visiting the Alps. And they also began to seek out the more modest peaks of their own country, in the Lake District, Scotland, and Wales, and to set down their impressions in journals, poems, sketches, and paintings.[53]

The sublime came into its own in the romantic period of the late eighteenth and early nineteenth centuries, a revolt against rationalism that took the form of a celebration of the individual quest for authentic experience. Poets were in the romantic vanguard, especially when it came to the search for the sublime. Percy Bysshe Shelley set the standard for mountain appreciation in his "Mont Blanc: Lines Written in the Vale of

Chamouni," composed during a visit in 1816. Although he described the mountain that towered above Chamonix as "still, snowy, and serene," as he elaborated it was clear that its viewer was not destined to come away from the scene feeling that same serenity: "How hideously / Its shapes are heap'd around, rude, bare, and high / Ghastly, and scarred, and riven."[54]

The distinctions that Burke drew between the categories of the beautiful and the sublime, carefully observed in Shelley's poem, tended to be drawn less sharply in the minds of Burke's American readers, who were not yet ready in the late eighteenth century to abandon the Enlightenment celebration of reason and order. For the scientifically minded Reverend Belknap, the scenery around Mount Washington was *both* "sublime and beautiful." For President Dwight of Yale, a squat little mountain like "Mount Taghconic," bearing scant resemblance with its tree-covered. rounded summit to "rude, bare, high" Mont Blanc, was nonetheless "sublime." Burke and Shelley, one suspects, would have disagreed with their American counterparts' aesthetic judgments. But for Americans of the late eighteenth and early nineteenth centuries, no soul-shaking sense of horror or terror need attend the act of observing mountains; instead, the experience of the sublime was regarded as a source of innocent pleasure and wholesome moral edification.[55]

Something else distinguished enthusiasts for the mountain sublime in America from their British counterparts. Shelley was writing about a foreign mountain; Dwight, about an American mountain. Mountains were not a defining part of the British national identity, which was instead tied up with seafaring and an island existence—"This sceptred isle . . . / This precious stone set in the silver sea," as Shakespeare put it in act 2 of *Richard the Second*. But the United States was located on and about to expand across a continent with many vast and lofty mountain ranges.

Timothy Dwight's *Travels in New-England and New-York*, chronicling his mountain-climbing adventures, was published in 1821 (among his numerous American readers was Henry David Thoreau, who went on to climb many of the same mountains). Dwight was a prolific and popular (if unmemorable) poet, as well as travel writer.[56] His poems celebrated American distinctiveness—indeed, its superiority to Europe. His "Prospect of America," published in 1785, included this catalogue of things that established a bright future for the nation:

> *Here spacious plains in solemn grandeur spread;*
> *Here cloudy forests cast eternal shade;*
> *Rich valleys wind; the sky tall mountains brave,*
> *And inland seas for commerce spread the wave* . . .[57]

For Dwight, as for many of his contemporaries in the first years of American independence, mountains were starting to evoke both the sublime and the patriotic. Tall and brave, they had become one of the landscape features defining American national identity. The association between mountains with natural character and mission became more pronounced in the century to come.[58]

THE NORTHWEST PASSAGE

Though Thomas Jefferson never traveled farther west than the Blue Ridge, it was through his efforts that American citizens first encountered two of their greatest western mountain ranges, the Rockies and the Cascades.

Jefferson inherited the dream of finding the Northwest Passage from his father, Peter. The senior Jefferson, a Virginia plantation owner, was one of the founders of the Loyal Land Company in 1749, six years after Thomas's birth; the partnership speculated in western lands and, according to the Reverend James Maury, later Thomas Jefferson's tutor, the company had considered sending "some persons . . . in search of that river Missouri . . . in order to discover whether it had any communication with the Pacific Ocean." [59]

Ever since the Missouri River's discovery by French explorers Louis Jolliet and Jacques Marquette in 1673, it had seemed the best remaining possibility for finding a navigable water route across the continent. A river so deep and turbulent at its confluence with the Mississippi River obviously flowed a great distance, and from some considerable height—most likely the as-yet-unseen Shining, Stony, or Rocky Mountains reputed to lie far to the west. And if those mountains were the source of a river flowing east across the continent, it seemed only logical that another great river must flow west from its heights, emptying into the Pacific—even if the mouth of such a river had yet to be discovered by sailors exploring the western coast of the continent.

So Jefferson believed, and in the years after the American Revolution he made repeated efforts to find someone who would lead an expedition up the Missouri (which, in *Notes on the State of Virginia*, he had described as the "principal river" of the West). Time and again he was disappointed.[60]

In 1792, Jefferson's belief in the existence of a Northwest Passage was strengthened when an American sea captain named Robert Gray, sailing out of Boston to the Pacific Northwest on a fur-trading voyage, discovered the mouth of a great river emptying into the Pacific. He named it the Columbia, after his ship the *Columbia Rediviva*. Gray didn't venture any great distance upriver, but he mentioned its existence to Royal Navy commander George Vancouver, who was on an exploratory voyage in the same region. Vancouver sent one of his subordinates, Lieutenant William Broughton, on an exploratory journey up the Columbia in a longboat. Broughton and his men sailed 100 miles inland, to a point just east of present-day Portland, Oregon. The lieutenant saw soaring snowcapped mountains in the distance and named two of them. The one to the south of the river he called Mount Hood; the one to the north, Mount Saint Helens.[61] Gray's discovery and naming of the Columbia River, and Broughton's voyage inland, left the United States and Great Britain each with vague and competing claims to the territory.

In 1801, Thomas Jefferson took the oath of office as third president of the United States. In one of his first official acts, he hired as private secretary a fellow Virginian, army captain Meriwether Lewis. Lewis lived in the White House for the next several years, and the two men frequently dined together and discussed matters of common interest.

In 1802, President Jefferson read a book recently published in England by Alexander Mackenzie, a Scottish-born employee of the fur-trading North West Company, based in Montreal. Mackenzie recounted his journey by canoe and by foot across western Canada to the Pacific Ocean and back in 1792–93. With a party of nine companions, he traveled up the Peace River to the foot of the Rocky Mountains and then crossed the Continental Divide. He made it sound easy, crossing the Rockies via a pass a mere 3,000 feet in elevation, and finding a river on the western slope within portaging distance (he did not, however, travel by water to the coast, but struck out overland). Mackenzie's description of his journey reinforced Jefferson's belief that the Rockies were simply the western equivalent of the Blue Ridge Mountains.

When Mackenzie reached the ocean, he painted on a cliff face the words "Alexander Mackenzie, from Canada, by land, the twenty-second of July, one thousand seven hundred and ninety three." Although the route he discovered to the Pacific was not practical for fur-trading purposes, and thus fell far short of the dreams of a Northwest Passage, he had succeeded in crossing the North American continent—the first time that feat had been achieved, at least by a white man. "By opening this intercourse between the Atlantic and Pacific Oceans," Mackenzie suggested, "and forming regular establishments throughout the interior . . . as well as along the coasts and islands, the entire command of the fur trade of North America might be obtained."[62]

This was exactly the outcome that Jefferson had feared since he first began promoting an expedition up the Missouri back in the 1780s. If Americans didn't find their own Northwest Passage, they might be shut out of expansion to the Pacific coast altogether. California was controlled by the Spanish, Alaska by the Russians, and now, it seemed, the territory in between would come under British rule.

Jefferson thus resolved to launch his long-planned expedition up the Missouri, this time under the auspices of the federal government. It would be the first official expedition ever undertaken by American citizens. And Jefferson found the ideal man to lead it: his secretary, Meriwether Lewis. Captain Lewis recruited as coleader a former army acquaintance, retired captain William Clark. The two men began organizing an expedition to explore the Missouri in the spring of 1804.

Adding impetus to the Lewis and Clark expedition was the surprise outcome of negotiations in Paris over the ownership of some key pieces of American real estate. The settlement that ended the American Revolution brought the border of the United States to the eastern bank of the Mississippi River. On the other side lay the Louisiana Territory, which, since 1763, had been controlled by Spain. But in 1801, Spain agreed with France, then under the rule of Emperor Napoléon Bonaparte, to return the Louisiana Territory to French control.

Jefferson was profoundly disturbed by the prospect of having French neighbors on the North American continent, and even more disturbed by the thought that they would again control New Orleans, providing Napoléon a potential choke hold on American trade passing down the Mississippi River to the Gulf of Mexico. On Jefferson's instructions, the US ambassador in Paris, Robert Livingston, initiated negotiations with the French government for the purchase of New Orleans. Negotiations took an unexpected turn in 1803 when Napoléon offered to sell the entire Louisiana Territory, from the Mississippi west to the Continental Divide, to the United States.

Jefferson jumped at the opportunity. For the bargain price of $15 million, the Louisiana Purchase brought into US possession the territory that, in the course of the nineteenth century, would become the states of Louisiana, Arkansas, Missouri, Iowa, Minnesota, South Dakota, North Dakota, Nebraska, Kansas, Oklahoma, and Montana, as well as about half the future states of Wyoming and Colorado. The new border of the United States, as defined by treaty in 1803, now ran up to the Continental Divide, culminating at the top of the eastern slopes of the greatest mountain range in North America.

TO THE CONTINENTAL DIVIDE

Two centuries after the establishment of the first British settlements in North America, and a quarter century since the United States won its independence, US citizens were about to have their first encounter with the Rocky Mountains, an interlocking chain of a score of ranges and groups of mountains that extend more than 3,000 miles from New Mexico north to Canada and Alaska. Within the present boundaries of the United States, some 3,000,000 square miles are covered by the Rockies. In places, the Rockies are more than 350 miles wide, with peaks ranging from 7,000 feet to more than 14,000 feet. The Rockies form the Continental Divide.

From their eastern flanks, water flows toward the Mississippi and from there to the Gulf of Mexico; from their western flanks, water flows to the Pacific.

Like the Appalachians to their east, the Rockies were created by the collision of tectonic plates, though much more recently in geological time. In the case of the Rockies, however, the collision was not between two slabs of continental crust as in the Appalachians, but between oceanic crust and continental crust. The mountain-building event that created the Rockies, known to geologists as the Laramide Orogeny, started in the Late Cretaceous (eighty million years ago) with the subduction of the oceanic Pacific Plate (and related plates) under the North American Plate. The less dense continental crust overrode the denser basaltic oceanic crust of the Pacific Plate. As the rocks of the Pacific Plate were pushed down into the mantle, some of the material carried along with them melted. The partially molten material moved upward toward the surface and formed igneous rocks—volcanic rock, if it emerged on the surface; intrusive rock, like granite, if it cooled below the surface. In the Rockies as in the Appalachians, great mountain peaks over 20,000 feet tall resulted, and then began to erode. Over tens of millions of years, the movement of the plates shifted direction several times, pushing up new ranges and creating other geological features, such as the Columbia River Plateau and the Snake River Plain.

Although sharing a common geological origin, the Rockies include more than a hundred named groupings of mountains. Geographers generally divide the Rocky Mountains into five sections. The Southern Rockies, found in New Mexico, Colorado, and southern Wyoming, include the Laramie, Medicine Bow, Sangre de Cristo, and San Juan Mountains, as well as the Colorado Front Range of the Rockies. The Middle Rockies lie in northwestern Colorado, northeastern Utah, and western Wyoming and include the Teton Range, as well as the Big Horn, Beartooth, Owl Creek Uinta, and Wind River Mountains. The Northern Rockies run through northwestern Wyoming, western Montana, central and northern Idaho, and eastern Washington to the Canadian border. They include the Bitterroot, Clearwater, Salmon, and Sawtooth Ranges, the Lost River Mountains, and the Front Range of Montana. The Canadian Rockies run north of the Canadian border through British Columbia and Alberta. Finally, to the north and west, the Columbia mountain group of the Rockies includes the Purcell and Cariboo Mountains of Canada (along with the nearby Selkirk Range, technically separate from the Rockies) and the Brooks Range of Alaska.[63]

LEWIS AND CLARK: "IMMENCE RANGES OF HIGH MOUNTAINS"

On May 14, 1804, Captains Lewis and Clark's expedition, officially the Corps of Discovery, set sail in a keelboat and two long canoes, known as pirogues, from their camp on the eastern shore of the Mississippi River and "proceeded on" up the Missouri River. Within a few days they had left the last white settlements along the river behind them. Their primary mission was to find out whether the Missouri was indeed the long-sought Northwest Passage, but Jefferson, ever the scientist, provided them with a long list of other duties, including recording the climate, plant and animal life, soil conditions, and evidence of volcanic activity they encountered en route. By October, they had established a winter camp near a collection of Indian villages at the confluence of the Missouri and Knife Rivers, in present-day North Dakota, the last known location along the Missouri that appeared on their maps. And on April 7, 1805, when the ice melted in the Missouri, they proceeded on once again, this time in the two pirogues and a half dozen dugout canoes—and into the unknown.

Some of the original members of the expedition returned to Saint Louis with the keelboat. Among the thirty-three who set off up the river, there were a few new members, including the only one of their number who had actually seen the Rocky Mountains before—Sacagawea, a teenage Shoshone woman who had been kidnapped as a child by the Hidatsa and brought east as a slave. Most of the men on the trip were from Virginia and Pennsylvania, with a few from New England and other scattered locales; thinking of what lay ahead of them, they had only the Appalachians as models for mountains.[64]

Captains Meriwether Lewis (left) and William Clark (right), commanders of the Corps of Discovery, 1803–6.

By mid-May, the Corps of Discovery had begun spotting mountains on the horizon, part of the Little Rocky Mountains, an outlying range detached from and well east of the real Rockies. In late May, they could see the Bears Paw, Judith, and Highwood Mountains in the distance. And by mid-July, after portaging around the Great Falls in Montana, they finally came in sight of the real Rockies.

On August 12, 1805, an advance party consisting of Lewis and three others followed a small stream, now known as Horse Prairie Creek, that they judged the "most distant fountain of the waters of the mighty Missouri." It led, Lewis recorded, to "the base of a low mountain or hill of a gentle ascent" that marked the eastern foot of the Continental Divide. Lewis hoped they were within a day's travel of "finding a passage over the mountains and of tasting the waters of the great Columbia" on the other side—an easy day's portage for the expedition. Instead, when they reached the summit of what was later called Lemhi Pass, 7,323 feet above sea level, a disappointed Lewis noted, "I discovered immence ranges of high mountains still to the West of us, with their tops partially covered with snow."[65] The Rockies were not the western Blue Ridge after all.

With help from the Shoshone Indians, whom the party met after descending the western side of Lemhi Pass, the Corps of Discovery acquired horses and a native guide to lead them through the mountains. They headed north over some low ridges to a valley later known as Ross's Hole and followed the Bitterroot River north, with the Bitterroot Range of the Rockies to their west. The Bitterroots are not the highest of the Rockies, topping out at 10,157-foot Trapper Peak, but the snow-dusted summits worried the captains, who knew they had to get up and over the mountains before deeper snow made them impassable.

On September 9, they reached a stream flowing down the western slopes of the Bitterroots, which they named Traveler's Rest Creek, since they took a day off on its banks (it is the present-day Lolo Creek). Two days later, the Corps of Discovery set out to cross the Bitterroot Mountains, following the Lolo Trail. Although Lolo Pass, at 5,233 feet, was considerably lower than Lemhi Pass, which they had climbed without difficulty in August, the passage of a month had brought inclement weather. For eleven cold, hungry, weary days they struggled across the mountains. Horses slipped on the steep footing and rolled down the hillsides, scattering the expedition's supplies. Eight inches of snow fell on September 16, prompting Clark, a Virginia man, to write in his journal, "I have been as wet and as cold in every part as I ever was in my life."[66]

Food ran short, and game was scarce. Sergeant Patrick Gass, a Pennsylvania man, expressed the common sentiment of the men toward mountains and mountain-climbing in an entry in his journal on the eighth day of their trek: "We have . . . some hopes of getting soon out of this horrible mountainous desert."[67] Finally, on September 20, Clark and an advance party reached the Weippe Prairie in Idaho, 160 miles from their starting point on the eastern slope of the mountain, and the rest of the party joined them on September 22. In his journal entry that day, Lewis, the first of his countrymen to encounter the Rocky Mountains, bid them an unfond farewell:

The pleasure I now felt in having tryumphed over the rockey Mountains and descending once more to a level and fertile country where there was every rational hope of finding a comfortable subsistence for myself and party can be more readily conceived than expressed.[68]

The group was much relieved to be back on the water in early October, in newly built dugout canoes, heading down the Clearwater River, from there to the Snake River, from there to the Columbia River, and finally to the Pacific Ocean. En route to their winter encampment on the coast, which they made a few miles south of the Columbia's mouth, they encountered the mountains first discovered in 1792 by Lieutenant William Broughton—Mount Hood and Mount Saint Helens—and a third, as-yet-unnamed snowcapped peak, Mount Adams, all part of the Cascade Range. They were better disposed to the Cascades than they had been to the Rockies, no doubt because they were sailing past them rather than climbing over them. Of Mount Saint Helens, Lewis wrote: It "is the most noble looking object of it's [sic] kind in nature."[69]

On the return trip, the Corps of Discovery spotted to the south another tall, white peak, until then unseen by white men. They called it Mount Jefferson, after the man who had sent them west. Not the least of the accomplishments of the Lewis and Clark expedition was the map of the west that Clark, a talented cartographer, published in 1814—the first to depict the Rockies as a series of ranges rather than a single continuous line of mountains, as well as depicting the location of some of the principal peaks of the Cascades. It remained the master map of the West from which most others were derived until the 1840s.[70]

TO THE COLORADO ROCKIES

Other expeditions headed westward as Lewis and Clark made their way up the Missouri and home again. Two expeditions set out under instructions from President Jefferson to explore the southern tributaries of the Mississippi River: the Dunbar-Hunter expedition of 1804, and the Freeman-Custis expedition of 1806. And, also in 1806, General James Wilkinson, governor of the new Louisiana Territory, ordered army lieutenant Zebulon Montgomery Pike to lead an expedition from Saint Louis across the plains to the southern Rocky Mountains, and then make his way back east via the Red River. (Pike was twenty-seven years old when he took on this assignment. Having previously led an expedition up the Mississippi River to find its headwaters in Minnesota, he was considered a seasoned explorer.)

Pike and twenty-two soldiers left Saint Louis on July 15, 1806, traveling by keelboat up the Missouri River and partway up the Osage River before switching to horses.[71] En route, they learned from a French trader of Lewis and Clark's successful return to Saint Louis in September—the news of which, Pike recorded, "diffused general joy through our party." They followed the Arkansas River across the plains. On November 15, shortly after crossing into present-day Colorado, Pike noted in his journal:

> At about two o'clock in the afternoon I thought I could distinguish a mountain to our right, which appeared like a small blue cloud. . . . When our small party arrived on the hill they with one accord gave three *cheers* to the *Mexican mountains.*[72]

The "Mexican mountains," still 150 miles distant, were the Front Range of the Colorado Rockies. Within the future boundaries of the state of Colorado were more than 1,500 peaks topping 12,000 feet, 637 over 13,000 feet, and 54 topping 14,000 feet. Seven of the ten highest peaks in the continental United States are in the Colorado Rockies.[73]

In contrast to Lewis and Clark, who detested the mountains they encountered en route to the Pacific, and who were never tempted to try for the summit of any of them, Pike was determined to climb at least one of those high peaks on the horizon, although that was not part of his original orders. On November 24, from a small fort near the site of present-day Pueblo, Colorado, Pike set off with the expedition's doctor and two privates to attempt to reach the summit of a "Grand Peak" in the range that lay before them. Distances proved deceptive: Pike thought he was close enough to climb the mountain and return to camp in a single day, but three days later he and his party had yet to reach the base of their intended mountain. Instead, on November 27 they decided to climb another, more accessible mountain, to the southeast of the one for which they had set out.

"Commenced our march up the mountain," Pike recorded in his journal, "and in about one hour arrived at the summit of this chain; here we found the snow middle deep; no sign of beast or bird inhabiting this region." Gazing at the mountain that was their original goal, and estimating its height at over 18,000 feet, Pike concluded "no human being could have ascended to its pinical." It is impossible to determine the mountain that Pike wound up climbing, but since the available candidates are in the 9,000-foot range, on that November day he and his companions established an altitude record in American mountaineering that finally eclipsed the one established by Darby Field in 1642.[74]

Pike's "Grand Peak," the one he didn't climb, would soon be renamed "Pikes Peak." At 14,115 feet, it is not the highest of Colorado's mountains (an honor that goes to 14,440-foot Mount Elbert, which is also the highest peak in the Rockies, and second-highest in the contiguous United States). But Pikes Peak is an impressive presence on the Front Range, standing apart from the surrounding peaks, and visible far to the east.

In search of the sources of the Arkansas and South Platte Rivers, Pike led his men into the mountains, via Currant Creek Pass, reaching the area later known as South Park, at elevations between 9,000 and 10,000 feet, and across Trout Creek Pass (9,346 feet), ascending the Arkansas River to a point close to present-day Leadville.[75] In January, seeking the source of what he thought was the Red River (and turned out to be the Rio Grande), he led part of his detachment south into the Sangre de Cristo Mountains. They suffered greatly from cold and hunger and in February were apprehended by a troop of Spanish cavalry from Santa Fe, taken into custody, and led south as prisoners to Chihuahua, Mexico. Their misadventure ended the following year when they were released to American authorities in Natchitoches, Louisiana.[76]

LONG'S EXPEDITION

During the War of 1812, Congress authorized the creation of a unit of army topographical engineers charged with military reconnaissance. Disbanded at the conclusion of the war, the unit was reorganized in 1816 as the Topographical Bureau and later renamed the Corps of Topographical Engineers. As such, it played a significant role in the exploration and mapping of the western United States. Among the corps's number was Stephen Harriman Long, a Dartmouth College graduate and military veteran of the War of 1812 who by 1819 held the rank of major in the Topographical Bureau.[77]

In May of that year, Major Long, accompanied by a small group of military topographers and civilian scientists, set out on the steamboat *Western Explorer* to catch up with a thousand-man military force commanded by Colonel Henry W. Atkinson. Atkinson's expedition, traveling by steamboat up the Missouri, was intended as a show of force to western Indians and to the British in Canada. But the steamboats proved unsuitable for the mission, since they were of too deep a draft to navigate the Missouri. The expedition made it only as far as Nebraska before it was time to halt for the winter's encampment. Embarrassed, authorities back east called it off.

Major Long got a new assignment. Instead of following the Missouri to the mouth of the Yellowstone, Long was now ordered to take his small party west along the Platte River to find its source in the Rocky Mountains, and return east by way of the Arkansas and Red Rivers. They would thus explore the Front Range of the Rockies north of the point reached by the Pike expedition in 1806–7.[78]

Long, who had traveled to Washington in the interim, re-joined his men at Council Bluffs, Nebraska, on May 27, 1820. He was accompanied by Captain J. R. Bell as his second in command, two artists (Titian Peale and Samuel Seymour), and Dr. Edwin James as expedition botanist (James would author the two-volume report of the expedition). On June 6, Long and his men set out on horseback overland, with only a month's supply of food carried by a few packhorses and mules. A Pawnee chief

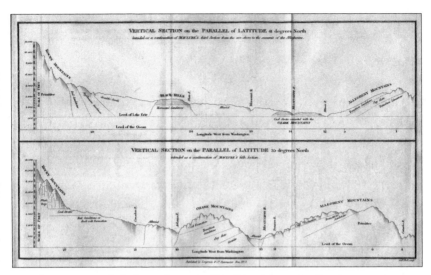

This illustration, included in Volume 3 of Dr. Edwin James's official report, *Account of an Expedition from Pittsburgh to the Rocky Mountains in 1819–1820*, gave eastern readers a glimpse of the disparity in height between eastern and western mountains when it was published in 1823.

they encountered en route named Long Hair paid them a backhanded compliment: "You must have long hearts," he told them, "to undertake such a journey with so weak a force."[79]

The expedition followed the Platte across the prairie to a fork in the river—the North Platte leading to present-day Wyoming; the South Platte, toward Colorado. Following the southern fork, on June 30, as James's account recorded, "we left the encampment at our accustomed early hour, and at 8 o'clock were cheered by a distant view of the Rocky Mountains."[80] By July 5, they had reached the site of present-day Denver. And along the Front Range of the Rockies, they spied a distinctive high peak that they named for their commander: Longs Peak.

At 14,259 feet the highest summit in the Front Range of the Rockies, Longs Peak remained unclimbed for decades. But not so Pikes Peak to the south. With two other men, Dr. James spent several days climbing the east face of Pikes Peak, and they reached the summit at 4:00 p.m. on July 14, 1820. When James and his companions stood at the top, 14,115 feet above sea level, they were 5,000 feet higher than Pike and his companions had climbed in 1806.[81] "From the summit of the Peak," James recorded, "the view towards the north, west, and southwest is diversified with innumerable mountains, all white with snow."[82]

After about a half hour, they set off downhill toward the camp they had made at a lower elevation, but darkness fell, so they bivouacked, warmed only by a small fire they managed to start in the near-freezing cold. They descended safely to the base of the mountain the following day, taking note of mountain columbine, horned toads, and house finches along the way. The explorers decided to call the mountain James Peak, but the fur traders who had begun pouring into the region called it Pikes Peak, which is the name that stuck. It has been called "the most famous single mountain within the United States."[83]

Following the Long expedition, the federal government lost interest in western exploration. It would be nearly a quarter century before the next official expedition was dispatched.[84]

RISE OF THE MOUNTAIN MEN

Though official interest in sponsoring western exploration faltered, the profit motive proved a powerful and durable incentive to the same end. Private individuals pursuing their private interests—the so-called "mountain men"—explored more of the West than Lewis and Clark, Pike, and Long put together. They had no interest in the act of climbing a mountain for its own sake, as Pike and Long had done, but they performed some significant feats of mountaineering nonetheless, in pursuit of beaver and other fur-bearing mammals.[85]

On their return trip on the Missouri River in the summer of 1806, Lewis and Clark encountered fur traders heading west up the river—more than a hundred, all told, passing them before they reached Saint Louis. With the captains' permission, expedition member John Colter had taken leave of the Corps of Discovery before the return to Saint Louis, instead heading back west to trap and trade for furs with two of the men they had met on the river.

Colter would become a celebrated figure, as would many mountain men to follow, including Jedediah Smith, Jim Bridger, and Kit Carson. At the height of the fur trade in the 1820s and 1830s, several thousand mountain men were active in the West, their ranks including French Canadians, Indians, and African Americans, as well as white Americans. And as they became heroes to their countrymen, the books that they wrote or that were written about them became the first popular mountaineering literature.[86]

Washington Irving was among the writers who chronicled the mountain men's exploits for the reading public back east. In his 1836 book *Astoria, or Anecdotes of an Enterprise beyond the Rocky Mountains*, Irving celebrated mountain men as "pioneers and precursors of civilization," who had penetrated

> to the heart of savage countries; laying open the hidden secrets of the wilderness; leading the way to remote regions of beauty and fertility that might have remained unexplored for ages, and beckoning after them the slow and pausing steps of agriculture and civilization.[87]

The mountaineering exploits of the fur trappers could fill many books. Consider two of the most remarkable: John Colter and Jedediah Smith.

After taking leave of Lewis and Clark in 1806, Colter headed back to the Yellowstone Territory and spent the fall and winter trapping along Clark's Fork of the Yellowstone River. In the spring of 1807, he once again headed down the Missouri for Saint Louis, and once again he decided not to go there, after he encountered and joined a large party of fur traders recruited and led by Saint Louis fur merchant Manuel Lisa. The Lisa party followed the Missouri back up to the Yellowstone, and the Yellowstone to the mouth of the Big Horn River, where they established a fur-trading post called Fort Raymond. From there, in October 1807, Colter set out alone to spread the word about the post's existence to surrounding Indian tribes.

In an incredible feat of solo exploration over the winter of 1807–8, totaling 500 miles of wilderness travel, Colter crossed the Wind River Mountains in present-day Wyoming, the first white man to travel through that mountain range. He may have stumbled upon the Teton Range, theretofore unseen by white men. And in northwestern Wyoming, he came across a region abounding in thermal hot springs. When he returned to Fort Raymond, no one believed him; the traders made jokes about "Colter's Hell." (Commonly assumed to be present-day Yellowstone National Park, "Colter's Hell" actually refers to an area on the Shoshone River near present-day Cody, Wyoming.)[88]

Colter went on to have another famous adventure in the western wilderness. In 1809 he was captured by a hostile party of Blackfeet Indians, who stripped him naked and let him run for his life. Amazingly, he survived the ordeal, outrunning most and overcoming one of his pursuers, and crossing 200 miles of rough terrain to make it back to Fort Raymond and safety. On his return to Saint Louis in 1810, Colter met with his old commander, William Clark, and told Clark of his discoveries, which Clark incorporated into his map of the western Louisiana Territory. Never returning to the mountains, Colter died in 1813 of illness.

In the 1820s, Saint Louis resident William Henry Ashley reorganized the fur-trading business in the West. Manuel Lisa's model, also followed by government-run "factories" along the Missouri, was to set up a system of permanent trading posts where Indians would bring furs to exchange for goods. Ashley did away with the trading posts. Instead, he recruited and equipped his own men as trappers, who became known as "Ashley men," sending them out on horseback throughout the Rockies. (Contrary to popular accounts, they traveled in sizeable groups for protection against the Indians, not as lone individuals.)

The Ashley men, sometimes working for a share of furs, sometimes for wages, would bring in a year's harvest of furs to an annual summer rendezvous, an event characterized by sharp trading and heavy drinking. Ashley's Rocky Mountain Fur Company proved immensely profitable, and he retired after a few years to pursue a political career in Missouri. Ashley's employees left their names upon some of the most storied landscape in the West: Jackson Hole, Wyoming (originally "Jackson's Hole"), for example, was named for Rocky Mountain Fur Company trapper David Edward Jackson.[89]

Jedediah Smith was among the most audacious of the Ashley men, and in the nine years he spent as a hunter, trapper, and trader, he established a record of exploration in western mountains and deserts second to none. Born in Bainbridge, New York, in 1798, as a teenager he read an account of Lewis and Clark's expedition and was drawn westward. He is supposed to have carried his copy of the Lewis and Clark journals with him on his subsequent western travels. He also carried a Bible with him, since, unusually for those in his line of work, he was a devout Christian.[90]

At the age of twenty-three, Smith arrived in Saint Louis and signed up as an Ashley man. He went with an Ashley party in 1822 up the Missouri to the mouth of the Yellowstone River. From the start, Smith quite consciously saw himself following in the path of earlier explorers, writing in his journal in 1822, "The country [surrounding the Missouri] has been well described by Lewis and Clark, therefore any observation from me would be superfluous."[91]

Like his distinguished predecessors, Smith had impressive skills as an outdoorsman and a leader, as well as a measure of luck: in 1823 alone, he survived a pitched battle between the Ashley men and hostile Arikara Indians, and a subsequent mauling by a grizzly bear. In the fall of 1823, he set out with a party of trappers across the Badlands and into the southern Black Hills of the Dakotas, where no whites had gone before. The group continued west through the Big Horn Mountains before turning south into the Wind River valley where they spent the winter of 1823–24.

In March 1824, Smith crossed the Continental Divide at South Pass, a 22-mile-wide opening rising gradually to a height of 7,550 feet in the Wind River Range. The first white man to "discover" the pass (well known to the local Crow Indians, who told Smith about it) had been fur trader Robert Stuart, returning from John Jacob Astor's outpost in Astoria, Oregon, in 1812. But the existence and importance of the pass had been overlooked since Stuart's crossing. The South Pass would prove as valuable to westward migration as the Cumberland Gap had done three-quarters of a century earlier.

In November 1824, the Little Rock *Arkansas Gazette* breathlessly reported the news that Smith's party had "discovered a passage by which loaded wagons can at this time reach the navigable waters of the Columbia River. This route lies South of the one explored by Lewis and Clarke [*sic*], and is inhabited by Indians friendly to us."[92] And in March 1826, the *Missouri Advocate and St. Louis Enquirer* found evidence of providential intervention in Smith's discovery of South Pass:

> Those great barriers of nature, the Rocky Mountains, have been called up in judgment against the practicality of establishing a communication between this point and the Pacific Ocean. But the Great Author of nature in His wisdom has prepared, and individual enterprize discovered, that "so broad and easy a way" that thousands may travel it in safety, without meeting any obstruction deserving the name of a MOUNTAIN.[93]

South Pass became a crucial link in the Oregon Trail, and hundreds of thousands of Oregon- and California-bound emigrants would make the crossing over the next four decades.

In August 1826, by that point a partner in his own trading company (Smith, Jackson & Sublette), Smith set out with a small party of men from a site near present-day Soda Springs, Idaho, heading southwest to the Great Salt Lake, on a route that took him through present-day Zion National Park in Utah. In a journal entry written a few years later, reflecting on this journey, Smith made it clear that by this point in his life it wasn't purely profit that motivated him: "I wan[ted] to be the first to view a country on which the eyes of a white man had never gazed and to follow the course of rivers that ran through a new land."[94] Smith's "Southwest Expedition," as it became known, traveled westward across the Mojave Desert to the southern California coast—the first US citizens to make an overland journey to California (the Spanish authorities were not pleased). The Southwest Expedition headed north toward Sacramento, and then east to the mountain range known as the Sierra Nevada, which, even though they blocked his way home, Smith described in his journal as a range of "unsurpassed grandeur and Sublimity."[95]

Smith hoped to find a pass through the mountains, but his advance up Kings Canyon was blocked by heavy winter snows. Finally in May 1827, while the main party remained behind, Smith and two other men headed for the crest of the Sierra from a base 300 miles farther north. The peaks were still buried in snow, but this time, following the American River, he found an 8,730-foot pass, later named Ebbetts Pass, that allowed him to cross the mountains out of California, marking the first time that white men had made a passage through the Sierra.[96]

Reaching the eastern side of the mountains, they were back in desert (later known as the Great Basin), and their crossing of this new obstacle was another first for white explorers. Finally, they reached the Great Salt Lake on June 27, 1827—the conclusion of an epic journey. Smith went on to further adventures as an explorer, but his survivor's skills failed him in the spring of 1831 when he was ambushed and killed by a band of Comanche while en route to Santa Fe.[97]

Francis Parkman would provide a fitting epitaph for Smith's generation of mountain men. The Harvard-educated scion of a prominent Boston family, Parkman would become America's first great historian to write about the frontier. In 1846, he traveled along the Oregon and Santa Fe Trails that Smith had done so much to open up. Along the way he encountered a number of mountain men, although the heyday of the fur trade had already passed. Parkman's account in his popular travel narrative *The Oregon Trail*, published the following year, helped cement the reputation of the mountain men as the knights-errant of the American West: "I defy the annals of chivalry to furnish the record of a life more wild and perilous than that of a Rocky Mountain trapper."[98]

MOUNTAINS AS COMMODITIES: LITERATURE, ART, TOURISM

In the West, the mountain men lived a hard and solitary existence. In the East, in the same years, it became possible for the first time to visit the mountains in comfort and in crowds.

Washington Irving's 1819 *Sketch Book* included his famous short story "Rip Van Winkle," which opens with a paean to New York State's Catskill Mountains: "Whoever has made a voyage up the Hudson must remember the Kaatskill mountains . . . swelling up to a noble height and lording it over the surrounding country."[99] Irving wrote the story while living abroad in England, drawing upon memories of visiting the region in younger years. "Of all the scenery of the Hudson," he would later recall, "the Kaatskill Mountains had the most witching effect on my boyish imagination."[100]

The Catskills, like the Adirondacks, are often mistakenly thought to belong to the Appalachian mountain range. They are, in fact, geologically separate—the product of millions of years of erosion along the eastern edge of a plateau formed by a tectonic collision that occurred between 400 and 325 million years ago known as the Acadian Orogeny. On their eastern edge they rise steeply from the valley, while their western edge is a gentle slope. Because of their location directly west of the Hudson River, the Catskills were the first North American mountain range to be glimpsed at close range by European explorers: Englishman Henry Hudson, exploring the river that would bear his name, sailed beneath them on board the *Half Moon* in September 1609. But early Dutch settlers in the region seldom ventured into their heavily forested hills.

The Catskills reach their highest elevation at 4,180-foot Slide Mountain and contain more than thirty peaks higher than 3,500 feet. The settlers of New Amsterdam called the mountains "Katskill," thought to be derived from the Dutch words for "Cat Cree," or perhaps "Wild Cat Creek." After the English took over the Dutch colony in the seventeenth century and renamed it New York, they also renamed the Catskills as the Blue Mountains (for the blue spruce, which was at that time one of the dominant species of trees growing in the region). But the new designation never fully took, and the popularity of Irving's stories about the "Kaatskill" region settled the matter for good.[101]

The Catskills also fired the imagination of another nineteenth-century American writer: novelist James Fenimore Cooper. In 1823, Cooper published *The Pioneers*, which introduced his readers to Natty Bumppo, a character who would reappear in four subsequent *Leatherstocking Tales*, including *The Last of the Mohicans*, and thus became the prototype for countless later depictions of frontiersmen. Natty was a rough-hewn character, educated by Indians in the ways of the wilderness, but illiterate and thus not likely to have come in contact with the ideas of an Edmund Burke. As imagined by Cooper, however, Natty had his own firm views on the aesthetic and spiritual benefits of viewing wild and high places. Thus, in *The Pioneers*, when he is an old man and is asked by a young acquaintance to describe his favorite vista, he replies that it can be found in the Catskill Mountains of central New York, "next to the river, where one of the ridges juts out a little from the rest, and where the rocks fall for the best part of a thousand feet." What, his young friend wanted to know, could he see from there? "'Creation!' said Natty."[102]

The high plateau from which Natty viewed creation is known as the Pine Orchard, atop the Catskill Escarpment, located near Palenville, New York (a community that, under the name of "The Village of Falling Waters" was the fictional home of Rip Van Winkle). And on that escarpment, in 1824, a year after publication of *The Pioneers*, a group of local merchants opened a three-story hotel called the Catskill Mountain House, to cater to the burgeoning influx of tourists who were riding steamboats up from New York City. The venture proved wildly successful and became the prototype for mountain tourist lodgings elsewhere in the Adirondacks, the White Mountains, and the Green Mountains.[103]

Among the visitors that the Catskill Mountain House attracted in its first year in business was a young New York City artist named Thomas Cole, an English immigrant whose paintings of the hotel and the surrounding Catskills region would launch his own successful career as a landscape artist, as well as the Hudson River School of landscape art, the first distinctively American movement in the visual arts. Cole would

Catskill Mountain House.

make his home, first in the summers and then year-round, in the village of Catskill, on the western bank of the Hudson River, his bedroom window providing a spectacular view of the Catskill Range a dozen miles farther to the west—and also the desolation that loggers, tanners, and farmers were wreaking on the no-longer primeval forested hills below.

The Hudson River School, including Cole protégés like Frederic Edwin Church, provided urban art and nature lovers a lovingly preserved and highly romanticized vision of a fast-disappearing eastern mountain wilderness. Cole's famous painting titled *The Falls of Kaaterskill* actually hung in the stateroom of the Hudson River steamboat *Albany* for many years, schooling tourists in the sublime vistas that awaited them at the end of the line (as long as they were prepared to overlook the accumulating evidence of civilization's depredations).[104]

The popularity of Irving's stories, Cooper's novels, and Cole's paintings both reflected and encouraged the emergence of a mountain-based tourism industry in the first decades of the nineteenth century. People were now willing to pay to be stirred by the views that could be had in wild places, which they had glimpsed at second hand in books and paintings—especially those wild places offering ease of access and comfortable accommodations to the traveler.[105]

An expanding and increasingly prosperous, literate, urban-based middle class came to regard America's wild landscapes, particularly its mountains, as emblematic of national identity. As Cole wrote for a magazine in his "Essay on American Scenery" in 1836:

> It is a subject that to every American ought to be of surpassing interest; for, whether he beholds the Hudson mingling waters with the Atlantic—explores the central wilds of this vast continent, or stands on the margin of the distant Oregon, he is still in the midst of American scenery—it is his own land; its beauty, its magnificence, its sublimity—all are his; and how undeserving of such a birthright, if he can turn towards it an unobserving eye, an unaffected heart![106]

In the White Mountains, scenery tourism began to develop around the same time as in the Catskills—but with a new development. In the Catskills, tourists came to contemplate mountains; in New Hampshire, many visitors came to climb them. That was something new on the American scene. Ethan Allen Crawford was the man who, more than any other individual, made it possible for them to do so.

Crawford's father, Abel, was one of the earliest settlers of the area west of Mount Washington that became known as Crawford Notch, moving there with his family, including infant Ethan, in 1793. Abel and his father-in-law, Eleazar Rosebrook, who moved to the region soon afterward, both supplemented their income as farmers by providing rough accommodations to travelers passing through the notch (the Reverend Timothy Dwight was one of Crawford's guests in 1803). In 1817, Rosebrook died, and Ethan Allen Crawford inherited his farm. The area was beginning to attract visitors from Boston, some of whom wanted to climb Mount Washington. Abel and Ethan both guided parties to the summit, as Rosebrook had occasionally. But their clients complained of the difficulty of making their way through the thick stands of trees and *krummholz* (German for "bent wood," the dwarf black spruce trees that grow just below tree line).[107] So the Crawfords decided to cut a trail up the western side of the mountain from the notch.

Still in use today, the Crawford Path was the first mountain trail in the United States built for recreational purposes. For the next thirty years, most of those who climbed Mount Washington did so on that trail (unlike the Belknap-Cutler party, which had climbed from the east). And Crawford, a powerfully built man, over 6 feet in height and known as the "Giant of the Hills," became the first professional mountain guide, advertising his services and attracting an ever-expanding clientele. Some were botanists interested in the mountain's plants (one of them, Amherst College historian and botanist Edward Tuckerman, left his name on a notable feature of the mountain, Tuckerman Ravine). But most were there to climb the mountain for its own sake, including, among others, Nathaniel Hawthorne, Daniel Webster, Henry David Thoreau, Ralph Waldo Emerson, Washington Irving, and Thomas Cole.

The life of a mountain guide was not an easy one, as a reminiscence by Ethan Crawford, preserved by his wife Lucy, makes clear:

In September [1820] . . . there came a number of gentlemen up through the Notch, and sent to me to prepare and furnish them with provisions and other necessaries for the expedition. I was accordingly fitted out, and when ready, my pack weighed eighty pounds. I carried it to the Notch on horseback, and when I arrived there the sun was setting, and the party had taken the path and gone along and left their cloaks by the way for me. I piled them on top of my load and budged on as fast a possible, and when I arrived at the camp it was dusk; there was no fire; wood was to be chopped, and supper to prepare, and when all this was done, I was tired enough to sleep without being rocked in a cradle.[108]

Crawford expanded his original inn, bought new ones, and built a second path farther north, while widening the original trail into a bridle path that allowed tourists to ride horseback to the summit. Although prosperity eluded him, he and his family left their mark on the region in many ways, including the book written by Lucy Crawford, *History of the White Mountains*, published in 1846, the first history devoted to chronicling American mountains.[109]

Thomas Cole visited the White Mountains on at least two occasions, and his paintings of New Hampshire's peaks popularized the region as a tourist destination with the same degree of success that his earlier paintings had done for the Catskills. He also painted mountain scenery in New York's Adirondacks and Massachusetts's Holyoke Range, as well as fantastic fictional mountainscapes illustrating scenes from *The Last of the Mohicans*. Cole and other members of the Hudson River School, which spanned several generations of nineteenth-century painters, gave many Americans the feeling that their landscape, as well as their republican institutions, set them apart from a decadent Europe.

Cole and some in his circle believed that America had been home to the Garden of Eden in biblical times, and they were thus living in what had been (and in some ways still was) paradise. In Europe, nature had been largely subdued and supplanted by man's works. But in the United States, God's message could still be read in millions of acres of unspoiled wilderness. Artists like Cole were given the power of revelation in their representations of nature. They encouraged well-off Americans to regard a visit to the easily accessible and none-too-daunting summits of Massachusetts's Mount Holyoke or New York's Catskill Mountain escarpment as a comfortable form of pilgrimage.[110]

NEGLECTED MOUNTAINS

While tourists had been visiting the Catskills and the White Mountains for several decades, New York State's highest mountains were still largely unknown and unvisited at the start of the 1830s. The Adirondack Range encompasses over a hundred peaks, some standing in isolation and others in groups across a region of more than 5,000 square miles. Forty-two of the peaks are over 4,000 feet in elevation—the highest, Mount Marcy, at 5,344 feet.[111] The Adirondacks are composed of a billion-year-old rock layer, part of the continental basement known as the Grenville Province, pushed to the surface between twenty and ten million years ago, relatively recently in geological terms, by an underlying hot spot in the magma. Unlike the Appalachians, the Adirondacks are still growing in elevation, by about a foot per century.[112]

The word "Adirondack" is of Mohawk origin, literally meaning "the eaters of trees" and used as a derogatory name for Indian tribes to the north of the Adirondacks with whom the Iroquois competed in the fur trade, and often fought. In the years before the arrival of the whites, local Indians ventured into the region only to hunt in the summer, never to settle.[113] The lack of navigable rivers or wide valleys bisecting the region discouraged exploration by whites, who began moving into the adjoining Champlain and Mohawk Valleys in the eighteenth century, and dense woods, thin soils, and a forbidding climate meant that the area was of little interest to farmers or land speculators who were opening up the rest of upper New York to development in the late eighteenth and early nineteenth centuries.

In June 1797, surveyor Charles Brodhead was the first to venture into the region later known as the High Peaks, climbing near or perhaps to the summit of 4,627-foot Giant Mountain, as well as crossing, if not summiting, a half dozen other 4,000-footers, including Rocky Peak Ridge, Lower Wolf Jaw Mountain, Table Top Mountain, Algonquin Peak, and Iroquois Peak, a formidable traverse even today, when established trails make the climbing easier. The Adirondacks had very few visitors over the next four decades apart from the occasional surveyor.[114]

In 1836, Ebenezer Emmons, professor of natural history at Williams College, and geologist James Hall, set off to explore the High Peaks region on behalf of the newly created New York State Geological Survey (official state surveys, usually inspired by a desire to locate potential sources of mineral wealth, were established by state legislatures in sixteen eastern states in the 1830s). It was Emmons who popularized the name Adirondacks to describe what had previously been known as the Great Northern Wilderness.

Hall led a group that included an independent scientist, William C. Redfield, through thick woods alongside the Opalescent River to Lake Colden and Avalanche Lake, an area never before visited by whites. From a hillside near Lake Colden, Redfield spied the previously unknown Marcy. Later that summer, Hall and Emmons made the first ascent of 4,867-foot Whiteface Mountain. They returned to the area the following summer, and on August 5, 1837, Emmons, Hall, Redfield, and several others reached the summit of the region's high peak via a route close to the modern Calamity Brook Trail. Emmons named the mountain for New York governor William Learned Marcy. According to Redfield's account of the ascent, "The aspect of the morning was truly splendid and delightful, and the air on the mountain top was found to be cold and bracing. Around us lay scattered in irregular profusion, mountain masses of various magnitudes and elevations, like to a vast sea of broken and pointed billows."[115]

Most of those mountain masses remained unvisited for the next few decades. Although Lake Placid to the north of Marcy, and Keene Valley to the east, began to attract small numbers of summer visitors, only ten of the forty-six 4,000-footers in the Adirondacks had seen their first ascents by 1861. That year, Orson Schofield ("Old Mountain") Phelps of Keene Valley, one of the first and the most famous of the Adirondack guides, carved the first trail to the summit of Mount Marcy, nearly four and a half decades after the Crawford Path was built to the summit of Mount Washington.[116]

MANIFEST DESTINY MOUNTAINEERING

"God has promised us a renowned existence if we will but deserve it," James Brooks wrote in a widely reprinted essay in the magazine the *Knickerbocker* in 1835, the same year that Thomas Cole published his "Essay on American Scenery." "He speaks this promise in the sublimity of Nature," Brooks continued. "It resounds all along the crags of the

Alleghanies," as well as in "the thunder of Niagara" and "the roar of two oceans." A continent so blessed with the beauty of the natural world was clearly intended by Providence as the site for a model society: "The august TEMPLE in which we dwell was built for lofty purposes. Oh! that we may consecrate it to LIBERTY and CONCORD, and be found fit worshippers within its holy wall!"[117]

In the 1840s the walls of the "august TEMPLE" of nature's nation were about to expand again, and a mountain-climbing explorer named John C. Frémont was in the vanguard of that expansion.[118]

Frémont came to be known as "the Pathfinder" (the title also of one of James Fenimore Cooper's *Leatherstocking Tales*, published in 1840) for his westward expeditions as an officer in the Corps of Topographical Engineers. Frémont was the son-in-law of Senator Thomas Hart Benton of Missouri, a leading proponent of the belief that it was the United States' "manifest destiny" to expand to the Pacific coast, at the expense of Mexico in the Southwest and California, and at the expense of the British, who still disputed American claims to the "Oregon Country" of the Pacific Northwest. To further his political agenda, Senator Benton helped wangle choice exploration assignments for Lieutenant Frémont, and he used his son-in-law's exploits to publicize westward migration.

With Benton's backing, Frémont set off in 1842 on an expedition to survey the trail along the banks of the Kansas and Platte Rivers, in command of a crew of mountain men, including the soon-to-be-famous scout Kit Carson and an able German immigrant surveyor and cartographer, Charles Preuss. Stretching his orders, something he was prone to do and, indeed, boasted of, Frémont led his expedition all the way to the Rockies and across the South Pass, and explored the Wind River Mountains.[119]

Senator Benton hoped that Frémont's expedition would draw the attention of potential settlers to the South Pass as a gateway to the Oregon Territory. Frémont's natural flamboyance made him the ideal figure to lead such a publicity-driven effort. When he reached the Wind River Mountains in Wyoming, he impulsively decided to climb a mountain that he called "Snow Peak," mistakenly believing it was the highest in the Rockies (at 13,745 feet, the mountain, known today as Fremont Peak, is only the third-highest in Wyoming, and scores of mountains in Colorado are higher still). Or perhaps not so impulsively—since he had included among his expedition's baggage the barometers, chronometers, and thermometers that were at that time the standard scientific equipment for mountain exploration.[120]

Riding mules to a high mountain meadow, and struggling on foot up the icy slopes above, his party reached the summit on August 15. From their commanding height they could see the Tetons to the northwest. They fired their pistols, drank brandy, and, in a grand and legendary gesture, planted a homemade US flag—or, as Frémont put it, "unfurled the national flag to wave where never flag waved before."[121]

Returning to Washington, DC, at the end of October, Frémont set to work on a report of his adventures. Written in the form of a daily journal and published by Congress the following spring, it proved wildly popular. Americans were fascinated both by Frémont's description of the ease of travel over the South Pass (which he compared to climbing Capitol Hill in Washington) and his thrilling account of the flag-raising on "Snow Peak"

COL. FREMONT
PLANTING THE AMERICAN STANDARD ON THE ROCKY MOUNTAINS.

John C. Frémont unfurling the flag to wave "where never flag waved before."

(which he would later rename after himself). A recent historical account of Frémont's 1842 expedition describes "this shrewd and beautiful report" as "one of the seminal works of American expansionism."[122]

Contemporary readers were especially taken with Frémont's whimsical description of a "solitary bee" that flew around the party while they were on the summit and settled on the knee of one of the men. Bumblebees were not native to North America; they had arrived in the cargo of European ships on the East Coast of the continent sometime in the seventeenth century and had been making their way westward ever since. Hence, they were seen by both whites and Native Americans as an indicator of the westward push of white settlement.

Frémont was clearly aware of the symbolic import of the insect's arrival at that precise moment on that precise peak where he now stood. "It was a strange place," Frémont wrote (perhaps with the collaboration of his literary-minded wife, Jessie Benton Frémont), "the icy rock and highest peak of the Rocky mountains, for a lover of warm sunshine and flowers; and we pleased ourselves with the idea that he was the first of his species to cross the mountain barrier—a solitary pioneer to foretell the advance of civilization."[123] In the months following its publication, Frémont's report helped create a popular sentiment known as "Oregon Fever."

Frémont's flag-raising atop "Snow Peak" wasn't the first time such a gesture had been made, but it was the first to capture popular imagination. And the fact that it happened in the Rockies helped make the mountains themselves patriotic icons (rather than simply a barrier to be passed through).

"We had accomplished an object of laudable ambition," Frémont concluded in his account of August 15, 1842:

We had climbed the loftiest peak of the Rocky mountains, and looked down upon the snow a thousand feet below, and, standing where never human foot had stood before, felt the exultation of first explorers.[124]

It had been two hundred years since Darby Field became the first to reach the summit of a North American mountain. For more than half of that time, mountains had been of little interest to Americans. That would change in the years to come, as subsequent generations of Americans came to share Frémont's ambition to put human foot where it had never stood before, as they pushed ever westward.

CHAPTER TWO

HARDY MOUNTAIN PLANTS, 1842–1865

Up!—If thou knew'st who calls
To twilight parks of beech and pine,
High over the river intervals,
Above the ploughman's highest line,
Over the owner's farthest walls!
Up! where the airy citadel
O'erlooks the purging landscape's swell!...
Bookworm break this sloth urbane;
A greater spirit bids thee forth,
Than the gray dreams which thee detain

—RALPH WALDO EMERSON, "MONADNOC," 1845

A mountain chain determines many things for the statesman and philosopher.

—HENRY DAVID THOREAU, *A WALK TO WACHUSETT*, 1842

On July 19, 1842, in the (unobserved) bicentennial year of Darby Field's failed quest for diamonds on the summit of the "White Hill" in the White Mountains, and only weeks before John C. Frémont's discovery of a lonely bumblebee atop "Snow

Peak" in the Wind River Range, a twenty-five-year-old Harvard College graduate named Henry David Thoreau set off on an expedition of his own. His predecessors had sought out mountains in hope of finding riches or fame. Thoreau's goal, in contrast, reflected lesser, or perhaps greater, ambition—that of spiritual self-discovery, climbing the means to that end. With his friend Richard Fuller, he left in the early morning from his hometown of Concord to walk to 2,006-foot Mount Wachusett, whose modest summit, visible from Concord in those days, lay 30 miles to the west in central Massachusetts.

Although Thoreau is best remembered for the two years and two months he spent just a few hundred feet above sea level in a cabin by Walden Pond, he was also a regular visitor to New England's mountains. On that July day in 1842, Thoreau and Fuller walked 25 miles, stopping occasionally to cool off by bathing their feet in the streams they passed. A sometime schoolteacher, sometime pencil maker, and full-time amateur naturalist, Thoreau liked to walk and aspired to write. He was taking mental notes on the journey for what would be his first published piece of travel writing, "A Walk to Wachusett," which appeared in the *Boston Miscellany* the following January.[1]

The two young men spent the night in an inn in the present-day village of West Sterling. At dawn the next day they arose and walked another 4 miles to the mountain's base. They then made their way up its slopes—a short and uneventful climb through stands of sugar maples and scrub brush—until reaching the rocky summit.

From their vantage point at the top, they admired Mount Monadnock to the northwest in New Hampshire, the White Mountains farther north, and the Berkshires and Green Mountains to their west. As night fell, they watched shadows fall in the valleys east and west until, it seemed to Thoreau, "the sun's rays fell on us two alone, of all New England men."[2]

They slept on the mountaintop. The next morning, as Thoreau recalled in the account he published of his adventure, he reflected on the role of mountains in American history:

A mountain chain determines many things for the statesman and philosopher. The improvements of civilization rather creep along its sides than cross its summit. How often is it a barrier to prejudice and fanaticism! In passing over these heights of land, through their thin atmosphere, the follies of the plain are refined and purified; and as many species of plants do not scale their summits, so many species of folly, no doubt, do not cross the Alleghenies; it is only the hardy mountain-plant that creeps quite over the ridge and descends into the valley beyond.[3]

Henry David Thoreau might himself be considered a species of "hardy mountain-plant." It did not trouble him that he was considered strange by some Concord neighbors for his lack of steady employment, his disinterest in material acquisitions, his nonattendance at church, his failure to marry, and his solitary ways. "But special I remember thee," he wrote in a poem embedded in his article about the climb, "Wachusett, who like me / Standest alone without society."[4] Thoreau's New England ancestors regarded mountains, among other things, as barriers to progress. Not so Thoreau. In their sturdy uprightness, he believed, they provided his fellow Americans models of righteous independence for winnowing out the follies of the plain.

Thoreau had no idea in July 1842 that Lieutenant Frémont was preparing to carry the national banner to the rooftop of the Rockies, and it was not the kind of gesture that necessarily would have gained his approval. The limit of Thoreau's own mountain exploration extended only from New England to the Catskills, and the notion that it was America's manifest destiny to push its borders westward to the Pacific, or southward into Mexican territory did not fill him with enthusiasm. But he was fascinated by exploration, actual and metaphorical. As a freshman at Harvard College, he had read Washington Irving's biography of Christopher Columbus, in addition to the Greek and Latin tomes required by the college's classical curriculum. As he later urged readers of *Walden*, they should each seek to become "the Lewis and Clark . . . of your own streams and oceans; explore your own higher latitudes."[5]

Henry David Thoreau.

TRANSCENDENTAL MOUNTAINEERING

Thoreau belonged to an informal cohort of New England intellectuals and writers, most living in or near the small town of Concord, Massachusetts, between the 1830s and 1850s, who were interested in social reform, liberal Christianity, literature, philosophy, and the natural world. The ideas of these "transcendentalists," although often ridiculed by their contemporaries, would come to have a dramatic impact on American culture, particularly on popular attitudes toward the environment.[6]

Transcendentalism developed as part of a broader romantic movement on both sides of the Atlantic that celebrated individual consciousness, intuition, and self-expression, against what its adherents felt was the excessive empiricism of the Enlightenment tradition. Europeans like the German idealist philosopher Immanuel Kant challenged the notion propounded by John Locke that all knowledge was absorbed through the senses, arguing instead that some of the most important forms of knowledge, especially a sense of right and wrong, were innate within human beings; some knowledge "transcended" the senses.[7]

That did not mean that either Kant or the transcendentalists rejected science; instead, they sought a balance between the knowledge that could be gained by empirical observation and that to be gained by personal revelation or pure thought. Thoreau filled his notebooks with observations of the natural world, including counting the rings on tree stumps, for thus, he exulted, "you can unroll the rotten papyrus on which the history of the Concord forest is written."[8]

Leading figures in the transcendentalist movement in the United States, including Unitarian minister Ralph Waldo Emerson, founded a Transcendental Club, which met periodically between 1836 and 1840, and launched a magazine, the *Dial*, published between 1840 and 1842 (and edited by Margaret Fuller, older sister of Richard, Thoreau's climbing partner on Wachusett in 1842). Although the transcendentalists borrowed ideas from European romanticism, their attempt to reshape philosophy was part of a continuing American debate over the meaning of wilderness and nature. For New Englanders of earlier generations, the Bible was the only appropriate guide to understanding the divine order, including its embodiment in the natural world. God revealed himself through his creations—but only if the viewer saw the world through a scriptural prism.

The transcendentalists turned this argument on its head; they believed that a close study and appreciation of nature revealed truths about life's meaning that could be only dimly understood from scriptural sources. "The happiest man," Emerson observed, "is he who learns from nature the lesson of worship."[9]

This wasn't nature worship exactly, since ultimately man would learn to rise above nature to fulfill his spiritual destiny. But it elevated the natural world to a realm nearly (and for some transcendentalists, actually) sacred. Emerson celebrated nature as a perfect creation of God.

Knowledge of the natural world was thus a crucial element in human self-discovery, self-knowledge, and self-cultivation.[10]

In harmony with these ideals, Emerson headed for the hills. On a trip to Italy three years before the publication of *Nature*, he climbed 4,203-foot Mount Vesuvius in 1833, among the first Americans to do so.[11] Closer to home, Emerson climbed Mount Washington in New Hampshire; 4,395-foot Mount Mansfield, the highest mountain in Vermont; and 3,489-foot Mount Greylock, the highest in Massachusetts.[12] His favorite mountain, to which he often returned, was 3,165-foot Mount Monadnock, in southern New Hampshire, visible from Concord in those days of cleared fields.[13] On one of those climbs, in May 1845, Emerson began composing a poem in which he imagined the mountain speaking to its human visitors in terms that suggested their mutual admiration:

> *Monadnoc is a mountain strong,*
> *Tall and good my kind among;*
> *But well I know, no mountain can*
> *Measure with a perfect man. . . .*[14]

The poem was much admired by nature-loving New Englanders, who felt it strengthened their region's claims to possess world-class mountains. Unitarian minister and mountain-climber Thomas Starr King wrote in 1859 that Monadnock "would feel prouder than Mont Blanc, or Chimbarozo, or the topmost spire of the Himalaya, if it could know that the genius of Mr. Emerson has made it the noblest mountain in literature."[15]

In the long run, it was Emerson's protégé, Henry David Thoreau, who would do most to ennoble the mountains—and American wilderness in general. Following his 1842 climb of Mount Wachusett, Thoreau climbed Mount Monadnock four times between 1844 and 1860, as well as Mount Greylock and various peaks in the Hoosac Range of western Massachusetts and the Catskills in 1844.[16]

Thoreau also climbed New Hampshire's Mount Washington twice—once with his older brother, John, in 1839, and again in 1858. On the first journey, after sailing a small boat up the Concord River to the Merrimack River, and taking to shore near Hooksett, New Hampshire, Thoreau and his brother visited Franconia Notch and Crawford Notch, where they stayed at the Crawford House. They climbed Mount Washington, most likely by the Crawford Path, but possibly along a more northerly route (the line taken by the present-day cog railway).

Thoreau described the trip in *A Week on the Concord and Merrimack Rivers*, a book he composed while living at Walden Pond in 1846–47, and published in 1849. The account was part travel narrative and part memorial for John, who died less than three years after the New Hampshire trip of complications from a minor infected wound—a loss that deeply affected Henry David. Clearly knowledgeable about the history of Mount Washington, Thoreau referred to it as "Agiocochook," the name the Pigwacket tribe had known it by two centuries earlier.[17] And in an entry in his journal written after his brother's death, he placed their climb squarely in the context of New England history:

> We had resolved to travel to those White mountain . . . the Chrystal hills which one John [Darby] Field an Irish man had visited—as [Governor John] Winthrop says.[18]

Thoreau's exploits on New England's gentle peaks were unremarkable as feats of mountaineering. Still, in climbing these mountains he managed to display his independent streak, preferring to chart his own compass-line route to the top rather than following established trails. And he extended his acquaintance with the mountains by sleeping at the summit of three of them—Wachusett, Monadnock, and Greylock—and just below the summit of a fourth, Katahdin.[19]

Mount Katahdin was Thoreau's most challenging climb. It is one of the rare mountains in the northeast retaining its Native American name, derived from the Penobscot Indians who lived in its vicinity and called it "Kette-Adene," meaning greatest or preeminent mountain.[20] At 5,268 feet, Katahdin is the highest mountain in Maine, and fifth-highest in New

England. It was long neglected by climbers because of its remote location, with surveyor Charles Turner Jr. and ten companions recording the first ascent in 1804.[21]

In the summer of 1845, two socially prominent Bostonians—the Reverend Edward Everett Hale (remembered as the author of the 1863 patriotic short story "The Man without a Country") and William Francis Channing (a friend of Emerson and Thoreau)—were the first to attempt Katahdin for no reason other than their own enjoyment. A furious thunderstorm on summit day kept them from reaching the top. Their example, however, inspired Thoreau to make his own attempt the following year.[22]

Thoreau's trip to Katahdin came in the midst of his year living at Walden Pond, and it was very much a part of his intent to "live deliberately." Leaving Concord on August 31, 1846, Thoreau traveled by railroad, steamship, buggy, bateau, and on foot, picking up a half dozen companions en route, some volunteers and some hired, and reaching the mountain's base on September 7. The others were not as experienced or enthusiastic as he was, so he led the way, taking a route never before climbed (and seldom attempted since, except by those who wished to follow in his footsteps).[23] The party camped below tree line that night, although Thoreau had gone on his own to open ground above tree line before returning to camp.

September 8 was summit day, or perhaps just-short-of-summit day, with Thoreau alone reaching the tableland between South and Baxter Peaks, the latter the mountain's true summit. Clouds obscured the view (Thoreau called the mountaintop a "cloud factory"), and it's not entirely clear from his account whether or not he believed he was standing on the top of Katahdin; he refers to being on the "summit" but also mentions catching a glimpse through the clouds of a "dark, damp crag to the right or left." Earlier biographers credited him with reaching the summit; later writers have not.[24]

Thoreau seemed to have felt some of the unease about Katahdin that had kept local Indians from climbing the mountain. His subsequent account, written in a series of articles for a New York periodical called

Sartain's Union Magazine and posthumously published as part of *The Maine Woods*, are some of the darkest reflections on nature to appear in his writings, and indeed in American mountaineering literature. "The tops of mountains," he reflected,

> are among the unfinished parts of the globe, whither it is a slight insult to the gods to climb and pry into their secrets, and try their effects on our humanity. Only daring and insolent men, perchance, go there. Savage races, as savages, do not climb mountains—their tops are sacred and mysterious tracts never visited by them.[25]

Thoreau left the summit and re-joined his party below. His unease only increased on the descent, alongside the Abol Stream. He came to a section of open land on the mountain slope, barren of trees because of some long-ago conflagration:

> Perhaps I most fully realized that this was primeval, untamed, and forever untameable Nature . . . while coming down this part of the mountain. . . . It is difficult to conceive of a region uninhabited by man. We habitually presume his presence and influence everywhere. And yet we have not seen pure Nature, unless we have seen her thus vast, and drear, and inhuman. . . . Nature was here something savage and awful, though beautiful. I looked with awe at the ground I trod on, to see what the Powers had made there. . . . This was that Earth of which we had heard, made out of Chaos and Old Night. Here was no man's garden, but the unhandselled globe. It was not lawn, nor pasture, nor mead, nor woodland, nor lea, nor arable, nor waste-land. . . . There was there felt the presence of a force not bound to be kind to man.[26]

Unlike Emerson's "Monadnoc," Thoreau's "Ktaadn" wasn't offering its visitors any hearty hail-fellow-well-met greeting. The mountain was no benign presence. Thoreau felt humbled in its presence, understanding its indifference to the tiny humans who ventured up its slopes (here he was tending closer to the original notion of the sublime, as revealed in Shelley's 1816 poem about Mont Blanc). Katahdin served no function for man ("not lawn, nor pasture, . . ."), and indeed was incapable of being converted to any such use; that was what made it a "force" in its own right. Thoreau returned twice to Maine in the 1850s, with the intention of returning to Katahdin's summit, but each time he changed his plans.

WESTERN MOUNTAINEERING AND MANIFEST DESTINY

While Thoreau was climbing Katahdin in 1846, Abraham Lincoln was campaigning in Illinois for a seat in the United States Congress. Other countrymen were fighting a war with Mexico that, when concluded in 1848, brought more than a million square miles of territory into the Union. Lincoln, who won his seat in Congress but served only a single term, opposed that war; so did Thoreau. In the aftermath of the war with Mexico, tensions between the North and the South increased dramatically, as Americans debated whether the territories gained in the conflict should be counted among the free or the slave states.

Included in the spoils of war were the Sierra Nevada of California, a range greater in area than the western Alps. The Sierra Nevada would play a singularly important role in the history of American (and, indeed, international) mountaineering—the proving ground for techniques and equipment that would redefine climbing standards in the twentieth century. The Sierra Nevada lie to the east of California's Central Valley, running 400 miles on a north–south axis between the gap below Lassen Peak to the north and Tehachapi Pass to the south, and averaging about 70 miles in width. The western slopes of the mountains rise gently, but sheer granite faces, ranging between 4,000 and 7,000 feet high, dominate the eastern front.

The origins of the mountain range date back 600 million years, with the formation of sedimentary rock along the western coast of North

America. About 220 million years ago, magma seeped into the sedimentary level from deep below, creating giant granite blocks. Beginning 80 million years ago, underground pressures split the granite blocks and uplifted a tilted line of the broken blocks high above the surface—what geologists call fault-block mountains. Interspersed among the granite peaks are outcroppings of metamorphic and volcanic remnants. Rivers and glaciers carved dramatic valleys through the range, including Kings River canyon, which is more than 8,000 feet deep. The Sierra Nevada constitute the longest continuous mountain range in the United States and encompass thirteen peaks over 14,000 feet, clustered on the southern end of the range and including Mount Whitney, at 14,505 feet the highest mountain in the United States south of Alaska. More than 120 peaks in the range are over 13,000 feet in height.[27]

The name "Sierra Nevada" means "snowy range" in Spanish. The California mountains are not the only ones so named. Portuguese explorer Juan Rodriguez Cabrillo, exploring the coast of California on behalf of the Spanish, sighted a range of coastal mountains and called them the "Sierra Nevada," although the name didn't stick; they became known instead as the Santa Cruz Mountains. The Spanish were slow to follow up on the early exploration of the region they called Alta California, but late in the eighteenth century, fearing the encroachment of imperial competitors like Britain and Russia, they began to move northward up the Pacific coastline.

In 1776, an expedition of Spanish colonists founded a mission at the site of a natural harbor to which they gave the name San Francisco. A Franciscan missionary who accompanied and chronicled the expedition, Father Pedro Font, climbed a hill above the new outpost and, looking to the northeast, spied a chain of mountains that he described as *una gran sierra nevada.*[28] This time the name stuck—deservedly, since in nondrought winters the mountains are buried in heavy snow, although most of it melts in the summer, and the range contains few glaciers or permanent snowfields.[29]

The Spanish settlers of California showed little interest in the Sierra Nevada over the next half century. In the interval, Mexico gained independence from Spain. But newly independent Mexico held a tenuous control over the northern provinces. A few score Americans found their way to California by the 1830s, and they encouraged others to join them. The first wagon train of American settlers arrived in the Mexican province in 1841, and by mid-decade there were over a thousand US settlers, about a tenth of the non-Indian population of the province. Americans in California were well aware of the similarity between their position and that of their compatriots in Texas who, a decade earlier, had forcibly wrested control of the province from Mexico. Americans back east took note as well. While manifest destiny's advocates in Washington, DC, had previously focused their attention on the Oregon Country of the Pacific Northwest, by the early 1840s it had occurred to them that California was the greater prize.

In March 1843, Lieutenant John C. Frémont of the US Army Corps of Topographical Engineers was in Washington, DC, completing the report of his 1842 expedition to the Rockies.[30] Now he was given a new assignment through the influence of his expansionist-minded father-in-law, Senator Thomas Hart Benton of Missouri. Frémont was to cross the Rockies to survey the trail followed by American settlers to the Oregon Country. Although the expedition he commanded was ostensibly scientific in purpose, some of Frémont's preparations suggested otherwise, including the fact that he requisitioned a cannon and 500 pounds of ammunition.

At the end of May, Frémont set off across the Kansas plain with thirty-nine men on horseback, cannon in tow. He hoped to find a route over the Rockies to the south of the established South Pass route. With a small contingent he explored the Cache la Poudre River canyon (near present-day Fort Collins, Colorado) in search of a pass, but without success. So he re-joined the rest of his company and crossed South Pass. Eventually, they made their way to the Columbia River and the Oregon Country.

Frémont's orders were to explore the Oregon Trail; they said nothing about California. But the ambitious young officer rarely felt constrained by the formal limits of his orders. Instead of turning back after reaching Oregon, he took his men south along the eastern slope of the Sierra Nevada, searching for the rumored (and nonexistent) San Buenaventura River, hoping it would provide an easy passage through the mountains. By late January 1844, he had given up that quest—but not the idea of crossing into California.

On January 29, Frémont's party headed into the mountains, though they had to leave their cannon behind. It took them a month to make their way through deep snow, killing off their horses one by one for food. En route, Frémont and the expedition's topographer, Charles Preuss took time off to make mountaineering as well as exploratory history. As Frémont recorded in his subsequent account, "The dividing ridge of the Sierra is in sight from this encampment. With Mr. Preuss, I ascended today [February 14, 1844] the highest peak to the right: from which we had a beautiful view of a mountain lake at our feet, about fifteen miles in length, and so entirely surrounded by mountains that we could not discover an outlet."[31] The mountain lake was Lake Tahoe; the mountain they climbed was 10,068-foot Red Lake Peak.

Six days later, on February 20, they made it across that final "dividing ridge," via 9,338-foot Carson Pass, later to become the major overland route to California for gold-seeking prospectors. When they descended the western slopes of the Sierra Nevada into the valley below, they were, as scout Kit Carson recalled, "naked and in as poor condition as men possibly could be."[32] After resupplying at Sutter's Fort, they rode south through the San Joaquin Valley, departing California in mid-April and crossing eastward via a pass in the Tehachapi Mountains. Frémont was greatly impressed by the climate and fertility of the San Joaquin Valley, thinking how pleasant it was in the "warm green spring to look up at the rocky and snowy peaks where lately we had suffered so much."[33]

Frémont's superiors in Washington were not displeased that he had stretched his orders to include a sojourn in California. Promoted to captain on the return, Frémont's public popularity grew apace. His mountain-climbing feats were singled out for praise. The *Cincinnati Chronicle* wrote that the expedition's "crossing of the Great North American Andes"—that is, the Sierra Nevada—"in the midst of winter [was] a feat far exceeding the passage of the Alps, by the ancient or modern warriors."[34]

The link between mountain exploration and American expansionist dreams, always an undercurrent in Frémont's ventures, came to the fore in

John C. Frémont, ca. 1859.

his third western expedition in 1845–46. In June 1845, he led fifty-five men westward from Saint Louis, officially to find the headwaters of the Arkansas River in the Colorado Rockies. Instead, by December his party had made the first winter crossing of a newly discovered 7,057-foot pass through the Sierra Nevada into California. (He and his men were lucky that the snows were late; the following year a hapless party of settlers led by Jacob and George Donner found themselves trapped in deep snow in November below what became known as the Donner Pass and resorted to cannibalism to survive.)[35]

Frémont and his party spent the next six months without apparent purpose, riding from place to place in California and Oregon, as if waiting for a sign. The sign arrived in May 1846, when a messenger from Washington, DC, caught up with Frémont at Oregon's Upper Klamath Lake, carrying confidential dispatches. What exactly they contained is unknown, but Frémont ceased dawdling and led his men south to support an armed rebellion by American settlers in California against the Mexican rulers of the province.[36] They would be joined by US forces landed by sea, and others crossing from Santa Fe, and by the end of 1846, California was in American hands. The Treaty of Guadalupe Hidalgo, signed on February 2, 1848, formally brought into the Union the territory (soon to be state) of California, along with the southwestern territory that became the states of Nevada, Utah, Arizona, Oklahoma, and New Mexico.

In February 1847, on the occasion of the annual observance of Washington's birthday, American warships in San Francisco Bay fired a salute to the founder of a nation that now stretched from coast to coast. Edwin Bryant, a veteran of Frémont's forces in the fight against the Mexicans, described the cannon fire as "a voice from the soul of Washington, speaking in majestic and thunder-like tones to the green and flowery valleys, the gentle hills and lofty mountains of California, and consecrating them as future abode of millions upon millions of the sons of liberty."[37] The nation's "manifest destiny" had been realized. And with all the other advantages, great new ranges of "lofty mountains" now became available for exploration.

DIXIE MOUNTAINEERING

The popular mountain resorts in the Catskills and the White Mountains had no counterparts below the Mason-Dixon line before the Civil War. Indeed, southerners were more likely to visit northern mountains for vacations than those in their own backyards, convinced that the northern climes were healthier places to be in summer. And they learned to speak what was by this point the conventional language of mountain aesthetics and appreciation on their northern journeys. "The ascent to the summit of this Mount," J. C. Myers of New Hope, Virginia, wrote of New Hampshire's Mount Washington in 1849, "is attended with considerable fatigue; but the wild and sublime character of the scenery induces a stranger to climb upward and onward, till he gains the summit when all is richly repaid . . . by the magnitude of the elevation, the extent and variety of the surrounding scenery, which is wild, picturesque and sublime on every hand."[38] Two "sublimes" in a single paragraph was indeed evidence of Burke's predominance in the rhetoric surrounding American mountains.

The best-known southern mountain-climber of the antebellum era was, in fact, a transplanted Yankee. Born in Connecticut in 1793, a graduate of Yale College, Elisha Mitchell went to the University of North Carolina in 1818 to teach mathematics and natural philosophy. A man of many parts (he was also an ordained Presbyterian minister), in 1825 he added the subjects of chemistry, geology, and mineralogy to his teaching load. Mitchell became fascinated with a peak in western North Carolina, which as early as 1828 he decided must be the highest in the region. The mountain he had in mind was located about 30 miles northeast of Asheville, part of the Black Mountain subrange of the Appalachians.

In July 1835 he made the first ascent of what he called the "Black Mountain." The ascent was difficult because of the "thick laurels" on the mountainside, "so closely set and their strong branches so interwoven, that a path cannot be forced by pushing them aside." This was typical of southern mountains, thanks to the warmer climate, and the fact that the mountains themselves had not been stripped of the layers of ground soil by the scouring action of glaciers, as in the White Mountains. Even at the summit, unlike Mount Washington, there were tall balsam firs. "The growth of the tree is such on these high summits," Mitchell recorded in his account of the ascent of Black Mountain, "that it is easy to climb to the top and taking hold of the highest branch look abroad upon the prospect."[39]

Mitchell measured the mountain on a subsequent trip in 1844 at 6,708 feet. The actual height was 6,684 feet, nearly 400 feet higher than New Hampshire's Mount Washington, which became a point of pride for North Carolinians in those years of worsening sectional tensions. Black Mountain is the highest mountain in North America east of the Mississippi River.

There was, however, a rival claimant for that title. Thomas Lanier Clingman, a prominent North Carolina politician from Asheville and a former student of Mitchell's, argued that a mountain he had recently climbed, Smoky Dome (later Clingmans Dome) in the Great Smoky Mountains on the border of North Carolina and Tennessee was over 6,900 feet, and thus taller than Black Mountain (Clingmans Dome's actual height is 6,643 feet). Mitchell returned to his own mountain on June 27, 1857, to measure it yet again. Mitchell was climbing alone below the summit when he was caught in a storm and died in a fall above a 40-foot waterfall. Searchers found his body several weeks later at the bottom of a pool in the Cat-tail fork of Caney River. He was among the first American climbers to die on a mountain.[40]

Mitchell was initially buried in the graveyard of the Presbyterian church in Asheville, but his remains were dug up a year later and he was reinterred on the mountain that, in the meantime, had been given his name. Local boosterism influenced the decision to rebury Mitchell's remains. "In view of the fact that he was the first to visit these mountains and to make known their superior height to any east of the Rocky Mountains," the Asheville *Spectator* editorialized in 1858, "no more fitting testimony of esteem could be offered his memory" than burial on the mountaintop.[41] A stone monument in his memory was erected on the mountain in 1888, and Mount Mitchell became North Carolina's first state park in 1916.[42]

THE CASCADES

The Oregon Treaty of 1846 brought within the boundaries of the United States the territory that would become the states of Oregon, Washington, and Idaho. It also brought possession of several active volcanoes, including 11,249-foot Mount Hood, which had erupted only a few decades before it was first spotted by Lewis and Clark in 1805, and 9,677-foot Mount Saint Helens, which had erupted briefly and mildly in 1842 as the first permanent American settlers were arriving in the Oregon Country. (The latter would erupt again, more spectacularly, in 1980, reducing the height of its summit to 8,364 feet.)[43]

Mounts Hood and Saint Helens are part of a chain of mountains, mostly of volcanic origin, stretching some 700 miles from Mount Lassen in northern California through Oregon and Washington and into south-western British Columbia. The origins of the range stretch back 40 million years or more, but relatively recent volcanic events (whose duration extends back only hundreds of thousands rather than tens of millions of years), account for the shape and bulk of the major peaks. The name "Cascades" was already being used to describe these mountains by the 1820s, probably inspired by the Columbia River, which was then full of rapids and falls, cascading through a break in the mountain range between present-day Oregon and Washington. The Cascade Volcanic Arc, as it is also known, is part of the "Ring of Fire" of volcanoes found on landmasses around the Pacific Ocean. Among their other distinctions, the Cascades are the most heavily glaciated mountain range in the contiguous United States.[44]

In some American mountain ranges, like the Sierra Nevada, it could take many days even to catch a glimpse of, let alone figure out the approach to, the principal mountains. The highest peak in the Sierra would not be identified until the mid-1860s. In contrast, the Cascades, including Rainier, Saint Helens, Adams, Hood, and Jefferson, stand in magnificent isolation from surrounding mountains, their gleaming snow slopes visible at considerable distance by land and sea. And, as white settlement increased in the Pacific Northwest, some of the principal cities of the region were established near the highest peaks—Portland just 50 miles from Mount Hood, Seattle just 60 miles from Mount Rainier. As a result, from the early days of settlement, the Cascades proved accessible to and attracted amateur climbers, in contrast to the Rockies and Sierra, where surveyors, military officers, and others with official or professional designations took the lead. Local settlers made the first ascents of Mount Saint Helens in 1853, Mount Adams in 1854, and Mount Hood in 1857.[45]

Mount Saint Helens was named by Lieutenant William Broughton of the Royal Navy, during his exploratory voyage up the Columbia in 1793. The mountain is clearly visible to the north from Portland, Oregon, and in 1853 Thomas Jefferson Dryer, founder of the city's first (and lasting) newspaper, the *Oregonian*, set out to climb it.

Traveling on horseback with three companions (known from Dryer's

subsequent account as "Messrs. Wilson, Smith [and] Drew"—possibly
John Wilson, an *Oregonian* employee, and Edwin P. Drew, an Oregon
Indian agent, with Smith's identity a mystery), Dryer's party reached the
south side of the mountain on August 25, 1853. The group climbed to the
summit the next day. Editor Dryer's subsequent account, published in his
newspaper, reflects the continuing, and by this point routine, influence
of Burkean aesthetics and Emersonian philosophy on mountaineering
writing:

> The appearance of the mountain upon a nearer approach is sub-
> limely grand, and impossible to describe. The blackened piles of
> lava which were thrown into ridges hundreds of feet high in every
> imaginable shape, with an occasional high cliff of primitive forma-
> tion, seeming to lift its head above the struggle to be released from
> its compressed position, impress the mind of the beholder with the
> power of Omnipotence, and the insignificance of human power
> when compared with that of nature's God.

From the summit, Dryer reported:

> The whole Coast and Cascade ranges of mountains could be
> plainly traced with the naked eye. The snow covered peaks of Mts.
> Hood, Rainier and two others seemed close by. These form a sort
> of amphitheatre on a large scale, diversified with hills and valleys.[46]

Mount Saint Helens was the first of the Cascades to be climbed in
the newly incorporated Washington Territory, and the highest mountain yet climbed on the Pacific Coast, although that record would not
last long.

The next Cascade to fall in the Washington Territory was 12,276-foot
Mount Adams. Sometime in August or September 1854, A. G. Aiken,
Edward J. Allen, and Andrew Burge, all of whom had been workers
employed in building a military road from the Columbia River to Puget
Sound, made the first recorded ascent of Adams, although their achieve-

ment was little noted at the time. A published account of their climb would not appear for more than a half century, and few details survive.[47]

The third of the Pacific Northwest giants to fall in the 1850s was Mount Hood—the highest mountain in Oregon and the fourth-highest of the Cascade volcanoes. Viewed from the Willamette Valley to its west, it displays itself as a model mountainscape, with symmetrical ridgelines culminating in a sharp peak. Hood was the best-known peak in the Pacific Northwest in the nineteenth century and had been so long before anyone tried to climb it. The mountain was also named by Lieutenant Broughton, in 1792, and it served as a beacon of trail's end to weary settler families in the wagon trains wending their way to the Oregon Country in the 1840s and 1850s.[48]

For the earliest settlers, Mount Hood was an obstacle. From The Dalles, a point on the Columbia River to the mountain's east, they were

This early photo of Mount Hood appeared in John Muir's *The Mountains of California* (1913).

forced to load their wagons onto rafts to complete their journey to the Willamette Valley. When a settler named Joel Palmer arrived at The Dalles in 1845 and discovered how expensive it would be and how long it would take to get a boat to take him around to the western side of the Cascades, he balked. Instead, he joined with a group of settlers led by Samuel Barlow to find a wagon route across a pass on the south side of the mountain.

On October 12, 1845, to get a better view of the surrounding hills, Palmer climbed above 9,000 feet on Mount Hood's south side in moccasins (and went on in bare feet when his footwear fell apart). His route took him up what would later be known as Zigzag Glacier and the rock formation of Mississippi Head, probably reaching the base of Crater Rock, a lava dome that is a prominent feature on the south side and that had been formed only a few decades earlier.

Palmer was interested in the practical problem of getting around the mountain, not in reaching its summit. But he did have some thoughts on that question, which he shared in a subsequent account of his climb. "The opinion heretofore entertained that this peak could not be ascended to its summit, I found to be erroneous," he declared confidently. "There is no doubt that, but any of the snow peaks upon this range can be ascended to the summit."[49]

Nine years passed before anyone again ventured to the higher elevations of Mount Hood. Having summited Mount Saint Helens in 1853, Thomas Dryer decided to add Mount Hood to his list of conquests the following year. On August 8, 1854, with six other men (including William Barlow, son of road builder Samuel Barlow), Dryer attempted to climb the mountain's south side. Several dropped out en route. At noon that day, according to Dryer, they reached the summit, from which they could see not only Mount Rainier, Mount Adams, and Mount Jefferson (the peaks he had already seen from the summit of Mount Saint Helens), but also Mount Shasta in California, and Fremont Peak in Wyoming. In reality, neither Shasta, nearly 300 miles away, nor Fremont Peak, even farther distant, are visible from the summit of Mount Hood. A host of other details about the climb (including Dryer's estimate of Hood's summit height at 18,361 feet) suggest that imagination outstripped mountaineering judgment.[50]

Three years later, Henry L. Pittock led the next party to attempt Mount Hood. Pittock was born in England but he had been raised in Pennsylvania and had emigrated to Oregon in 1853, where he went to work as a typesetter for Dryer's *Oregonian*. On August 6, 1857, accompanied by four others, Pittock climbed the south side of the mountain and reached the summit by what remains today the most popular route, past Crater Rock, up the steep snow ridge known as the Hogsback, and then through another chute to the final summit slope.

For a group of completely inexperienced climbers, it was an impressive piece of route-finding on snow and ice. And while it presents no serious technical difficulties, the route is not without dangers to the unwary and the unlucky, including rockfall and a yawning bergschrund (the crevasse formed at the head of the glacier, where it pulls away from mountain bedrock), both especially treacherous in late summer. To put Pittock and his companions' achievement in perspective, it was only two years earlier that English climbers had first reached the summit of Mont Blanc unaccompanied by local guides. And, unlike Mont Blanc, which been ascended scores of times by 1857, Hood had been climbed, at most, once before.[51]

Pittock and his climbing partners found that the summit of Mount Hood bore little resemblance to what Dryer had described three years earlier. They concluded that Dryer's claim to a first ascent was unjustified. His description suggests that he reached only the "Crow's Nest" above Steel Cliffs, high on the mountain's southeast ridge, but still 350 vertical feet below the summit by the challenging Wy'East route.[52]

For their part, the members of Pittock's party left a flag on the summit and carved their names on a rock to ensure that their own claim to Hood's conquest would stand up. On their return to Portland, one of the climbers, James G. Deardorff, announced their achievement in the pages of the *Democratic Standard*, a rival to Dryer's *Oregonian*. Deardorff's account was not without its own misleading details (Shasta again allegedly in view), but the description of the summit itself, including its precipitous drop-off on the northern side, gives the Pittock party a much more plausible claim to the first ascent. Not that Dryer would admit as much. In the pages of his own *Oregonian* a week later, he grumbled about "these young gentlemen," who dared challenge "the veracity of those far their seniors in years, experience and standing," out of "their own panting desire for fame."[53]

YOSEMITE REVEALED TO CALIFORNIA'S NEW CONQUERORS

The days when the Oregon Country was the main destination on the West Coast for American settlers ended abruptly with the Mexican War. The Spanish and Mexicans had controlled California for nearly three-quarters of a century without venturing into the mountains, and they had not suspected that there might be riches in the northern hills. The California gold rush following the discovery of flakes of the precious metal at Sutter's Mill on January 24, 1848, brought tens of thousands of prospectors to the newest American territory within a year—some by sea, but many finding their way over Sierra mountain passes.

It is likely that more Americans found themselves climbing mountains in the first two years of the gold rush than in all the years prior to 1848. Not that many of them took any enjoyment from the experience. T. H. Jefferson, who made the five-month, 2,000-mile journey from Independence, Missouri, to San Francisco in 1846, crossing the Sierra Nevada, published a map and booklet in 1849 describing the route and its hardships, warning prospective emigrants that they should make sure to be across the range by October, lest they be trapped by snow, and that the "western descent of those mountains is the most rugged and difficult portion of the whole journey."[54]

The newcomers found more than gold on the western slopes of the Sierra. Prospectors began to explore the tributaries of the Tuolumne River by 1849, and by 1850 an enterprising miner named James Savage had opened a trading post on the Merced River, 10 miles to the west of a deep valley first glimpsed from its northern rim by fur trader Joseph Walker in 1833. Skirmishing broke out between the prospectors and the local Indians. In the late winter of 1851, white volunteers in a local militia founded by Savage and called the Mariposa Battalion tracked a band of Ahwahneechee Indians westward into the mountains to the wilderness valley where they were rumored to be hiding.

On March 27, 1851, the pursuers came upon a vista, later called Inspiration Point. From that flat granite shelf at 5,300 feet, they saw a cleft in the earth spread below them, a mile wide and 7 miles long, framed by steep granite walls and distinctive rock formations rising 3,000 feet from the valley floor. Two of the latter, soon named El Capitan and Half Dome, became among the best-known rock formations on earth. Huge waterfalls, including one to be named Bridalveil, fell from the rim, and a river, later named the Merced, flowed placidly through the verdant meadows of the valley floor.

"The grandeur of the scene," one of the Mariposa Battalion volunteers, Lafayette Bunnell, wrote, "was softened by the haze that hung over the valley—light as gossamer—and by the clouds that partially dimmed the higher cliffs and mountains." Bunnell, who suggested they call the valley "Yosemity," the supposed name of the tribe they were pursuing, was moved to tears by the sight.[55]

It took the White Mountains of New Hampshire two hundred years to go from howling wilderness to genteel tourist attraction. It took Yosemite Valley a little over four years to make the same transition. The difference reflected the shift in attitude toward mountains between the seventeenth and nineteenth centuries, as well as the self-interested efforts of a number of California promoters, eager to replicate the success enjoyed by their eastern counterparts in the thriving tourism industry. In July 1855, James Mason Hutchings, a transplanted Englishman who had made and lost a fortune as a gold prospector, and who saw a new opportunity to get rich in promoting California's scenic wonders, organized the first tourist party to visit Yosemite.[56]

By 1856, the first crude hotel had been constructed in the Yosemite Valley, and two others were erected by 1859. Early visitors to Yosemite were also attracted by the discovery of giant trees nearby: the Mariposa grove of sequoias, some of them more than 2,000 years old and 200 feet in height. The flat valley floor, cut by the wandering Merced River, was an ideal pastoral parkland, and the stark granite walls that surround the floor provided a sense of welcome separation from mundane civilization.

So the tourists came—at first a few score a year, then hundreds, then thousands. Among them was Thomas Starr King, who had celebrated the White Mountains of his native New England in his widely read *The White Hills: Their Legends, Landscapes and Poetry*, published in 1859. He moved to San Francisco the following year to open the city's first Unitarian church. In the four years before his death at thirty-nine from illness, the young minister became one of California's leading citizens and best promoters. Bringing a Boston-bred transcendentalist sensibility to bear on California's scenic beauties, he persuaded many eastern readers that California was truly a promised land. The Sierra, in particular, delighted him, and he described them in letters to the *Boston Transcript* in terms of sacred landscapes.

King's first glimpse of the range, from a steamer on the Sacramento River in 1860, seemed "like a vision from another world, like the street and wall of the New Jerusalem." On his first trip to Yosemite Valley later that same year, King experienced "that which the Israelites felt amid the passes of the Sinai when the Divine glory was at the mount."[57] King felt Yosemite surpassed in grandeur any other mountain setting in the world. Describing El Capitan (then known as Tutucanula), the granite monolith on the north side of the Yosemite Valley, he struggled to find a comparison that would be meaningful to his New England readers:

Probably you have been in "The Glen" among the White Mountains, and you remember the sharp peak of Mount Adams, whose pyramid is so symmetrical. . . . Imagine Mount Adams cloven by Omnipotence midway from its apex to its lowest stone, so that you could ride on horseback within a few yards of the smooth wall, and look up from plinth to crown![58]

And in a letter to an eastern friend written from the Sierra, King derided his earlier romantic celebration of the White Mountains: "Poor White Mountain Notch! Its nose is broken. If you can find any copies of King's book on the New Hampshire ant-hills, I advise you, as a friend of the author, to buy up the remaining edition."[59]

Visual artists, like the New York–born photographer Carleton Watkins, and the German-born and -trained landscape painter Albert Bierstadt, visited Yosemite in the 1860s and made their own contributions in enshrining the valley to the status of national wonder. Watkins's photographs were displayed in eastern galleries and sold to the public in a series of stereoscopic views, while Bierstadt's golden-lit paintings *Valley of the Yosemite* (1864), *Looking Down Yosemite Valley* (1865), and *Domes of Yosemite* (the latter completed in 1867 and sold for a then astounding $25,000) were widely viewed and helped solidify the image of Yosemite as an unspoiled Garden of Eden.[60]

Carleton Watkins's photos of Yosemite were popular subjects for viewing by stereoscope, as in this panoramic view of Yosemite Valley from Inspiration Point.

MOUNTAINEERING AND GEOLOGY

"Genesis governed geology," Marjorie Nicolson wrote in *Mountain Gloom and Mountain Glory*, her 1959 account of changing attitudes toward mountains from the Middle Ages to the modern world.[61] That the world had existed only six thousand or so years since the moment of creation was a given for Christians on both sides of the Atlantic in the late eighteenth century and into the early nineteenth century. And that opinion survived, notwithstanding such anomalies as the mountaintop discoveries of fossils of long-extinct animals, including those of seashells and fish. Yale College professor of chemistry and natural history Benjamin Silliman wrote in 1829, "Respecting the deluge"—that is, Noah's flood—"there can be but one opinion . . . geology fully confirms the scripture history of that event."[62]

In line with the need to defend theological orthodoxy, most geologists (whose discipline began to emerge as a distinct field of study in the early nineteenth century, and no longer as simply part of a more general "natural science") argued for a "catastrophic" explanation of land formations: Given the short duration of the earth's existence, when change came to the landscape it must have done so suddenly and chaotically—in the form of floods, volcanic eruptions, and the like. Noah's flood was an all-purpose explanation for any phenomenon that was otherwise difficult to explain.

There were dissenters. In Britain, Scotsman James Hutton published a work entitled *Theory of the Earth* in the late eighteenth century, offering a much longer timeline for the earth's existence, as well as a different theory for changes in the earth's surface features. Hutton's version, known in the history of geological thought as uniformitarianism, discarded the catastrophic model for one in which the earth's surface was understood as the product of gradual and continuous (and thus "uniform") changes that could be observed and measured in the present, such as the movement of glaciers, the erosion caused by rivers, winds, the annual cycle of freezing and thawing, and other natural phenomena. The earth was thus a work in progress, a living laboratory where the processes that had shaped the planet in the past—a past now believed to extend tens of millions of years rather than a few thousand—could still be seen unfolding in the never-ceasing modification of surface features.[63]

Hutton's ideas were developed and popularized by another Scotsman, Charles Lyell, an Oxford-trained lawyer who became a professor of geology at Kings College London in the 1830s. His three-volume work *The Principles of Geology*, published between 1830 and 1833, had its thesis clearly summarized in its subtitle: *An Attempt to Explain the Former Changes of the Earth's Surface by Reference to Causes Now in Operation*. The book's publication represented a watershed in scientific and popular understanding of the earth's past, influencing, among many others, Charles Darwin and Henry David Thoreau. It also helped spur interest in recreational hill-walking and mountaineering, as amateur geologists set forth, hammer in hand, to collect fossils and rock specimens. Evidence of the earth's ancient origins stirred a sense of wonder in the educated classes akin to the earlier celebration of mountains as sublime. As Robert MacFarlane argues in *Mountains of the Mind*, for Victorians geology "came to suggest both a healthy outdoorsiness and a romantic sensibility; not just tinkering with old bones and stones."[64]

Lyell visited the United States in 1841 and again in 1845. He was fascinated by American democracy, appalled by southern slavery, and intrigued by the question of how the Appalachians came into existence (a process of uplift caused by underground magma pools was his best guess). On his second trip he ascended Mount Washington by the bridal path on its western flank, and he suggested that the origins of the rocks on the summit were "lost in times of extreme antiquity."[65]

Another European geologist who visited the United States in those years was a friend of Lyell's named Louis Agassiz. Unlike Lyell, Agassiz decided to stay. The Swiss-born Agassiz, a protégé of the Prussian naturalist Alexander von Humboldt, made his reputation in European scientific circles with his exploration of the glacial systems of the Bernese and Valaisian Alps. Agassiz proved an intrepid mountaineer, making the fourth ascent of the 13,642-foot Jungfrau in the Swiss Bernese Alps in 1841.[66]

In the course of his glaciological studies, Agassiz developed the concept of the "Ice Age," which he announced to the world in an 1840 book. The notion that a long period of global low temperatures had, in the not-so distant past, led to the expansion of vast sheets of ice over much of the Northern Hemisphere, gave both geologists and lay readers a valuable tool for understanding the world around them.

Glaciers are the workhorses of the mountains, extremely efficient at eroding, transporting, and depositing rock. In North America, the glacial record is visible in U-shaped valleys, striated rock formations, and glacial erratics. Although an interest in slow-moving glaciers would seem to suggest an allegiance to the new doctrine of uniformitarianism, Agassiz was actually more of a catastrophist and a supernaturalist, in that he believed that repeated catastrophes like the ice age had wiped out previously existing species—part of God's plan to clear the way for new and favored species, including man. Abandoning Noah's flood as an all-purpose earthmover, Agassiz announced that glaciers were "God's great plough" for reshaping the landscape.[67]

In 1846, Lyell helped Agassiz secure a contract to deliver a series of public talks on natural history in Boston. The wildly popular lectures led to Agassiz's appointment as professor of geology and zoology at the newly created Lawrence Scientific School at Harvard. Agassiz's ice-age theory won adherents, although proponents of alternate flood theories fought a stubborn rear-guard resistance for decades. Henry David Thoreau was among those influenced by Agassiz, corresponding with him and collecting rock specimens to send along to him at Harvard.[68]

Agassiz married into Boston society and was among the instigators of a prestigious literary and dining society, called the Saturday Club, that also counted Ralph Waldo Emerson as a member.[69] In 1858, Saturday Club members Agassiz, Emerson, poet James Russell Lowell, and seven others traveled to Follensby Pond, between Raquette Lake and Tupper Lake in the Adirondacks, for a month-long summer outing. The Boston campers devoted themselves to hunting, fishing, and canoeing, along with campfire seminars in the evening devoted to their shared interests in natural history (Agassiz discovered a freshwater sponge previously unknown to scientists during the excursion). This "philosophers' camp" received widespread attention in the press and helped awaken easterners to the recreational potential of the still largely unexplored Adirondack mountainous wilderness in their own backyard.[70]

Thanks to the celebrity status of leading geologists like Agassiz, and thanks to the practical uses to which its findings could often be put, the discipline attracted ambitious and talented students. The first professional association of geologists was founded in 1840. The rise of geology as a scientific discipline coincided with the exploration of the newly acquired territories of the United States and drew some of the best and brightest geologists westward.

THE WEST OF WHICH I SPEAK

For Americans in the mid-nineteenth century, daily life seemed to move at an ever-accelerating pace. Railroads crisscrossed the northeastern states, hurtling passengers from destination to destination at speeds of 20–30 miles an hour, and it was only a matter of time before the iron rails would cross the Continental Divide and link the East to the West Coast. The transcontinental telegraph, completed in 1861, made it possible for news to race across the country in hours.

Henry David Thoreau was a fan of neither the transportation nor the communication revolutions he was living through. "We do not ride on the railroad," he wrote in *Walden*, "it rides upon us." The sound of a locomotive whistle from the nearby Fitchburg Railroad, disturbing the tranquility of his cabin in the woods, was like "the scream of a hawk sailing over some farmer's yard." And in another famous passage he wrote, "We are in great haste to construct a magnetic telegraph from Maine to Texas, but Maine and Texas, it may be, have nothing important to communicate."[71]

For all of his rejection of conventional religion, Thoreau was a latter-day Jeremiah, a prophet dismayed by the false idols his fellow Americans found worthy of worship. In April 1851 he delivered to his neighbors gathered at the Concord Lyceum a newly composed lecture, entitled "The Wild," that was at once an affirmation of the transcendentalist celebration of nature, and a condemnation of the effects of overcivilization. "I wish to speak a word for Nature," he began,

> for absolute freedom and wildness, as contrasted with a freedom and culture merely civil,—to regard man as an inhabitant, or a part and parcel of Nature, rather than a member of society. I wish to make an extreme statement, if so I may make an emphatic one, for there are enough champions of civilization: the minister and the school committee and every one of you will take care of that.[72]

Thoreau delivered the lecture many times in the last decade of his life, in the process adding new material and splitting it into two separate parts—one called "Walking," the other remaining "The Wild." In the spring of 1862 he revised and sold the two lectures to the *Atlantic Monthly*, which ran them as a single article in June, just a month after his death from tuberculosis. In his lectures and in his final article, Thoreau looked westward for a purified vision of the American dream, even as he acknowledged, in that second year of fratricidal war, the breakdown of the Union:

> To Americans I hardly need to say,—
>
> "Westward the star of empire takes its way."
>
> As a true patriot, I should be ashamed to think that Adam in paradise was more favorably situated on the whole than the backwoodsman in this country.
> Our sympathies in Massachusetts are not confined to New England; though we may be estranged from the South, we sympathize with the West. There is the home of the younger sons . . . .
>
> The West of which I speak is but another name for the Wild; and what I have been preparing to say is, that in Wildness is the preservation of the world.[73]

Although Thoreau's words linking "Wildness" and "the preservation of the world" are often quoted, the context in which the linkage was made—in a nation in the midst of civil war—is less often remembered. But clearly, as Thoreau prepared his final essay for publication, the "estranged" relationship between North and South was much on his mind. The question of the future of the West, slave or free, was chiefly responsible for that estrangement. Thoreau looked westward and to "the Wild" as a metaphor for the process through which the "younger sons" of New England could come to the self-knowledge that would permit them to carry on the highest values of the nation—its open-mindedness, its love of liberty, its independence from age-old superstitions and conventions. The promise of "Wildness" was "the preservation of the world"—and it also held hope for the redemption of the nation in its moment of greatest crisis.[74]

THE CALIFORNIA GEOLOGICAL SURVEY, 1860–1863

Some of those "younger sons" of New England were exploring western lands as Thoreau lay dying in Concord—among them Josiah Dwight Whitney and the band of scientist-mountaineers he assembled under the aegis of the California Geological Survey. Whitney, born in 1819 in Northampton, Massachusetts, and educated at Yale College and in France and Germany, had won renown as a geologist and mining consultant in the East when, in 1860, he successfully lobbied the California state legislature to fund a state survey, and to appoint him as its director (Whitney secured the backing of many of the nation's leading geologists, including Harvard's Louis Agassiz, to support him in his lobbying). Whitney hired New York–born William Henry Brewer, who had been trained as a chemist at Yale's Sheffield Scientific School and in Europe, as his chief assistant. The two of them arrived by ship in San Francisco in November 1861. Soon afterward, Whitney met a German engineer and topographer named Charles F. Hoffman, who had been living in California since 1858, and brought him into the survey as mapmaker.

Unlike their predecessors (Lewis and Clark, Pike, Long, and Frémont), who had passed through or over mountains, but always in transit, Whitney's explorers intended to stay in the California mountain ranges for as long as it took to survey them thoroughly—the first sustained exploratory mountaineering effort in North America. They discovered, named, mapped, and made first ascents of many of the most spectacular and challenging peaks in the United States. Until the California Geological Survey, most American mountaineers were men of limited education. Afterward, there would be a strong and ongoing connection between the world of higher education, particularly the sciences, and that of mountaineering.[75]

A dozen years after the initial California gold rush, the state's lawmakers hoped that Whitney's survey would point the state's mining interests to new sources of underground wealth, as the original gold fields were tapped out. Although he was eager to please his benefactors, Whitney had different priorities. The Latin motto of the survey was *Altiora Petimus*, "We Seek Higher Things," and Whitney and his associates sought to reveal and catalogue the landforms, plant life, fossil record, and mineral composition of the state for the sake of scientific knowledge, rather than for mere commercial exploitation. The survey left behind detailed maps and extensive specimen collections (including a treasure trove of ancient seashells found atop the coastal mountains south of Santa Barbara) but, to the increasing dissatisfaction of the state legislators, no new gold fields.

Whitney's surveyors began their efforts in southern California in 1861 and worked their way northward. By 1862 they had reached Mount Shasta in northern California, an object of intense interest because it was believed to be the highest mountain in the state (at 14,179 feet it is actually the fifth-highest). Although they did not know it when they started to climb the mountain, theirs would not be Shasta's first ascent. That had taken place eight years earlier on August 14, 1854, when Captain Elias Pearce, leading an eight-man party up the southwest side of the mountain, raised an American flag on the summit. Pearce and his men beat the old altitude record for an American climb—set in 1820 on Pikes Peak—by 64 feet.

Shasta's height was still a matter of conjecture in 1862. Israel S. Diehl, who made the first solo ascent of the mountain in 1855, estimated that its summit reached 17,500 feet.[76] Whitney and Brewer lugged barometers up the mountain and came up with a more reasonable 14,400-foot figure. As they took their measurements, it was obvious to them that they were not the first to reach the summit, finding it strewn with a "mixture of tin cans and broken bottles, a newspaper, a Methodist hymn book, a pack of cards, an empty bottle, and various other evidence of a bygone civilization." Brewer was also disappointed by what he reported as the lack of glaciers, though Shasta has seven sizable glaciers, one of them, later named the Whitney glacier, the longest of any in California. These were not present on or visible from the south side of the mountain, the route of the early climbers. But Israel Diehl had spotted them when he was on the summit seven years earlier. In general, as proven on other occasions, Brewer and Whitney seemed to have a blind spot when it came to glaciers.[77]

In the summer of 1863, Whitney, Brewer, and Hoffman shifted their focus to the High Sierra. They began by exploring the region around Yosemite Valley and Tuolumne Meadows. They made a first ascent of 10,885-foot Mount Hoffman.[78] Continuing eastward, they climbed another mountain, this one 13,061 feet in height and providing a spectacular view from its summit. "Hundreds of peaks were in sight," Brewer recorded, to the north, the west, and the south, including, he estimated, fifty that were over 12,000 feet. Farther east, in the desert, they could see Mono Lake. When Brewer and Whitney returned to the scene the following day, according to Brewer, Whitney "thought the view the grandest he had ever beheld, although he has seen nearly the whole of Europe."[79]

Whitney honored the eminent scientists of his day by naming peaks in the Sierra after them; thus, he named the mountain they had just climbed Mount Dana, for James Dwight Dana, whose influential textbook *Manual of Geology* was published in 1863.[80] After that ascent, Whitney returned to San Francisco, but Brewer and Hoffman pushed on, attempting 13,120-foot Mount Lyell (named for Charles Lyell), but stopping short of the summit. Later in the summer, on his own, Brewer climbed 9,985-foot Pyramid Peak, west of Lake Tahoe.[81] At the end of a season of first ascents, Brewer headed out of the mountains to Sacramento, where he boarded a steamer to San Francisco and had an encounter fateful to the future of American mountaineering.

CLARENCE KING AND THE ASCENT OF MOUNT TYNDALL

Clarence Rivers King was born in Newport, Rhode Island, in 1842. His father was a successful merchant, but King scarcely knew the man, who was usually off in China on business and died abroad when his son was just five years old. King was doted on by his mother. He was short but strong, a natural athlete, and popular with his schoolmates. As a high school student in Hartford, Connecticut, he became best friends with a boy a few months younger named James Gardner. In 1859, Gardner went off to Rensselaer Polytechnic Institute in Troy, New York, while King took a position with a flour company in New York City. While living in New York, King frequented the New York Art Academy, where he was much taken by an exhibit of Albert Bierstadt's paintings of the Rocky Mountains.

In September 1860, King enrolled at the Scientific School at Yale College (soon renamed the Sheffield Scientific School after a wealthy donor), where he studied chemistry under Professor George Jarvis Brush and geology under Professor James Dwight Dana (the same Dana honored by the naming of a peak in California). King was particularly taken by a lecture of Dana's that recounted a journey on horseback through northern California in 1841, during which he had had the opportunity to view Mount Shasta from the west. Dana's visit to California had established him as a pioneer in the scientific study of western mountains; he had contributed a sketch of Mount Shasta to Benjamin Silliman's *American Journal of Science and Arts* and published a study of the geology of the Shasta region in 1849.[82]

King graduated from Yale in 1862, returning to New Haven in the fall of that year to visit his old professor, George Brush. It so happened that Brush had just received a letter from one of his old Yale classmates— William Brewer, currently engaged in the business of surveying for something called the California Geological Survey. Brush read the letter aloud, including its account of Brewer and Whitney's recent ascent of Mount Shasta. King was again entranced. He had to see this Shasta for himself.[83]

In April 1863, King, his friend James Gardner, and another friend left for California. They bore with them a letter of recommendation from Professor Brush addressed to Brewer. After various misadventures, King and Gardner reached California at the end of August. And by happy coincidence, they ran into Brewer on September 1, on the paddle-wheel steamer carrying the geologist on his return from his summer's explorations in the Sierra. Brewer immediately recruited King as a volunteer worker for the survey.

Four days later, Brewer and King were off on an expedition to northern California. On September 26, just a month after arriving in California, King accompanied Brewer to the summit of the first mountain he had ever climbed, in the second recorded ascent of 10,457-foot Mount Lassen, the southernmost outcropping of the Cascade Range. From its summit, he gazed rapturously at the fabled Mount Shasta, now only 75 miles away. At Yale, King had read John Ruskin on mountain aesthetics. Now, he exclaimed, "What would Ruskin have said if he had seen *this!*"[84]

In 1864, the California surveyors shifted their attention to the area around Kings Canyon in the southern Sierra Nevada. The party, led by William Brewer, included King, James Gardner, Charles Hoffman, and Richard Cotter. They racked up another impressive string of first ascents, climbing west to east from one crest of mountains to the next. On June 28 they climbed an 11,258-foot peak on the crest of the Kings-Kaweah Divide, which they named Mount Silliman for Benjamin Silliman Jr., a geologist at the Sheffield Scientific School, and the son of the famed Yale chemist.

From Silliman's summit they spotted a mountain crest 10 miles to the southeast that they initially thought to be the Sierra Crest, the highest of the range's ridgelines. But on Sunday, July 2, when Brewer and Hoffman made their way to the crest (later known as the Great Western Divide) and climbed 13,576-foot Mount Brewer, they were startled to see the actual Sierra Crest 8 miles farther east. Only then did the true dimensions of the

From left to right: James Gardner, Richard Cotter, William Brewer, and Clarence King, in a photograph that appeared in Brewer's *Up and Down in California in 1860–1864.*

Sierra Nevada become clear to its explorers. "Such a landscape!" Brewer enthused in describing the mountains surrounding the summit his companions named for him. "The view was wilder than any we have ever seen before. . . . A hundred peaks in sight over thirteen thousand feet—many very sharp—deep canyons, cliffs in every direction . . . sharp ridges . . . on which human foot has never trod."[85]

Among the mountains now in view was a 14,025-foot peak they named for John Tyndall, a distinguished British geologist and leading figure in the golden age of alpine climbing.[86] And there was an even higher peak— one they decided must be the highest in the United States—to which they gave the name Mount Whitney, after their absent chief. Brewer thought that the rough terrain between the Great Western Divide and the Sierra Crest was impenetrable, but King wanted to attempt Whitney. From his reading of Tyndall's alpine exploits, he had concluded that "no place was inaccessible."[87] The supposed scientific objective of the survey had little to do with King's ambitions. "Professor Brewer asked me for my plan," he would later write, "and I had to own that I had but one, which was to reach the highest peak in the range."[88]

With Brewer's reluctant approval (he actually thought the effort "madness"), King and Cotter spent July 3 preparing their push into the unknown. King was an impetuous mountaineer in some respects; once in motion, he tended to charge ahead without fully considering his route. But he was meticulous in his preparations for a climb. "Our walking-shoes were in excellent condition," he noted in retrospect,

> the hobnails firm and new. We laid out a barometer, a compass, a pocket-level, a set of wet and dry thermometers, note-books, with bread, cooked beans, and venison enough to last a week, making two knapsack-shaped packs strapped firmly together with loops for the arms, which, by Brewer's estimate, weighted forty pounds apiece.[89]

King and Cotter also packed a rope to take with them, a piece of equipment not previously employed (or at least mentioned) by American mountaineers. The next day, July 4, King and Cotter set off for Mount Whitney. What lay ahead of them King described as "the most gigantic mountain-wall in America, culminating in a noble pile of Gothic-finished granite and enamel-like snow."[90] They headed south along the ridgeline, looking for a likely route down the Great Western Divide's eastern slope. Francis P. Farquhar placed what came next into historical perspective in his *History of the Sierra Nevada*:

> When Clarence King and Dick Cotter bade good-bye to their companions on the shoulder of Mount Brewer they began a new era in

American mountaineering. Never before had anyone attempted to traverse such a complex maze of ridges and canyons as those that confronted them. To venture into such unknown country, scantily equipped and without experience on steep snow and precipitous rock, required more than ordinary courage.[91]

They found a lower ridge or, more accurately, a line of connected crags, now known as the Kings-Kern Divide, bridging the Great Western Divide and the Sierra Crest. They used their rope to lower the packs down the steep slope that led them to the cross ridge. They camped that night under an overhanging rock (a wise precaution, as rock and ice tumbled down on their shelter through the night). The next morning they set off again before dawn along the divide, heading for its high point. They cut steps up an icy snowfield with Cotter's bowie knife, crossed rock fields, and edged their way up a cliff on a diagonal ledge. At one point, stymied in how to ascend a rock face that blocked further progress, they used the rope to lasso a granite spike above them.

Neither man had previous experience in rock-climbing; indeed, the concept barely existed, in Europe or America. Most climbing in the Alps during the "golden age of alpinism" consisted of following routes on mountain ridges involving some cutting of steps in snow and ice, and hand-over-hand scrambling over rocks. Ropes were used routinely in alpine climbing for protection, but not for what would only later be called "aid climbing" (that is, artificial means of ascent, not relying entirely on hands and feet.)

In his subsequent description of the climb, King employed dramatic language that exaggerated the dangers they faced. When, nearly a century later, a teenage California climber named Royal Robbins got a look at the route that King and Cotter were following, he "lost a climbing hero," because it "turned out to look a lot easier than King had described it."[92] But, to be fair to King and Cotter, who were each in their first year of serious mountain-climbing, they still managed to anticipate climbing techniques yet to be attempted or perfected on either the American or the European continent. King went first up the rope and reached a shelf.

He hauled up their gear and then dropped the rope back down to Cotter, who came up with the same arm-over-arm technique, without a stop. And then they continued on to the cross ridge.

But their troubles weren't over. Eastward from its high point, the ridge was broken and unstable. If they dropped off the ridge to the north, into the upper drainage of the Kings River, they would find themselves trapped in a bewildering maze of canyons. On the other hand, looking to the south into the upper Kern River drainage, they saw a potential route that offered a fairly direct line of ascent to the highest peak on the Sierra Crest. The complication was that the way down the southern side was a nearly sheer rock face. So again they innovated, tying the rope to a rock, lowering themselves one at a time to small ledges on the cliff face, and then whipping the rope off the top hold. They did not believe they could climb back up the way they were descending; as King put it, stepping off the ridge "cut off our connection with the upper world."[93]

Even more daunting, the first ledge they reached on the rock face offered no place to tie off the rope. So they improvised again, this time inventing what was, in essence, the concept of the belay (a technique as yet unpracticed by mountaineers in the Alps). King tied the rope around his chest, and Cotter, bracing himself against the cliff, let it out gradually as King climbed downward. At one point, losing his balance, King reported that he felt he must surely fall, but he found a gooseberry bush firmly rooted in a crack and used it to steady himself. Cotter then tied in to the rope and climbed down to King, this time with King pulling in the slack.

Several hours of such maneuvers brought them, to their relief, to the base of the cliff. They camped that night in a grove of pines about a mile from the base of the north face of the mountain that was their destination. The next morning, July 6, they again set out in darkness, leaving their packs behind. There were more challenges, including an ice tower in which they again cut steps (another innovation, at least in the United States). At noon they were on the summit, triumphant.

But they were not, as they had hoped, on the summit of the state's highest peak. They could see two higher peaks nearby, one of which, about 2 miles to the east, they named Mount Williamson for Lieutenant

Robert Stockton Williamson, a topographical engineer who had taken part in the prewar railroad surveys in California. At 14,389 feet, Mount Williamson is the second-highest peak in California. The highest peak in the state, topping out at 14,505 feet, lay about 6 miles to the southeast: the real Mount Whitney, which they had hoped to climb before losing track of it on their approach and winding up on the wrong mountain. Making the best of what they had already accomplished, King would later write, "I rang my hammer upon the topmost rock, we grasped hands and I reverently named the great peak MOUNT TYNDALL."[94]

Even if it wasn't Whitney, Mount Tyndall, the tenth-highest peak in California, was a notable prize for a pair of novice mountaineers making their way through remote, previously unexplored, and rugged terrain. When King and Cotter reached its summit, they stood on the tallest mountain yet climbed in the Sierra Nevada. It was only the second recorded ascent of a 14,000-foot mountain in California, the first being the Cascades' Mount Shasta ten years earlier.[95]

King may have exaggerated the challenges of the climb in his subsequent account, but as William Brewer noted judiciously, "It was by far the greatest feat of strength and endurance that has yet been performed on the [California] Survey."[96]

King remained determined to reach the summit of Mount Whitney. Brewer gave him permission to make another attempt, accompanied by two soldiers and enough food for fourteen days. This time King tried to approach the mountain from the southwest, but he struggled to make his way to its base and then encountered an apparently unclimbable wall, hundreds of feet high. King gave up the attempt that day, but not the ambition to someday climb California's highest peak.[97]

YOSEMITE PARK AND
NATIONAL REDEMPTION

On June 30, 1864, one week before King and Cotter reached the summit of Mount Tyndall, President Abraham Lincoln signed into law a bill granting the Yosemite Valley and the Mariposa Grove of Giant Sequoias

Stereoscopic view of Yosemite's El Capitan by Carleton Watkins.

to the state of California, some 40,000 acres in all, to be "held for public use and, resort, and recreation for all time."[98] This was the first law in the history of the world protecting an area from development for the purpose of preserving its wilderness character. The bill had influential backers: the nation's most celebrated landscape architect, Frederick Law Olmsted, who had moved to California during the war and had been moved by Yosemite's natural beauty, was among them; so was Israel Ward Raymond of the Central American Steamship Line, who had the vision to imagine Yosemite Valley as a postwar tourist destination. Reverend Thomas Starr King, Jessie Benton Frémont, and US senator John Conness from California also played important roles.[99]

President Lincoln had other pressing matters on his mind in the spring and summer of 1864. In the two months before the Yosemite bill reached his desk, more than fifty-five thousand Union soldiers had fallen as casualties in the fighting in Virginia between General Ulysses S. Grant's Army of the Potomac and Robert E. Lee's Army of Northern Virginia. Lincoln's prospects for reelection that fall looked grim. And unlike some of his predecessors in the White House, such as Thomas Jefferson, Lincoln never displayed much interest in mountain scenery or nature. He was a practical man of politics, and certainly no transcendentalist.

On the other hand, the Civil War had begun in 1861 as a contest over the future of the United States' western territories, with Lincoln determined to preserve them as free soil. California's admission into the Union as a free state in 1850 had secured the Pacific coast for the free-soil cause. And Lincoln had carried the state handily in the 1860 election. All of this may have inclined him to look favorably on a proposal to create a wilderness park for the benefit of the state's—and the nation's—citizens.

During the war, Lincoln wondered often about God's intentions for the United States. Perhaps he felt that the preservation of Yosemite, with its ancient trees and even more ancient rock formations, was a redemptive gesture in a time of great suffering and sacrifice, an act of affirmation of his hopes for the future of the nation.[100]

Within months of the end of the war, Frederick Law Olmsted suggested a link between wartime concerns and the interest in preserving Yosemite. As he wrote in August 1865:

> It was during one of the darkest hours, before Sherman had begun the march on Atlanta or Grant his terrible movement through the Wilderness, when the paintings of Bierstadt and the photos of Watkins . . . [gave] the people on the Atlantic some idea of the sublimity of the Yo Semite.[101]

This assertion of federal power to secure an area of sublime beauty for the enjoyment of future generations reflected a belief that the role of enlightened government was to benefit ordinary people. It became the precedent and model for the subsequent creation of the national park system.

INTO THE SUNLIGHT

In the fall of 1864, Clarence King, James Gardner, and Richard Cotter spent several weeks surveying Yosemite Valley and the surrounding mountains to determine the boundaries of the new state park, turning over their findings to Frederick Law Olmsted in December. The California Geological Survey's feats of heroic exploration in the Sierra were drawing to an end. William Brewer resigned from the survey in the fall of 1864 to take a position as professor of agriculture at Yale, and Josiah Whitney moved to Boston to write up the survey's geological findings. King and Gardner both went back east later that winter to visit family and friends, although they planned to return to California the following year. King was still on the East Coast in April 1865 when the Army of Northern Virginia surrendered at Appomattox to the Army of the Potomac, an event followed within days by Lincoln's assassination at Ford's Theatre in Washington, DC, by John Wilkes Booth. Twenty years later, King reminisced how, in 1865, "The nation and its people went out as from some black tragedy into the sunlight of every day, and resumed a suspended life."[102]

In the 1840s, Henry David Thoreau predicted that as the United States expanded westward, its citizens would leave prejudice and fanaticism behind. The thin atmosphere of the mountains would, hopefully, refine the follies of the plain. He was being too hopeful, as the events of 1861–65 made all too clear. But following four years of bitter conflict—somewhat like a hardy mountain plant "that creeps quite over the ridge and descends into the valley beyond"—the nation survived.

In the postwar era, a reunified United States would become ever richer and more powerful. More and more, its citizens resided in great commercial and industrial cities, where the middle and upper classes enjoyed a level of material comfort that their ancestors could not have imagined. But their affluence, combined with the frantic pace of modern urban existence, left many of them dissatisfied and searching for a larger sense of meaning and community. And for that, some turned to the mountains—not as explorers or scientists, but as the first generation of recreational climbers.

CHAPTER THREE

GOOD TIDINGS,
STRENUOUS LIFE,
1865–1903

Walk away quietly in any direction and taste the freedom of the mountaineer. . . . Climb the mountains and get their good tidings. Nature's peace will flow into you as sunshine into trees.

—JOHN MUIR,
OUR NATIONAL PARKS, 1901

It is only through strife, through hard and dangerous endeavor, that we shall ultimately win the goal of true national greatness.

—TEDDY ROOSEVELT,
THE STRENUOUS LIFE, 1899

On July 22, 1893, thirty-three-year-old Katharine Lee Bates set off in a horse-drawn wagon for the summit of Colorado's Pikes Peak. A descendant of one of the oldest Puritan families in New England, daughter of a Congregationalist minister, Bates was an alumna of and professor of literature at Wellesley College in Massachusetts. She might have been referred to in her era as a "spinster lady," a single woman past the likely age of marriage, although, in fact, she was in a long-term romantic relationship with another female Wellesley professor. Adventurous and energetic, Bates traveled in Europe and the Middle East, as well as within her own country.

That summer of 1893, she had crossed two-thirds of the United States by railroad to teach her academic specialty, medieval literature, at Colorado College in Colorado Springs. En route, she stopped off at Niagara Falls, as well as at the Columbian Exposition (the Chicago World's Fair) then being held to celebrate the four hundredth anniversary of the discovery of the New World. While in Colorado, Bates explored the Front Range of the Rockies, including Garden of the Gods and Cripple Creek. Her trip up Pikes Peak was the "supreme day" of her summer's adventures, offering "the most glorious scenery" she had ever beheld. And something else made the day memorable:

> It was then and there, as I was looking out over the sea-like expanse of fertile country spreading away so far under those ample skies, that the opening lines of the hymn floated into my mind.[1]

The "hymn" she refers to became known as "America the Beautiful," its opening stanza, slightly revised, as familiar to subsequent generations of Americans as the first lines of the Declaration of Independence and the Gettysburg Address:

> *O beautiful for halcyon skies*
> *For amber waves of grain,*
> *For purple mountain majesties*
> *Above the enameled plain.*
> *America! America!*
> *God shed his grace on thee,*
> *Till souls wax fair as earth and air*
> *And music hearted sea.*

Bates's "hymn" was published on July 4, 1895, in a Boston religious magazine, the *Congregationalist*, under the title "America." In 1904, with a new title and some new phrasing ("halcyon" giving way to "spacious," "enameled" to "fruited," and so forth), it was set to music that composer Samuel Augustus Ward of New Jersey had originally written in the 1880s for another religious hymn: "O Mother, Dear Jerusalem."[2] Many Americans believed then—and many still believe—that "America the Beautiful" should be the country's official national anthem, although it lost that distinction to "The Star-Spangled Banner" in 1931.

PURPLE MOUNTAIN MAJESTIES

Prior to the Civil War, that greatest dividing line in American history, some citizens of the United States ascribed spiritually redeeming qualities to mountains. But for the most part, these people belonged to a well-educated and unconventional minority in New England, like Henry David Thoreau. Others identified mountains, particularly in the far West, as symbols of American national greatness and destiny—but, for the most part, they belonged to a select corps of intrepid explorers, like John C. Frémont. Following the Civil War, these two ways of viewing mountains—the spiritual and the nationalist—blended into one, in a patriotic sacralization of mountain landscapes that became commonplace in Gilded Age America.[3]

In May 1865, a few weeks after the Confederate surrender at Appomattox Court House, Samuel Bowles set off to see the West. Bowles, like Bates a native New Englander, was the publisher of the influential Springfield, Massachusetts, *Republican*. The letters he wrote describing his journey across the newly reunified United States, first by railroad, then by horse-drawn coach, were published in the *Republican* and later gathered together as a best-selling travelogue entitled *Across the Continent*. Like other visitors, before and since, Bowles was stirred by the view of the Front Range from the Plains, the summit monoliths and great walls of the Colorado Rockies towering above the intervening foothills. He had seen high mountains before, having spent two months touring the Swiss Alps in 1862—but to his mind the glorious palisade of mountains stretching a hundred miles from Longs Peak to Pikes Peak eclipsed their European counterparts. His appreciation of the mountainscape was spiritual as well as aesthetic. "No town that I know of in all the world," Bowles wrote,

> has such a panorama of perpetual beauty spread before it as Denver has in this best and broadest belt of the Rocky Mountains, that rises up from the valley in which it is built, and winds away to the right and to the left as far as the eye can see. . . . These are visions that clear the heart of earthly sorrow and lead the soul up to its best and highest sources.[4]

"Earthly sorrow," to our ears, may sound like one of those high-minded platitudes that dot (and clot) the rhetoric of nineteenth-century prose. But Americans reading those words in the summer of 1865, just weeks after the surrender of General Robert E. Lee's Army of Northern Virginia, would be reminded of the deaths of as many as three-quarters of a million of their countrymen in the preceding four years of civil war, as well as the recent assassination of President Abraham Lincoln. Bowles transformed the mountains that formed the Continental Divide into a symbol of national unity, as well as spiritual redemption, leading the souls of Americans to their "best and highest sources."

Three years later, Bowles returned to Colorado and found the perfect mountain to illustrate his point. On this second visit, he climbed 14,278-foot Grays Peak near Loveland Pass. It was not the mountain's first ascent; botanist Charles Parry had reached that summit eight years earlier, and by the time Bowles came along it was possible to reach the top by horse trail.[5]

What made the day memorable was Bowles's discovery of another peak visible from the summit of Grays, about 40 miles away at the northern end of the remote Sawatch Range. That 14,009-foot mountain was known to early Spanish explorers and priests as Santa Cruz. Blocked from view from the east by 13,237-foot Notch Mountain, it had subsequently gone unnoticed and unnamed by the American explorers (Pike, Long, and Frémont) who came along before the Civil War.

Bowles was the first to describe the long-forgotten peak in print, and what caught his eye just below its summit was a cross-shaped snowfield, roughly 1,500 feet high and 750 feet across. The vertical line of the cross was formed by a couloir (a steeply angled gulley) running up the mountainside, the horizontal line by an outward-sloping bench, each holding snow longer into the summer season than the surrounding rock, and thus forming the impression of a white cross superimposed on the dark granite gneiss face. Was this natural feature fashioned by mere happenstance? Bowles thought otherwise. "It's as if God has set His sign, His seal, His promise there," he wrote in a widely read account of his discovery, "a beacon upon the very center and height of the Continent to all the people and all its generations."[6]

But had God blessed America? President Lincoln certainly had his doubts. In his second inaugural address, delivered on March 4, 1865, he asked his countrymen to consider the possibility that the bloodletting they had endured over the previous four years had been a judgment by God on both sides in the conflict, an affliction on the entire nation for having tolerated the sin of slavery. In the aftermath of that war, and Lincoln's martyrdom on Good Friday, April 14, 1865, it was thus comforting to think, as Bowles suggested, that a symbol affirming God's eternal covenant with the American nation existed on this mountainside on the Continental Divide.

The following year, in 1869, William Henry Brewer, of California Geological Survey fame, made his own way up Grays Peak and, spotting the same cross-bearing mountain, gave it the name by which it continues to be known: the Mount of the Holy Cross. Four years later, in 1873, the Mount of the Holy Cross had its first recorded ascent, by J. T. Gardner and W. H. Holmes, two members of a surveying expedition to the region led by geologist (and former Union army surgeon) Ferdinand Hayden. Gardner and Holmes climbed the mountain for scientific rather than religious purposes; they had been dispatched by Hayden to establish a geodesic station on its summit.

Another member of the expedition, photographer William Henry Jackson, a Union army veteran of Gettysburg, took a picture of the cross-bearing peak from Notch Mountain that reinforced the mountain's religious aura. As it turned out, God's handiwork needed a little tweaking on

William Henry Jackson's 1873 photograph of the Mount of the Holy Cross; image reversed in 1900 print.

Jackson's part; back east in his studio, Jackson discovered that the cross's right arm looked crooked in his photograph, so he retouched the negative to make it come out right. The resulting image created a public sensation in 1876, the nation's centennial year, marking the hundredth anniversary of the adoption of the Declaration of Independence. The centennial observances focused attention on a war that Americans, both northern and southern, could celebrate: the War of Independence. Jackson's photograph won acclaim and an award when displayed in a prestigious exhibit of artwork at the 1876 International Exposition in Philadelphia, a world's fair marking the centennial.[7]

The 1876 Philadelphia fair also featured a 7-by-5-foot oil painting of the Mount of the Holy Cross by Thomas Moran, an English immigrant to New York City and a disciple of the Hudson River School of heroic landscape painting. Moran brought his sketchbook to Colorado's Sawatch

Range in 1874, and on his return to the studio, he reproduced and embellished the Mount of the Holy Cross in his oil painting, complete with a halo of wispy clouds around the summit. Collectively, the four eastern-bred visitors to the Rockies—Bowles, Brewer, Jackson, and Moran—fashioned the Mount of the Holy Cross into a shrine to the nation's providential mission to explore and settle the West, making it a destination for pilgrims for decades to come.[8]

THE GREAT SURVEYS

The last third of the nineteenth century brought the culmination of three centuries of western exploration and settlement in North America. The discovery of gold, first in California in 1848 and then in the Colorado Rockies in 1858, the passage of the Homestead Act in 1862, the completion of the transcontinental railroad in 1869, and the abundant economic opportunities that came with the growth of western mining, lumber, and other extractive industries lured tens and then hundreds of thousands of Americans westward, many of whom found themselves living in the shadow of great mountains. But as late as the 1870s, at least from an easterner's perspective, the nation's West still could seem exotic and mysterious. As the *New York Times* commented in an editorial in 1871:

> There is something romantic in the thought that, in spite of the restless activity of our people, and the almost fabulous rapidity of their increase, vast tracts of the national domain yet remain unexplored. As little is known of these regions as of the topography of the sources of the Nile or the interior of Australia.[9]

A determined federal effort, led by a new generation of scientist-explorers, filled in those remaining blank spots on the map.

Before the war, the official exploratory parties sent westward by the federal government had been military operations, led by US Army officers, starting with Captains Lewis and Clark in 1804–6. Those early expeditions sometimes included trained scientists, but the civilians played subordinate roles. After the war, following the pattern set by the California Geological Survey, the civilian scientists took the lead.[10] In January 1867, Clarence King, veteran of two years of exploration in the Sierra, returned east and persuaded powerful men in Washington, DC, of the need for a survey of resources, mineral and otherwise, along the route of the transcontinental railroad from the Sierra east to the Rockies. He opened the way for the launch of a broad campaign of federally supported scientific exploration.[11]

Between 1867 and 1879, four separate geological and geographical surveys, collectively known as the Great Surveys, explored the vast West. Only one was led by a military officer, Lieutenant George M. Wheeler, who oversaw the United States Geographical Surveys West of the One Hundredth Meridian. The other three were headed by civilian scientists: Clarence King's Geological Exploration of the Fortieth Parallel (which, like Wheeler's survey, was undertaken under the auspices of the US War Department); Ferdinand V. Hayden's Geographical and Geological Survey of the Territories; and John Wesley Powell's Geographical and Geological Survey of the Rocky Mountain Region (the latter two conducted under the auspices of the Interior Department).

The survey staff, even in Lieutenant Wheeler's survey, consisted almost entirely of civilians. The surveys overlapped in territory and mission, and they competed for funding and personnel, until 1879, when government-sponsored surveying was consolidated under the aegis of the United States Geological Survey (USGS), whose first director was Clarence King, succeeded by John Wesley Powell. Although mountain-climbing had not been specified by Congress as the mission of the Great Surveys, the surveyors climbed a lot of mountains.[12]

CLARENCE KING, SHASTA, AND WHITNEY

In 1867, twenty-four-year-old Clarence King was appointed director of the Geological Exploration of the Fortieth Parallel. His initial assignment was to survey an 80,000-square-mile territory, in a corridor stretching from the eastern slopes of the Sierra Nevada to the eastern slopes of the Rockies. Over the next six years he would take his surveying parties along that corridor all the way to Cheyenne, Wyoming, where the Union Pacific Railroad tracks crossed the South Platte tributary of Crow Creek. And, taking on additional assignments, King and his surveyors also roamed up and down the Pacific coast, climbing some of the region's highest mountains in the process.

King hired a photographer, Timothy H. O'Sullivan, to record the expedition's findings. O'Sullivan was already widely known for his photographs of the Gettysburg battlefield; his *Harvest of Death*, showing the Union dead, remains one of the iconic images of the patriotic sacrifices demanded by the war. Now his photographs (and those of other photographers who accompanied the Great Surveys, including such figures as Carleton Watkins, William Henry Jackson, E. O. Beaman, and John K. Hillers) recorded, celebrated, and helped popularize the far reaches of the American West. O'Sullivan's portfolio for the King survey included never-before-photographed mountain vistas, from the Sierra's Donner Pass to Utah's Wasatch Range and Nevada's Humboldt Mountains. O'Sullivan (or possibly another photographer, Andrew J. Russell, who briefly joined the survey in 1869) also took a picture of King making a roped descent of a cliff in Utah's Uinta Mountains—the first photographic image in the United States of a rock climb in progress, albeit one that looks a little staged for effect.[13]

King described Mount Shasta as "the magnet" that originally attracted him to California in 1864.[14] But six years later he still had not climbed the mountain. He finally got his opportunity when congressional authorization came in the summer of 1870 for his surveyors to explore the volcanic mountains along the Pacific coast. King headed for Shasta in September 1870, while other parties from the survey were assigned to climb Mounts Hood and Rainier. Timothy O'Sullivan had shifted his efforts to the Wheeler survey by then, so King hired Carleton Watkins to accompany him to Shasta, along with a local guide, Justin Hinckley Sisson. They climbed first to the top of Shastina, a subsidiary volcanic cone on the western side of Shasta, which at 12,330 feet would be the third-highest of the Cascades if it were not part of the Shasta massif. From there they made their way across a 12,000-foot saddle to the summit of Mount Shasta itself.[15]

En route they spied something that Brewer and Whitney, after their 1862 ascent, had declared did not exist on the mountain: an active glacier—in fact, California's longest glacier. Brewer and Whitney had climbed from the relatively glacier-free south side. The route King and his companions followed offered a very different perspective:

> We clambered along the edge toward Shasta, and came to a place where for a thousand feet it was a mere blade of ice, sharpened by the snow into a thin, frail edge, upon which we walked in cautious balance, a misstep likely to hurl us down into the chaos of lava blocks within the crater. Passing this, we reached the north edge of the rim, and from a rugged mound of shattered rock looked down into a gorge between us and the main Shasta. There, winding its huge body along, lay a glacier, riven with sharp, deep crevasses yawning fifty or sixty feet wide, the blue hollows of their shadowed depth contrasting with the brilliant surfaces of ice.[16]

King named his discovery the Whitney Glacier after his former employer. He also spotted three more of Shasta's seven active glaciers before descending. Many American climbers had previously stood upon or been in the vicinity of glaciers, on Shasta itself and elsewhere, but science had failed to take official notice. King's report of what he found on Shasta, published in the *American Journal of Science* the following year, is thus often described as the first sighting of an American glacier.

King meanwhile was at work on an account of his mountaineering adventures since 1864, initially published as a series of articles for the *Atlantic Monthly* magazine, and then in 1872 as the first widely read book about climbing in America: *Mountaineering in the Sierra Nevada*. King recalled in vivid detail his ascents of Mount Lyell in 1864 and Mount Shasta in 1870.

The concluding chapter was devoted to his return to Mount Whitney, the mountain he had thought he was climbing in 1864 when he actually climbed Lyell—an attempt followed by another unsuccessful effort to climb Whitney that same year. Seven years later, in the company of Paul Pinion, a French-born mountaineer he happened to meet en route, King headed back for a third attempt. On the first day of their climb, June 21, 1871, the two men forged their way upward through clouds and rain, and on June 22 they reached the summit, still shrouded in mist. King was disappointed to discover that he and Pinion were not the first to reach the top, for they found there "a small mound of rock," which had "solidly built into it an Indian arrow-shaft, pointing due west." But King said that he did not begrudge his "Indian predecessor," identity unknown, "the honor of first finding that one pathway to the summit of the United States, fifteen thousand feet above two oceans."[17]

Like many of King's tales, this one was well told and, unlike some, unembellished by exaggerated peril. "On the whole," he reported, "this climb was far less dangerous than I had reason to hope. Only at the very crest, where ice and rock are thrown together insecurely, did we encounter any very trying work."[18] This achievement of a quest nearly a decade in the making must have seemed to King a good way to end his book. And so it might have proved to be, except that, on that cloudy June day in 1871, he was—once again—standing on the summit of the wrong mountain. King and Pinion had actually climbed a peak of 14,032 feet about 5 miles to the southeast of Whitney. Later named Mount Langley, the mountain stood nearly 500 feet below Mount Whitney in elevation. King had even seen and named this mountain before, calling it in 1864 "Sheep Rock" for the flocks of bighorn sheep that dotted its slopes.[19]

Thus it came as a blow to King's mountaineering reputation when, two years later, another two-man party—W. A. Goodyear and M. W. Belshaw—reached the summit of Langley on July 27, 1873. There they found a silver dollar that, as King had recorded and they had read in *Mountaineering in the Sierra Nevada*, he had inscribed with his and Pinion's names and left behind as a token of what they supposed was Whitney's first recorded ascent. Goodyear and Belshaw, unlike King, had climbed Mount Langley on purpose and on a clear day, and looking to the northwest they could clearly see the real Mount Whitney. Goodyear, who knew and disliked King, reported the error to the California Academy of Science.

So, Whitney remained unclimbed. Embarrassed, King hurried back to the southern Sierra to climb the true Whitney, reaching its summit in September 1873 on what was his fourth attempt. But he was a month too late for a first ascent, for on August 18, 1873, another party—Charles Begole, A. H. Johnson, and John Lucas, residents of the nearby town of Lone Pine—had reached the summit of the highest mountain in the United States outside of Alaska. "All honor to those who came before me," King wrote graciously, but probably gloomily, in a note he left behind on the summit.[20]

THE HAYDEN AND WHEELER SURVEYS

The Wheeler survey spent more of its time in deserts and on the Colorado River than exploring mountains, but still left its name on two western mountains: 13,065-foot Wheeler Peak in Nevada, and 13,167-foot Wheeler Peak in New Mexico, the latter the highest mountain in the state. The Hayden survey was most famous for its exploration of the Yellowstone region in Wyoming, an endeavor that influenced Congress in its decision in 1872 to create the first national park.[21] Members of the survey also explored the adjacent Teton Range in Wyoming.

A fault-block range thrust upward by the stresses of plate tectonics, the Tetons are of relatively recent geological origin, dating back less than ten million years, youngest of all the Rockies. The range includes sixteen peaks above 11,000 feet, seven at about 12,000 feet, and one closing in on 14,000. The tallest three are Grand Teton, Middle Teton, and South Teton.[22] James Stevenson (Hayden's chief assistant) and Nathaniel Langford (newly appointed as superintendent of Yellowstone National Park) claimed to have reached the summit of 13,775-foot Grand Teton on July 29, 1872, but discrepancies in Stevenson's published account raised questions about his achievement.[23]

JOHN WESLEY POWELL
AND LONGS PEAK

John Wesley Powell, who headed up the fourth great survey, made his most important contributions to western exploration before assuming the directorship of the federal Geographical and Geological Survey of the Rocky Mountain Region in 1870. Born in New York State, Powell had grown up in the Midwest and picked up a smattering of college geology before serving as an officer in the Union army in the Civil War (losing an arm at the Battle of Shiloh). Following the war, he taught geology in Illinois colleges, traveling during the summers of 1867 and 1868 to Colorado on privately sponsored expeditions to the Rockies.[24]

On his 1867 trip, Powell had climbed Pikes Peak and, spotting Longs Peak to the north, he had vowed to climb it, too, when he returned the following summer. Longs Peak had been known to Americans since the 1823 publication of the *Account of an Expedition from Pittsburgh to the Rocky Mountains*, describing the discoveries of the Stephen Harriman Long expedition. But so formidable was Longs' appearance that whites arriving in the region waited more than four decades before attempting to climb it.[25]

The first serious attempt came in 1864, when botanist Charles Parry teamed up with William N. Byers, the editor of Denver's newspaper, the *Rocky Mountain News*. Byers was early Denver's most enthusiastic promoter (in 1870 he was instrumental in bringing a railroad line to Denver, which had been bypassed by the original transcontinental railroad), and an equally determined mountaineer; in 1863 he had guided the painter Albert Bierstadt in the first ascent of 14,265-foot Mount Evans in the Front Range.[26]

Parry and Byers's exact route on Longs Peak in 1864 is unknown, although it may have been through the "Keyhole," the route up Longs' north and west sides that is today the standard way up the mountain. At the end of a long day of scrambling, they were still a thousand vertical feet from the top. A second attempt the next day by Byers and another climber from the east was similarly frustrated. Byers reported gloomily,

"We are quite sure that no living creature, unless it had wings to fly, was ever upon its summit, and we believe we run no risk in predicting that no man ever will be."[27]

But meeting Powell in Denver in the summer of 1868, Byers was inspired by the geologist's single-minded determination to climb the mountain. As Lewis Keplinger, one of the students who accompanied Powell that summer, recalled, "Before leaving Illinois it was understood that whatever else we might or might not accomplish, we would ascend the Peak."[28]

The group that gathered at Grand Lake to approach the mountain included, in addition to Powell and Byers, Powell's brother, Byers's brother-in-law, and two other college students, as well as some others who would not be part of the final summit party. They set off on horseback on August 20, abandoning their horses after two days of riding westward. The next day, on foot, they made first ascents along the Continental Divide

Geologist John Wesley Powell made the
first ascent of Longs Peak.

of 13,310-foot Mount Alice and 13,579-foot Chiefs Head Peak before descending into Wild Basin. From there, on the fourth day, they were in position to make their summit attempt.

Setting off at 6:00 a.m., they set a brisk pace, climbing via the south side up a couloir scouted the previous day by Keplinger (and bearing his name today), exiting to the left before the notch to finish on what is now known as the Home Stretch on the Keyhole Route. The route required hands as well as feet; as Byers wrote, "life often [depended] upon a grasp of the fingers in a crevice that would hardly admit them."[29] The route must have been especially challenging for the group's leader, who had only one hand with which to grasp the available holds. Nevertheless, Powell and the others reached the summit at 10:00 a.m., having accomplished a very rapid ascent of the most difficult mountain yet climbed in the United States.

Powell, son of an itinerant Methodist preacher, had been named for the founder of Methodism. As an adult, he had largely forsaken his parents' faith, finding a substitute for religious piety in the strict rationalism of the natural sciences.[30] Nonetheless, there was something about being on top of this great mountain, atop the Continental Divide, that suggested to him an appropriate moment for the moral edification of the young students who accompanied him. "As we were about to leave the summit," Keplinger would remember,

> Major Powell took off his hat and made a little talk. He said, in substance, that we had now accomplished an undertaking in the material or physical field which had hitherto been deemed impossible, but that there were mountains more formidable in other fields of effort which were before us, and expressed hope and predicted that what we had that day accomplished was but an augury of yet greater achievements in such other fields.[31]

Perhaps he had in mind the journey that he was planning for the following year, when he and a small group of companions would make a thousand-mile voyage in three wooden boats down the Green and

Colorado Rivers, including the length of the Colorado through the Grand Canyon. Powell made a second journey down the Colorado in 1871, this time as leader of his federal survey, and the account of the two trips, published in 1875 as *Exploration of the Colorado River of the West* secured his reputation as one of the most daring of the post–Civil War explorers.[32]

In reaching the summit of Longs Peak in 1868, Powell was carrying out his professional duties, which were scientific in inspiration, not romantic. Still, even for this man of science, it was now a commonplace to think of climbing as a fitting metaphor for human and national achievement.

AMERICAN ALPINISM

John Wesley Powell's climbing partner on Longs Peak in 1868, William N. Byers, did not climb the mountain for science. He climbed for the sake of climbing, calling himself a "mountain tramp."[33] It wouldn't have occurred to him to call himself something as exotic as an "alpinist," a word that made its first appearance in an English publication in 1860.[34] Those individuals who climbed regularly in the American West in the decades following the Civil War did so for a variety of reasons—some, like Powell, as surveyors and scientists; others, like Byers, for the satisfaction of reaching high and inaccessible places—but in neither case did they believe they were engaged in an activity that was governed by a shared tradition, with commonly recognized forms of expertise and technique. The notion of mountaineering as a sport called "alpinism," an athletic endeavor with a well-developed set of rules just like cricket or tennis, first developed among English climbers in the Alps. With few exceptions, it had yet to cross the Atlantic.

Only a handful of Americans made their way to the European Alps with the intention of climbing in the first half of the nineteenth century— but then, neither did all that many Europeans. Two native-born residents of the Chamonix Valley below Mont Blanc—Michel-Gabriel Paccard and Jacques Balmat—made the first ascent of that 15,781-foot peak in 1786. Thirty-three years later, in 1819, Dr. William Howard of Baltimore, Maryland, and Dr. Jeremiah Van Rensselaer of New York City, became the first Americans to stand on Mont Blanc's summit, guided by Joseph-Marie Couttet, in what was only the eighth ascent of the mountain.[35] Afterward, they collapsed in their hotel in Chamonix, exhausted from two arduous days of climbing but proud of the accomplishment. As Howard wrote in a pamphlet entitled *Narrative of a Journey to the Summit of Mount Blanc* (the first published report from an American climber abroad), "five of the loftiest of the Alleghanies piled on each other, would scarcely reach to the height I have attained."[36]

Thirty-five years later, in 1854, a noted English barrister named Alfred Wills reached the summit of the 12,134-foot Wetterhorn in the Swiss Alps (although widely believed to be the mountain's first ascent, there had actually been at least two prior ascents by local climbers). The publicity generated by this achievement kicked off a decade that came to be known in climbing history as the "golden age of alpinism." Mountaineering emerged as a popular pastime with well-off Britons, the result of easy rail access across France to the Alps (with travel time from London to Chamonix reduced from twelve days in the prerailroad era to a mere two days by 1851), increased leisure time among the professional classes, and the Victorian obsession with putting England's mark upon the world.

Scores of first ascents and new routes were put up by British climbers throughout the western Alps in the decade following Wills's achievement on the Wetterhorn. British alpinists hired local Swiss, Italian, or French climbers to lead them up the mountains, even though some of the "clients" became mountaineers as capable as or more capable than the "guides." The guides broke trail, cut steps on icy slopes, and were, at least technically, in charge of deciding the route to be taken by their clients. Guideless climbing was considered by guides and clients alike a breach of alpine ethics down to the 1890s.[37]

In 1857, a devoted band of British climbing enthusiasts established the Alpine Club in London, the world's first climbing club, dedicated to "the promotion of good fellowship among mountaineers." Lawyers, clergymen, university dons, doctors, civil servants, and businessmen, along with the occasional aristocrat, paid a guinea a year for the privilege of attending the club's annual banquet in London and subscribing to its journal, *Peaks, Passes and Glaciers* (renamed a few years later as the *Alpine Journal*). The Alpine Club was, in the words of its most knowledgeable chronicler, "a Who's Who of the educated and professional classes of Victorian England."[38] It served as a model for similar organizational ventures in Europe, North America, and elsewhere, but pride of place allowed it to always remain *the* Alpine Club, without adopting a national prefix.

American tourists began making the Alps a stopping point on their grand tours of Europe in the nineteenth century; James Fenimore Cooper visited the Swiss Alps in 1828 and 1832; Harriet Beecher Stowe visited Chamonix in 1853, two years after the publication of *Uncle Tom's Cabin*; and Mark Twain visited Zermatt in 1878. Twain professed bafflement at many aspects of alpine mountaineering in his travelogue *A Tramp Abroad*. "Evidently it is not considered safe to go about in Switzerland, even in town, without an alpenstock," he observed. "If the tourist forgets and comes down to breakfast without his alpenstock, he goes back and gets it, and stands it in the corner."[39]

Cooper, Stowe, and Twain, like most of their countrymen visiting the Alps in those years, showed little interest in climbing the mountains that towered over the comfortable resorts below. But a few proved more adventurous. In the second half of the nineteenth century, more than a hundred Americans summited Mont Blanc, and scores climbed other peaks in France, Switzerland, and Italy.[40] Their enjoyment of the experience varied, as an entry in a mountain shelter's visitor book in September 1866 by Charles Morrison of Philadelphia suggests:

> Attempted the summit of Mont Blanc yesterday . . . but being overcome by fatigue, and at the same time, met by a sharp wind and stinging hail which rendered rest impossible, was obliged to acknowledge myself defeated. . . . Had I known the difficulty of the ascent, the attempt had never been made.[41]

British climbers displayed a patronizing attitude toward the Americans who turned up in Chamonix. Leslie Stephen, a prominent member of the Alpine Club (its president from 1865 to 1868), classified them as a disagreeable species of interlopers that also included "kings, cockneys, persons traveling with couriers" and "commercial travelers."[42]

Stephen made an exception for one young American, James Kent Stone, praising him as "one of the best walkers it has ever been my fortune to meet." Born in Boston, Stone had spent several summers as a teenager in the White Mountains. In 1856, not yet sixteen years old, he enrolled at Harvard but withdrew because of vision problems and instead traveled to Europe, where he attended a German university. In 1857 he climbed Mont Blanc. He returned to Harvard but, before graduating, spent another year traveling in Europe. In 1860, Stone was back in the Alps, having what he described to his father in a letter that fall as a "strange, wild summer." As he proudly recounted, during his climbing exploits:

> I believe I "used up" one of the stoutest guides in Switzerland. Towards the end I had to lead the way myself on the slopes of ice & snow. Why I went to work so wildly I cannot well tell you. I heard something constantly whispering with me, "The Mountains, Kent,—the mountains," and I followed the voice eagerly. From Mont Blanc to Monte Rosa & over to the heart of the great Oberland, I know every wrinkled glacier and every proud summit. I made the Alps my friends.[43]

Stone also made friends with the British climbers he encountered that summer, and they elected him as the first American and the youngest member of the Alpine Club. Returning to the United States, he graduated with the Harvard class of 1861, just in time to be swept up in the Civil War, fighting at the Battle of Antietam. Stone survived the war but gave up serious mountaineering afterward.[44]

A few other American climbers in the Alps also won the respect of their British counterparts. Marguerite "Meta" Brevoort became the first American woman to climb Mont Blanc in 1871, and the second woman of any nationality to climb the 14,692-foot Matterhorn. (She would have been first, but a British rival, Lucy Walker, hearing of Brevoort's plans, got to the mountain and to its summit first; however, Brevoort did make the first traverse of the mountain by a woman, ascending from Zermatt and descending the Italian side.) From a wealthy background—she had first come to Europe as a student in a convent school in Paris—Brevoort was a feisty character who never married, and she began her serious climbing career at the age of forty. When she reached the summit of Mont Blanc in 1865 in her first season of climbing, Brevoort sang the revolutionary anthem "Marseillaise" (banned in France at the time).[45] She was also noted for wearing knickers under her skirts when she climbed, flouting the prevailing standards of female modesty for comfort and practicality.[46]

In another notable contribution to the history of mountaineering, Brevoort introduced her nephew, William August Brevoort Coolidge, to the sport when he was fifteen; the two of them, with Swiss mountain guide Christian Almer, racked up an impressive list of climbs over the next several years, including the first winter ascent of the Wetterhorn on January 23, 1874, helping to popularize winter climbing in the Alps. Meta Brevoort died two years later, but her nephew, who became known by his initials, W. A. B. Coolidge, carried on, making over twelve hundred climbs in the Alps, including the first winter ascent of the Jungfrau. The second American to be accepted as a member of the Alpine Club, Coolidge spent the rest of his life in England, as an academic and eventually an Anglican priest. He also served for a decade as the editor of the Alpine Club's *Alpine Journal*, earning a reputation as a diligent if disputatious chronicler of alpine climbing history.[47]

In time, Americans who climbed in Europe began to import the techniques and language of the new sport of alpinism to their own country. Frederick Hastings Chapin, a prominent Hartford, Connecticut, businessman, visited the Swiss and French Alps in 1877 and 1882, summiting Mont Blanc on his first visit. In the mid-1880s, he began to explore the possibilities for recreational climbing in the Colorado Rockies, reaching the summits of Pikes and Longs Peaks among others, and in 1889 he published a book about his Colorado exploits, in effect the first Rocky Mountain guidebook. Chapin believed that most of his fellow climbers from the East were more familiar with the Alps than with the Rocky Mountains; for the high valleys of Switzerland are so easy of access, and the distances are so small, that one can cross many glacier passes and ascend important peaks with much less trouble than he can visit such an out-of-the-way place as Estes Park and climb the mountains which surround it.[48]

Although Americans were beginning to climb their own mountains for the sheer pleasure of doing so, "alpinism" as such, remained a distinctly European pastime.

EQUIPMENT AND TECHNIQUE

For Americans at home who could not afford the expense of European travel, an opportunity came in 1871 to experience alpinism vicariously when the popular American monthly *Lippincott's Magazine* serialized Edward Whymper's *Scrambles among the Alps* in 1871–72. Whymper's book recounted his attempts to climb the Matterhorn, an effort crowned with success and tragedy in 1865 (after his party of seven made the first ascent of the mountain, four of Whymper's companions, roped together, fell to their deaths). *Scrambles* thrilled readers on both sides of the Atlantic and was the most widely read mountaineering book of the nineteenth century. Four separate editions of the book would be published in the United States between 1872 and 1899.[49]

Apart from its appeal as an adventurous narrative, *Scrambles* offered readers practical instruction in climbing technique. Whymper described step cutting, glacier crossing, and crevasse rescue. He particularly emphasized rope craft—not surprising, given his memories of the Matterhorn disaster—noting that "a man must either be incompetent, careless, or selfish if he permits the rope to dangle about the heels of the person in front of him."[50]

It would be another twenty years before the first formal guide to mountaineering technique appeared, in an 1892 volume published in England in a series called the "Badminton Library of Sports and Pas-

A young Teddy Roosevelt had this photo taken
in climbing apparel following his ascent of the
Matterhorn in 1881.

times." Much of the Badminton volume on mountaineering was written
by Clinton Thomas Dent, a prominent figure in British climbing circles.
It included detailed descriptions and illustrations of the use of ropes for
mountain rescue as well as climbing.[51]

Nineteenth-century British climbers had little in the way of
purpose-designed clothing or equipment. The ropes they carried could
be found in households and barns; their boots were ordinary walking
shoes with hobnails hammered to the soles; their clothing consisted of
the same linens and woolen (and, beginning in the 1880s gabardine) outer
garments they might have worn on a blustery day's walk in the English
countryside, with perhaps an extra layer or two for insulation. The two
specialized pieces of equipment they employed were alpenstocks, long
wooden poles with sharp iron tips on the bottom, and, sometimes in

addition, an ice ax, with a pick and adze of equal lengths mounted atop a long wooden pole. The alpenstock was used for balance and support, the ax to cut steps on snowy or icy slopes. British climbers also would have been familiar with "creepers," the four-pronged crampons that French hunters sometimes wore on the lower alpine mountain slopes, but they were rarely used by those attempting to reach the summits of mountains.[52]

Climbing techniques that were becoming standardized in the European Alps remained haphazardly practiced in the New World. Climbers in the Northeast had no glaciers to contend with and thus saw no point in lugging around a lot of useless gear. An 1882 guide to climbing in the White Mountains (the first such ever published) advised readers that alpenstocks "are seldom carried by the stronger pedestrians in the White Mountains, as they find them more of a hindrance than a help; but the novice is advised to take one at first, and when he finds himself sufficiently strong and sure of foot he can leave it behind."[53]

On the snowy volcanoes of the Pacific Northwest, specialized alpine gear was of greater utility. In 1857, a twenty-nine-year-old US Army lieutenant, August Valentine Kautz, who was stationed at Fort Steilacoom in Washington Territory, decided to attempt a first ascent of 14,411-foot Mount Rainier, the fifth-highest mountain in the pre–Alaska Purchase United States. Perhaps because he was German-born (his parents brought him as a young child to the United States), he planned his climb with European precedents in mind. As he wrote of his Rainier venture:

> I made preparations after the best authorities I could find, from reading accounts of the first ascent of Mount Blanc and other snow mountains. We made for each member of the party an *alpenstock* of dry ash with an iron point. We sewed upon our shoes an extra sole, through which were first driven four penny nails with the points broken off and the heads inside. We took with us a rope about fifty feet long, a hatchet, a thermometer, plenty of hard biscuit and dried beef.[54]

The soldiers who accompanied him, along with their Indian guide, soon tired and turned back on the day of the summit attempt, but Kautz came remarkably close to making a solo first ascent of Rainier. Climbing from the south up a glacier that now bears his name, he reached an elevation of perhaps 13,000 feet, when darkness fell and he was forced to abandon the effort.[55]

Thirteen years later, in August 1870, a retired military officer (and winner of the Congressional Medal of Honor during the Civil War) named Hazard Stevens made the next attempt on Rainier. He was accompanied by two other climbers, Philemon Beecher Van Trump and Edmund Coleman, along with a Yakima Indian guide named Sluiskin. Van Trump was a fellow American (employed as private secretary to the governor of Washington Territory, who was Stevens's brother-in-law). Coleman, however, was English, a landscape painter, and a charter member of the Alpine Club with climbing experience in the Alps, including two ascents of Mont Blanc. In 1868, Stevens led the party that made the first ascent of 10,781-foot Mount Baker in northern Washington Territory.[56]

As Stevens would later acknowledge, Coleman was the most knowledgeable member of the group, and he saw to outfitting the party for the challenge of tackling a large, glaciated mountain:

> There was a strong rope to which we were all to be tied when climbing the snow-fields, so that if one fell into a chasm the others could hold him up. The "creepers" were a clumsy, heavy arrangement of iron spikes made to fasten on the foot with chains and straps, in order to prevent slipping on the ice. [Coleman] had an ice-axe for cutting steps, a spirit lamp for making tea on the mountains, green goggles for snow-blindness, deer's fat for the face, alpine staffs.[57]

Given his climbing résumé and expertise, Coleman might have been expected to play a leading role in the conquest of Rainier. As things turned out, he did not get along well with his American companions, who were younger and stronger, and he had difficulty keeping up with them on the approach march. The two Americans took to deriding their English companion as an "alpine tourist." Coleman either decided on his own to turn back, as Stevens and Van Trump would later suggest, or, perhaps, was abandoned by them.[58] But he made his contribution to the success of the climb: when the two Americans reached the summit on August 18, they did so cutting steps with Coleman's ice ax, and making use of his rope to cross a yawning crevasse.[59]

Both Stevens and Van Trump remained active mountaineers, and both would climb Rainier again. Van Trump was the first person to guide parties up the mountain; John Muir was among his clients.[60] Thirteen years after his first Rainier ascent, as reported in a Tacoma newspaper, Van Trump instructed a group of novices in the climbing arts. His lesson plan suggests that American mountaineering still remained in an era of improvisation, with no commonly accepted set of rules when it came to considerations of safety or style. "When you commence the descent of the steep and dangerous places," Van Trump advised,

> let your leader plant his alpenstock firmly in the snow and tie one end of the rope firmly to the staff low down near the snow, and then let the rope hang full length down the line of descent, the leader getting a firm footing and bracing the upright staff. Now let each of the other mountaineers, in turn, take the strand of rope and carefully descend the length of it.

That this technique left the leader stranded above the others, with no one able to protect him on his own descent, did not seem to occur to Van Trump. He proudly proclaimed the superiority of his system to foreign rivals: "I much prefer this method to the Alpine or Swiss plan of the company being constantly tied together when climbing or descending. It is slower, but it is safer. The leader is always braced and looking out for a slip or fall on the part of the man descending."[61] American exceptionalism did not always prove the wisest climbing strategy.

On slopes where roped descents were unnecessary, some Americans learned a faster means of descent: a standing glissade. An innovation of climbers in the Alps, the "glissade" is a controlled standing or seated slide down a slope, using an ice ax or alpenstock as combination rudder and brake. Clarence King used the term in his 1872 *Mountaineering in the Sierra Nevada* to describe his descent from a ridgeline en route to Mount Tyndall in 1864. But what he described was hardly an orthodox glissade, since it involved "turning now and then a somersault."[62]

Thirty years later, Yale University student Yandell Henderson displayed a better grasp of the technique. With four fellow students he made a number of first ascents in the Canadian Rockies in the summer of 1894. He had read the Badminton guide to mountaineering, and two of his companions had previously climbed in the Alps. In a letter to his family, he reported that he had overcome his fear of snow slopes, for they were "far easier and safer" to ascend "than grass or rock." And easier to get down as well:

> In descending, providing there are no [berg]schrunds and the bottom is all right, you glissade, that is you hold your legs stiff with the toes bent down and slid[e]. You check your speed by digging your heels or ax in the snow. It is great sport. The first time I tried it my feet were continually sliding out from under me, but in snow a fall doesn't hurt as it does on rocks; it only makes you wet.[63]

Although a few American climbers in the last decade or so of the nineteenth century were acquiring the terminology and techniques of European alpinism, most just went out and did what seemed to work.

JOHN MUIR

The greatest figure in American mountaineering, in the nineteenth or any other century, was himself a European import, born a Lowland Scot in the coastal town of Dunbar on the North Sea in 1838. Although John Muir emigrated with his family to the United States at the age of eleven, he spoke with a Scottish accent throughout his life. Scotland proved formative in another way. "When I was a boy in Scotland," Muir wrote in the opening lines of his memoir of childhood and youth, "I was fond of everything that was wild, and all my life I've been growing fonder and fonder of wild places and wild creatures."[64]

Muir was a man of contrasts: a practical-minded inventor who was also a dreamer and wanderer. He would be compared in his lifetime and ever afterward to that other loner and lover of nature, Henry David Thoreau, and it is fair to say that Muir was the Thoreau of California, Yosemite his Walden Pond. But for all his love of solitary treks to wild places, Muir was also a man who knew how to win friends and influence people. He developed the skills of a master publicist and was a cultivator of powerful allies, and he used both talents to affect public environmental policy at the national level. He founded and led the most significant outdoors organization in American history. A keeper of journals, he would not publish his first book until age fifty-five, but later he turned them out on a regular basis, and through his articles and books he found the popular audience that had always eluded his Concord counterpart. Unlike that lifelong bachelor Thoreau, Muir eventually married happily and into money, despite his taste for solitude.[65]

After coming to America in 1849, Muir grew up on the family farm in Wisconsin, chafing under the harsh domestic rule of a dour and pious father. Muir enrolled in the fateful year of 1861 at the University of Wisconsin in Madison, where he discovered a love of botany. But the prospect of being drafted into the Union army and having to kill, even for a cause he regarded as just, drove him to cross the border into Canada in 1864, where he spent the next two years exploring the northern woodlands.

On his return to the United States in 1866, Muir worked in a factory in Indianapolis, until an injury nearly cost him his eyesight and convinced him to devote the remainder of his life to the study of nature. He set off on a cross-country trek from Indianapolis to Florida that took him into his first mountains, the Great Smokies of the southern Appalachians. Along the way, he shed the narrow evangelical doctrines of his family, although not his spiritual yearnings. And then, fatefully, rather than following his

John Muir, 1902.

original plan to explore tropical forests in the Amazon, he took ship for California, arriving there in late March 1868.[66]

Muir did not linger in San Francisco. Setting off on foot for the Sierra, he arrived at Yosemite at the start of May, a month past his thirtieth birthday. He wrote of his first view of the valley, "Never before had I seen so glorious a landscape, so boundless an affluence of sublime mountain beauty."[67] He had found his spiritual home. To support himself, he took the only employment he could find locally, as a sheepherder, and then as a sawmill operator—two activities that he deplored as despoiling the landscape, and that also got him thinking that the state of California was not a suitable custodian for the glories of Yosemite. Despite these qualms, the summer of 1869, when he was herding sheep in an area stretching from the rim of Yosemite Valley to Tuolumne Meadows, was perhaps the happiest of his life.[68]

The year that Muir arrived in Yosemite was also the year of the publication of Josiah Whitney's *The Yosemite Book*, which, among other observations, categorically denied the possibility that the valley had been carved by glaciers. Instead, Whitney suggested that a catastrophic geological event, perhaps a collapse of the bedrock, had opened a great rift in the landscape. Muir had little training as a geologist, but he could read landscape. In his very first published article in 1871, "Yosemite Glaciers," which appeared in the New York *Daily Tribune*, he took on the distinguished founder of the California Geological Survey. The great valley, he argued, was not the product of a single moment of chaotic destruction, but "was brought forth and fashioned by a grand combination of glaciers" over a long period of geological time in a previous ice age.[69]

Whitney, and his protégé Clarence King, scoffed at this theory; Muir, King declared, was an "ambitious amateur" whose writings on geology were "hopeless floundering."[70] In his own private journals from 1864, however, King had independently noted "unmistakable" evidence of glaciation in Yosemite Valley, and in 1870 he would find existing glaciers on Mount Shasta, another place where Whitney had declared their nonexistence. But in the acrimonious dispute with Muir, King evidently felt obliged out of loyalty to Whitney to state what he knew to be false. It was not his finest moment as a scientist. And although Muir erred in thinking Yosemite the product of only a single ice age rather than many, he was, of course, in his most important point, vindicated by later research.[71]

Muir understood the mountains with scientific detachment, which he somehow combined with a lyric celebration of their beauties. He consciously linked himself with the earlier transcendentalists, carrying a copy of *The Prose Works of Ralph Waldo Emerson* in his knapsack. He also read Thoreau with care, borrowing freely from his prose; from Thoreau's account of his 1846 Katahdin climb, Muir took the phrase "unhandselled globe" to describe California's Hetch Hetchy Valley, a place he thought more beautiful than Yosemite, and from Thoreau's 1860 "Walking" address, Muir adapted as his own the motto "In Wildness is the preservation of the world."[72]

In a symbolic transfer of authority from the founders to the new generation of nature romantics, Muir encountered Emerson when the aging philosopher came to Yosemite on his first and only visit in 1871. Muir took him around the valley floor and the Mariposa Grove but was disappointed when Emerson's companions would not allow him, at age sixty-eight and in declining health, to accompany Muir on a camping trip to the surrounding High Sierra. "You are yourself a sequoia," Muir told Emerson. "Stop and get acquainted with your big brethren."[73] But that was not to be. Emerson and Muir corresponded afterward, and the sage of Concord came to regard the sage of Yosemite as a worthy successor in the transcendentalist tradition.[74]

In the course of the next two decades, turning to his journals for source material, Muir published scores of articles in eastern magazines like *Scribner's*, the *Century*, and the *Atlantic Monthly* about the natural wonders of California, the Pacific Northwest, Wyoming, and Alaska, helping to create a new constituency among the educated middle classes for a movement that had not yet found its name: conservationism (or in Muir's version, "preservationism").

By the 1870s, almost every peak in and around Yosemite Valley had been scaled, usually by an easy, unroped scramble from the rim of the valley, but the sheer faces and spires had not been attempted. In 1865, Josiah Dwight Whitney said of Half Dome, rising 4,737 feet above the valley floor, that it was "perfectly inaccessible, being probably the only one of all the prominent points about the Yosemite which never has been, and never will be trodden by human foot."[75] Actually, Half Dome would be climbed ten years later, but only by unorthodox means.

In 1875, George C. Anderson, a carpenter and, like Muir, a Scottish-born immigrant, drilled a line of 6-inch holes some 900 feet up the final steep section of Half Dome's northeast shoulder, pounding in iron eye-bolts and then linking them into a rope line to the summit. (Anderson's ropes rotted away over the next few decades and were replaced in 1919 by a cable system that is still in use.) Anderson is sometimes credited with being the first American to engage in aid climbing, although any climber in more recent times who relied exclusively on a ladder of drilled bolts to ascend a rock face would be condemned for a grave violation of climbing ethics.[76]

Muir sought out more challenging climbs and pushed the limit of the imaginable in the valley and in the Sierra. He explored and climbed mostly on his own. Very few could have kept up with him, or accepted the privations that he did (usually climbing without tents or blankets, and with little to eat), or would be willing to take the risks that he did (though he scorned those mountaineers who, he felt, sought out risk for its own sake—having Clarence King chiefly in mind). In September 1869, during his sheepherding summer in Tuolumne Meadows, Muir undertook a solo first ascent of 10,916-foot Cathedral Peak, climbing a crack to surmount a 30-foot-high rock blocking his path—a pitch that in years since has rarely been climbed unroped or solo.[77]

In October 1872, Muir set out to make the first ascent of 13,143-foot Mount Ritter in the eastern Sierra, a mountain that King had tried and failed to climb in 1866. Muir ran into trouble in a steep couloir a little short of the summit. There, he remembered,

> I found myself at the foot of a sheer drop . . . which seemed abso-lutely to bar further progress. It was only about forty-five or fifty feet high, and somewhat roughened by fissures and projections. The tried dangers beneath seemed even greater than that of the cliff in front; therefore, after scanning its face again and again, I began to scale it, picking my holds with intense caution. After gaining a point about halfway to the top, I was suddenly brought to a dead stop, with arms outspread, clinging close to the face of the rock, unable to move hand or foot either up or down. My doom appeared fixed. I *must* fall. There would be a moment of bewilder-ment, and then a lifeless rumble down the one general precipice to the glacier below.

Heart pounding, limbs trembling, mind clouding, he awaited death. But then, a feeling of calm acceptance descended upon him:

> I seemed suddenly to become possessed of a new sense. The other self, bygone experiences, Instinct, or Guardian Angel,—call it what

you will,—came forward and assumed control. Then my trembling muscles became firm again, every rift and flaw in the rock was seen as through a microscope, and my limbs moved with a positiveness and precision with which I seemed to have nothing at all to do. Had I been borne aloft upon wings, my deliverance could not have been more complete.[78]

He scrambled to the summit and admired the spectacular Sierra vistas that spread out around him, including Mount Whitney to the south.

The following year, in 1873, Muir set out to climb that mountain, which had its first ascent in August of that year. Like Clarence King, he wound up first ascending Mount Langley by mistake. Unlike King, he recognized his mistake. Spying the true Whitney in the distance, he descended Langley and climbed the right mountain. Despite Whitney's pride of place as the state's tallest mountain, Muir did not find it a particularly interesting climb compared to Ritter, and he wondered what all the fuss was about. A year later, in November 1874, he climbed Shasta but on the way down was caught in a snowstorm. Untroubled, he spent several days sheltering under some firs and was disappointed when a rescue party reached him, ending his solitary communion with the mountain.

He returned to Shasta the next spring with surveyor Jerome Fay, this time reaching the summit twice. On the second climb, on April 30, he and Fay were caught in another storm on the descent, and they spent a long and uncomfortable night sheltering for warmth close to some noxious-smelling fumaroles, alternately feeling frozen and scalded. Muir, indefatigable, reassured his companion on that last night of April that "to-morrow we go a-Maying."[79] And later, looking back on the experience, Muir noted, with characteristic optimism, "Healthy mountaineers always discover in themselves a reserve of power after great exhaustion. It is a kind of second life only available in emergencies like this, and having proved its existence, I had no great dread that either Jerome or myself would fail."[80] Muir did not seek out danger, discomfort, and life-threatening experiences for their own sake, but he was stoically prepared to accept them in the pursuit of mountaineering.

In September 1877, Muir again returned to Shasta, his favorite California mountain, this time in the company of Harvard botanist Asa Gray, along with fellow Scotsman Joseph Hooker (the latter a friend and associate of Charles Darwin). They gathered alpine plant specimens and, in Muir's account, "had a fine rare time together . . . camping out & enjoying ourselves in pure freedom." When a particularly grand view opened before them on the mountainside, Muir, to the bemusement of his distinguished guests, began to dance ecstatically, commanding them to "Look at the glory! Look at the glory!"[81]

THE FIRST MOUNTAINEERING CLUBS

Muir's Sierra Club would become the most influential mountaineering group in the United States, but it was not the first in the field. In 1902 Charles E. Fay, a founder and past president of the Appalachian Mountain Club, contributed an article to the *Outlook* magazine entitled "Mountaineering as an Organized Sport." A few decades earlier, virtually no one in the United States would have described the act of climbing a mountain as "sport," let alone an organized one. Fay attributed the change to London's Alpine Club and the similar organizations that had sprung up around the world, including in the United States, which by 1902 boasted three important regional climbing clubs: Fay's Appalachian Mountain Club in New England, the Mazamas in Oregon, and the Sierra Club in California.[82]

Middle- and upper-class professionals were the lifeblood of these organizations, with a strong contingent from the expanding ranks of university and college graduates and faculty members. Academic certification was becoming important to many careers that had previously been based largely on apprenticeship, such as law and medicine. And to pursue a professional career also increasingly meant to be a member of one or more professional organizations. The American Medical Association predated the Civil War, but city and state bar associations did not appear until the 1870s, capped by the creation of the American Bar Association in 1878. The following decade saw the organization of such national academic organizations as the American Historical Association, the Modern Language Association, and the American Economic Association.[83]

Middle-class leisure and recreation, as well as professional careers, displayed the same organizational impulse in the latter decades of the nineteenth century. In those years, Boston alone spawned scores of athletic societies, associations, and clubs devoted to yachting, rowing, baseball, bicycling, and other sports. Intercollegiate athletics, which barely existed before the Civil War, grew robustly in the years that followed, with rival colleges fielding teams in baseball, football, track and field, tennis, and basketball.[84]

Climbing enthusiasts shared the general impulse to band together with like-minded souls. The first such organization appeared in April 1863 in western Massachusetts: the Alpine Club of Williamstown, founded by Albert Hopkins, professor of natural philosophy and astronomy at Williams College, brother of the college's famous president, Mark Hopkins. In contrast to its namesake in Britain, but typically for American mountaineering groups to come, the club admitted both men and women into its ranks. In fact, perhaps because able-bodied men tended to be in uniform in 1863, women accounted initially for nine of the twelve members of the Williamstown group. Club members made numerous outings to local Berkshire summits, especially Mount Greylock, as well to the Green Mountains in Vermont and Mount Washington in New Hampshire.[85]

Similar local groups sprang up in Portland, Maine, in 1873, and in Denver in 1875. Like the one in Williamstown, they were small and short-lived, but their very existence indicated a growing interest in organized outdoor adventure, or "tramping" as it was sometimes called. A founding member of the White Mountain Club of Portland, John M. Gould, published a book in 1877 entitled *How to Camp Out*, the first such guide to appear in the United States. Gould counseled campers not to worry about their appearance in the wilderness: "When you are camping, you have a right to be independent."[86]

The real organizational history of American mountaineering begins in 1876, with the founding of the Appalachian Mountain Club. On January 1 of that year, Edward Charles Pickering sent letters to fifty individuals in the Boston area, inviting them to come to a meeting "of those interested in mountain exploration" a week later at the Massachusetts Institute of Technology (then located in Boston's Back Bay). After several preliminary meetings, in which the discussion centered on the appropriate name for the organization ("New England Mountain Club," "White Mountain Club," and "Mountain Exploration Society" among the contenders), the Appalachian Mountain Club held its first regular public meeting on February 8. At that gathering the founding members elected Pickering as president and adopted a statement declaring the club's mission to be "the advancement of the interests of those who visit the mountains of New England and adjacent regions, whether for the purpose of scientific research or summer recreation."[87]

President Pickering was a Harvard University graduate, astronomer, and physicist, then teaching at MIT and soon to assume the directorship of the Harvard College Observatory. He was sufficiently eminent in his academic field to have craters named for him on the moon and on Mars; closer to home, he was devoted to exploring the White Mountains. Samuel Hubbard Scudder, entomologist and paleontologist, and a graduate of Williams College and Harvard University, was the AMC's first vice president. Both men traced their family origins to the earliest settlers of New England, as did most of the club's rank and file.

In June 1876, the first issue of the club's journal *Appalachia* appeared; it included a list of over a hundred members who had joined since the start of the year, with old New England names predominating. In terms of professional affiliation, Harvard and MIT faculty were amply represented. The selection process for new members reinforced the group's social exclusivity. According to the club's constitution, applicants for "active" membership had to be nominated by at least two current members, and the nomination approved first by a majority of the club's governing council, and then by majority vote at a regular meeting. Only residents of New England were considered eligible for active membership. Even with these restrictions, by 1890 membership had grown to eight hundred; by 1900 it was more than thirteen hundred.[88]

As with the Alpine Club, the AMC's monthly meetings were the occasion for the reading of papers on mountain-related topics, including accounts of climbs recent and past, the geology of the White Mountains, and the like. But unlike the Alpine Club, the AMC also became known for gathering its members together, including both men and women, on well-attended group mountain outings. Scores of AMC members would regularly head off to New Hampshire by railroad for a day of climbing fellowship. In 1887, in another lasting innovation, the AMC sponsored its first "August Camp," a two-week camping trip. This first one, held at the base of Maine's Mount Katahdin, attracted nineteen AMC members, ten of them women. In subsequent years, in ever-larger gatherings, the camp shifted between the White Mountains and the Adirondacks.[89]

Foreign observers were struck by the integration of women into American climbing circles. Emily Thackeray, an English visitor to the White Mountains, wrote in a local New Hampshire newspaper in 1889:

> In the conservative, masculine mind, particularly in Europe, it has been a mooted point whether a woman could climb, camp out and "rough it" with any pleasure to herself or comfort to the "lords of creation." But to-day in America, things are greatly changed; mountain-tramping has become a "fad" among ladies and they are greatly encouraged by their brothers, their cousins and their uncles.[90]

In still another innovation in 1888, the AMC built its first "hut," a stone cabin, on the col between Mount Madison and Mount Adams in the White Mountains. Modeled on European mountain refuges, which some AMC members had encountered in the Alps, Madison Spring Hut provided an overnight way station for those climbing from the valley floor at Randolph, New Hampshire, to the summit of Mount Washington. For most of its first two decades, the hut offered its visitors few amenities beyond a roof to shelter beneath. It was open to anyone who came along, AMC member or nonmember, without fee. In 1906 the AMC hired a caretaker to spend the summer in the hut, and to offset the additional cost the club began charging guests fifty cents a night. Six years later, the hut began serving meals.

Madison Spring Hut, constructed in 1888.

By that time, an emergency refuge been constructed near the old Crawford Path, at Lakes of the Clouds on the side of Mount Washington (replaced by a stone hut in 1915). The collection of AMC huts in the White Mountains eventually grew to eight, spread at one-day hiking intervals along 56 miles of trails, as well as two lodges in surrounding valleys. (So important were the huts to the club's profile and finances by the late twentieth century that some disgruntled members began referring to it as the "Appalachian Motel Club.")[91]

The AMC encouraged New England climbers to take full advantage of their local mountains. In addition, from the club's earliest days, AMCers found their way to and helped popularize climbing in other ranges, in the United States and abroad. Frederick Chapin, the Hartford, Connecticut, climber, had joined the AMC by 1881, and he became a prolific contributor to its journal *Appalachia*, with articles chronicling his climbs in the Alps and the Colorado Rockies; the AMC brought out his *Mountaineering in Colorado* in 1889, as the club's first published book.[92]

CHARLES E. FAY AND
THE CANADIAN ROCKIES

Members of the Appalachian Mountain Club—chief among them Charles E. Fay—also played an important role in the exploration and early mountaineering history of the Canadian Rockies.

Born in Roxbury, Massachusetts, on March 10, 1846, son of a Universalist minister, Fay enrolled at Tufts College in 1864, an institution with which he would be associated for the rest of his long life. He was a pioneering figure in the teaching of modern languages, proficient in French, German, and Italian at a time when most colleges offered instruction only in the "dead languages," ancient Greek and Latin. He was a founder of the Modern Language Association and capped a distinguished academic career with over a decade's service as dean of Tuft's School of Graduate Studies.[93]

Fay spent the academic year 1869–70 in Europe mastering his command of western European languages. On his return and over the next decade and a half, he climbed exclusively in the White Mountains. Then, in 1888, at the age of forty-two, Fay traveled west, where he not only climbed Longs Peak but, with some others, including Frederick Chapin, made a first ascent of 13,514-foot Ypsilon Mountain in the Mummy Range of the Colorado Rockies.[94]

A charter member of the AMC, chairing its first organizational meeting, Fay was elected club president on four occasions, the first in 1879, and for a half century served as the editor of its journal *Appalachia*. As corresponding secretary of the club, Fay established ties with European mountaineering groups and with prominent figures in the international climbing community, including Matterhorn conqueror Edward Whymper and Italian mountain photographer Vittorio Sella. Fay would make his final climb just six months before his death at age eighty-four.[95]

Fay enthusiastically promoted mountaineering for the opportunity it offered to admire what he called "the grand cathedral of Nature" in his 1879 presidential address to the AMC. Fay placed himself in the tradition of Burkean aesthetics and the New England transcendentalism, as he proclaimed that upon reaching the summit of a mountain, the climber experienced "an influence akin to religious exaltation. We call it the sentiment of the sublime."[96]

Fay made his most significant contribution to mountaineering history when he was well into middle age, accomplishing more than a dozen first ascents in western Canada's mountains.

The Canadian Rockies, like their American counterparts, form that nation's Continental Divide, with the drainage from the western slope making its way to the Pacific via the Columbia and Fraser Rivers, and from the eastern slope to the Atlantic via the Great Lakes and the Saint Lawrence River. The Columbia River loops around the geographically separate but nearby Selkirk Range to the west of the Rockies, in what is called its Big Bend. Topping out at 11,545-foot Mount Sir Sandford, the Selkirk Range is home to forty peaks over 10,000 feet. The Canadian Rockies top out at 12,972-foot Mount Robson, with eighteen peaks over 11,000.

Neither range offers mountains as high as the Wyoming or Colorado Rockies. But the Canadian mountains, unlike their southern counterparts, are heavily glaciated, thanks to the prevailing west winds carrying moisture from the Pacific, with the snow line between 5,000 and 10,000 feet.[97] It was a commonplace by the late nineteenth century to call the Colorado Rockies the "Switzerland" of America, but that was an accurate comparison only seasonally, given the melting of the snows every summer. The Canadian Rockies, with year-round snow like the Swiss Alps, better deserved the title. They would earn it, once the railroad came along.

Twenty-two years after the golden spike was driven marking completion of the transcontinental railroad in the United States, construction on the Canadian Pacific Railway began, with the intent of linking the new Canadian province of British Columbia with the Atlantic coast. The main obstacle was, of course, the collection of Swiss-like mountains in western Alberta and eastern British Columbia. Railroad surveyors found a good route through the main chain of the Rockies at Kicking Horse Pass, but the tangle of peaks in the Selkirks proved more difficult to pierce. A Massachusetts-born surveyor, Major Albert Bowman Rogers, who directed the construction of the mountain section of the Canadian Pacific Railway, found a pass through which tracks could be laid; today it bears his name.[98]

The completion of the Canadian Pacific Railway in 1885 made it possible for passengers to cross Canada in just seven days. Before long, accommodations for visitors opened in the mountains, including Glacier House at Rogers Pass in the Selkirks, along with a more modest accommodation, referred to as a chateau, on the shore of Lake Louise. In 1888, the much grander Banff Springs Hotel opened its doors. Banff emerged as the first true equivalent in North America of alpine resort communities like Chamonix, complete with a corps of Swiss and Austrian professional guides recruited by the Canadian Pacific Railway to drum up trade with mountain-oriented tourists. (The only equivalent community in the United States at the time was, perhaps, Conway, New Hampshire, linked by rail to Boston in 1871, but with nowhere near the opportunities for genuine mountaineering that surround Banff, and no staff of European guides in residence.) As in France and Switzerland in the golden age of alpinism, mountaineers could now explore and ascend an abundance of unclimbed peaks, with comfortable accommodations at their disposal as they made their preparations and on their return. And it was only a four-day trip by railroad from this mountaineering paradise to Boston.[99]

It took a few years for Bostonians to figure that out. Fay was the first to see the possibilities. In 1890, at age forty-four, Fay accompanied Harvard astronomer J. Rayner Edmands on a railroad journey across the United States to the Pacific coast, where Edmands was investigating a site for a new observatory. (Edmands, who had accompanied Fay on the 1888 first ascent of Colorado's Ypsilon Mountain, was also celebrated among New England mountaineers for his trail building in the White Mountains, and he was a past president of the AMC.) Fay and Edmands returned to the East Coast via the Canadian Pacific Railway, on September 5 stopping for the night at Glacier House.

The next morning, Fay set out alone to explore the approach to 10,774-foot Mount Sir Donald, which had had its first ascent only a few days earlier by Swiss climbers Emil Huber and Carl Sulzer, along with their

Charles E. Fay (center, with beard), with members of the Canadian Alpine Club.

porter Harry Cooper. Fay did not have time to follow their footsteps to the summit, but he did reach a ridgeline about 7,500 feet up the mountain before turning back to catch his train. He was struck by the beauty of the region and determined to return and explore what he now described as the "new Switzerland."[100]

There were no more first ascents to be made in the old Switzerland, and no American climber could claim any first ascent anywhere in the European Alps. But there were hundreds of first ascents still to be made in the Canadian Rockies, including eighteen unclimbed peaks over 11,000 feet and four over 12,000 feet, with another three peaks in the Selkirks over 11,000 feet.

It was five years before Fay returned. In the meantime, another AMC member, the Reverend Harry Pierce Nichols, made his own trip to the region. In the summer of 1893, he stayed in Glacier House and climbed 10,486-foot Mount Fox in the Selkirks, the tenth-highest mountain in that range. Nichols, who had climbed in the Swiss Alps a decade earlier, reported on his Canadian adventure at a meeting of the AMC in Boston in October of that year, declaring happily, "We Americans have, hard at hand, without sea sickness, without great expense, a range of mountains rivaling the Alps, furnishing all the cherished features of mountaineering."[101]

Two Yale undergraduates, Walter Wilcox and Samuel Allen, also visited the region in 1893. The students were unsuccessful in attempts that summer on Mount Victoria and Mount Temple, but they did succeed in making the first ascent of 9,003-foot Fairview Mountain south of Lake Louise, followed by first ascents of 9,363-foot Eagle Peak and 8,468-foot Cheops Mountain in the Selkirk Range. The western Canadian mountains were still so little visited that even two casual summer tourists could stumble upon significant discoveries. Wilcox and Allen were the first white men to view Lake Moraine and its ten surrounding peaks. Allen, recalling his feelings on stumbling upon "this unknown and unvisited spot," called the moment "the happiest half hour of my life." A philologist by training, Allen gave all ten peaks names from the local Stoney Indian language, although most were subsequently changed—one of them, 10,622-foot Mount Fay, renamed for Charles Fay; another, 10,830-foot Mount Allen, renamed to honor Allen himself.[102]

Returning to New Haven after their summer's adventure, Wilcox and Allen sought recruits among their friends for a return to the Canadian Rockies the following summer. In the summer of 1894, undergraduates Yandell Henderson, George Warrington, and Louis Frissell joined them in a newly constructed chalet on Lake Louise (an earlier, cruder, log structure had housed visitors to the lake before this). Unlike Wilcox and Allen, the three newcomers to what they were now calling the "Lake Louise Club" were novices. According to Henderson's account, written many years later:

> As regards mountaineering: the pages of the "Badminton Volume on Mountaineering," read after we reached Lake Louise, were our only source of information. We read up the night before and the next morning applied our information in practice on the mountains that are in some respects the most dangerous in the world.

We had hobnailed boots, ropes and ice-axes. We also had that spirit of adventure that gets boys into tight places and generally gets them out again.[103]

Early that summer, before all the members of the Lake Louise Club assembled, Wilcox, Henderson, and Frissell went out for a day's practice on Mount Lefroy. Frissell took a tumble when he dislodged a large rock while ascending a steep couloir. The Badminton mountaineering guide, with its instructions on mountain rescue, proved its value that day. Wilcox described their descent with their incapacitated comrade:

Uncoiling the full length of the rope, one end was fastened round his waist, and the other round mine. With an ice-ax buried to the head in the snow as an anchor, I paid out the rope and lowered our helpless friend fully fifty feet. Then Henderson went down and anchoring himself in like manner, held him while I came down. This operation, repeated a number of times, brought us soon upon the comparatively level glacier.[104]

Wilcox set off for help from the chalet. Frissell's injury turned out not to be as serious as feared. Within a few days he would re-join his companions on the slopes. Together they would complete several first ascents, including that of 11,627-foot Mount Temple, the highest mountain yet climbed in Canada.[105]

Charles E. Fay finally returned to the Canadian Rockies in 1895. He did so in the company of a number of fellow AMCers, including twenty-eight-year-old Philip Stanley Abbot. The younger man was already one of the most experienced climbers in the United States, having climbed in Switzerland, Mexico, Norway, and Yosemite. Born in Brookline, Massachusetts, in 1867, Abbot grew up in Cambridge and Milwaukee, graduating from Harvard College in 1890 and from Harvard Law School in 1893, and he was working as a railroad corporation attorney. His fellow AMCers expected great things of him.[106]

On July 30, 1895, Fay, Abbot, and Charles Thompson made the first

Philip S. Abbot in the Canadian Rockies, summer of 1895.

ascent of 11,135-foot Mount Hector. "So far as the Club is concerned," Abbot reported to *Appalachia*'s readers the next winter, "Mt. Hector is the first alpine peak . . . which has been conquered for the first time by an Appalachian [Mountain Club] party, as such, climbing without guides."[107] The three followed this triumph with another, less than two weeks later, on August 10, when they made the first ascent of 9,108-foot Mount Castor. Thompson's enthusiastic recounting of the Castor climb to *Appalachia*'s readers revealed the continuing infiltration of European mountaineering jargon into American climbing narratives, at least those written by educated easterners:

> At the col a surprise awaited us. On the névé snow, just beyond the arête, lay a tiny lake, deepest blue in the centre, shading shoreward to lightest green, a sapphire girt with emerald set in a frozen sea.[108]

The one great disappointment for Abbot and his companions that summer of 1895 lay in two foiled attempts to climb 11,231-foot Mount Lefroy. Abbot returned to his career as an attorney in Boston but remained obsessed with the unclimbed peak. He had spotted a possible route up its western face and, along with Fay and Thompson, vowed to return the next summer for another try.[109]

So it was that, at the end of July 1896, the three AMCers, joined by George T. Little, were reunited at Glacier House.[110] They set out to conquer Lefroy on the morning of August 3. Departing the chalet on the shore of Lake Louise, the four men rowed across the lake to the base of the mountain at dawn. By noon they had reached the high col, just under 10,000 feet, linking Mount Victoria (then known as Mount Green) and Mount Lefroy.[111] After lunch, as Fay recorded, "we again set forth to complete, as we fondly believed, the largest enterprise in the way of mountaineering that has ever been accomplished on Canadian peaks."[112]

This was most definitely alpinism in the European style, apart from the absence of a professional guide. The men took a zigzag course up the icy slopes of Lefroy's western face, cutting steps as they went. They proceeded in a single roped line, each equipped with an ice ax, with one climber at a time heading uphill while the others braced themselves to hold any fall. Abbot, the most proficient, led most of the way.

At about 5:30 in the afternoon, they found their path blocked by a steep rock cliff about 200 vertical feet below Lefroy's summit. Fay and Thompson unroped so that Abbot and Little could find a way around the obstacle. A falling rock nearly severed the rope connecting the two lead climbers, and Little untied himself and came up beside Abbot. For all their caution at lower elevations, the AMC climbers now began to make imprudent choices. Abbot moved out ahead and alone into a gulley, confidently reassuring his partner, "I have a good lead here."[113] A moment later, however, he lost his footing and hurtled down the slope past a horrified Little. Abbot tumbled 900 feet before coming to rest on a flat surface below.[114]

By the time his companions reached Abbot's side several hours later, he was barely clinging to life, with blood draining from a deep cut on the back of his head. Fay, Thompson, and Little tried to carry their wounded companion to safety, but he died before they could get far. With darkness falling, they felt they had no choice but to leave the body behind and make their own descent. Before long they were in complete darkness and forced to bivouac overnight on the col between Lefroy and Victoria. At dawn they resumed their descent, returning to the hotel with the sad news. Abbot's body was subsequently retrieved from the mountain and shipped home by railroad for burial in Mount Auburn cemetery in Cambridge, Massachusetts.[115]

Abbot is sometimes mistakenly described as the first mountaineering fatality in North America. He was, indeed, the first to die in Canada, but others had died before him in the United States.[116] He was certainly the most socially prominent American to die in a climbing accident as of the 1890s, and also the first member of an American climbing club to do so—factors that attracted widespread public attention. News of Abbot's death initially provoked criticism of the climbers for their foolhardiness, and even calls for banning the pastime. Reporting on Abbot's "tragic death," the *New York Times* commented that he and his companions had ignored the advice of "residents of the district" to abandon their attempt on the mountain, "a feat so difficult and dangerous that few have attempted and fewer have accomplished it." (In reality, no one had yet accomplished it.)[117]

At a memorial meeting for Abbot in October in Boston, Charles Fay offered a detailed account of the accident that had ended the young climber's life—and also a defense of mountaineering in the face of continuing controversy. Abbot's family had a tradition of patriotic selflessness; he was named for an uncle who had dropped out of Harvard as an undergraduate to join the Union army during the Civil War and had been killed at Gettysburg. Fay suggested that Abbot's death on Lefroy, far from meaningless, was, in its own way, a noble form of self-sacrifice, in a new cause:

> After duly weighing all that is urged against Alpine climbing, and while appreciating, none more profoundly, the value of the rare life that went out on Mt. Lefroy, we maintain that the gain therefrom

for the general and the individual life in an age of growing careful-
ness for ease and luxury must be held to outweigh the deplorable
losses, and that this casualty should not call a halt in American
alpinism.[118]

WEST COAST MOUNTAINEERING CLUBS

In the late 1880s and early 1890s, the organizational impulse that had
led to the creation of the Appalachian Mountain Club in Boston in 1876
made the leap across the Continental Divide, first to Oregon and then to
California.

Throughout the nineteenth century, Mount Hood was the most frequently climbed of the Pacific Northwest's mountains, as it has remained
to the present. It was only a day's journey on horseback or by wagon from
Portland along the old Barlow Road to Government Camp, on the mountain's south side. And from there, then and now, Hood can be summited
in a single day. In contrast, in 1888, when John Muir set out to climb
Mount Rainier, it took him three days of riding and hiking over rough
terrain simply to reach timberline, and then another day and a half to
reach that mountain's summit.[119]

Hood was also distinguished from comparable peaks by the number
of new routes that climbers had followed to its summit; by the 1890s,
in addition to the standard south-side route first climbed by the Pittock
party in 1857, there had been ascents via four more challenging routes—
two on the mountain's north side, one on the northwest, and one on the
east side.[120]

William Gladstone Steel's efforts to popularize the Oregon Cascades
are comparable to those of his better-known contemporary and friend
John Muir in the Sierra. Born in Ohio, Steel moved to Portland with
his family as a teenager in the 1870s. His mother and father had been
abolitionists before the Civil War; they sheltered runaway slaves. In 1881
the *Oregonian* associated mountain-climbing with freedom fighting, in
an editorial that praised the Steels "and others of the early abolitionists"
for having "stood on the mountain tops, and beholding the goodly land

of a freeman's republic, followed their principles through storm and sunshine."[121]

Steel shared his parents' energy and idealism, pouring it into the causes of wilderness preservation and mountain tourism, while pursuing an eclectic career as an ironworks pattern maker, journalist, mailman, and real estate developer. It was largely through his efforts that Crater Lake and its surroundings in southern Oregon became the fifth national park in 1902, and he later served as the park's superintendent.[122]

Starting in 1870, and on other occasions over the next decade and a half, Portlanders attempted unsuccessfully to light bonfires and set off fireworks high up on Mount Hood, with the hope that the flames would be visible from the city 50 miles to the west. Steel and some friends decided to try their hand in 1885. While Steel stayed in Portland to publicize the forthcoming illumination, his friends set up an elaborate device intended to spill a bottle of inflammable liquid onto a pile of incendiary powder atop a rocky outcrop at 9,534 feet on the mountain's southwest flank. But the effect was spoiled when an avalanche prematurely triggered the fireworks in daylight.

Steel was back two years later, and this time, beside a large rock at an elevation of 9,800 feet, he managed to set off 100 pounds of an incendiary known as Red Fire on the night of July 4, 1887. The display was clearly visible in Portland and the state capital, Salem—a spectacular bit of alpine pyromania that made the front page of the *New York Times*, as well as the cover of the popular magazine *Frank Leslie's Illustrated Weekly*. The rock at the site of their triumph remained ever afterward "Illumination Rock," while Steel's name was preserved on another nearby landscape feature, Steel Cliff. The publicity generated by the illumination made Mount Hood a nationally recognized symbol of Oregon.[123] As Steel wrote a few years later, the mountain was "the idol of Oregon, the paragon of beauty, at whose feet it is but human to bow, and bless the God that gave such grandeur."[124]

Building on the publicity from the successful illumination, a few months later Steel helped organize the Oregon Alpine Club. Like its East

Coast predecessor, the AMC, the Oregon group sponsored lectures and mountain excursions. The club put the first summit register atop Mount Hood and listed 650 members within a few years.

Steel's dream was to develop Mount Hood as a tourist mecca, comparable to Mount Washington in New Hampshire. In 1892 he proposed the construction of a rail link from Portland to Government Camp, and from there a cog railway like the one that had opened in 1869 on Mount Washington, to carry passengers to within a thousand vertical feet of the summit. "Within 60 miles of our city stands Mount Hood," he proclaimed enthusiastically in an 1892 interview in the local paper. "It is a place where pure air and water, together with pleasant weather and grand scenery, combine to form a summer resort with few equals and no superiors." (As for its eastern rival, Mount Washington, Steel noted disparagingly that Washington's summit was "about equal to the timberline on Hood.")[125]

Despite Steel's boosterism, the Oregon Alpine Club fell on hard times within a few years. There were no requirements for membership, and active climbers felt its ranks included too many nonclimbers for whom the club was merely a social outlet. By 1892 the club was all but moribund.[126]

So Steel decided to found a new club. With his usual flair for public relations, and to guarantee that this time only active climbers would join, he determined to hold the group's organizational meeting *on top* of Mount Hood. Following a preliminary meeting in Portland in March 1894, 250 climbers gathered at Government Camp on July 18 for dinner and a musical program, before setting out on a mass climb to the summit at 2:00 the next morning. A total of 155 climbers, including 38 women, reached the top (the onset of a storm discouraged others). The summit delegates adopted a constitution and elected officers for a club to be known thenceforth as the Mazamas, the name derived from the Spanish for "mountain goat." The Mazamas restricted membership to those who, like themselves, had climbed a glaciated mountain.[127]

As with the AMC, mass outings became a signature activity of the Mazamas. An English journalist offered an amused report on the Oregon climbers for his readers in 1897: "At first one hardly knows whether to take the Mazamas, a comparatively new mountain club of the Pacific

Climber on Mount Hood, 1902.

Northwest, wholly in earnest, for there are many fireworks and flags and hurrahs, there is much 'hustle,' and rhetoric, and apparent sensationalism in the reports they make of themselves, and their mountain climbing seems to be done in crowds."[128]

FOUNDING OF THE SIERRA CLUB

Unlike William Gladstone Steel, John Muir was not given to hustle, fireworks, or climbing in crowds. But Muir was persuaded by his friend Robert Underwood Johnson, an editor of the influential eastern magazine the *Century*, to abandon what Johnson called his "gentle hermit" ways for a larger goal. Johnson understood that Muir's nature writings over the previous two decades had given him a significant moral stature among educated middle-class readers in the East—a reputation that could now be turned into political capital.

Together, Muir and Underwood launched a campaign to save Yosemite Park from the abuses that its California state commissioners were overlooking—especially commercial and agricultural development. Largely as a result of Muir's articles in the *Century* and Johnson's lobbying efforts, Congress established Yosemite National Park in September 1890, expanding the boundaries of the original 1864 park to close to 1,200 square miles, although for the moment leaving Yosemite Valley and the Mariposa Grove under the authority of the state of California.[129]

Thanks to Muir's increasing fame as a writer, and his role in the creation of the third national park in the United States (Sequoia National Park in the southern Sierra was the second, created just a week before Yosemite National Park), he was asked by outdoors-minded faculty members at the University of California at Berkeley (including the influential professor of geology and natural history Joseph LeConte), along with others at Stanford University, to preside at a meeting to form a California alpine club. Muir agreed to do so, and on June 4, 1892, twenty-seven delegates founded what they decided to call the Sierra Club, with the purpose, as defined by its articles of incorporation, "to explore, enjoy, and render accessible the mountain regions of the Pacific Coast," as well as to preserve "the forests and other natural features of the Sierra Nevada mountains."[130]

When the Sierra Club held its first public meeting in September, 250 people were in attendance to hear John Wesley Powell report on his exploration of the Colorado River. The club was an instant success, its ranks, like those of its eastern cousin the AMC, on whom it was modeled, drawn from the well-educated middle class—professors, scientists, and businessmen.[131] Summer outings in the mountains were an opportunity for Sierra Club members, like their AMC and Mazama brethren, to put aside the trappings of social status for the rude democracy of tent and campfire—with certain exemptions, as can be seen in the instructions for the annual outing of 1905:

No tips, gratuities, or other considerations shall be paid by any one participating in the Outing to any person in the employ of the Club. (This rule does not apply to payment for washing done by Chinamen.)[132]

Sierra Club and Appalachian Mountain Club members climb Mount Lyell in the Sierra.

Like the AMC back east, and rather more than the Mazamas to the north, the Sierra Club was influenced by the example of the Alpine Club in London, and by European alpinism more generally. Among the charter members was David Starr Jordan, founding president of Stanford University, who a decade earlier had been one of the first Americans to climb the Matterhorn. A portrait of Edward Whymper hung in the club's headquarters in San Francisco's Academy of Sciences.[133]

Although regionally based, the Sierra Club from the beginning addressed conservation issues on a national rather than a state basis, calling for the creation of a national park centered on Mount Rainier in Washington (which would be established in 1899).[134] Muir's own instincts emphasized the preservation of wilderness for its own sake, without regard to human advantage. But with the organization of the Sierra Club, he spoke more frequently of the benefits that wilderness preservation and appreciation represented for his fellow citizens. As he wrote in his 1901 book *Our National Parks*:

> Camp out among the grass and gentians of glacier meadows, in craggy garden nooks full of Nature's darlings. Climb the mountains and get their good tidings. Nature's peace will flow into you as the sunshine into the trees. The winds will blow their freshness into you, and the storms their energy, while cares will drop off like autumn leaves.[135]

REDEMPTIVE MOUNTAINEERING

Long before Muir first saw Yosemite, Thoreau and Emerson had expressed similar sentiments about Monadnock and Katahdin (and, indeed, the "good tidings" passage in Muir's *Our National Parks* echoed, probably intentionally, the rhythms of the closing paragraph of Emerson's 1836 *Nature*).[136] What was different as the twentieth century came on the horizon was that Muir's readers were prepared to apply his familiar enthusiasms as a prescription for personal and national redemption.

In 1890, the year that Yosemite National Park was established, the US Census Bureau issued what remains its most famous announcement: that it could no longer find a continuous line of frontier anywhere in the United States. Less than a century had passed since President Thomas Jefferson in his 1801 inaugural address had enumerated the blessings enjoyed by the United States, including enough unexplored and unsettled land to the west "for our descendants to the thousandth and thousandth generation."[137] As it turned out, it took only three generations to populate that vast reserve.

On July 12, 1893, ten days before Katharine Lee Bates stood on the summit of Pikes Peak, University of Wisconsin professor Frederick Jackson Turner delivered a paper entitled "The Significance of the Frontier in American History" at a meeting of the American Historical Association in Chicago. Turner's essay made him the most influential historian of his generation. In an often-cited peroration, Turner argued that the announcement of the frontier's demise would prove a watershed in the American national experience:

> What the Mediterranean Sea was to the Greeks, breaking the bond of custom, offering new experiences, calling out new institutions and activities, that, and more, the ever retreating frontier has been to the United States. . . . And now, four centuries from the discovery of America, at the end of a hundred years of life under the Constitution, the frontier has gone, and with its going has closed the first period of American history.[138]

Turner traced his family line in the New World back to a Puritan settler in the Massachusetts Bay Colony in 1634. His ancestors, huddled along the northeastern coast of the vast unmapped North American continent, would have rejoiced at the prospect of the taming of that howling western wilderness. Turner and his contemporaries weren't so sure. What now was left that made America exceptional? With teeming cities filled by a polyglot mix of immigrants and, looming on the horizon that summer of 1893, the mass unemployment and labor unrest of the country's worst economic depression to date, could the United States really claim to be all that different from the class-stratified nations of Europe? What, if anything, could take the place of the nation- and character-building experience of exploring and settling the western frontier, so recently thought limitless, now finally vanquished?[139]

Perhaps the answer lay in the American mountains, celebrated in Katharine Lee Bates's hymn and John Muir's essays, and in those casual summer outings sponsored by the recently established mountaineering groups. Frank Branch Riley, a former president of the Mazamas, contributed an article to the club's journal in 1914, reminiscing about the early days of the club's summer encampments in the Cascades in the 1890s:

> Life in camp was a joyous riot of democracy. Reduced to frank equality in dress and general appearance, we were none the less

so in spirit. Titles and formal salutations were forgotten. College presidents, eminent surgeons, celebrated naturalists, and men of letters, were, for a time, mercifully spared that deference which it is their lot to endure in classroom and clinic; they answered promptly to their nick-names, and helped to select appropriate sobriquets for the others.[140]

Riley's recollection of the list of professions likely to be represented at a Mazamas encampment, starting with college presidents and eminent surgeons, underlined the actual social exclusivity of the club for all his celebration of "frank equality." Nevertheless, outdoor fellowship for these affluent professionals represented a kind of ritualized (if romanticized) return to earlier versions of American democratic community that Turner believed had thrived on the frontier.

And what was good for the community was also good for the individual. The so-called Gay Nineties might have been better labeled the "Anxious Nineties," as the urban middle classes took a morbid interest in a variety of nervous disorders, or "neurasthenia," that they felt themselves at risk of contracting.[141] Dr. George Beard, in his wildly popular 1881 book *American Nervousness; Its Causes and Consequences*, described his fellow countrymen as enduring an epidemic of "insomnia, flushing, drowsiness, bad dreams, cerebral irritation, dilated pupils, pain, pressure and heaviness in the head," and a myriad of other symptoms that took a full page and a half to list.[142]

A decade later, the influential psychologist G. Stanley Hall warned of the dangers of "over-civilization," particularly for American boys who were being pampered by luxury and overprotected by their mothers. For their future psychological health, males needed to acquire the toughness that came from contact with the primitive: a healthy boy, Hall asserted, was given the opportunity to repeat "the history of his race," from barbarism to civilization.[143]

Muir was likely among both Beard's and Hall's readers, for on the very first page of *Our National Parks*, he offered a simple solution to the problems they described:

Thousands of tired, nerve-shaken, over-civilized people are beginning to find out going to the mountains is going home; that wilderness is a necessity; and that mountain parks and reservations are
useful not only as fountains of timber and irrigating rivers, but as
fountains of life.[144]

In the first centuries of American national existence, the wilderness
had been a problem to be solved by civilization; in the last decade of the
nineteenth century and the start of the twentieth century, it began to
seem to many Americans that civilization was a problem to be solved by
wilderness.[145]

A STRENUOUS LIFE

The most influential proponent of that point of view was also the most
prominent American of the early twentieth century: President Theodore
Roosevelt. Second only to Thomas Jefferson among American presidents
in his fascination with the natural world, Roosevelt was second to none in
his familiarity with and love for American mountains.

Born in New York City in 1858, Teddy Roosevelt had been a sickly
child, suffering from asthma and other ailments. He remade himself into
a physically strong and active adult through his own willpower and his
family's considerable economic resources. At age eleven, he was taken on
a yearlong grand tour of Europe, during which he hiked in the Swiss Alps.
He spent his summers as a teenager in outdoor settings, in the Hudson
River valley, the North Shore of Long Island, the Adirondacks, the White
Mountains, and the Maine woods. In August 1879, at age twenty, he
reached the summit of his first big mountain, Mount Katahdin, in the
company of a backwoods guide who remained a lifelong friend. "I find I
can endure fatigue and hardship pretty nearly as well as these lumbermen," he boasted afterward.[146]

In the summer of 1881, after graduating from Harvard, marrying, and
beginning Columbia Law School, Roosevelt traveled to Europe with his
wife, Alice, on a belated honeymoon, and climbed both the Matterhorn

and the Jungfrau. Part of his motivation for climbing in the Alps was to prove to the English travelers he met in Switzerland that Americans were their equals as mountain climbers. Of the Matterhorn, he wrote home to his sister Anna: "It was like going up and down enormous stairs on your hands and knees in nine hours."[147]

Roosevelt inherited his interest in the natural world from his father, a founder of the Museum of Natural History in New York City. A collector of stuffed birds, shells, snakeskins, and the like as a boy, he had aspirations when he left for his first year at Harvard College of a career as a naturalist or biologist. Instead, he became a politician. Returning from the Alps in 1881, he won his first elected office as New York State assemblyman from the twenty-first district in New York City.

Energetic and ambitious, Roosevelt rose to national prominence in the years that followed, with a career that included stints as Dakota rancher, civil service commissioner, police commissioner of New York, assistant secretary of the navy, US Army cavalry officer, governor of New York, and, as of the spring of 1901, vice president of the United States. He had held that office barely six months when, on vacation in the Adirondacks on September 13, 1901, shortly after he reached the summit of Mount Marcy, a messenger arrived bearing bad news. President William McKinley, recovering from an assassination attempt the previous week in Buffalo, New York, had taken a sudden turn for the worse. Teddy Roosevelt descended the mountain to ascend to the presidency of the United States.[148]

Two years earlier, on April 10, 1899, still governor of New York, Roosevelt had given a speech to the Hamilton Club in Chicago, a well-heeled Republican social club, at its annual banquet commemorating the anniversary of the Confederate surrender at Appomattox. He told his audience that he had come to preach "the doctrine of the strenuous life, the life of toil and effort, of labor and strife." Success would come only to the man (and by extension only to the nation) "who does not shrink from danger, from hardship, or from bitter toil, and who out of these wins the splendid human triumph."

In part a call for the United States to protect and expand the overseas empire it had obtained the previous year in the Spanish-American War, the speech was also a criticism of the spirit of materialism and the love of luxury that, Roosevelt felt, had animated the nation's wealthiest and most prominent citizens in the years since the Civil War. In contrast, Roosevelt pointed to the example of the "highest type" of men who had led the nation through the war—men like Abraham Lincoln and Ulysses S. Grant who, though "they toiled to win a competence for themselves," devoted their lives to "loftier duties—duties to the nation and duties to the race."[149]

The speech was widely circulated in the years that followed, and not just because its author was such a prominent citizen. It struck a nerve with the public. Its theme and language found their way into the writings of mountaineers, as well as politicians, including Charles E. Fay of the Appalachian Mountain Club. Mountaineering's "contempt of hardships," Fay suggested in a 1902 essay, and its

> acceptance of a certain element of personal danger to be averted by judgment and coolness, its alluring invitations to conquest in which the heart need not harden as it exultantly strengthens in tenacity of purpose, render it not only the king of sports for strenuous man, but the one theoretically the best adapted to develop fearless leaders.[150]

In his 1879 AMC presidential address, Fay had emphasized the Burkean sublime as the best reason for climbing a mountain, while in his 1896 memorial elegy for Philip Stanley Abbot, he had defended mountaineering from its critics as an antidote to sloth and luxury. Now, under Roosevelt's influence, he placed even greater emphasis on the sport's sterner values.

MUIR AND ROOSEVELT, 1903

Muir and Roosevelt had very little in common. Muir was a pacifist; Roosevelt was a warrior. Muir worshipped nature, including its living creatures; Roosevelt was a big-game trophy hunter. And although no American president did more for the cause of national parks, Roosevelt (and his chief of the US Forest Service, Gifford Pinchot) had little sympathy for Muir's absolute commitment to the preservation of wilderness for its own sake. Their version of conservationism held that the nation's natural resources should not be squandered heedlessly, but neither, outside of particularly spectacular settings like Yosemite and the Grand Canyon, should they be locked up in their original condition forever. Accordingly, Roosevelt and Pinchot were prepared to make trade-offs between pristine wilderness and public utility—as shown in their support for the proposal to dam the Sierra's Hetch Hetchy Valley to provide a reliable source of drinking water to San Francisco.[151]

But that unhappy controversy was a few years in the future, when Roosevelt wrote to Muir in the spring of 1903 to secure his company on a trip he planned to take to Yosemite Valley. In April, Roosevelt had embarked on a two-month national speaking tour that took him to more than half the states in the nation. Much of the tour was devoted to engagements in cities, big and small, but he also visited Yellowstone Park, and the rim of the Grand Canyon, before arriving in California, where he headed for his rendezvous with John Muir. "I do not want anyone with me but you," Roosevelt wrote to Muir, "and I want to drop politics absolutely for four days and just be out in the open with you."[152]

Roosevelt seldom did anything without political calculation. When he and Muir headed toward Yosemite, first by buggy and then on horseback from the train station at Raymond, California, on May 15, 1903, reporters and photographers were not far behind (one of the latter took the famous picture of Roosevelt and Muir two days later, atop 7,214-foot Glacier Point, with its commanding view of Half Dome and the Yosemite Valley).

Most of the presidential entourage stayed behind at the Wawona Hotel on the valley floor, while Roosevelt and Muir headed for the hills. The two men spent their evenings around a campfire and slept in the open with only blankets as shelter—the first night at the Mariposa Grove, the second high on the valley rim near Sentinel Dome, and the third at Bridalveil Meadow on the valley floor, with a view of El Capitan across the Merced River. Muir tutored the president on the glacial origins of the valley, while Roosevelt tried to interest Muir in the local birds and their songs (one of Muir's rare blind spots when it came to appreciating nature). Muir, who had his own political agenda for the trip, lobbied for a federal takeover of the original park granted to California, arguing that the state was mismanaging it. "I never before had a more interesting, hearty and manly companion," Muir wrote his wife. "I stuffed him pretty well regarding the timber thieves, the destructive work of the lumbermen, and other spoilers of the forest."[153] (The payoff came three years later when Roosevelt signed the Yosemite Recession Bill, which placed Yosemite Valley and the Mariposa Grove under federal jurisdiction.)

Americans were delighted with the image of their president roughing it in the company of the nation's most famous wilderness advocate. "The President in the Yosemite Park," readers of the *New York Times* learned

Teddy Roosevelt and John Muir, enjoying the view of the Yosemite Valley from Glacier Point, 1903.

in a headline on May 16, 1903: "Gets Dusty Riding in Stage, and Goes Mountain Climbing and Horse Back Riding."[154] Roosevelt held a press conference on the morning of May 17 and pronounced the Yosemite trip a "bully" experience. "Just think of where I was last night," he exulted to reporters, pointing toward Glacier Point. "Up there, amid the pines and the silver firs, and the Sierrian solitude, in a snowstorm, too, and without a tent. I passed one of the most pleasant nights of my life."[155]

Muir and Roosevelt, good tidings and strenuous life. These were not entirely compatible men, nor entirely compatible ways of thinking about mountains. But for three nights in May 1903, the differences blurred and the two coexisted comfortably in their Sierran solitude.

CHAPTER FOUR

BROTHERHOOD OF THE ROPE, 1900-1946: PART I

A leader . . . does not fall. It is the first condition of his hegemony that he must not.

—GEOFFREY WINTHROP YOUNG, *MOUNTAIN CRAFT*, 1920

The rope . . . transforms an individualistic into a higher social enterprise . . . developing comradeship and the consciousness of standing solidly together, under stress, for a common cause. This is one of the finest experiences that mountaineering can afford.

—ROBERT UNDERHILL, "ON THE USE AND MANAGEMENT OF THE ROPE IN ROCK WORK," 1931

American mountaineering came of age in the first half of the twentieth century, assimilating and improving upon advanced European techniques. Not coincidentally, in the same half century, the greatest generation of American climbers emerged—a roster that included, to name but a few seminal figures, Albert Ellingwood, Alan Carpé, Terris Moore, Robert Underhill, Joe and Paul Stettner, Kenneth Henderson, Brad Washburn, Fritz Wiessner,

Charlie Houston, Bob Bates, Bill House, Paul Petzoldt, Norman Clyde, Bestor Robinson, Jules Eichorn, Dick Leonard, Raffi Bedayn, Arnold Wexler, and Dave Brower.

Individuals climb for many reasons—most obviously, of course, to reach summits. But considered as a social endeavor, there always has been more to mountain-climbing than simply gaining altitude and a good view. Seen from the bottom up, as it were, mountaineering both reflects and helps define a society's values and priorities. Nineteenth-century mountaineering in the United States combined both a sense of national manifest destiny and a quest for personal transcendence. Less important was any particular sense of comradeship among climbers.

Climbers went out on their own, or with random associates, but the experience was an individual one. John Muir, who did most of his climbing solo, once declared, "No mountaineer is truly free who is trammeled with friend or servant, who has the care of more than two legs."[1] Between 1900 and 1946, climbing took on an additional meaning: a social vision centered on the ideal of a "brotherhood of the rope," the intense bonds of comradeship and trust that developed among climbers who relied upon one another for both safety and success.

There were good reasons why, in the nineteenth century, no one talked about a brotherhood of the rope. Ropes were haphazardly deployed and sometimes, as in the fatal case of the Matterhorn climbers in 1865, represented as much a threat to climbers as a source of security. But in the first half of the twentieth century, the climbing rope became the most important tool and the moral core of the mountaineering endeavor. When Robert Underhill, who played a significant role in raising the standards of alpinism among his countrymen, wrote in 1931 that the climbing rope transformed "an individualistic into a higher social enterprise," it was just two years after the stock market crash of 1929 and just ten years before Pearl Harbor.[2]

Like their fellow Americans, the greatest generation of American mountaineers confronted the challenges of the Great Depression and the Second World War. For American mountaineers, the higher social enterprise of mountaineering offered the satisfaction of demonstrating mastery over a danger-filled natural world, "standing solidly together, under stress, for a common cause," at a moment when the economic and political worlds sometimes seemed to be spinning, fatalistically, out of human control. According to Charlie Houston, who coined the phrase "brotherhood of the rope," mountaineering represented

> the chance to be briefly free of the small concerns of our common lives, to strip off nonessentials, to come down to the core of life itself. Food, shelter, friends—these are the essentials, these plus faith and purpose and a deep and unrelenting determination.[3]

Another change for American climbing in the first half of the twentieth century was the shift in what might be called its regional hegemony. Since the founding of the Appalachian Mountain Club in Boston in 1876, easterners of an Anglophile bent, men of means who could afford a season or two exploring the European Alps, had defined what it meant to be a climber. Robert Underhill certainly fit that description, a man much in the mold of the patrician founders of the AMC. Underhill, Brad Washburn, and Charlie Houston—all Harvard-educated easterners—continued to play important roles in opening new routes and employing new techniques in the United States and elsewhere. But by the beginning of the Second World War, a cadre of young Sierra Club climbers, many of them students at or alumni of the University of California at Berkeley, were coming to the fore in American mountaineering.

GROWTH OF AMERICAN MOUNTAINEERING CLUBS

To be a climber in the United States in the early twentieth century meant, almost by definition, joining one or more organizations devoted to the endeavor. Clubs were the places where climbing techniques and ethics were passed on to new generations of climbers, climbing partners found, climbing tales swapped.

In the nineteenth century, American climbers joined regional clubs: the Appalachian Mountain Club, the Mazamas, and the Sierra Club. There was no equivalent of Britain's Alpine Club, the premier national organization of the British climbing elite. In the second half of the nineteenth century, other nationally organized alpine clubs were coming into existence across Europe, appearing in Italy in 1863, in Germany in 1869, in France in 1874.

At the turn of the century, American mountaineers on the East Coast, who looked to Europe for guidance in things alpine, decided to form a similar group. In May 1901, a dozen eastern climbers and explorers, led by Professor Angelo Heilprin, a geologist at the Academy of Natural Sciences in Philadelphia, met at the Geographical Society headquarters in Philadelphia to form a committee of organization. Through their efforts, the American Alpine Club (AAC) came into existence the following year with forty-five founding members. The AAC was not intended to supplant the regional groups, from which it drew many of its members. Charles E. Fay, of the Appalachian Mountain Club, served as AAC president from 1902 through 1907, and was succeeded by John Muir of the Sierra Club, who served from 1908 to 1910.[4]

The AAC set high standards for new recruits, who had to be nominated by existing members and then judged by an admissions committee on the quality of their climbing résumé (or, in the case of a few polar explorers, their Arctic and Antarctic experience). In January 1917, Henry S. Hall, a Harvard College student with some alpine climbs behind him, wrote to AAC secretary Howard Palmer, himself a Harvard graduate, to inquire about the possibility of joining.[5] Palmer responded politely but with scant encouragement: "While I do not think there would be much point in applying to the Club at present, I would be glad to know the actual peaks which you have ascended." Since the "chief activity of the Alpine Club, its annual meeting and dinner, has just taken place and there really is nothing more until the end of this year," it would make more sense for Hall to wait for the following autumn to apply, said Palmer, "to include any conquests you may make this coming summer."[6] Undiscouraged, Hall applied again following military service as an infantry officer in the First World War and was finally accepted, going on to serve as club secretary from 1932 to 1946, and president from 1950 to 1952.[7]

In its early years the AAC functioned as an elite social club to which few applied and even fewer were accepted; a decade after its founding there were only sixty-seven members, and a decade after that membership barely topped a hundred. As Palmer's letter to Hall suggests, the AAC's main activity centered on the sponsorship of an annual December meeting and banquet, usually held in its headquarter city of New York. In 1907 the AAC launched a short-lived publication, *Alpina America*; the more enduring and now venerable *American Alpine Journal* first appeared in 1929. The journal had few readers, but those few read it with great care. In a sport (to the extent that climbing deserves that label) that had no organized competitions, championships, or other formal rewards, the reports of first ascents published in the journal were the one sure way in which climbers could burnish status and assert authority.[8]

Annual dinner of the American Alpine Club in the Hotel Vendome, Boston, 1909. AAC President Charles E. Fay is seated fifth from the left in the front row.

The regional clubs set looser standards for members than did the AAC, if not socially (their members were generally drawn from local elites), at least in terms of climbing qualifications. Their signature activity was the outdoor group excursion rather than the black-tie banquet. Although the regional clubs in their formative years had often announced lofty goals of scientific exploration, by the early twentieth century the emphasis was on casual fellowship and informal fun—thus the nickname for AMC members, first appearing around 1918, as the "H'Appies" (later shortened to "Appies").[9]

In an era when even a relatively accessible mountain, like Oregon's Mount Hood or Washington's Mount Rainier, might attract no more than a few hundred climbers annually, club-sponsored climbs accounted for a large proportion of total ascents. Club members, accordingly, came to regard their favorite mountains with a proprietary affection. In July 1905, twenty-seven members of the Appalachian Mountain Club and eighty-three members of the Sierra Club traveled from their home states to the Pacific Northwest at the invitation of the Mazamas. After a mass ascent of Mount Hood, the climbing legion traveled on to the newly established Mount Rainier National Park in pursuit of another summit. "Great hilarity prevailed" around the campfires that night, AMC member William Brooks reported in *Appalachia*,

> and songs, college yells, and ten-minute speeches by members of the three clubs went far to cement a union that it is hoped will prove in the future to be a powerful factor in the furtherance of American mountaineering, and a love of the mountains and the woods by others who may follow.[10]

Over the next several decades, the three original regional clubs were joined by scores of others, including the Seattle-based Mountaineers in 1906 (an offshoot of the Mazamas), the Vermont-based Green Mountain Club in 1911, the Denver-based Colorado Mountain Club in 1912, and the New York–based Adirondack Mountain Club in 1922. In 1916, nine mountaineering clubs joined together to form a federation called the

136 On the Summit of Mt. Copeland.

Colorado Mountain Club members on the summit of 13,176-foot Mount Copeland, at the southern end of the newly founded Rocky Mountain National Park, August 1916. Women outnumber men in the party.

Associated Mountaineering Clubs of North America; by 1925 there were nearly seventy affiliated groups.[11]

Around the same time, university climbing clubs began to form. First in the field was the Harvard Mountaineering Club, established in 1924 (by Henry S. Hall, among others), followed by the Yale Mountaineering Club in 1932, and the Dartmouth Mountaineering Club in 1936. By the later 1930s, university clubs were supplanting regional clubs as sponsors of and recruiting depots for cutting-edge expeditionary mountaineering in remote regions, particularly Alaska and the Himalaya.[12]

ANNIE PECK AND FANNY BULLOCK WORKMAN

Like the regional climbing clubs in the United States, the American Alpine Club included women among its members from the very beginning (in contrast to the Alpine Club in London, which began allowing women to join only in 1975). Of the four charter AAC members who were women, two played pioneering roles in exploring some of the world's highest and most formidable mountains: Annie Peck in the Andes, and Fanny Bullock Workman in the Himalaya.

Peck (born in 1850) and Bullock Workman (born in 1859) had much in common. Both were the descendants of early New England settlers, with Annie tracing her family back to Rhode Island founder Roger Williams, and Fanny to the Pilgrims of Plymouth Colony. Both were from socially and politically prominent families: Annie, the daughter of a Providence, Rhode Island, Republican legislator; Fanny, the daughter of the Republican governor of Massachusetts. Both were, to varying degrees, inclined to defy the conventions governing their sex. Despite these similarities, they came to develop an intense loathing for one another. No sisterhood of the rope for those two; theirs would prove one of the most vituperative climbing rivalries in the history of American mountaineering.

Peck climbed Mount Shasta with her brother George in 1888. Her passion for mountaineering soared while she was pursuing a graduate education in classical studies in Europe. In 1895 she became the third woman to climb the Matterhorn. That exploit made her famous—in part because she scandalized public opinion by wearing pants, as she would do on all of her subsequent climbs. The male journalists who covered the story also had difficulty imagining a middle-aged woman capable of pulling off such an exploit: "A Yankee Girl Climbs the Matterhorn," the *New York Times* proclaimed in its headline, as if Peck were a plucky teenager, rather than, in reality, a matronly forty-five-year-old.[13]

Peck proved a pioneer in other and more significant ways. She was among the first professional mountaineers in America, and certainly the first of her sex. Until the beginning of the twentieth century, to be a "professional mountaineer" (a term no one used at the time) meant being a guide. Peck had no large inheritance to live off of and never married, so after deciding to leave teaching following a brief career, she had to find another way to support herself. She did so by making a career out of her mountain exploits, developing a keen eye for commercial opportunities. She funded her expeditions by selling articles to newspapers and magazines, writ-

Annie Peck in climbing apparel (including pants) in a studio photograph.

ing an expedition book and a guidebook, giving lectures, and endorsing products—all strategies employed by today's professional mountaineers.

She also pioneered in making her main field of mountaineering endeavor the still largely unexplored Cordillera Blanca, a 112-mile-long and 20-mile-wide mountain range in the western Peruvian Andes. The range includes twenty-nine summits higher than 20,000 feet—the greatest concentration of high peaks in the Western Hemisphere. The elevation and scale of the mountains made their exploration and ascent a challenging proposition. Highest of all the Peruvian Andes, as it turned out (although this wasn't known when Peck first set eyes upon it), was 22,205-foot Huascáran.[14]

Peck climbed with a political as well as a mountaineering agenda. As she wrote in the preface of *High Mountain Climbing in Peru & Bolivia: In Search of the Apex of America*, "Being always from earliest years a firm believer in the equality of the sexes, I felt that any great achievement in any line of endeavor would be of great advantage to my sex."[15]

Peck's first big climb in the Western Hemisphere came two years after her Matterhorn ascent when she climbed the Pico de Orizaba, at 18,491 feet the highest mountain in Mexico, in a trip funded by the *New York World*. The mountain had first been climbed by American soldiers in 1848, and numerous times since, so this was by no means a first ascent. Peck was, however, the first woman to reach the summit, and in doing so she established a world altitude record for women, at least in terms of recorded climbs.[16] Then, after two unsuccessful attempts to climb Bolivia's 21,490-foot Mount Sorata, she set her eyes on a more glittering prize: the first ascent of Huascáran. Four times she set out, and four times she was defeated—not for lack of mountaineering skill, but for her habit, perhaps dictated by insufficient funds, of hiring unqualified male companions to accompany her. Undaunted, she planned a fifth expedition to the mountain in 1908.[17]

Annie Peck's altitude record on Pico de Orizaba lasted just two years before it was bested by Fanny Bullock Workman. Unlike Annie, Fanny never had to worry about making a living. She was from a wealthy family, and at age twenty-two she married William Hunter Workman, a doctor twelve years her senior. Hunter Workman, as he preferred to be called, introduced Fanny to climbing in the White Mountains. In 1889, when Dr. Workman retired, the family, which included now a young daughter, and eventually a son, moved to Germany and began a life of strenuous adventure. They climbed in the Alps, where Fanny followed Annie Peck's footsteps to the summit of the Matterhorn, as well as climbing Mont Blanc and the Jungfrau. And then they went farther afield, to Algeria, Indochina, and India.[18]

In 1895 the Workmans coauthored their first travel book, *Algerian Memories*. Seven more would follow, including five devoted to their exploration of the Himalaya.[19] The Workmans were strong hill walkers but not really climbers; by hiring the world's best mountain guides, however, they left their mark on the early history of Himalayan mountaineering. Past the prime of their own lives (well past, in the case of William), they ventured onto remote terrain previously visited by only a handful of European explorers. The year 1898 found them in India, where they decided to make an attempt to circumambulate 28,169-foot Kangchenjunga, summoning the famous Swiss guide Rudolf Taugwalder from Zermatt to accompany them. Despite lavish expenditures on equipment and manpower, that expedition did not get very far.

Undiscouraged, the Workmans returned the following year to the region, this time to the Karakoram, a range of mountains lying southwest of the Tibetan Plateau, geologically distinct from but usually considered part of the Himalayan ranges. The highest mountain range in the world, with an average elevation of 20,000 feet, along a continuous rampart of 300 miles, the Karakoram includes four of the fourteen mountains in the world topping 8,000 meters, including K2, whose summit at 28,251 feet is second only to 29,029-foot Everest in height. Despite the efforts of early British explorers, including Henry Haversham Godwin-Austen, Francis Edward Younghusband, and Martin Conway, much of the region at the turn of the century was still unmapped, its preeminent peaks—with the sole exception of 26,660-foot Nanga Parbat—never attempted, let alone climbed.[20]

As her husband aged, Fanny took the initiative in planning and leading their adventures. Strong willed and with a powerful sense of racial and class entitlement, she dealt imperiously with the native peoples whose countries she visited, regarding them as one more impediment to the exploration and conquest of mountain summits.[21] Fortunately, the Workmans could afford to hire good (European) help. In their 1899 trek, this time accompanied by the Swiss-Italian guide Matthias Zurbriggen, they traveled north from the Indian city of Srinagar, over the Skoro La (a 16,643-foot pass in the Gilgit-Baltistan region, in the northern edge of what would become Pakistan) to Askole on the Braldu River. From there they ascended the Biafo Glacier to the Hispar Pass.

After a temporary retreat to Askole (to allow Zurbriggen, who was suffering from altitude sickness, to recover), they returned to the wide cirque under the Skoro La pass, where they climbed three peaks in succession, including making the first ascent of 20,997-foot Koser Gunge, a formidable looking massif overlooking the Shigar Valley. And in doing so, although she overestimated Koser Gunge's height, Fanny Bullock Workman bested Annie Peck's two-year-old claim to the women's high-altitude record.[22]

Year after year, the Workmans returned to the Karakoram. Their illustrated books were popular, if, as subsequent generations of explorers discovered, marred by considerable geographical confusion.[23] In 1906, exploring the region around the Nun Kun massif, the Workmans set their sights on what they thought was the second-highest peak on the massif (but is actually the third-highest): 22,735-foot Pinnacle Peak (whose height Fanny mistakenly calculated to be 23,300 feet). In any event, by reaching Pinnacle's summit, she set an altitude record for women that would last for the next twenty-eight years. This was only a hundred feet shorter than the highest mountain definitely known to have been climbed by a man at the time, 22,837-foot Aconcagua in the Andes, ascended by none other than the Workmans' guide Matthias Zurbriggen in 1897.[24]

Meanwhile, Annie Peck prepared to undertake her fifth expedition to Huascáran. She was aware of Fanny Bullock Workman's well-publicized Himalayan achievements, including the altitude record on Pinnacle Peak. Whether that was what drove Peck to reach what she believed to be an even higher summit is unclear. But her next attempt would put her on a collision course with the imperious Mrs. Workman.

Peck herself was enough of a celebrity that, stopping off in Washington, DC, in early June prior to departing for Peru, she requested and received a White House audience with Teddy Roosevelt.[25] Avoiding her past error of haphazardly hiring climbers on arrival in Peru, and with adequate funding for once, Peck brought along two experienced Swiss guides: Rudolf Taugwalder (who had been with the Workmans on their abortive trek around Kangchenjunga) and Gabriel Zumtaugwald.

They made their first attempt on Huascáran in early August. As she toiled up the slopes, Peck chewed coca leaves, like the Indian porters who carried their supplies. Her account of the climb included a vivid description of altitude sickness, saying it bore "much resemblance to seasickness, usually having the form of a headache, often with nausea and vomiting."[26] It was Peck's two professional guides who suffered the most, forcing the party to turn back at 16,000 feet, an altitude higher than any of the Alps the guides were accustomed to climbing.

The group returned several weeks later, and this time, on September 2, 1908, Peck reached her long-sought summit. The only thing spoiling her triumph was that Taugwalder, in violation of guiding ethics, preceded his employer to the top (she had been preoccupied with a pressure hypsometer, a device for measuring altitude, a short distance below the summit). "I resolved," she recalled, "that if we ever got down to give that man a piece of my mind."[27] In the end, she relented: on their descent Taugwalder suffered acute frostbite, costing him several fingers and half a foot—as well as his profession.

The summit Peck reached that day with her guides was the 21,812-foot northern peak of Huascáran; the southern peak, which she did not attempt, is actually higher, and remained unclimbed until 1932. But Peck believed (or at least claimed in some subsequent interviews) that she had been much higher. As she told a reporter from the *New York Times* on her return to the United States in December 1908, "I reached the summit of the highest peak of Mount Huascáran in Peru, a height of over 24,000 feet." In doing so, she claimed, she not only had reclaimed the women's altitude record in mountaineering, but had surpassed anything ever done by a man. "The greatest height ever before reached," she told the reporter, "was one of 23,800 feet by W. W. Graham in the Himalayas."[28]

In the fall of 1908, Peck's boast reached Fanny Bullock Workman, who was off on yet another Himalayan expedition. Outraged and incredulous at the claim that her 1906 altitude record on Pinnacle Peak had been surpassed, Bullock Workman set out to discredit Peck. She enlisted the help of the Société Générale d'Études et de Travaux Topographiques of Paris, arranging to have a four-man survey team sent to Peru at her own $13,000 expense (more than triple the amount that Peck's Huascáran expedition had cost). The French team carried out a complete triangulation of the

Huascáran massif and fixed the height of the north summit (the one Peck had climbed) at 21,812 feet—far lower than the altitude she thought she had reached. Bullock Workman had purchased the pleasure of disproving Peck's claims in an article in *Scientific American*. Fanny Bullock Workman also proved she was not a woman to cross.[29]

The Peck and Bullock Workman competition was fought over rival claims to altitude records, but also over questions of female propriety. Here, Peck was more of a pioneer than Bullock Workman. The unmarried Peck climbed on her own, while Fanny Bullock Workman climbed with her husband. Bullock Workman, like Peck, was a supporter of women's suffrage, and she was photographed in the Karakoram holding a sign reading "Votes for Women." But in her campaign against Peck, she felt no scruples about reminding the public that her rival was a woman who notoriously

Fanny Bullock Workman in climbing apparel (including skirts), at 21,000 feet in the Himalaya, advocating the vote for women.

climbed in pants. An article in the *Trenton Evening News* in 1909 offered a sympathetic portrait of Bullock Workman, noting, "Her vigorous life has not served to make her unfeminine in appearance or manner, nor has she the slightest desire to be considered mannish." The article noted that Bullock Workman spoke of her rival with "subtle scorn," declaring "I have never found it necessary to dispense with the skirt" while climbing.[30]

Annie Peck continued to climb. In 1911 she attempted to reach the summit of Peru's second-highest mountain, 21,079-foot Nevado Coropuna, failing to do so but raising at the top of a subsidiary peak her own "Votes for Women" banner.[31] Before leaving on that expedition, Peck again spoke with a reporter from the *New York Times*. Peck conceded that she had been mistaken in estimating Huascáran's height, but unrepentantly defended her mountaineering achievements. Climbers from other nations had reached greater heights, but she and her chief rival had reached summits as yet unmatched by any male American.[32]

INNOVATION AND RISK IN EUROPEAN MOUNTAINEERING

In 1918, Howard Palmer, the American Alpine Club's secretary, contributed a chapter on mountain climbing to the *Handbook of Travel* (an eclectic guide to adventurous travel, including separate chapters on the use of sled dogs, packhorses, and camels for transportation). In the climbing chapter, Palmer offered some thoughts on route-finding, a key skill for mountaineers:

> It is an axiom of mountaineering that arêtes [ridges] are selected as routes wherever favorable, since nothing can fall upon a party there, a wider view is to be had of one's surroundings, and there is a better chance to take advantage of any easier way that may appear.[33]

But by 1918, Palmer's "axiom" had long since been rejected by cutting-edge climbers on the European continent, and within another decade or two it would seem antiquated to many American climbers as well. Finding the "easier way" to a mountaintop ceased to be regarded as a significant achievement.

Americans had long regarded British climbers as the master authorities of alpinism. But Italian, German, and Austrian climbers, perfecting their craft on the steep rock faces of the eastern Alps and Dolomites rather than the gentler snowy slopes of the western Alps, were developing new and—for the climbing gentry of the Alpine Club in London—controversial techniques. With few notable exceptions, the British remained wedded to Victorian notions of genteel amateurism, with a strong aversion to innovation or risk.

In contrast to the British insistence on "free climbing" (using only hands and feet to get up a mountainside) as the only legitimate form of mountaineering, Continental climbers began to experiment with "aid climbing" or "direct aid" (the technique of placing man-made devices as artificial hand- or footholds or to rest on midclimb). And just as important, the Germans, Austrians, and Italians forged a new ethic of climbing, one that valued the difficulty and the purity of a route more than simple success via the "easier way." They moved off the ridges, usually the most accessible path to the summit, and took to the faces. Climbing became a test of skill and endurance, which could be precisely measured by the route taken.

In 1894 an Austrian climber named Fritz Benesch developed the first system of grading the difficulty of a rock climb; revised by Munich climber Willo Welzenbach in 1923, the six-rank numerical system, with each addition marking a higher level of difficulty and danger. (More elaborate variations of the original six-rank system continue to be used by climbers around the world.) As they matched themselves against the new grading scale, Germans, Austrians, and Italians displayed a willingness to accept levels of risk shocking to the traditionalists across the English Channel.[34]

Roped climbing in the nineteenth century had posed many dangers to its practitioners. The hemp ropes of the era were of unreliable quality, and prone to breaking under stress. In addition, there was no widely accepted system for climbers to belay one another from a secure stance.

If a lead climber fell, there was a strong likelihood that he would pull his unanchored partner or partners below him in a mutual plunge to injury or death. Even in the best of circumstances, in which the belayer stopped a fall, the lead climber would drop twice the length of the rope played out between him and his belayer. Thus, a leader who was 10 feet above his belayer and fell would, assuming no intervening obstacles to break the fall, drop 20 feet straight down. The impact of a sudden halt to a fall that long could break ribs and damage internal organs.

Thanks to the innovations of the Continental climbers (or "Munich School," as they were later known), climbing paradoxically got safer even as it got riskier. By the 1890s, climbers in the eastern Alps began to employ a device known as the piton, a flat or angled metal spike with a metal ring fitted through a small hole at its end. After the spike was hammered into a rock wall, a cord would be used to tie the climbing rope to the ring. In the event of a fall, the lead climber on belay from below would be, in theory, caught after traveling twice the distance he was above his last hammered piton or protection (his "running belay" as it came to be called), instead of twice the distance between him and his belayer, as he would without the piton in place. Thus, if the leader was 10 feet above his belayer but had placed a piton/running belay at 5 feet above the belayer, he would drop only 10 feet instead of 20 in the event of a fall. Moreover, the direction of the pull on the rope in the belayer's hand would be upward (toward the running belay point), rather than downward (as the leader plummeted past his belayer)—an easier force for the belayer to control.[35]

In 1908, Tyrolean guide Hans Fiechtl improved the piton, giving it its modern form by getting rid of the metal ring and substituting an eye hole at the end of the spike. That same year, coincidentally, Munich climber Otto Herzog adopted as a climbing aid the carabiner, a steel loop with a spring-loaded gate on one side, then in use by German firefighters and bricklayers.

Now, instead of the tedious process of binding rope to piton (which was also tedious to undo), the lead climber could simply clip the carabiner to the piton and run the rope through the carabiner. As the lead climber advanced up the wall, he placed protection at regular intervals.

His belayer, following behind, could easily unclip the carabiner from the piton as he followed (in the United States this process became known as "cleaning the pitch"). The result of these innovations was to greatly reduce the chance of death or serious injury if the leader fell. And accordingly, the leader could take on more daunting challenges, including vertical and exposed cliffs, and even overhanging rock.

Around this same time, Munich climber Hans Dülfer developed a new and improved method of descending a rocky face, known as the *Dülfersitz*. With the rope looped around a secure anchor like a rock or a tree or through a carabiner attached to a piton, and wrapped around the body (around the hips, across the chest, over the shoulder, and then pulled forward between the legs), a climber could walk (or run, or even bounce) backward down a cliff, using friction to control the rate of descent, in what was variously known as an abseil or a rappel.[36]

Except for the *Dülfersitz*, which won widespread acceptance across the channel as well as on the Continent, British climbers (and the Americans who looked to them for guidance) regarded these inventions and those who made use of them with disdain. The Munich School was mocked as the "dangle and whack school."[37] Unlike the old-school European guides in the western Alps who regarded it as a professional duty to defer to their social betters, the Munich School climbers—some of them students, others from working-class backgrounds—appeared to Anglo-American traditionalists as brash, arrogant upstarts. And, of course, many of them were also from Germany and Austria, countries that had been Britain's enemies in the First World War.[38]

"Artificial aids have never been popular with us," Geoffrey Winthrop Young (future president of the Alpine Club) wrote in *Mountain Craft* in 1920, a book that served as a standard guide to the sport in Anglo-American climbing circles. "In ascending, a peg [piton] is no protection to a leader, although its insertion may tempt him perilously to go beyond what he should." *To go beyond what he should*—the language could have been lifted from a Puritan sermon or an evangelical tract. The use of pitons was unsafe, possibly immoral, and definitely unaesthetic. It spoiled rock, Young declared, "with blacksmith's leavings."[39] If the use of pitons for protection was immoral, their use for *direct aid* was even more unacceptable. Young insisted that the guiding principle of mountaineering was, as it had always been, that the leader must not fall. Most American climbers, at least in the first few decades of the twentieth century, agreed.[40]

EARLY MOUNTAINEERING IN ALASKA

On July 16, 1741, a Russian naval officer on board the ship *St. Peter*, part of Vitus Bering's exploratory expedition to the coast of Alaska, caught sight of a high mountain to the northeast. The Russians named the cape on the Alaska coast below the mountain Saint Elias, and the name in time came to apply to the mountain itself. Forty years later, in 1781, British explorer James Cook was on his own voyage of discovery along the Pacific Northwest coast and spotted the same mountain, estimating its height at 18,100 feet, higher by far than any mountain in western Europe or encountered to that time in North America.

The estimate was off by only a few feet, for Mount Saint Elias, on the border of the Canadian Yukon, British Columbia, and the state of Alaska, stands at 18,008 feet, the second-highest mountain in both Canada and the United States. It is part of several ranges of mountains that came to be known as the Saint Elias Mountains and include 19,551-foot Mount Logan the highest mountain in Canada; 17,192-foot Mount Lucania, the third-highest in Canada; plus three more peaks topping 16,000 feet and an additional six above 15,000 feet.[41]

Alaska has sixteen mountains over 14,000 feet (compared to fifty-three in Colorado), but that number includes four of the ten highest mountains in North America: seven over 15,000 feet, three over 17,000 feet, plus one at over 20,000 feet, representing the continent's crowning height. Even the lower peaks, in the 10,000- to 13,000-foot range, are challenging because of their remote location, heavy glaciation, extreme cold at high latitude, and dangers like severe storms, icefall, and avalanche. Alaska has fourteen distinct mountain ranges. In the first half of the twentieth century, most mountaineering was concentrated in three regions: the Saint Elias Mountains, in southeastern coastal Alaska and extending into the Canadian Yukon and British Columbia; the Wrangell Mountains, a southeastern inland range, largely volcanic in origin with one still active volcano; and the Alaska Range, the highest mountain range in the world outside of the Himalaya and the Andes.[42]

The accessibility of Mount Saint Elias, located only a dozen miles from the coast, made it a tempting prize to American mountaineers. Between 1886 and 1897, five expeditions set out for the mountain, the first an American party led by Lieutenant Frederick Schwatka. The *New York Times* sponsored the expedition, hoping for a story of triumph for its front page. "What the difficulties of this may be no man can say," the *Times* declared, "and it is conceivable that they may prove to be too great to be surmounted. If pluck and endurance can surmount them, however, Lieut. Schwatka will . . . crown this great unclimbed peak with shoe leather of American make."[43]

As it turned out, the shoe leather that reached the summit would be of expensive Italian make instead. In 1897, Prince Luigi Amadeo di Savoia, Duke of the Abruzzi and the brother of the king of Italy, snatched away the first ascent of Mount Saint Elias. It was a formidable feat of mountaineering (the mountain would not be climbed again for nearly a half century)—although the one fact about the duke's expedition that everyone remembers is that his team of porters carried an iron bedstead up to the 12,000-foot level on the mountain, so that he could enjoy a good night's sleep before summit day.[44]

Alaska's greatest prize remained to be claimed. In 1794, fifty-three years after the Bering expedition caught sight of Mount Saint Elias, George Vancouver, the British explorer, spotted what he described as "distant stupendous mountains covered with snow and apparently detached from one another."[45] Though visible from the coast, they seemed all but inaccessible, lying about 125 miles from Vancouver's vantage point at Cook's Inlet. Vancouver did not name the two mountains, but one was 17,400-foot Mount Foraker, and the other, a 20,237-foot giant known to inland Alaskan natives as "Denali." That is the name by which it shall be called in this account, although it was renamed in 1896 by prospector William A. Dickey as "Mount McKinley" after the recently nominated Republican presidential candidate from Ohio, until renamed Denali by President Barack Obama in 2015.[46] Although Denali is lower in height than Mount Everest, the distance from its base to its peak is actually greater than that of Everest.

The first white man to set foot on Denali was United States Geological Survey explorer Alfred H. Brooks in 1902. Exploring the Alaska Range, Brooks left his men camped some 15 miles to the north of the mountain, while he set off to explore its lower slopes, reaching an elevation of 6,300 feet before turning back. That left only about 14,000 more vertical feet to reach the summit—about the height of Mount Whitney, highest point in the lower United States. In a subsequent article for *National Geographic Magazine*, Brooks argued that an approach from Denali's north, rather than striking east from the coastline, offered the best chance for success.[47]

The following year, in 1903, federal judge James Wickersham set out with four friends from Fairbanks on the first serious attempt to climb the mountain, choosing one of the most difficult routes imaginable, the 14,000-foot-high north face of the mountain, subsequently known as the Wickersham Wall. The climbers made it to just above 8,000 feet before concluding that to continue upward was suicidal. They did spot a glacier to the north of the mountain (called the Muldrow Glacier after an earlier Alaskan explorer) that they thought might offer a more promising route than the one they had chosen.[48]

Later that year, a second expedition attempted the mountain. It was led by a Brooklyn doctor and founding member of the American Alpine Club, Frederick A. Cook, possibly the most notorious figure in the history of American mountaineering. Cook had impressive credentials as an explorer, having taken part in two Arctic expeditions in the 1890s—one led by Robert M. Peary, the second by Roald Amundsen. He hoped to lead an expedition of his own to the Arctic, and to be the first to reach the North Pole. But first, in part to burnish a reputation as a successful expedition leader, he decided to tackle Denali. Cook's 1903 expedition, which included not a single experienced mountaineer, halted at about 11,000 feet on Denali's Northwest Buttress, but his little party did manage to circumnavigate the mountain—a first, and a genuine achievement.[49]

Three years later Cook was back, this time paired as expedition leader with a Columbia University professor of electrical engineering, Herschel C. Parker, who had climbed extensively in the Alps and Rockies. The party also included, among others, Belmore Browne, a formally trained artist with previous climbing experience in the Pacific Northwest.[50] It was a stronger expedition than Cook's first and stood a better chance of success, but it wasted much time on an ill-chosen approach. In September, after three months of effort, the group retreated back to the coast, its members preparing to go their separate ways.

But then there was an unplanned development, or at least one that took expedition coleader Parker by surprise. Cook, and another member of the expedition, Edward Barrill, a horse packer from Montana, along with a local prospector, John Dokkin, took a boat up the Susitna and Tokositna Rivers back toward Denali, telling the departing members of the expedition that they wanted to spend a few more weeks doing a reconnaissance of the mountain, along with the surrounding glaciers and river systems. However, in a telegram Cook sent secretly to one of the expedition's financial angels back east, he proclaimed another goal: a "last, desperate attack on Mount McKinley."[51]

Two weeks later, according to the story Cook would tell on his return, on September 16, 1906, he and Barrill were standing on top of Denali, having ascended the mountain by its East Buttress. And he had the photographs to prove it.

When his former expedition mates, Browne and Parker, heard Cook's claim, they instantly disbelieved him, though they kept their doubts to themselves for the moment.[52] Cook published his account of the climb in *Harper's Monthly Magazine* and as a book, and he gave many illustrated lectures.[53] Hailed as a hero, he attracted another wealthy patron and, with his aid, set off for the North Pole, which he claimed to have reached on April 21, 1908. Unfortunately for Cook, his old expedition leader, Robert M. Peary, was also after the title of first at the North Pole, claiming to reach it the following April. Peary undertook a campaign to discredit Cook's claim (as it turned out, ironically, Peary's claim to have reached the North Pole was also disputed).

The resulting controversy brought Cook's alleged Denali ascent under renewed scrutiny. In reality, he and Barrill had not been anywhere near Denali's summit. Subsequent investigation revealed that Cook's "summit shot" was actually taken 20 miles from the true summit, and at an elevation of a mere 5,000 feet. Cook was summarily drummed out of the American Alpine Club, which was heartily embarrassed to have been taken in by one of their own. Cook is the only AAC member ever to have been expelled.[54]

The Cook affair fascinated and scandalized the citizens of Fairbanks, Alaska. Among them were a group of "sourdough" prospectors (so-called for the sourdough starter they carried with them in the wild to bake bread and pancakes), who decided that they would set out to climb the mountain themselves, to prove Cook a liar, and to show that Alaskans could succeed where outsiders from the east had failed. There was a bet involved, placed by local saloonkeeper Bill McPhee, who pledged to pay $500 (or, in some versions, $5,000) if they made it to the summit.[55]

Welsh-born Tom Lloyd assembled a seven-man team, and the Sourdough Expedition, as it came to be known, set off in December 1909, with a mule, five horses, and a dog sled carrying the gear. One of the seven, Charles McGonagall, had earlier discovered a pass (now bearing his name) providing access to the Muldrow Glacier. By February the expedition was preparing to make its way up the glacier, the foot of which lay 20 miles from the summit of Denali, when a fistfight broke out in camp over some long-forgotten issue. Three of the prospectors headed back to Fairbanks, leaving Lloyd, McGonagall, Pete Anderson, and Billy Taylor to carry on.

None of them were climbers, but three of them were extraordinarily hardy outdoorsmen. Lloyd, the expedition's erstwhile leader, proved the exception. He lingered at base camp while the others pressed on. In a remarkable feat of mountaineering, they carved a nearly 4,000-foot staircase in the ice and snow leading up to the summit ridge—all the more impressive given that they lacked real ice axes and instead made do with a wood-chopping ax, a shovel, and some alpenstocks. They had no rope, but they were equipped with primitive six-point creepers (crampons). After a false start a few days earlier, on April 3, 1910, the intrepid three—McGonagall, Anderson, and Taylor—carrying little but thermoses of hot cocoa and some doughnuts, set off for the summit, dragging behind them a 14-foot spruce pole, which they hoped would be visible from the mining camps to the north and provide proof of their success.

They made the northeast ridge (now Karstens Ridge) and crossed over the Grand or High Basin (now Harper Glacier) to the flank of the north peak, from where they made their way up Sourdough Gulley to the ridgeline. And there they attached a flag to their spruce pole and set it up at 18,700 feet. McGonagall decided he had had enough and stayed by the pole. Anderson and Taylor pressed on and, at 3:25 p.m., reached the North Summit, at 19,470 feet. From below, that had appeared to be the highest point on the mountain, but now they could see that the South Summit, at 20,237 feet, was Denali's true summit. But it lay 2 miles away, the day was waning, and it was 30 degrees below zero, so that prize was left for another day and other climbers.

The sourdoughs had pulled off an outstanding feat of mountaineering. They had ascended 8,000 vertical feet in a single day and then come down the same route. (In comparison, summit days on Denali today usually involve a 3,000- to 4,000-foot ascent, by climbers who are far better equipped, traveling on an easier route, and not encumbered on the ascent with a 14-foot pole.) Unfortunately, the spruce pole was not visible from below, and Tom Lloyd complicated matters by returning to Fairbanks before the main party and boasting that all four of them had reached the main summit together. As a result, many discounted their story.[56]

Later that summer of 1910, two parties approached the mountain from the southeast, the route Dr. Cook had allegedly followed to the summit four years earlier. The first party, led by Herschel Parker and Belmore Browne, veterans of the 1906 expedition, was determined to prove Cook a liar; the second, a party of Mazamas led by Claude Rusk, was determined to vindicate Cook's account. Both, in the end, came to the same conclusion—that Cook could not possibly have climbed the mountain in the time and by the route he had claimed to, and the Parker-Browne party found the exact rocky knob, 15,000 feet shorter than Denali, on which Cook had staged his summit photo.[57]

Two years later, in 1912, two expeditions once again set out for

Denali. One, organized by the *Fairbanks Daily News* and led by telegraph editor Ralph Cairns, made an unsuccessful attempt via what would later be called Pioneer Ridge.[58]

The second party was led, once again, by Herschel Parker and Belmore Browne. Although starting from the coast and approaching the mountain from the southeast, rather than beginning in Fairbanks and approaching from the north, they would follow the route of the Sourdough Expedition of 1910 up the Muldrow Glacier to the High Basin (Harper Glacier) once they got to the mountain. From the upper glacier, however, they set their sights on the South Peak, Denali's true summit. On the day of their summit bid, June 29, they reached a point over 20,100 feet, a new altitude record in North America. But the weather turned nasty, and they were still roughly 200 vertical feet below the summit. As Browne recalled, "The last period of our climb is like the memory of an evil dream."[59]

Exhausted by their previous efforts, nauseated by a diet of fatty pemmican, battered by blizzard conditions, and floundering in deep snow, they did not have it within them to stagger up the last remaining slope to the summit. Two days later they tried again, but again they ran into blizzard conditions and gave up. It was a heartbreaking defeat for Parker and Browne, on their third Denali expedition, and the tenth expedition to attempt the mountain all told.[60]

Mountaineering is a collective as well as an individual enterprise. The Sourdough climbers and Parker and Browne had fought their way through the passes, gulleys, glaciers, and ridgelines that, taken together, led to the summit of Denali. It was only a matter of time before someone would follow their footsteps and go the extra few hundred feet beyond.

Ever since coming to Alaska in 1904, the Reverend Hudson Stuck, Episcopal archdeacon of the Yukon, had dreamed of climbing the mountain that he always preferred to call Denali (or sometimes "Tenali"), against the custom of the time. As he wrote in 1906, "I would rather climb that mountain than discover the richest goldmine in Alaska."[61] And he was not idly dreaming. He had considerable climbing experience already, in Europe as well as the Sierra Nevada, the Colorado Rockies, the Cascades, and the Canadian Rockies. And, for a man of the cloth, his was a distinctly nonsedentary vocation, usually involving up to 2,000 miles of backcountry dog-sled travel each winter to visit his scattered parishioners.[62]

Stuck, born in London in 1863, immigrated to the United States in 1885. After stints as a cowboy and schoolteacher, he attended seminary and was ordained an Episcopal priest. His first parish was in Texas, where he gained a reputation as a social reformer, even a bit of a radical, for preaching against child labor and the lynching of blacks—both common practices at the time. When he came to Alaska, many of his parishioners were Native Americans, and he supported their rights as well.[63]

Stuck assembled a first-rate expeditionary party, which set out from Fairbanks for Denali in March 1913. In the party was thirty-four-year-old Harry Karstens. Chicago-born, Karstens had come to the Klondike in 1897 to mine for gold and had stayed on as a guide, packer, and dog-sledder. Although Karstens had no previous mountaineering experience, Stuck would later describe him as the real leader of the expedition, and he said he would prefer Karstens's companionship on a mountain "to any Swiss guides" he had known in the Alps or the Canadian Rockies.[64] Other members were twenty-one-year-old Tennessee-born Robert G. Tatum (an Episcopal postulant) and twenty-year-old Walter Harper (a native Alaskan and half Indian), as well as two teenage Athabascan Indians (the job of the latter would be to help relay supplies and tend to the sled dogs).

Well-informed about the route taken by previous expeditions, they found the pass onto the Muldrow Glacier without difficulty. But when they came to scale the northeast ridge, it was nothing like the "steep but practicable snow slope" that Browne and Parker had described and surmounted in only a few days; instead it was a nightmarish "jumbled mass of blocks of ice and rock," which they came to realize must have been the product of an earthquake that hit the mountain shortly after Browne and Parker had descended the previous summer.[65] Reverend Stuck's party, in a sense, was now climbing a different mountain.

Finally, after three weeks of effort, on May 27 Karstens and Harper found a way through the debris to the top of the ridgeline (Karstens Ridge). Now they could climb up to and into the High Basin (Harper Glacier). Stuck's plan was to place more and better-stocked camps than his predecessors had employed—five in total—as they worked their way up the glacier from 15,000 to 18,000 feet, ferrying up 40-pound packs from their lower camps. En route they solved one of the mysteries of Denali's climbing history when they spotted the Sourdough Expedition's flagstaff near the top of North Summit, putting an end to any controversy about that party's success in reaching one of the mountain's two peaks.

On June 6, they went to bed early (in the nearly continuous daylight of that time of year), rising at 3:00 a.m. on June 7 for their summit bid and departing an hour later. Harper took the lead, for the others were all suffering from high-altitude ailments. They had just over 2,000 feet of elevation to gain to reach the summit.

Archdeacon Stuck would afterward publish some very eloquent thoughts about his feelings that day, but there is something in the unpublished diary of his young companion Tatum that, despite its abbreviations and occasionally eccentric spelling, best conveys the sense of awe that came to them on the moment that they emerged, the native-born Alaskan Walter Harper still in the lead, on the highest point in North America:

1913 Saturday June 7th
Today stands a big red litcer [letter?] in my life as our party of four Hudson Stuck Harry Phillipp Karstens Walter Harper & my self reached the summit of Mount McKinley (Denallis) some 20600 feet above the sea level the highest mountain in a on the N. American continent. I was quite sick & so was Mr. K[arstens] but we left this morn at 400 a.m. and reached the summit at 100 pm Arch d[eacon] was very short winded and had great difficulty ascent but we took it very slowly. Walter reached the top first Mr. K next Archd. third & I last. I had made a flag an raised it. First of all after we all shook hands with congratulations. Arch deacon offered a prayer of thanks. Then the Instruments were read and I raised the flag and Archd. photographed it. Then while I took some angles with the prysmatic compas W. & Mr. K erected a cross. And set it up. And we all gathered around it and said "Te Deun"[66]

As for Stuck, his memory of the moment they reached the summit conveys a surprisingly modern attitude to the business of reaching the top of an unclimbed peak. There was, he wrote,

> no pride of conquest, no trace of that exultation of victory some enjoy upon the first ascent of a lofty peak, no gloating over good fortune that had hoisted us a few hundred feet higher than others who had struggled and been discomfited. Rather... that a privileged communion with the high places of the earth had been granted.[67]

An hour and a half after arriving, they headed down the mountain. It would be another two decades before anyone else stood where they had been that day. Four years later Walter Harper, Native American and the first man on the summit, whom Stuck regarded as an adopted son, died in a steamboat accident. Stuck himself would die in 1920, two years after the

The Stuck party making its descent from Denali's summit, the Muldrow Glacier visible below. (From Stuck's expedition account, *The Ascent of Denali* [1918].)

publication of his account of the expedition, *The Ascent of Denali*. In 1921, Harry Karstens became the first superintendent of the newly created Mount McKinley National Park, and three years later he was one of two Americans nominated for membership in the 1924 British Everest expedition (on which George Leigh-Mallory and Andrew Irvine lost their lives). Although it is not clear how serious a chance he had of actually being included in the party, at age forty-five, eleven years older than when he had led the way up Denali, Karstens in any case thought it better to decline the honor.[68]

Looking back in 1914 on the history of Alaskan climbing from the ascent of Mount Saint Elias in 1897 to that of Denali the previous year, USGS surveyor Alfred H. Brooks wrote in *Alpina Americana*, the American Alpine Club's periodical:

> Here is a field where there are no explored routes, no well-trained guides, packers, or established precedents. Every mountaineer must be his own guide and often his own beast of burden. Though three of the highest summits have been mastered, there are scores of high peaks whose snow and ice-clad summits will test the endurance and skill of the most experienced mountaineers.[69]

ALBERT ELLINGWOOD AND THE FIRST PITON IN AMERICA

In 1930, Colorado climber Albert Ellingwood contributed an article to the first volume of the *American Alpine Journal* entitled "Technical Climbing in the Mountains of Colorado and Wyoming." In recent years, he noted, the "more energetic climbers" in the region had "turned their attention to ascents which were attractive because of their technical interest rather than because of altitude."[70] No climbers in the region were more energetic or accomplished than Ellingwood, and none played a larger role in introducing new standards and techniques of climbing to the Colorado Rockies.

Ellingwood was born in Cedar Rapids, Iowa, and raised in Colorado, graduating from Colorado College in Colorado Springs in 1910. Awarded a Rhodes Scholarship, he studied at Oxford University's Merton College for the next three years, receiving a degree in civil law. While in England, Ellingwood joined the Oxford University Mountaineering Club, climbing in England's Lake District, in Wales, and in the Swiss Alps, where he learned the use of ropes and pitons.[71] Later he earned a PhD in political science from the University of Pennsylvania and pursued an academic career that eventually took him to Northwestern University. Virtually every summer, Ellingwood returned to his beloved western mountains.[72]

In the nineteenth century, rock-climbing in the United States was, with rare exceptions, understood and practiced as an adjunct to mountaineering, rather than a separate sporting endeavor. Some mountains required a certain amount of scrambling up steep rock slopes or slabs, even the occasional ascent of a rocky cliff. Clarence King and John Muir had tackled problems in the Sierra that today would certainly be called rock-climbing. But that's not what they called it, and there is nothing to suggest they thought about the effort as anything other than a means of overcoming an obstacle when no other more convenient route presented itself, the point of the exercise being to reach the summit. A 1907 AMC guidebook contained the first published suggestion in the United States that climbing rocks was something people might be interested in doing for its own sake; Huntington Ravine on Mount Washington, the book suggested, offered "interesting bits of climbing even to veteran rock climbers."[73]

In the Colorado Rockies there was no tradition of rock-climbing when Ellingwood returned from England with a few pitons stowed away in his baggage.[74] As long as mountaineering was thought of as the effort to reach a summit by the most accessible route available, it was an unnecessary skill. As Ellingwood suggested in his 1930 *American Alpine Journal* article, "Under normal conditions anyone of average physique, reasonable stamina and a modicum of determination can *walk* up most of the peaks in the American Rockies."[75]

Most, but not all peaks. About the time the first easterners were drawn to Mount Washington's Huntington Ravine for rock-climbing, a few intrepid residents of the college town of Boulder, Colorado, began to climb the distinctive uptilted sandstone rock formations just south of the city. Five in number, what are today known as the Flatirons were called the "Crags" in the early twentieth century—and they most definitely could not be walked up. In 1906, Floyd and Earl Millard, members of the Boulder-based Rocky Mountain Climbing Club, scaled the Third Flatiron, which rises nearly 1,300 feet from its base. They did so unroped; indeed, down until the 1920s it was considered poor sportsmanship by local climbers to bring a rope along on an ascent of the Flatirons.[76]

About 100 miles farther south along the Front Range of the Rockies, and 13 miles east of Pikes Peak, Colorado Springs had its own collection of spires of soft, red sandstone, some of them 300 feet high, known as the "Garden of the Gods." Until Ellingwood showed up in 1914, they were much admired, but unclimbed. With a hemp rope and pitons, he set out to change that, and he taught a generation of local climbers alpine technique, including such future Colorado mountaineering notables as Robert Ormes and Carl Blaurock. Ellingwood popularized the idea that in technical rock-climbing, reaching the summit was subordinate to the challenge of the route. In theory, he was committed to the British ethic of minimal use of pitons. But, employing his pitons as direct aid (he had no carabiners, so he could not use them for protection), he was able to climb at a standard not before seen in the United States.[77]

Ellingwood systematically climbed his way through the Colorado Rockies. In 1916 he made first ascents of the three remaining unclimbed 14,000-ers in Colorado: 14,171-foot Kit Carson Peak, 14,294-foot Crestone Peak, and 14,203-foot Crestone Needle. He was accompanied by various climbers on these outings, including, notably, Eleanor Davis, a Massachusetts-born physical education instructor at Colorado College, three years Ellingwood's elder. Under Ellingwood's tutelage, she would become a skilled climber in her own right—and, unusually in a male-female climbing partnership in those years, theirs was a platonic relationship. In Fred Beckey's judgment, together they were "likely the most experienced American climbers" of the 1920s.[78]

In the summer of 1920, Ellingwood decided to attempt 13,119-foot Lizard Head, in the San Juan Range. It is by no means the highest or most beautiful mountain in Colorado; instead it is a shabby, eroded volcanic plug—precisely what had kept other climbers away from it and made it an interesting challenge to Ellingwood. "A rottener mass of rock is inconceivable," he wrote.[79]

And that was not the only obstacle. There was no road to anywhere near Lizard Head. So in August 1920, Ellingwood and partner Barton Hoag hiked 8½ miles from the nearest railroad stop, carrying 80-pound packs, 100 feet of rope, and three metal spikes, which they were using in place of pitons.

On August 28, Ellingwood and Hoag launched their assault. After trying several routes and finding them unsuitable, they settled on a chimney near the southeast corner of the tower. Ellingwood led the climb, occasionally hammering in a spike as a still uncertain foothold in the rotten rock. The two men climbed while roped together, and Ellingwood belayed his partner from whatever secure stances he could find. Near the top, Ellingwood climbed onto Hoag's shoulders, and from there,

> probed all things within reach for what must have seemed an interminable time to him [Hoag]. At last I found holds at arm's length, but it was a strenuous pull to reach the crack. Equally strenuous it was, though not difficult technically, to wriggle up the narrow cleft with a very crowded back-and-knee crossbrace. This was the safest stretch of the day, and the hardest physical work.
>
> At the extreme limit of the rope I reached a large, safe anchor rock at the south end of the summit arete, and saw that we had won. Shouting down the glad tidings, I told Hoag to come on. . . . From this last anchor rock there is an easy ascent northwards along a fairly sharp ridge of loose rock, across a small gap where one gets a sensational view down the sheer east cliffs, and finally a careful climb over a few large rocks to the top, which is perhaps fifty feet above the anchor rock.

Albert Ellingwood on the summit of Lizard Head, 1920.

The summit was tiny, and rocks kept sliding off on all sides. "The situation," he concluded modestly, "was not without its thrills."[80]

Ellingwood left his mark elsewhere in the West as well, including Wyoming, where in August 1923 he made the first ascent of 12,804-foot Middle Teton and, that same day, with Eleanor Davis, the first ascent of 12,514-foot South Teton. He and Davis also climbed Grand Teton, with Davis the first woman to reach its summit.[81] The two returned to Crestone Needle in 1925, which they had first climbed in 1916, and, with two other climbers, attempted the northeast ridge, which featured "a superb array of formidable buttresses, seamed by tempting cracks and set off from each other by steep plunging chimneys."[82]

Ellingwood led the way up those cracks and chimneys, more than 2,000 feet of technical climbing, without piton or metal spike to aid his way, to reach the summit—a route thereafter known as Ellingwood Ledges, or Ellingwood Arête.[83] It remains an appropriate monument to a distinguished climbing career, which came to a premature end when Ellingwood died following an operation in 1934, at age forty-six.[84]

IMPACT OF THE AUTOMOBILE

The first Model T Ford rolled off the assembly lines of Henry Ford's factory in Dearborn, Michigan, in 1908. Ford pledged to keep the price of his new automobile at so affordable a level "that no man making a good salary will be unable to own one—and enjoy with his family the blessings of hours of pleasure in God's great open spaces."[85] Six years later, in 1914, Appalachian Mount Club president John Ritchie Jr. reported on the impact of Henry Ford's invention on the White Mountains, previously accessible only by railroad or horse-drawn wagon:

> The automobile has been this summer an important adjunct to mountain climbing in New Hampshire. With its mobility it puts places within striking distance of any given centre that are out of the question if walking be relied on and with loss of time at the outset if the horse be employed, that may seriously affect the day's programme.[86]

Roads were extended and improved to make previously remote areas accessible by automobile. In the eyes of some mountaineers, this was not an unmitigated blessing. Yosemite National Park issued the first permits allowing automobiles into the valley in 1913. Shortly thereafter, more visitors were arriving by automobile than by railroad. The 1921 edition of the Sierra Club's guide to the area, *Yosemite and Its High Sierra*, reported that 13,418 private automobiles carrying 46,074 passengers had visited the valley the previous year, and that since the admission of automobiles to the park in 1915, "the congestion of hotels and hotel camps, and even of

Automobile passengers enjoying mountain scenery in New Hampshire in the 1920s, with the Old Man of the Mountain rock formation visible in the background.

the public camping grounds has grown apace." The valley, the guidebook reported, "was not planned by Nature for the bivouac of a city's population." The opening of Highway 140 in 1926, reducing the time it took to drive to the valley from the Bay Area to six hours or so, dramatically increased the number of visitors.[87]

Easier access by automobile had a similar impact on the Tetons. Grand Teton National Park officially opened in 1929. Fritiof Fryxell and Phil Smith, who put up many of the new routes in the range in the 1920s, became the first park rangers that year, staffing the ranger headquarters at Jenny Lake. To manage the influx of auto-borne climbers, Fryxell and Smith initiated several new practices, including having climbers report in to the ranger station before setting off on climbs, and recording new routes. Fryxell and Smith also became the preeminent chroniclers of early Teton climbing history. They counted five ascents of Grand Teton in 1929, thirteen in 1930, and twenty-six in 1931.[88]

YUKON/ALASKAN PIONEERS: ALLEN CARPÉ AND TERRIS MOORE

By the start of the twentieth century, few mountains in the United States were more than a day's hike from a road or railway. The exceptions were to be found in the far Northwest, in the Alaska Territory, as well as the adjoining Canadian Yukon. In the far Northwest, mountaineering required a full-scale expedition, capable of surviving in remote regions for weeks or months with no opportunity for resupply. Alaskan and Yukon climbing helped school a generation of American climbers in the basics of remote, high-altitude exploratory mountaineering that would prepare them for tackling the Himalaya in the decades to come.

In 1925, Allen Carpé was a member of an eight-man Canadian-American expedition that sought to make the first ascent of 19,551-foot Mount Logan in the southwestern Yukon. Logan is the highest mountain in Canada and the second-highest, after Denali, in North America. It is so remote and set in such a rugged interior landscape that its existence went unnoted until 1891, nearly a century after the first documented sighting of Denali. The scale of the mountain and the challenges it posed put Carpé and his fellow climbers in mind of other expeditions that had recently taken place:

> We talked sometimes of the Mount Everest expeditions with their hundreds of porters and pack animals [and] their march of seven miles up the East Rongbuk glacier. How different things are in the North. On Logan, the nearest settlement 150 miles away, a journey of eighty miles over glaciers, an ascent of 17,000 feet from the ice level to the summit. Save for the physiological effects of high altitude, ours was probably the bigger job.[89]

Allen Carpé was the most accomplished exploratory mountaineer in the United States in his own short lifetime. He was born in 1894 in Chicago, great-grandson of Ezra Cornell, the founder of both the Western Union telegraph company and Cornell University. As a teenager, Carpé studied in Germany before returning to complete a degree in electrical engineering at Columbia University. While in Europe he climbed in the Carpathian mountains and the eastern Alps, centers of climbing innovation. During World War I he saw combat in France as an artillery officer in the American Expeditionary Force, and was wounded and gassed. After the war he worked as a design engineer for Bell Laboratories, playing an important role in the development of the telephone system. He also returned to mountaineering.[90]

The 1925 expedition to Mount Logan was inspired by and, to an extent, modeled upon the British Everest expeditions between 1921 and 1924, and it was undertaken at the initiative of the Canadian Alpine Club (which had been founded in 1906, five years after the American Alpine Club). The AAC, in its most ambitious effort yet to become something more than a social club for climbers, provided extensive financial support for the expedition, and helped recruit the climbing party, which was heavily seeded with Americans.[91]

In addition to Carpé, the expedition included Americans Norman Read, Robert M. Morgan, and Henry S. Hall. Leading the climb was American-born Albert MacCarthy, a retired US Navy officer and banker who had moved to British Columbia the previous year. The winter before the expedition was set to depart, MacCarthy reconnoitered the approach route to the mountain, using dog-sled teams and cached supplies en route.[92]

Setting off at the start of May, the expedition traveled by ship from Seattle to Alaska, then by train to McCarthy, Alaska, the closest human settlement to Logan, still 140 miles distant. From there they continued on foot down the Chitina valley with a packtrain of horses and mules for 90 miles. Once they reached the foot of the Chitina Glacier in mid-May, the horses and mules were sent back to McCarthy. The eight climbers had to ferry 2 tons of supplies by sled and on their backs across 50 miles of glacier to the foot of the Logan massif. "As we worked in toward the savage cliffs of Logan," Carpé wrote, "we entered a new world of appalling grandeur, and our little band seemed insignificant and very much alone. We had no support behind us, no organization of supply, no linkage at all with the outer world. We were on our own."[93]

At the beginning of June, the climbers launched an Everest-style siege operation on the west side of the mountain (later known as the King's Trench route, for a 6-mile-long and 1-mile-deep glacial trench that provided access to Logan), hauling supplies to ever-higher camps. Unlike on Everest expeditions, of course, they had no Sherpas to help them with the carries. The route was nontechnical, with no rocky cliffs or steep ice to surmount, but it involved a gain of 6,000 feet in elevation from their advance base camp to the summit plateau and a distance of more than 8 miles. There were occasional sunny days, but more often the climbers battled snow, high winds, or deep fog, while the temperature dropped to as low as −37 degrees Celsius. In addition to climbing, Carpé was in charge of shooting film for a motion picture documenting the expedition—a first in North American mountaineering.

Another innovation of the expedition was the use of willow wands to mark the route; the climbers brought a thousand wands, which proved not quite enough to reach the summit. On June 22, six climbers established their high camp at 17,900 feet on the summit plateau. By then, Robert Morgan was suffering from frostbitten hands and feet, and Henry Hall gave up his own summit bid to help Morgan down the mountain. The following morning, the six remaining climbers set off for the summit. They topped what turned out to be the false summit (now known as the Weak Peak) late in the afternoon and still had 2 miles to go to reach the real summit (High Peak), which they could see in the distance.

"We were 19,800 [actually 19,400] feet high and it was 4.30 in the afternoon," Carpé recalled. "Could we go on and climb that other peak? I doubt if the question ever entered our minds—certainly it did not mine. Probably I was the weakest of the lot, but we had gone through too much to give in now, although it was clear that we could not get back to camp that night if we went on."[94]

The six climbers—leader MacCarthy, Canadians Fred Lambart, Andy Taylor, and William Foster, and Americans Carpé and Norman Read—finally reached their goal at 8:00 p.m., dangerously late in the day, with a storm approaching and no wands within sight to guide their descent. Carpé filmed the scene with his motion picture camera. After twenty minutes on top, they set off down the mountain, in what turned into an epic of endurance, stumbling through the night, briefly bivouacking in snow caves, despairing of ever finding the way down the mountain.

Finally, late the next day, they stumbled upon their line of wands. It was still another full day before they were all safely back at base camp, all of them exhausted and most of them suffering from frostbite. Carpé began his report on the expedition for the *American Alpine Journal* (published posthumously in 1933) with the statement, "The ascent of Mt. Logan in 1925 was perhaps the most arduous feat of mountaineering ever undertaken in North America," which, if immodest, was not inaccurate, as measured by the intensity and duration of the effort.[95]

The following year Carpé returned to the region, this time to attempt the first ascent of 15,325-foot Mount Fairweather on the Alaska–British Columbia border, part of the Saint Elias Range. He was accompanied by William Ladd (future president of the American Alpine Club), and Andy Taylor (sourdough prospector and veteran of the 1925 Logan expedition). Approaching from their landing place at Sea Otter Bight, about 5 miles west of Cape Fairweather on the coast, they attempted to climb the mountain's west ridge but were halted at just over 9,000 feet by a seemingly uncrossable notch.[96]

At the start of the next decade, Carpé gained a new climbing partner who would also leave his mark on Alaskan climbing: Terris Moore. Moore was born in Haddonfield, New Jersey, in 1908 and attended Williams College. Upon graduation with a degree in geology in 1929, he headed for Ecuador, where with his father (a zoology researcher doing fieldwork in that country) and a school friend, he climbed 20,564-foot Chimborazo and then made the first ascent of 17,388-foot Sangay, an active volcano.[97]

Moore enrolled that fall in Harvard Business School, receiving his master's degree in business administration in 1933, and a doctorate in

1937. He joined the Harvard Mountaineering Club. And he was invited to give a talk about his South American adventure to the annual meeting of the AAC, held that year in Boston. There he met Carpé, who asked if he was interested in climbing in Alaska.[98]

In 1930, Carpé, again accompanied by Sourdough climber Andy Taylor, and joined this time by Moore, made the first ascent of 16,552-foot Mount Bona in Alaska's Saint Elias Range, climbing from the west and reaching the summit on July 2.[99]

The following spring, five years after Carpé, Taylor, and Ladd had attempted and failed to climb Mount Fairweather, they went back, this time joined by Moore. They landed on the coast at Lituya Bay and ferried their supplies 13 miles to the base of Fairweather. It took five weeks of effort to establish their base camp on May 24 at 5,000 feet. In a brief interval of the "fair weather" for which the mountain was inaccurately named, they moved swiftly up a ridge on the mountain's south side to establish a high camp on May 26 at 9,000 feet. But six days of heavy snow forced them back to base camp. On June 2, the four climbers were back in position at the high camp, and this time they launched their summit bid. Once again they were enveloped by a storm and retreated to their high camp, guided by the willow wands they had placed along the route. They were now running low on food. Ladd and Taylor generously gave up their own hopes for reaching the summit, retreating to base camp and leaving Carpé and Moore at the high camp to outwait the storm.

Finally, on June 7, trudging through deep snow, the pair made another summit bid and this time reached the top—"the most demanding and technical route yet done in North America," in the judgment of Steve Roper and Allen Steck's authoritative *Fifty Classic Climbs in North America*.[100] When Carpé and Moore reached the summit, their starting point on the coast was 15 miles away—meaning they had gained a thousand vertical feet, on average, for each mile traveled from sea level.[101] The deeply corniced southern ridge they ascended would thereafter be known as Carpé Ridge.

One thing that disturbed Moore about Carpé's climbing style on Fairweather was his reluctance to rope up. Perhaps this practice reflected carelessness, or a certain fatalism bred by his wartime experience on the western front.[102] The practice did not serve Carpé well the following year on Denali. This time he was back in Alaska, not with the goal of reaching a summit, but as part of a scientific expedition sponsored by the University of Chicago, studying cosmic radiation. Carpé and a Sierra Club climber named Theodore Koven had been ferried by a ski-equipped plane to the Muldrow Glacier, which landed them and their equipment at just below 6,000 feet on the east side of the mountain across from McGonagall Pass. Three other climbers were to join them later. Carpé and Koven headed off on skis up the glacier to establish a high camp at 11,000 feet on Karstens Ridge.

On May 11, climbers from another party, descending from the summit along the ridge after making the second ascent of Denali, came across Carpé's and Koven's tents, fully equipped but unoccupied.[103] Seeking clues, they read the two men's diaries and noted that the last entries had been four days earlier, on May 7. Continuing their descent, the party of climbers came upon Koven's body about a mile and a half below camp. Carpé's body was never found, but from tracks leading to a nearby crevasse, they concluded that he and Koven, traveling unroped, had both fallen in, with Koven managing to climb back out before succumbing to his injuries and exposure. Theirs were the first deaths ever recorded on Denali.[104]

ROBERT UNDERHILL AND CALIFORNIA ROCK-CLIMBING

Bestor Robinson, a California climber, along with two Bay Area friends, pulled off the first technical ascent of a rock formation in Yosemite Valley in the spring of 1934. Writing in the *Sierra Club Bulletin* shortly afterward, Robinson paid tribute to another climber, an easterner who wasn't there the day of their triumph, but whom he nevertheless felt deserved much of the credit:

The seed of the lore of pitons, carabiners, rope-downs, belays, rope traverses, and two man stands was sown in California in 1931 by

Robert L. M. Underhill, a member of the Appalachian Mountain Club, with considerable experience in the Alps. That seed has sprouted and grown in California climate with exuberant vigor.[105]

Robert Lindley Murray Underhill, the Johnny Appleseed of advanced climbing technique, was born in Sing Sing, New York, in 1889, graduating from Haverford College in 1909 and receiving a PhD from Harvard in 1916, where he subsequently found employment as an instructor in mathematics and philosophy. Not until after graduating from college did he climb his first mountain, in the Swiss Alps in 1910.

On subsequent trips to the Alps, he climbed the classic routes on the Jungfrau and Piz Bernina, and on a guided climb in 1928 he accomplished the first traverse of the Aiguilles du Diable, a rugged series of rock formations on Mont Blanc's southeast ridge, together with his future bride, Miriam O'Brien. (O'Brien, an experienced climber in her own right, a feminist known for her advocacy of "manless climbing," nevertheless did much of her future climbing in the company of her husband, including the first winter ascent of all forty-eight 4,000-foot peaks in the White Mountains.) In Courmayeur that summer, on the Italian side of Mont Blanc, Underhill also met a German climber named Fritz Wiessner, with whom he would later undertake some notable climbs in New England. Underhill was one of a very few American climbers whose name European alpinists might have recognized in the 1920s.[106]

Underhill became a member of the Harvard Mountaineering Club and the Appalachian Mountain Club. He edited the latter group's journal *Appalachia* from 1928 through 1934. And he was a devoted teacher, not only in Harvard classrooms, but on New England cliffs. The Appalachian Mountain Club organized a rock-climbing committee in 1928, with Underhill as its chairman. Rock-climbing had been growing in popularity in New England over the previous decade (the first continuous roped climb of a New England cliff took place in 1910), but few Appies knew much about alpine-style rope techniques.[107] Underhill, along with his frequent climbing partner Kenneth Henderson, set out to change that.

Henderson, a founding member of the Harvard Mountaineering

Club, was an investment banker and dressed like one even when he was climbing. His 1929 article, "Some Rock Climbs in the White Mountains," which appeared in *Appalachia*, described routes that he and Underhill had pioneered on Mount Washington's Huntington Ravine, on Mount Willard, and on Franconia Notch's Cannon Cliff, and helped popularize rock-climbing among AMC members. Several routes in the White Mountains, he declared, "will tax the capabilities of the most expert. Even those trained in the hard schools of Chamonix or the Dolomites will not despise them."[108]

To tax their own considerable capabilities, Underhill and Henderson headed west in the summer of 1929, bringing their pitons and carabiners to the newly opened Grand Teton National Park. The Teton Range was still largely unknown to American climbers; there were unclimbed mountains in the range, and Grand, Middle, and South Teton had until then been summited by only a single route. On July 22, Underhill and Henderson made the first ascent of the east ridge of Grand Teton. Their route required a glacier crossing, roped rock-climbing, step cutting up icy couloirs, and at one point, a *court-echelle* (shoulder stand) to surmount a rocky obstacle just short of the summit. They then went on to complete a traverse of the mountain by descending the traditional Owens-Spalding route. Albert Ellingwood, who had been defeated in his own attempt to find a way up the east ridge, described their achievement in the pages of the *American Alpine Journal* as "undoubtedly . . . one of the finest climbs in the Rockies."[109]

The following summer, Underhill and Henderson returned to Wyoming and, with park rangers Fritiof Fryxell and Phil Smith, made the first ascent of 12,928-foot Mount Owen, the second-highest peak in the Teton Range. After they reached the summit and were preparing to descend, Henderson and Underhill showed the two park rangers the *Dülfersitz* method of rappelling that they had picked up in the Alps. Fryxell and Smith, no strangers to the mountains, had never used the technique or even known it existed.[110]

Later that summer, Underhill headed to the Canadian Selkirks on a Harvard Mountaineering Club outing in which he attempted Mount

Robson by the unclimbed Emperor Falls Ridge. In treacherous conditions he got to within 300 vertical feet of the summit with brother-in-law Lincoln O'Brien, who, looking at the distance still to be traveled, remarked drily, "Robert, if our objective in life is making first ascents, I believe we will make more of them if we avoid making this one." They turned back.[111]

While in the Selkirks, Underhill met Francis Farquhar of the Sierra Club. (Farquhar was Massachusetts-born and had attended Harvard before moving to California; he and Underhill had corresponded previously, as the editors, respectively, of *Appalachia* and the *Sierra Club Bulletin*.) Underhill showed Farquhar new climbing techniques, including the rappel. Farquhar, impressed, solicited an article for the *Bulletin* on rope management.[112]

Underhill's article, published in February 1931 with the prosaic title "On the Use and Management of Rope in Rock Work," is one of the most famous and consequential articles devoted to climbing technique ever to appear in an American mountaineering journal. Illustrated with photos and drawings, the article outlined the proper technique for coiling and carrying ropes, tying on to ropes, belaying fellow climbers, and rappelling.

Beneath all the minutiae about knots and anchors, philosophy tutor Underhill was signaling a deeper set of concerns about what it meant to be a climber. If this was a manifesto, however, it was in some ways a very conservative one. Notably absent was any discussion of "hardware," or the use of pitons and carabiners. Throughout, just as British orthodoxy insisted, it was assumed that good style and safety required that the leader of a climbing party must not fall. Underhill believed a belay was a moral gesture rather than a meaningful safety measure. The leader essentially was on his own. "The effective strength of a party," he insisted, "lies very largely in its leader, and the strength of the leader is in turn very largely due to his social function . . . the trusted forefront of his party, its selected delegate and instrument."[113]

Underhill also insisted, as Geoffrey Winthrop Young had a decade earlier, that the sole legitimate uses of the rope in climbing were for safety while ascending, or as a means of descent—but never for artificial aid.

The only legitimate form of climbing was free climbing, without artificial aids.[114]

Despite these traditional elements in Underhill's climbing philosophy, he broke new ground in two significant ways. First, he insisted that climbing was a science, with formal and highly rational rules that needed to be observed to obtain the best results. A climber ignorant of correct technique, and lacking the appropriate gear, was a risk to himself and to his fellow climbers and had no business on a mountainside. Second, Underhill emphasized that climbing on a rope represented more than a variation on unroped climbing; it implied the acceptance of a new and higher ethical bond. There was a hierarchy in a climbing party that still saw the leader in an exalted role, but at the same time there was a web of mutual obligation linking all members in a dangerous yet exalted enterprise:

> A bevy of unroped climbers, attacking a peak each for himself, will enjoy the pleasures of independence and self-sufficiency, but they will very likely pay for these by the less pleasant elements of personal competition and rivalry, under conditions ill-suited to them. With the roped party an entirely new set of attitudes and values supervenes. There is no question of rivalry, for each member has a definite position in the party, with definite responsibilities. Instead, the opportunity is fully given for developing comradeship and the consciousness of standing solidly together, under stress, for a common cause.[115]

Comradeship and common cause, not independence and self-sufficiency (however much the latter two were enshrined in national myth and creed), were at the heart of the climbing enterprise. "This," Underhill famously pronounced, "is one of the finest experiences that mountaineering can afford." Unlike some other of his climbing contemporaries, Underhill was no radical politically. Still, his rhetorical choices may not be completely coincidental, as he sorted out the values of climbing in the shadow of the rapidly deepening Great Depression.

In any event, Underhill's article stirred considerable interest in Sierra Club circles, and it led to an invitation from Francis Farquhar to join Sierra Club members on the annual summer High Trip and teach the new techniques in person.[116] Underhill agreed, but first he headed back to the Tetons, and to the beginning of a remarkable season of climbing achievements.

Underhill spent six weeks in the Tetons that summer, the high point of which was a remarkable five-day series of first ascents. On July 15, 1931, Underhill, along with park ranger Phil Smith and Harvard Law School graduate Francis Adams Truslow, made a first ascent of the southeast ridge on Grand Teton, thereafter known as Underhill Ridge.

On that same day, Paul Petzoldt, who had arrived in Jackson Hole as an itinerant teenager in 1923, promptly climbing Grand Teton and launching a career as a pioneer guide in the Teton Range, led an Austrian couple up the standard route. And twenty-year-old Glenn Exum, who began the day as an assistant guide with the Petzoldt party and was clad in cleated football shoes, branched off to climb the mountain solo by the southwest ridge, thereafter Exum Ridge, the most popular route on the mountain. A "dramatic day" in a "memorable season," Fritiof Fryxell recorded in his indispensable history of early Teton climbing, in which "three parties climbed the Grand Teton by three distinct routes, two of them entirely new, and in the early afternoon met on the summit."[117]

Two days later, on July 17, Underhill, this time paired with Fryxell, made the first ascent of Middle Teton by its north face and then, traversing the mountain, descended by the southwest ridge and southwest couloir.[118] Three days later, July 20, in the culmination of this remarkable week, the two climbers returned to Grand Teton, to attempt its unclimbed north face (their route is today called the North Ridge). They approached the mountain from the east via the Teton Glacier, crossing the bergschrund, following steep ledges that gave access, after a messy scramble, to the face that rose 2,000 feet to the summit. Their greatest challenge came in a chimney, with a vertical rise of 15 feet, blocked at the top by a chockstone.

In a similar situation on the east ridge of Grand Teton in 1928, Underhill and Kenneth Henderson had resorted to a shoulder stand to surmount an obstacle. Underhill and Fryxell now used the same tactic, at first with the lighter Fryxell standing on Underhill's shoulders. When that failed, according to Fryxell's subsequent account in the *American Alpine Journal*, the two climbers "decided that now if ever the use of pitons was justified," to protect their route. Underhill drove in the first piton at the limit of his reach standing on his own feet and then, climbing to a perch on Fryxell's shoulders, drove in a second. Searching for a foothold, Fryxell sensed his partner's unsteadiness and urged Underhill, at least this once, to violate one of his cherished precepts, the prohibition of using the piton for direct aid: "Step on the piton!" he called up insistently.[119]

Whatever ethical qualms he may have experienced in doing so, Underhill obeyed Fryxell's command. Working his way up the chimney, Underhill, according to Fryxell, "raised his left foot onto the upper piton, made a quick shift around to the side of the chockstone, and sprawled over upon it." That proved the toughest move, although there were still several difficult pitches before they reached the summit.[120]

While Underhill and others were making climbing history in the Tetons, the stalwarts of the Sierra Club had already embarked on their annual summer outing to Yosemite National Park. On July 12, Francis Farquhar led what he described as the "first properly roped climb made in the Sierra," accompanying two teenagers named Jules Eichorn and Glen Dawson up the jagged north face of 10,823-foot Unicorn Peak above Tuolumne Meadows.[121] By the first week of August, the High Trip had moved on to Garnet Lake, in the shadow of Banner Peak and Mount Ritter, which is where Underhill, carrying his collection of pitons and carabiners, the first ever seen in California, joined the Sierrans.

While most of the High Trip participants contented themselves with the traditions of camp life and easy scrambles, Farquhar assembled an elite squad for Underhill including Dawson, Eichorn, and Bestor Robinson, later joined by veteran climber Norman Clyde (the latter in a long career racking up more than 160 first ascents in the region).[122] They practiced belaying and rappelling on 13,143-foot Mount Ritter and 12,945-foot Banner Peak, and Underhill and Eichorn made a first ascent of Banner's east face.

The Palisades climbing school, 1931. Standing, left to right: Francis Farquhar, Bestor Robinson, Glen Dawson, Neil Wilson, Lewis Clark. Front row, left to right: Robert Underhill, Norman Clyde, Jules Eichorn, Elmer Collett.

The party moved south to the Palisades and, on August 13, set out to climb what was then called the "Northwest Peak of North Palisade," the one remaining unclimbed 14,000-foot peak in California. In rapidly deteriorating weather, Dawson and Eichorn reached the pinnacle summit. The lightning bolts that pursued them in their descent led to the renaming of the 14,009-foot mountain, which was thereafter known as Thunderbolt Peak.[123]

Underhill's climbing camp culminated on August 16, when he, Clyde, Eichorn, and Dawson made the first ascent of Mount Whitney's 2,000-foot-high, white-granite east face in just three hours. Underhill's subsequent account of the climb for the *Sierra Club Bulletin* was notably blasé: "The rock work was not really difficult," he wrote, predicting that a "good climbing party that knew the route" could make the same climb in half the time.[124] This was perhaps too modest an assessment. Although not as challenging as some other climbs that Underhill had made in the Tetons that summer, it was the first big-wall climb in the Sierra and, in

Steve Roper and Allen Steck's opinion, "the most difficult High Sierra climb" of the decade.[125]

At the end of the summer, Underhill returned to his home in Cambridge, Massachusetts. His role in the transformation of California rock-climbing had come to an end. From then on, native Californians, particularly Jules Eichorn and Glen Dawson, stepped to the forefront. Eichorn taught Berkeley friends the techniques he had learned about climbing from Underhill, including the running belay and the *Dülfersitz* rappel.

Among the initiates, and soon to be a leader, was Richard "Dick" Manning Leonard, who was born in Ohio in 1908 and moved to Berkeley with his family at age fourteen. He attended the University of California at Berkeley as an undergraduate and in the spring of 1932 was completing his law degree at UC Berkeley's School of Law, Boalt Hall. He also helped found a small informal climbing group, called the Cragmont Climbing Club, named for a rock formation in the Berkeley Hills that offered local climbers a good place to practice.[126]

Orthodoxy dictated that the leader must not fall. Leonard wondered why not? He was fascinated by falls, and with his rock-climbing buddies he made a specialty of understanding the consequences of a fall. On a 15-foot overhanging cliff at the Cragmont rocks, they would set a firmly anchored belayer on top. Then, belayed climbers would take turns deliberately falling 5–10 feet on the rope. As Leonard explained in an article in the *Sierra Club Bulletin* in 1934, the "ten-foot falls give one quite a vivid realization of what a fall of a leader would mean." Not only that, but falling those 10 feet, with no serious consequences, gave climbers the confidence to attempt riskier moves: "He realizes more accurately than he could otherwise just what causes his falls and just how far he can go without falling."[127] In other words, one could become a better climber not by *avoiding* all falls, but, paradoxically, through *practicing* falls.

By the fall of 1932, Leonard and his friends in the Cragmont Climbing Club decided to affiliate with the Sierra Club, becoming the Rock Climbing Section (RCS) of the Bay Area chapter of the Sierra Club. Leonard served as chairman, a position he would hold for the remainder of the decade, and joined the club's board of directors in 1938. The RCS members took themselves and their group very seriously; they kept formal minutes of their meetings and dropped members who failed to show up for at least four meetings in a given year.[128]

A southern California chapter of the Rock Climbing Section was formed in 1934, and in the mid-1930s it began putting up challenging new routes on Tahquitz, a 1,000-foot-high white-granite formation on the western slope of Mount San Jacinto, to the east of Los Angeles. As in Yosemite Valley, Tahquitz rock consists of exfoliated granite, but without the glacial polishing it has in Yosemite. Within a few years the southern Californian climbers had put up a dozen routes, mostly on the west face and of moderate difficulty, but including the challenging Mechanic's Route on the south face, first climbed by Glen Dawson and Richard Jones in 1937.[129]

Within a year the northern California RCS attracted more than fifty climbers, mostly young professionals or students—many of them, like Leonard, connected to the University of California at Berkeley. To name a few of the most significant members of the group, Bestor Robinson was a lawyer, having attended UC Berkeley as an undergraduate, and then Harvard Law School; Hervey Voge was a chemistry graduate student at UC Berkeley; Jules Eichorn was an undergraduate music major at UC Berkeley (studying piano with Ansel Adams, the latter a Sierra Club member just embarking on his career as America's paramount mountain photographer); and Dave Brower was briefly a UC Berkeley undergraduate, before dropping out after his sophomore year. Raffi Bedayn was the one prominent non-UC exception, the son of a Nob Hill grocer in San Francisco who was too poor to send him to college in the midst of the Depression.[130]

As climbers, the Berkeley crowd displayed a taste for experiment and innovation. The standard belay stance of the time, the European technique that Underhill had imparted to the young Sierrans, involved wrapping the rope over a belayer's shoulder or under his armpits, a dangerously unsteady position. Notwithstanding the understandable prestige involved in following European precedent, the Berkeley RCS climbers worked out a new belay stance, with the belayer crouching, and the rope wrapped around the hips, offering far more stability. In another innovation, they began experimenting with what came to be called the "dynamic belay." Rather than tightening a grip on the rope to the belayed climber in the event of a fall, this technique called for allowing the rope to slip through gloved hands, slowing the fall before catching it firmly, thus lessening the chance for the rope (or the falling climber's ribs) to break.[131]

Up until this time, the greatest Sierra climbers often climbed solo. John Muir and Norman Clyde rarely sought out climbing partners. A young and up-and-coming Sierra Club member, San Francisco lawyer Walter Starr Jr., also preferred solo climbing—and in 1933 he met his death alone on Michael Minaret, one of a group of jagged peaks called the Minarets in the Sierra's Ritter Range. In contrast, the RCS climbers would not dream of climbing alone, for the sake of both safety and companionship.[132]

If they rejected some European techniques, the young Sierrans were still eager to absorb Continental teachings, particularly on the question of the best gear to employ. They were much influenced by an article that appeared in translation in the newly launched English *Mountaineering Journal* in 1933 and was written by a leading German climber of the 1920s and early 1930s, Leo Maduschka (the article's appearance was posthumous; between the publication in German in 1931 and its appearance in English, Maduschka died climbing the north wall of Monte Civetta in the Dolomites in 1932).

Maduschka offered a list of the "essential working tools" of rock-climbing, including ropes, "pitons, hammer, and swivel hooks [carabiners]," plus "slings for sitting, belaying, abseiling [rappelling], and other purposes." In his article, Maduschka also discussed and illustrated climbing techniques still virtually unknown to American climbers, like the pendulum traverse (in which the leader, lowered some distance on a rope from a fixed pivot point—usually a carabiner anchored by a piton—swings back and forth to reach easier terrain on one side or the other). Maduschka also explained the use of Prusik knots to ascend a rope.

Ascending via the Prusik knot, which became a standard part of the

Sierran climbing repertoire by the end of the decade, involves attaching a short loop of rope to the climbing rope via a simple hitch; the other end of the loop is clipped to the climber by a chest loop or harness. Two other Prusik knots are then attached to the rope and to foot slings. The special quality of the Prusik knot is that it slides easily up the climbing rope, but that it grips tightly when downward pressure is applied. By placing his weight alternately on one loop and then the other, a climber can climb a fixed rope up a cliff, sliding his chest loop and the foot loops upward as he goes.[133]

This was all very exciting to the Sierrans, but where were they going to find the "essential working tools" of modern climbing? Nothing on Maduschka's list, with the exception of ropes, was currently being manufactured in the United States. They had to turn to European suppliers, particularly a climbing store founded in Munich in 1914 called Sporthaus Schuster.[134] The Sierrans' quest in the mid-1930s to acquire the latest in climbing equipment marked the beginning of what would become a characteristic and even dominant trait of coming generations of climbers: an obsession with gear.

As the Berkeley Sierrans perfected their craft, they looked for greater challenges—and brought the first real rock-climbing to Yosemite Valley, now just a six-hour drive to the east by automobile. Seven carloads from the Sierra Club set out from San Francisco for the valley at the start of Labor Day weekend in 1933. "The caravan," Steve Roper noted drily, "containing the most overtrained rock climbers in America, was at last approaching the granite of Yosemite Valley." Before the weekend was over, they introduced roped climbing to the region that would, in time, become the most famous rock-climbing center in the world.[135]

For eighty years, since white men first viewed them, Yosemite's granite faces and spires had gone unclimbed. Despite their accessibility, greatly increased since the advent of the automobile, their sheer scale was sufficient to deter challengers. Half Dome, for example, towered nearly 5,000 feet above Mirror Lake on the valley floor.[136]

Scale wasn't the only obstacle. There was also the lack of obvious hand- and footholds. There was nothing to grab on to on the glacier-polished rock, and the first generations that explored the valley simply could not conceive of making use of the vertical-crack systems that were also a feature of the rock faces to ascend them. The technique known as "jamming" (forcing a fist, elbow, knee, or foot into a crack to provide tension) was both difficult and little practiced by early rock-climbers. And the absence of horizontal cracks and ledges meant that if a vertical-crack system petered out, it was difficult to move to the right or left along the rock face to a more promising route.[137]

The RCS climbers were now sufficiently confident of their skills, however, to give those vertical-crack systems a try. Leonard, Eichorn, Robinson, and Voge, the most dedicated climbers in the Bay Area RCS, made their first attempt that Labor Day weekend on Washington Column, which itself towers 1,900 feet above the valley floor, without success.[138] Then they turned their attention to Higher Cathedral Spire on the south side of the valley. There is also a Lower Cathedral Spire, and the two, the tallest freestanding spires anywhere in California, were among the few rock formations in the valley that lacked any easy scrambling approach, and thus remained unclimbed.

This was a transitional moment in Yosemite (and, soon, American) rock-climbing—a mixture of new and old. The Sierrans' goal was no longer just to get to the summit; the goal was to reach the summit by the most challenging route possible. A new concept came to the fore in their consciousness: the "crux move," or "crux pitch"—that is, the most difficult portion of a climb. The summit had become an afterthought; overcoming the problems presented by the crux was the real point of the climb. Thirty years later a Yosemite climber of another generation, Royal Robbins, wrote to friend and fellow climber Steve Roper to describe a particularly daring new route on El Capitan, illustrating the importance of this concept: "The best way to sum it up is to say that there were at least a dozen pitches which on almost any other climb would be the crux pitch."[139]

The Sierrans climbed roped on their first attempt at Higher Cathedral Spire, using their new belay stance, and, when descending, using the Dülfer rappelling technique. What they didn't have were any pitons, for protection or aid. So instead they hammered 10-inch nails of dubious reliability into the cracks. The nails weren't enough to get them to the top that first time.

The group, minus Voge, returned in November for another attempt, on both Lower and Higher Cathedral Spires. They failed to reach the top of either one, but they worked their way another 180 feet higher on the taller spire than in their previous effort, making use of a few pitons for direct aid that they had purchased in the meantime from Munich's Sporthaus Schuster.

Over the winter of 1933–34 they carefully studied photographs of the higher spire's west uphill face, planning a renewed attack in the spring. They acquired still more German climbing gear. For their third attempt, on April 15, 1934, Leonard, Eichorn, and Robinson came equipped with fifty-five pitons, thirteen carabiners, and three step slings—probably the most complete set of advanced climbing gear assembled to that date in the United States.

Previously, even climbers who made use of pitons, like Robert Underhill, prided themselves on their restraint in placing them; on the 1931 ascent of the east face of Mount Whitney, for example, his party had hammered in only a single piton.[140] The three Sierra Club climbers, in contrast, prided themselves on their extensive deployment of the new hardware. "Of primary importance on any climb is the question of safety," Leonard wrote afterward in *Appalachia*. "On the Spires we achieved this by practically nailing ourselves to the solid granite wall with spikes of steel."[141]

While Francis Farquhar watched approvingly from below, they worked their way up the cliff. Halfway up they stopped for lunch and contemplated the void beneath them. "There is a real thrill," Robinson wrote, "in munching an orange while perched on a one-foot ledge . . . and watching orange-peels drop perpendicularly to the talus below without once touching the mountainside."[142] After nine hours, just before dusk, they reached the top, attaching an American flag to a huckleberry oak branch to mark their achievement. "Looking back upon the climb," Robinson concluded in the *Sierra Club Bulletin*,

we find our greatest satisfaction having demonstrated . . . that
by the proper application of climbing technique extremely difficult ascents can be made in safety. We had practiced belays and
anchorages; we had tested pitons and ropes by direct falls; we had
tried together the various maneuvers which we used on the peak,
until three rock-scramblers had been coordinated into a team. The
result was that there was no time on the entire climb, but that
if any member of the party had fallen, his injuries would, at the
worst, have been a few scratches and bruises.[143]

Later that summer they returned to ascend Lower Cathedral Spire,
accomplishing the two most significant rock climbs in California to
date—significant, as climbing journals on both coasts noted, both for what
was climbed and the way it was climbed. (One tactic they employed on
the lower spire, chipping out footholds on a particularly difficult stretch
with a piton hammer, was not destined to become part of the repertoire
of acceptable rock-climbing techniques.)[144]

Western climbers had traditionally paid their eastern counterparts
a certain amount of deference as America's most knowledgeable practitioners of the arts of mountaineering (that is, the most likely to have
climbed in the Alps with European guides)—hence Francis Farquhar's
1931 invitation to Robert Underhill to instruct the Sierrans in rope craft.
An October 1935 letter from the young Sierran David Brower to the
venerable Norman Clyde suggests that deferential attitude was on the
wane. Recounting a Sierra Club expedition that unsuccessfully attempted
British Columbia's 13,186-foot Mount Waddington the previous summer,
Brower offered a few friendly but slightly mocking observations about the
party's one East Coast member:

Farnie Loomis, the Harvard man, was second youngest. Just 21.
Cultured, likeable, enthusiastic. We liked him because he was
willing to forget the comforts wealth can afford, and to come out,
rough it, and be a regular guy. He had spent two summers in the
Alps, but still didn't hold his ice axe right. Pronounces "can't" as

"cahwnt," as all Harvard men are reputed to do. We forgave him. On his trip back down the Franklin glacier he dropped his ice axe down a pinched, narrow, flooded crevasse. There it was, 12 feet under clear, blue ice water. What did he do but strip and go after it. Got it, too.[145]

In terms of mountaineering prestige and technique, it seemed, a summer in Yosemite now trumped a summer in the Alps.

The Sierrans went on to other triumphs in the second half of the 1930s—nowhere more dramatically, or with more public attention, than on New Mexico's Shiprock in 1939. A volcanic plug on a Navajo reservation, Shiprock rises nearly 1,583 feet above the surrounding desert. It is so named because to early white settlers it appeared as a clipper ship under full sail. It turned back a dozen parties in the 1930s, including a group led by Colorado climber Robert Ormes in 1937. Ormes was a protégé of Albert Ellingwood, and it was Ellingwood who had suggested to him that Shiprock was a worthy goal for an aspiring mountaineer. On the 1937 attempt, his third, Ormes fell 30 feet when a foothold broke while he was leading a difficult pitch. He owed his life to a piton he had placed for protection—and his subsequent account for the *Saturday Evening Post*, entitled "A Piece of Bent Iron," introduced the general reading public to the new techniques of rock-climbing.[146]

Among those interested to read Ormes's account were the hard-core Sierran rock-climbers—Dave Brower, Raffi Bedayn, Bestor Robinson, and John Dyer—who drove to the mountain from Berkeley in October 1939. Since the summer, aided by fellow Sierran Dick Leonard, they had carefully researched the mountain, corresponding with Ormes about his attempt. In September, Ormes wrote to Leonard and made a practical suggestion that raised an ethical dilemma:

I might remark that you will not be successful with the climb unless you are willing to make use of drilling techniques which are frowned on by most climbers. There is but one approach to the summit, and that is by the tower on the northwest, the third highest spire of the massif. . . . From my general experience of the type of rock, I think it doubtful whether either of these cracks will ever succumb to anything short of rape.[147]

The use of pitons no longer seemed like cheating to the country's leading rock-climbers. But that technique still depended on taking advantage of the natural features of the rock, requiring the lead climber to find a crack that would hold a piton. What Ormes was advocating—with what was obviously a slightly guilty conscience, given the reference to "rape"—was to take the next step for protection (and perhaps direct aid) and change the rock face by drilling into it and then screwing an expansion bolt (used in construction) into the resulting hole, to which a carabiner could be clipped.

The Sierrans took up the suggestion, equipping themselves with drills and bolts, and in doing so they foretold a major shift in climbing ethics—although one whose full force would not be felt for another decade and a half. Dave Brower understood the magnitude of what they were preparing to do, writing to a friend just before their departure:

> We place our hopes in the attempted application of "illegitimate" rock-engineering. . . . We shall try, throughout our attempts, to remain pure—using the expansion bolts only for safety, not for hand and footholds, but there's no telling to what extent our morality will slip, once we're in the field.[148]

They set off with 1,100 feet of rope, fifty-four pitons, eighteen carabiners—and several drills and expansion bolts, all of which came into use before they stood atop the mountain on October 12, 1939, after days of climbing. They used their bolts, as Brower had promised, only for protection, not for direct aid, and placed only four of them.[149] The distinction between using bolts for protection versus for direct aid was important to the prewar Sierra Club climbers, but the technique proved controversial to their contemporaries (and it would continue to be in decades to come). Bestor Robinson's subsequent account in the *American*

Alpine Journal offered a spirited defense against the climb's critics: "The Puritans, it is said, 'came to America to worship as they pleased, and see to it that no one else did the same.' The mountaineering purists have followed in their intellectual footsteps."[150]

The Californians were setting a new standard for American climbers. As mountaineering historian Joe Benson has written: "By World War II the Sierrans had evolved into arguably the most advanced rock-climbers anywhere."[151]

CHAPTER FIVE

BROTHERHOOD OF THE ROPE, 1900–1946: PART II

IMMIGRANT CLIMBERS IN THE 1920s–1930s

In the nineteenth century, most Americans who climbed were native-born; the exceptions—John Muir prominent among them—were born in the British Isles. Beginning in the 1920s, central European political upheavals prompted a stream of young and talented mountaineers to seek a new life (and new climbing opportunities) in the United States.

In 1926, Munich-born Joe Stettner emigrated to Chicago, followed shortly afterward by his younger brother, Paul. Both had climbing experience in the Bavarian and Austrian Alps. Both were eager to leave behind a Germany that they believed was flirting with disaster (their father had been killed by right-wing extremists shortly after the end of the First World War). With a cache of German climbing hardware, they set off from Chicago by motorcycle for Colorado in the late summer of 1927. After riding their bikes to the summit of Pikes Peak, they headed north up the Front Range, until they reached Estes Park. They purchased a rope and headed for Longs Peak, and on September 14 they tackled the mountain's east face.

There were already two established routes on the face, but the brothers embarked up steep rock slabs that previous climbers had not imagined could be climbed—and in a new style, hammering in pitons and clipping their rope into carabiners for protection. That the leader must not fall was not their climbing philosophy. Paul, in the lead, took a fall; Joe, belaying from below caught him, and they proceeded on to the summit. In seven hours they ascended 2,000 feet, setting a standard that would not be surpassed for the next two decades. They descended by the north face, thus traversing the mountain as well as climbing it. Their route would eventually become known as Stettner Ledges. But only eventually, because they told only a few acquaintances of the climb, and published nothing about it—a modesty typical of their climbing over the next decade.[1]

Thirteen-year-old Wolf Bauer arrived from Germany a year before the Stettners, in 1925. His contribution to American climbing started a decade later. His family emigrated to Seattle, where he taught himself climbing technique by reading German mountaineering books. In his twenties he began teaching a climbing course sponsored by the Seattle Mountaineers. Among his students were Lloyd Anderson, founder of the Recreational Equipment Incorporated (REI) cooperative, and George "Ome" Daiber, who would invent Sno-Seal, as well as other outdoor gear. The year he began offering the class, in 1935, Bauer and one of his students, Jack Hossack, were the first to climb Mount Rainier from the north.[2]

Dr. Otto Trott left Germany in 1937, shortly after earning his medical degree at the University of Freiburg, when Nazi authorities decided he was insufficiently Aryan (there was a Jewish ancestor on his family tree) to practice medicine. He began a medical residency at a Seattle Hospital and soon joined the Mountaineers, eager to resume the climbing he had loved in his native land. But he was amazed to discover that it was still considered good technique among fellow members of the Mountaineers to work their way up icy slopes by cutting steps with their ice axes, even though they were wearing crampons. He gave them a demonstration of the standard technique in the eastern Alps: walking with flexed ankles so that all ten spikes on the bottom of the crampon were at right angles to and in contact with the ice. "Thus," he wrote, "did I introduce modern ice climbing technique to the Pacific Northwest."[3]

In 1939, with Austrian-born Andreas "Andy" Hennig, then a ski instructor in Sun Valley, Trott made the first ascent of the north wall of

9,131-foot Mount Shuksan in the North Cascades, the Hanging Glacier route, which set a new standard for technical ice- and rock-climbing in the Cascades.[4] In 1948, Dr. Trott, along with Wolf Bauer, Ome Daiber, and others, would found the Mountain Rescue Council (later known as Seattle Mountain Rescue), modeled on Austrian precedents.[5]

Norman Dyhrenfurth, born in Germany, emigrated to Switzerland with his parents, Günther and Hettie Dyhrenfurth, both pioneering Himalayan climbers. In 1937 Norman moved to the United States, where he began to make a name for himself in climbing circles, but his greatest impact would come several decades later in connection with American mountaineering in the Himalaya.[6]

The most famous of the immigrant climbers was German émigré Fritz Hermann Ernst Wiessner. Wiessner submitted an application for membership to the American Alpine Club in 1933. There was little question that he would be accepted, for few prospective or accepted AAC members could match his climbing vita. On the application form, he listed eight new routes he had put up in the Dolomites between 1925 and 1928, plus his participation in the 1932 German-American Nanga Parbat expedition, on which he reached an altitude of 23,500 feet on the mountain's northeast ridge.[7]

Wiessner was born in Dresden, Germany, in 1900. With his father as instructor, and practicing on the local Elbe sandstone towers, he became a proficient climber by his teenage years. Dresden climbing traditions differed in the 1920s from those of the then-dominant Munich School, placing an emphasis on free climbing, while minimizing the use of pitons for protection or direct aid. Wiessner's specialty was wide-crack, or off-width, climbing (so called because it involves cracks too wide to be surmounted by jamming a hand or foot in them, but too narrow to be entered by the climber's entire body). Short and stocky, but strong and agile, he moved quickly and efficiently up such crack systems. Wiessner emigrated to the United States in 1929, settling in New York City, where he started a successful chemical business (among other products, his company produced a ski wax called Wiessner's Wonder Wax). He became an American citizen in 1939.[8]

Fritz Wiessner, climbing on Crow's Nest Cliffs, on the western shore of the Hudson River town of Highlands, New York, 1930s.

After a two-year hiatus, Wiessner returned to climbing in 1931, beginning in the Hudson Highlands, the mountains lining both shores of the Hudson River between Newburgh and Haverstraw Bays, much beloved by painter Thomas Cole in the nineteenth century. On a climb of Breakneck Ridge in the Hudson Highlands in the spring of 1935, Wiessner spotted the long, high ridgeline of the Shawangunks to the north. He decided to investigate and drove there the next weekend. He was struck by the solidity of the steep quartz conglomerate faces along the ridgeline, with "sharp holds and ledges which allow the climber to put up routes of the greatest variety on the often vertical or overhanging cliffs."[9] He established the first route in the Shawangunks in 1935, which he named the Gargoyle, for a rock projection near the top of the cliff.[10]

That was only the beginning of Wiessner's contributions to climbing history in North America and elsewhere. Before the decade was over, he had put up scores of new routes, in New York, New Hampshire, Connecticut, British Columbia, and Wyoming. Extremely versatile, he was happy climbing on little traprock mountain ridges like 761-foot Ragged Mountain in Connecticut and on 8,000-meter peaks in the Himalaya. Experienced American climbers like Robert Underhill were awed by his performances on rock, and he was equally skilled on snow and ice.[11]

Wiessner regarded none of the young partners he took on as equals; he insisted on leading almost every climb he undertook (he would later make an exception for Hans Kraus in the Shawangunks). Laura and Guy Waterman, the chroniclers of northeastern climbing, concluded that Wiessner could not be considered as transformative a figure in American climbing in the 1930s as, say, Underhill, because what Wiessner "was doing was so far ahead of what others were willing to try that he did not significantly improve the general standard."[12]

Among Wiessner's American climbs, one of the most notable was the ascent of 13,186-foot Mount Waddington, in British Columbia's largely unexplored Coast Mountains. Volcanic in origin, linked geologically to coastal mountains in Alaska and the Pacific Northwest, the coastal range stretches nearly 500 miles long in British Columbia, and is 75–100 miles wide. Although pierced by the Canadian Pacific Railway, much of the range was inaccessible in the 1920s except by a long hike inland from the coast through dank, heavy woods.[13]

Mount Waddington, only 175 air miles from Vancouver, and the largest mountain in the range, remained undiscovered until 1925. Canadian climbers Don and Phyllis Munday were the first to spot it, dubbing their discovery the "Mystery Mountain," and it became a highly coveted prize for both Canadian and American mountaineers over the next decade. The Mundays made several attempts on their own in the late 1920s, reaching the north peak, but not the higher south peak, the true summit. In the mid-1930s the couple joined forces with American climber Henry S. Hall, veteran of the 1925 Mount Logan expedition, and guide Hans Fuhrer, but again were unsuccessful.[14]

Other climbers, Canadian and American, also failed in their attempts, and in 1934 a talented Canadian climber, Alec Dalgeish, lost his life in a climbing accident on the mountain. The following year an eight-man team including the Sierra Club's rising stars Richard Leonard, Bestor Robinson, Jules Eichorn, and David Brower, along with Bill Loomis of the Harvard Mountaineering Club, headed for the mountain. They conceived of the climb above the glaciers as a rock-climbing problem and equipped themselves accordingly with 120 pitons, 700 feet of rope, plus ample carabiners, piton hammers, and the like. They made it within a day's climb of the summit but never enjoyed two consecutive days of good weather, and they had to abandon the effort when their food ran out. "Can Mount Waddington be climbed?" Robinson asked at the conclusion of his report for the *Sierra Club Bulletin*. "Serious doubts have been expressed by some. Thirteen unsuccessful attempts, involving the loss of one life, strongly support this viewpoint."[15] Still, the Sierrans resolved to return the following summer.

But they did not have the mountain to themselves that summer of 1936. The Sierra Club group (this time with Robinson and Leonard joined by Raffi Bedayn) would launch a cooperative effort with a group from the British Columbia Mountaineering Club led by William Dobson. And there was a third, smaller party as well, from the northeastern United States, led by Fritz Wiessner and including two members of the Yale

Mountaineering Club (Bill House and Alan Willcox) along with Olympic skier Betty Woolsey.[16]

The first challenge all the groups faced was getting to the mountain. Wiessner's group, the last to arrive, set off inland from the mouth of the Franklin River on the British Columbia coast on July 4 and, with the aid of two local hunting guides, hauled 700 pounds of food and gear through 8 miles of dense, untracked woods in pounding rains. Then they had to cross another dozen miles of glacier to reach the base of the mountain. By July 19 they were in position in a high camp just below the bergschrund on the southern side of the mountain.[17]

But they held off their own summit attempt for another day. Since the Sierra Club and the British Columbia Mountaineering Club had arrived on the mountain earlier, Wiessner's party had agreed even before setting out to let them attempt the first ascent. All day they watched their rivals, who tried pushing three different routes with three separate roped parties, run into insuperable obstacles. Their failure cleared the way for an attempt the next morning by the party's two strongest climbers, Wiessner and House. Wiessner had decided on the approach march to attempt a couloir on the face that could lead them to the southeast ridge, and from there to the summit block. Their first attempt, on July 20, via a couloir to the west of the summit failed; as Wiessner recorded, the couloir turned out to be "nearly vertical," with "a rotten rock structure," whose "every little crack and unevenness was glazed with ice."[18] They had to turn back.

Fortunately, unlike the Sierra Club's experience the previous year, the favorable weather they had enjoyed on the twentieth held on for another day. On July 21 they tried a different route, setting off from their high camp shortly before 3:00 a.m. for a couloir to the east of the summit. This one did the trick, bringing them first to the hanging snowfields atop the face, and then to the final challenge of a steep, forbidding rocky formation that stretched 1,000 feet above them to the summit. Wiessner's determination, route-finding ability, and versatility pulled them through.[19]

House was fortunate to be following Wiessner; he might not have been able to lead the final pitches on his own. But Wiessner was fortunate in having a partner who was a highly competent rock-climber in his own right. Wiessner changed into a pair of rope-soled climbing shoes and gave his ice ax and the extra 300-foot rappel rope he was carrying to House to carry the rest of the way to the summit. Finding the available belay stances too narrow, Wiessner put aside his usual distaste for pitons, hammering them in for an extra measure of protection. There was lots of loose rock, and Wiessner was hampered in his progress by the need to place each foot with great care, lest he set loose a barrage of falling stones on his partner. Wiessner led up an icy chimney and over an overhanging rock, which finally permitted the two climbers to reach the southeast ridge and then the summit. They stood atop the mountain in the late afternoon, thirteen hours after setting out, and did not reach their high camp until 2:00 a.m., concluding a twenty-three-hour day.[20]

Wiessner and House, along with Lawrence Coveney (a New York businessman, and future president of the American Alpine Club), pulled off another dramatic first ascent the following year, although in a very different setting, by reaching the summit of 5,114-foot Devils Tower in northeastern Wyoming. (An igneous intrusion, the tower is famous for many reasons, including its role as alien landing zone in the 1977 film *Close Encounters of the Third Kind*.) It was one of the first dramatic climbs of a desert rock formation. The torrid heat they encountered in their day's efforts toiling upward (placing only a single piton en route, per Wiessner's preferred climbing style), kept them from lingering at the summit. "It was not until the cool of the evening," House recorded for readers of the *American Alpine Journal*, "after we had found much cool beer that we began to feel like human beings again."[21]

Wiessner and House would each go on to play important roles in Himalayan mountaineering, both of them involved with American efforts to reach the summit of K2 in the Karakoram—though not on the same expedition.

EXCLUDED FROM THE "BROTHERHOOD"

Joining an American climbing club in the first half of the twentieth century, as has been noted, was not a simple matter of mailing in an application form with a check enclosed for annual dues. To join the American Alpine Club or the Sierra Club or the Appalachian Mountain Club, applicants needed to come recommended by existing members, who could attest to their qualifications, not all of which, at least in the case of the regional clubs, had to do with their mountaineering résumé. Social lineage figured largely in the recommendation for one successful AMC applicant in 1933:

> He is a member of the Harvard Club of Boston and of New York, and a Director of the Cambridge YMCA, and belongs to the Congregational Church. He is also a member of the American Alpine Club and the Harvard Mountaineering Club. . . . He graduated from Brown & Nichols School, and in 1919 from Harvard College.[22]

Well into the twentieth century, as a result, there continued to be a considerable overlap between the membership of the AMC (and other climbing clubs) and that of the General Society of Mayflower Descendants.

In April 1939, twenty-year-old Irving N. Feigin, who did not trace his ancestry to the *Mayflower* passenger list, died in a gruesome climbing accident while rappelling down to a ledge on Breakneck Ridge, a 1,260-foot summit 6 miles north of West Point on the eastern bank of the Hudson River. On his descent, dangling below a rocky overhang, he became entangled in the rope and was strangled while struggling to free himself. The following summer the AMC journal *Appalachia* ran a detailed account of the accident as a cautionary tale of what could happen to even relatively experienced climbers like Feigin and his partner, who were using the approved rappelling technique.[23]

Out on the West Coast, Dick Leonard read the article and, out of his interest in climbing safety, wrote to Robert Underhill to ask whether Feigin had been a member of an eastern climbing club and, if so, whether he had been properly trained. Underhill, who did not know the accident victim personally, nevertheless responded that "you can safely assume [Feigin's] training was very haphazard." How could he be so sure? He elaborated:

The A.M.C. has a New York Chapter, but the members are so afraid of getting stuck with kikes and others that they deliberately suppress any publicity it might have and make it almost impossible for new people to join! One can't be sure some special Jewish psychology didn't enter into this accident, at least fundamentally. It isn't so usual for Jews to go in for mountaineering, and when they do I can conceive that they are conscious of invading what they may look upon as the other man's sport, and consequently that they feel unduly impelled to make themselves felt by undertaking the spectacular.[24]

Being Jewish, Feigin was not admitted to the AMC, and not having been instructed by the AMC in proper rope craft, he was not qualified to make such a risky climb; thus ran Underhill's circular logic in condemning the victim for pursuing "the other man's sport." Of course, well-trained AMC members also died in rock-climbing accidents in those years. A year and a half after Feigin's death, in October 1940, Don Babenroth, the chairman of the New York chapter of the AMC's rock-climbing section, died on a climb in Arden, New York, because of a fall resulting from an unstable belay stance.[25]

The Feigin accident was not the only occasion that Underhill proclaimed anti-Semitic sentiments to his fellow climbers.[26] He was evidently confident that it would be no discredit to thus reveal his own attitude toward Jews. Nor was the AMC the only outdoor organization practicing ethnic, religious, or racial discrimination. As Leonard recalled in an interview years later, until the end of the Second World War the "Southern California chapter [of the Sierra Club] deliberately refused to allow blacks, Chicanos, Orientals, or Jews to be members." Leonard was one of a group of younger Sierra Club leaders who helped put an end to that policy.[27]

BRADFORD WASHBURN: "GOING PLACES"

In December 1936, Charlie Houston, recently returned to the United States from a successful expedition to India's Kumaon Himalaya, dropped a note to Bradford Washburn, with whom he had climbed three years earlier in Alaska:

> Bistrich [Bob Bates] and I were talking over the people you really started on expeditions, and we calculated there were at least eight who are doing big things, and half a dozen more whom you started in the climbing game. That's quite a record. You certainly started Bob and me going places.[28]

In the 1930s, Henry Bradford "Brad" Washburn Jr. succeeded Allen Carpé as the leading figure in Alaskan mountaineering. He pioneered the art of aerial mountain photography and cartography. Apart from Annie Peck several decades earlier, he was the first American to earn a significant portion of his income from writing and lecturing about his mountaineering exploits. And as Charlie Houston suggested, already by 1936 Washburn had become mentor to a rising generation of expeditionary mountaineers, who were "going places" and "doing big things" from Alaska to Asia to the Andes. No climber did more to shape American expeditionary culture and, in particular, the American preference for lightweight alpine-style approaches to big, remote mountains instead of grand siege-style expeditions. He would earn the nickname of "Mr. McKinley," and well into his eighties, succeeding generations of would-be Denali summiters sought his opinion and approval for new routes on that mountain and other Alaskan peaks.[29]

Born in Cambridge, Massachusetts, in 1910, Washburn was a minister's son who hailed from a very proper New England background.[30] Washburn's immediate family was not wealthy, but the generosity of relatives (and later, his earnings from royalties and on the lecture circuit) saw him educated at prestigious private schools, including Groton prep school and Harvard College, while enjoying extended summer excursions to the White Mountains and the Alps.

A precocious writer, with an engaging style and an unlimited sense of self-confidence, Washburn had authored a privately published guidebook with his own maps entitled *Trails and Peaks of the Presidential Range* by the time he turned sixteen. That same summer of 1926, Washburn traveled with his family to Chamonix, where he was instructed in the art of technical climbing by the local guides. Before the summer was over, he had reached the summits of Mont Blanc and the Matterhorn, and the following year he brought out a book, this time with a commercial publisher, chronicling his adventures in 1926 and on a return trip to Chamonix in 1927, entitled *Among the Alps with Bradford*.[31]

On yet another trip to Chamonix, in 1929, the summer before he started college, he made a first ascent of the north face of the 13,524-foot Aiguille Verte, part of the Mont Blanc massif, with guides George Chalet and Alfred Couttet.[32] While in Chamonix, Washburn developed an enthusiasm for photography. Late in life he said of himself, "I'm a photographer who climbs, not a climber who photographs."[33]

An illustrated talk at Groton in 1926 by John Noel, veteran of the 1924 British Everest expedition, fired Washburn's ambition to test himself against the big Himalayan peaks—and also his growing interest in mountain photography. But the following year Allen Carpé's presentation at the annual meeting of the AAC about his failed attempt to climb Mount Fairweather got Washburn thinking about Alaska. And when he arrived at Harvard in 1929 and joined the Harvard Mountaineering Club (later becoming its president), he came under the influence of the club's founder, Henry S. Hall, who told him about his own great adventure in 1925 on the Yukon's Mount Logan. Still a teenager, Washburn was hooked on the idea of being an Alaskan mountaineer.[34]

Hooked, but not really prepared. In the summer of 1930, at the age of twenty, Washburn led his first expedition. (As Washburn's friend and biographer David Roberts has noted, it tells us something interesting about the man that he "never went on an expedition led by anyone but himself.")[35] But on that Alaskan expedition, his attempt to climb Mount Fairweather with five even more inexperienced Harvard buddies proved a fiasco. Slogging heavy loads from their coastal landing point at Lituya Bay, first through thick, trackless forest and then up 20 miles of an icy glacial trench they called Desolation Valley, they found their path completely blocked by an impassable ice cliff at 6,500 feet, nearly 3,000 feet lower than the height Carpé's party had reached in 1926.[36] "Mountaineering in Alaska is still little short of Arctic exploration," Washburn wrote in *National Geographic Magazine* a few years later, "with all of its attendant difficulties and hardships."[37]

In the summer of 1931, Washburn accepted a commission to make a documentary film about an ascent of Mont Blanc. In the meantime, Allen Carpé pulled off the first ascent of Fairweather, five years after his initial effort. Washburn resolved to make the second ascent of the mountain, assembling a team of Harvard climbers for the summer of 1932. Remembering the difficulties encountered in 1930, he decided to land his party and their supplies by floatplane on a lake near the mountain. But the lake was frozen, so they had to fly back to the coast to land, once again making Lituya Bay their base camp. Undiscouraged, Washburn made a snap decision to attempt a different and unclimbed mountain, 12,726-foot Mount Crillon, southeast of Mount Fairweather, and the second-highest peak in the Fairweather Range. As in 1930, the long approach march inland exhausted the party and its supplies, leaving too little time for a serious attempt.[38]

Two wasted summers might have discouraged a less determined character, but Washburn was back in the summer of 1933, with another team drawn from the ranks of the Harvard Mountaineering Club, including students who would soon play key roles in Himalayan mountaineering: Robert "Bob" Bates (who had been on the 1932 expedition), Charles S. "Charlie" Houston, and H. Adams "Ad" Carter. With Washburn, they were four of the group of climbers later dubbed the "Harvard Five," the absent Terris Moore was the fifth. There were also several Dartmouth students on the 1933 expedition, conducting a geological survey of the region and a study of glacier movement—hence the designation "Harvard-Dartmouth Alaskan Expedition."

This time Washburn's party found a suitable landing spot for its pontoon-equipped Lockheed Vega seaplane, setting down on Crillon Lake, 300 feet above sea level. Rather than spending weeks hauling themselves and their supplies over rough terrain, at the end of a single day of air transport they were perched at the base of the mountain.

The expedition thus got off to a strong start. The newcomers were impressed with Washburn's methodical preparations, including the then innovative method of dividing rations into bags sufficient to support two climbers for three days high on the mountainside: "It was an exact science with Washburn," Houston recalled.[39] But two strong-willed individuals like Washburn and Houston, in the forced intimacy of expedition life, were almost bound to find a way to disagree, which they wound up doing in an argument over route-finding. As expedition leader (and two years Houston's elder), Washburn prevailed.

There seemed to be other divisions in the ranks, although the issues remain unclear; in subsequent letters, both Houston and Carter made it clear they were on opposite sides of a personal dispute.[40] In any case, the six climbers were poised for a summit bid when, as so often happens, blizzard conditions hit them; three—Houston, Carter, and Bill Child—descended to base camp, while Washburn, Bates, and Everett remained high on the mountain hoping to catch a break in the weather, which never came.[41] Washburn's first three Alaskan expeditions thus could all be counted as failures—the one promising development being that he was failing at ever-higher altitude.[42]

Before heading back to Cambridge to begin graduate studies at Harvard's Institute of Geographical Exploration, Washburn, in a plane piloted by Gene Meyring of Alaska Southern Airways, flew over Crillon to find a more likely route to the summit, as well as to take aerial photos of the coastal range. He wrote home ecstatically to his parents on August 24:

Yesterday dawned CLOUDLESS—as I have never hoped or expected to see Lituya Bay or the mountains and not a cloud was in the sky ALL DAY. We surveyed like the dickens till noon when the plane arrived at last amid our wild cheers. Then Dick, Walt and I jumped aboard and flew to Icy Point 25 miles south, climbing to an altitude of 5000 feet. We returned opposite the range over the ocean at this height taking *overlapping photographs the whole way*! Then we kept inland the whole way to Yakutat Bay. . . . Then we continued over the Malaspina Glacier till we were right opposite Mount Saint Elias and Mount Logan and took the first aerial pictures ever taken of them and the largest piedmont glacier in the world—magnificent moraine pictures as well as unbelievable peaks—The second and third highest in North America—18,000 and 19,539 feet high! Then back to the bay over the coast range at 9000 feet with another overlapping set of everything all the way with the sunset shadows on the peaks. The most superb day of photography that I have ever had in my life. What an experience.[43]

Nineteen-thirties climbing might be described as the age of mentoring. Robert Underhill mentored the youth of the Sierra Club, while Brad Washburn (himself still a youth) mentored even younger members of the Harvard Mountaineering Club. However, Washburn's protégés differed from Underhill's. Although Houston, Bates, Carter, and others headed for Huntington Ravine on Mount Washington for rock and ice climbing during their undergraduate years, they thought of that activity as off-season conditioning, preparing them for more interesting challenges in big and remote ranges. They were moving to the fore in expeditionary mountaineering, rather than in technical climbing.[44]

The second Harvard-Dartmouth Mount Crillon expedition set off for the mountain in the summer of 1934. It was Washburn's largest expedition, with four members from each school, and three others. Almost all of them were newcomers; Ad Carter was the only veteran of 1933 on the expedition. Washburn's innovations this time around included the use of a shortwave radio at base camp to communicate with the outside world, plus the use of walkie-talkies to communicate between camps on the mountain—a first on any expedition. The increased possibility for communication was a boon and a burden; Washburn described these "radio telephones," in *National Geographic Magazine* as "weighing less than 20 pounds apiece."[45] Washburn also arranged an airdrop of supplies at 5,600 feet on the west slope of Crillon, which he figured saved two weeks of hauling supplies by the climbers.

By the second week of July, the expedition had ferried supplies up to the next-to-last high camp, at about 6,300 feet, prior to a summit attempt. Things were going so well that Washburn took a day off from climbing to make another aerial photographic reconnaissance of the coastal range, and he circled the summit pyramid of Crillon to check on snow conditions. He brought the same characteristically bold approach to photography that he brought to climbing. With the plane's door removed, tied in with a rope, Washburn leaned far out with his large-format aerial camera to get his shots.[46]

Climbing resumed on July 15 with a cache of climbing ropes and other supplies hauled up to 8,000 feet. Two days of snow followed, but on July 18 the climbers returned in sun to their high camp. And at 2:00 a.m. on July 19, four climbers set out for the summit plateau, fixing ropes along the way. Washburn and Henry Woods made up the first roped pair, followed by Ad Carter and Howard Kellogg as the second, with Waldo Holcombe and Edward Streeter waiting below. Despite having to surmount an icy cliff, the four climbers quickly made the first 2,000 feet, bringing them to the summit plateau by 6:45 a.m. That was as far as they had originally planned to go that day, with the summit still 4 miles and 4,000 feet away.

But the climbing conditions were ideal; for once it was sunny and still, and the snow below their feet was still frozen. So in a spur-of-the-moment decision, Washburn and Carter, the most experienced climbers, took all the chocolate and lemon drops from the other two and pressed on ahead on their own, following a route that Washburn had picked out from the air. Everything went smoothly until they were 200 feet below the summit, where they found their way barred by "a huge, yawning crack with an upper lip that overhung far above our heads."[47]

The weather was deteriorating, and they had to struggle upward waist deep in powder snow. But they worked their way out onto an icy ridge that led them around the edge of the crack, and at 12:30 p.m. they stepped out onto the summit, descending after only two minutes because of the gathering storm. Three days later, Washburn returned to the summit in perfect weather, accompanied by Holcombe and Carter. They brought with them a movie camera, as well as an American flag and a Harvard banner to plant on top. This time, writing to "Dear Dad and Mother" on July 25, Washburn could announce complete success. Of the second summit day, he wrote:

> The day was cloudless from sunrise till sunset. We saw everything. The only obstacle to vision was the curvature of the earth! The ocean was cloudless—everything was as clear as crystal. There is no other way up Crillon than ours—the other ridges that drop from the summit are truly sickening: the giddiest drops that I have ever seen anywhere.[48]

Washburn had emerged a master of expeditionary mountaineering. He never knew an unsuccessful summit attempt thereafter. Among his achievements over the next several years was an epic first ascent of 17,192-foot Mount Lucania, Canada's third-highest mountain, in 1937, in the company of Bob Bates; followed by their traverse of 16,614-foot Mount Steele, Canada's fifth-highest mountain, and an arduous 100-mile wilderness trek to return to civilization; first ascents of 13,250-foot Mount Marcus Baker in Alaska's Chugach Mountains and of 16,208-foot Mount Sanford in Alaska's Wrangell Mountains in 1938; the first ascent of 10,182-foot Mount Bertha in the Fairweather Range in 1940 (in the company of his bride, Barbara, on their honeymoon—her first climb); and the first ascent via the difficult north ridge of 13,740-foot Mount Hayes in the Alaska Range in 1941, again with Barbara. In the meantime he had assumed the directorship of the venerable but moribund museum of the Boston Society of Natural History in 1939, which he would, over the next forty years, transform into the dynamic Boston Museum of Science.[49]

AMERICANS IN THE HIMALAYA

After Fanny Bullock Workman and her husband, Hunter, completed their final Himalayan expedition, an exploration of the Siachen Glacier in the Karakoram in 1912, twenty years passed before an American expedition returned to the region. Himalayan expeditionary mountaineering was largely a British enterprise through the 1920s. But in the course of the 1930s, Americans began to move to the forefront of climbing in the region.

In 1932, several Americans accompanied an expedition to attempt a first ascent of 26,659-foot Nanga Parbat, the ninth-highest mountain in the world. The so-called German-American Nanga Parbat expedition was, in reality, a German expedition with a couple of Americans invited along, perhaps to make the whole idea of Germans and Austrians climbing in a region under British control more palatable to the authorities.

The expedition was led by Munich climber Willi Merkl, an outstanding proponent of the Munich School of bold rock-climbing employing direct-aid techniques. Merkl assembled a talented team of alpine climbers—none, however, with previous Himalayan experience. From the United States came Fritz Wiessner, at the time still a German citizen; Wiessner's friend Elbridge Rand Herron, who, although American-born, had grown up in Italy and Switzerland, where he had gained considerable alpine experience; and Elizabeth Knowlton, who also had alpine experience and came along as expedition historian. She would reach 20,000 feet on Nanga Parbat but was not allowed by Merkl to go any higher.[50]

Plagued by porter troubles, food shortages, heavy snowfall, and inexperience, the expedition was a failure, although three members, including Wiessner, reached a respectable 23,000 feet on Rakhiot Ridge, establishing the route by which the mountain would eventually be climbed twenty-one years later. Nanga Parbat would cost the lives of many good climbers in the next few years (including Willi Merkl in 1934). None died on the 1932 expedition, but on the way home to the United States, Rand Herron stopped off for a visit to Egypt and, ironically, died in a fall while descending the Pyramid of Chephren, second tallest of the Pyramids of Giza.[51]

In mid-October 1932, when Herron had his fatal pyramid encounter, another band of American climbers was heading toward the summit of a different Asian peak, 24,789-foot Minya Konka (today Mount Gongga), highest mountain in China's Szechuan Province. Not technically part of the Himalayan range, but of similar scale, it is the third-highest mountain outside of the Himalaya and Karakoram. Terris Moore and Art Emmons, both of the Harvard Mountaineering Club (with Emmons succeeding Brad Washburn as HMC president), were joined on the expedition by Richard Burdsall, a mechanical engineer and graduate of Swarthmore College, and Jack Young, a Chinese-born journalism student at New York University. Moore, with three first ascents in Alaska to his name—two of them in the company of Allen Carpé, and one with British Everest climber Noel Odell—was the most experienced climber, but the expedition members deliberately refrained from choosing a formal leader. Democratic decision making would prove to be a hallmark of expeditions in which HMC alumni played leading roles.[52]

Moore and his companions had originally dreamed of making a lightweight attempt on Everest, which had been off-limits to climbers of any nationality since the failure of the 1924 British expedition, but the British, who were planning a return engagement of their own traditional siege operations (dispatching fourteen climbers to the mountain in 1933), refused permission. As an alternative, the Americans decided to tackle Minya Konka, a mysterious mountain about which little was known; some speculated that it stood even taller than Everest.[53]

Expedition histories are often a form of escapist literature, designed to allow the reader the opportunity to ignore politics, the economy, and other worldly cares. That, interestingly, was not the case with the account of the Minya Konka climb, *Men against the Clouds*, written by Emmons and Burdsall, a forgotten classic of mountaineering literature. It took the four Americans seven weeks to travel across China to reach the base of the mountain in early September. En route they were constantly reminded of the conflicts engulfing China: Japanese gunboats on the Yangtze river, and Communist banners condemning foreign imperialism and the Kuomintang government.[54]

When two-month-old mail from the United States miraculously reached the group by courier in mid-October at Camp 1, the young Americans were delighted by personal news from home. But they were also interested to learn, according to Emmons, "how Hoover's campaign was progressing and how devastating was the Depression."[55] Later, descending the mountain and resting at a missionary's home, they learned by shortwave receiver of the outcome of the 1932 presidential contest, and the election of Franklin Delano Roosevelt.[56] The vision of mountaineering presented in *Men against the Clouds* was above the world but definitely not removed from it.

Once the expedition arrived at the mountain, six Tibetans were hired to help ferry supplies to a base camp at 14,000 feet, two of whom continued to carry supplies up to 17,000 feet, where Camp 1 was placed. Beyond that the climbers were on their own. "We would have given much for a corps of stout Darjeeling Sherpas," Emmons confessed in the expedition book.[57] Instead, they ferried their own supplies to ever-higher camps on the mountainside, each at an interval of about a thousand-foot elevation gain. The final camp, from which they would make their summit bid, was placed at 22,000 feet on the mountain's northwest ridge.

The climb took its toll. Emmons's feet were showing signs of frostbite by the time they established their final camp, while Burdsall was suffering from poor acclimation. And then, on the day before they were to make their summit attempt, Emmons badly cut his hand while trying to slice a frozen biscuit. He was forced to remain at Camp 4 while Burdsall and Moore set off alone on the summit attempt at 5:00 a.m. on October 28. They reached the top nine and a half hours later. As Moore would write: "Flag-waving was certainly not one of the purposes of our expedition, yet, since this was the highest point of land . . . which Americans had ever reached, we flew the American flag for a few brief seconds from my inverted ice-ax while Dick photographed it."[58]

The summit altitude record attained that day in 1932 would not be surpassed by another American expedition until 1958. But there were costs. Baring his hands to take summit photos, Burdsall suffered frostbitten fingers. Emmons's feet froze while he waited for the two summiters at Camp 4. Burdsall kept his fingers, but Emmons lost all his toes.[59]

Apart from the altitude record, the Minya Konka climb was notable for style. Four climbers pulled off the ascent without porters, on a mountain that had never before even been reconnoitered, let alone attempted. As the Harvard Mountaineering Club's journal noted in an issue highlighting the expedition's success:

In contrast to the large unwieldy Himalayan expeditions with their complicated problems of transport, it placed emphasis on lightness of equipment and mobility of organization. Whether such tactics could be effectively employed on the greater Himalayan peaks is an open question, as yet unanswered.[60]

NANDA DEVI

Another mountain, this one located in the Garhwal Himalaya of India, would help answer that question. Nanda Devi, at 25,642 feet the highest and also holiest of Indian mountains, was named for a Hindu goddess, the consort of Lord Shiva. Given its setting, it is not surprising that Nanda Devi should have inspired such myths. It seemed unapproachable and unknowable. The mountain is completely surrounded by two enclosing circles of mountain ramparts, mostly in the 20,000-foot range—a near-continuous wall with no apparent entryway. Within the second ring of mountains lies an "inner sanctuary," 240 square miles of glacier and alpine pasture, never trodden on by the foot of man. Until 1934 that is, when the intrepid British duo of Eric Shipton and Bill Tilman, two of the greatest Himalayan climbers of all time, and a sterling example of the brotherhood of the rope, searched for the elusive entryway to the sanctuary.

The previous year Shipton had been on the first British expedition to attempt Everest since the deaths of George Leigh-Mallory and Andrew Irvine high on the mountain in 1924. Shipton was one of eleven climbers involved in the 1933 expedition, which had also included a transport officer, two wireless radio operators, two doctors, 170 Sherpas and other porters, and 350 pack animals.[61] In contrast, Shipton and Tilman set off on their 1934 expedition accompanied by just three Sherpas and twelve porters. They didn't reach the summit of Nanda Devi, but that was not their intent (nor were the British able to reach Everest's summit on any of the four expeditions they launched in the 1930s).

Shipton and Tilman found what they were looking for: the entrance to the sanctuary via the Rishi Gorge. They spent three idyllic weeks exploring the inner sanctuary, their only company the wild sheep and goats that had somehow found their own way through the deep, intimidating cliffs. At the end of June, the human visitors were forced out of the sanctuary by the onset of the monsoon, but Shipton and Tilman returned in September for another look. On that trip they reached an altitude of 21,000 feet on the mountain's southeast ridge and concluded that with a slightly stronger party, the mountain could be climbed.

Shipton and Tilman were determined to return the next year but were diverted by Everest, taking part in the 1935 British expedition (chiefly notable in retrospect because a nineteen-year-old Sherpa named Tenzing Norgay was hired on as a porter, on his first Everest expedition). In 1936 Shipton was given leadership of the next Everest expedition, but Tilman was judged physically unfit by the British climbing establishment, so he could not accompany Shipton to Tibet.[62]

Tilman might have sat out the 1936 climbing season had it not been for the ambitions of some American climbers to return to the Himalaya. Despite having lost his toes on Minya Konka, Art Emmons was lobbying fellow Harvard Mountaineering Club members to pull together another expedition. Sometime in the fall of 1935 he proposed the idea of a Himalayan climb to Ad Carter (who had reached the summit of Alaska's Mount Crillon with Brad Washburn in 1934) and William Farnsworth ("Farnie") Loomis, who had been part of the unsuccessful 1935 Sierra Club expedition to Mount Waddington. They in turn spoke to Charlie Houston, who had been on Washburn's 1933 attempt on Mount Crillon, and who in the summer of 1934 had pulled off the first ascent of Alaska's 17,400-foot Mount Foraker, the third-highest peak in the United States.[63]

Houston was interested but, for the moment, distracted by the demands of his first year in medical school, so Emmons and Loomis undertook the main organizational responsibility, with the latter dispatched to London to negotiate with British authorities to obtain permission for their climb.[64]

Loomis was also charged with finding some British climbers to go with them. He started with Scottish climber T. Graham Brown, whom Houston had first met in a hotel in Chamonix in 1932 and then recruited to his Foraker expedition. Brown provided access to the cream of the

British climbing establishment, who otherwise might not have had time for the American college boys and their grand ambitions. In the standard historical telling, which follows Houston's own account, the youthful American *naïfs* had decided that the mountain they would like to attempt was Kangchenjunga, third-highest peak in the world, which had turned back three European expeditions between 1929 and 1931. They were then gently steered to another more attainable goal, or so Houston's self-deprecatory story went, by older and wiser British climbers.[65]

However, a letter from Houston to Henry S. Hall written in the spring of 1936 complicates the story. Houston reported to Hall that he and his compatriots were indeed seeking permission for an attempt on Kangchenjunga that summer, but he added: "Since no one at any time has been very sanguine about our securing the permission, [Loomis] also asked [Eric] Shipton if he minded our trying Nanda Devi; to which the answer was 'By all means go ahead.'"[66] The young Americans on their own had apparently come up with Nanda Devi as an alternative goal, but they were hesitating because of what they regarded as Shipton and Til-man's proprietary right to the mountain. Reassured that Shipton would not resent their intrusion, they applied to the India Office in London for approval of their expedition, and got it.

Meanwhile, Loomis recruited four British climbers to join what was now being called the British-American Himalayan Expedition. The new (but more experienced) recruits were Brown; Noel Odell, who knew the Harvard Mountaineering Club circle from his time teaching geology at the university; Peter Lloyd, a rising star in the Cambridge University Mountaineering Club; and, most important, Bill Tilman.[67]

It was going to be a Tilman-style expedition or, one could also say, a Brad Washburn/Harvard Mountaineering Club–style expedition, rather than one on the grand Everest scale. As in the Shipton-Tilman partnership, and on Minya Konka, there would be a lack of formal hierarchy. "We certainly will be very respectful of whatever peak we take, and decidedly not over-optimistic of our chances," Houston wrote to Hall. "Traveling light, very light, as we are, and being all very close friends, we feel we have a strong, flexible and responsible party." No leader had been selected. "We all feel that friends should be able to travel making committee decisions, perhaps a naïve belief, but we intend to try it until it fails."

Houston added what, in the light of subsequent events, would prove an interesting postscript. Apparently, a ninth climber had been under consideration for inclusion in the expedition: Fritz Wiessner. In the end he had been rejected, although not for a lack of climbing qualifications or Himalayan experience. As Houston explained: "We feel that a British-American crowd is more homogenous and sympathetic without the introduction of a German; for that reason Wiessner was not included."[68]

In the spring of 1936, the expedition members set off from the United States and Britain for India. They arrived in stages. Tilman, one of the first to arrive, recruited two Sherpas and fourteen local porters. With this company, in June he and Loomis ferried 900 pounds of supplies through the Rishi Gorge to a cache in the inner sanctuary.

By the end of June, most of the other climbers had arrived at the expedition's staging point, at Ranikhet. They set to organizing their supplies, weeding out inessentials (many of the expensive delicacies the Americans had brought along, for example), and packing what remained into 60-pound loads. Tilman also cut one nonessential expedition member: Houston's father, Oscar (a wealthy New York lawyer who had accompanied his son on the Mount Foraker expedition, though not on the ascent). Toeless Art Emmons would come along (the expedition having been his idea to begin with) but would restrict his own role to base-camp manager.[69]

The little expedition left Ranikhet for Nanda Devi, 175 miles distant, on July 10 (Ad Carter, the one member still absent, would catch up with them en route). Porter troubles along the way caused delays and additional pruning of expedition supplies by Tilman, who still thought they were traveling too luxuriously. Finally, on August 4, they established a lower base camp at 15,000 feet on a high moraine shelf above the mountain's southeast glacier. The next camp went in at 19,200 feet on the southeast ridge that Shipton and Tilman had scouted two years earlier. Camp 2 went in at 20,000 feet, Camp 3 at 21,000 feet. By the time they reached Camp 3, all the expedition's Sherpas had succumbed to one or another of the afflictions these ventures were prone to (dysentery, snow blindness), leaving the American and British sahibs to face the wrath of the "Goddess" alone.

As Houston had written to Hall back in the United States that spring, the expedition had intended to make decisions by consensus, each man's voice as important as any other's. But now that they were in striking distance of the summit at 21,000 feet, they decided to elect a leader, with Tilman the unanimous choice. He, in turn, chose Houston and Odell as the first summit team. After waiting out several days of blizzard, Houston and Odell established Camp 4 at 21,800 feet.

On August 25, initially accompanied by Tilman, Loomis, and Lloyd, the summit team cut steps up the steep ridge, with Lloyd leading a difficult rock pitch via a chimney. At 4:00 p.m., the three not named to the summit team headed back down to Camp 4, while Houston and Odell continued upward.

The mountain was shrouded in mist on August 25, and those waiting anxiously in Camp 4 could see nothing of and heard nothing from the men above them. But the following morning, they heard a yodel from Noel Odell far above. Carter yelled up to find out what Odell was trying to tell them, and he thought he heard Odell bellow, "Charlie—is—killed." Distressing news indeed, or so it seemed until Tilman and Brown reached the bivouac where Houston and Odell had spent the night. Charlie wasn't killed; he was "ill" (which is what had confused Carter, the preferred American term being "sick"), poisoned by a rancid portion of a tin of corned beef he had shared the previous night with Odell. So, while others helped Houston down, Tilman took his place. Odell and Tilman moved the bivouac higher, to 24,000 feet, and on August 29 made their summit bid. A little over nine hours of climbing brought them to the highest point in British India, where, in Tilman's immortal note of understated self-mockery, "we so forgot ourselves as to shake hands."[70]

Charlie Houston may not have made the summit, but he came within 300 feet of it. The young Americans from Harvard, along with their British compatriots, had participated in a successful first ascent of a Himalayan giant in elegant simplicity of style, without the elephantine trappings of the expeditions regularly trouping off for Everest. When Shipton, who had led the most recent failed expedition to Everest that spring, learned of the successful ascent of Nanda Devi, he called it a "model of what such an expedition should be."[71] It would shape the Himalayan expeditions that Houston led in years to come.

On the return trip, two of the Harvard Five who had cut their expeditionary teeth on Brad Washburn's 1933 Crillon expedition wrote to their mentor, each independently suggesting that the other had become a better person in the interval since that somewhat dispute-prone effort. According to Ad Carter, writing in September from Ranikhet:

> Charlie was a prince. I had been a bit afraid about how I should get on with him after Crillon but we are now the best of friends. He has learned a pile on Foraker and seemed much less moody and never got grouchy at anyone. I have never seen such an unselfish person in my life.[72]

And Charlie Houston wrote to Washburn a month later:

> We had a grand trip too this summer, and you'll be interested to hear that Ad worked out splendidly on the trip; evidently he profited a great deal by two trips with you after [Crillon].[73]

K2, 1938

Following the triumphant ascent of Nanda Devi, Bill Tilman led a (relatively) lightweight expedition to Everest. He had hoped to invite Charlie Houston along, making him the first American on Everest. But the British climbing establishment wouldn't approve the idea, and Houston would be otherwise engaged on another Himalayan giant.

In 1936, Fritz Wiessner and Dick Burdsall brought a proposal to the American Alpine Club to sponsor an expedition to attempt K2, the first such since the Duke of the Abruzzi had explored the mountain in 1909. With the aid of the American consul in Calcutta, permission was secured for a small party to attempt K2 in the summer of 1938. For business reasons, Wiessner felt he could not leave on such short notice, yielding leadership of the expedition to Charlie Houston, while planning to lead a subsequent expedition himself in 1939. The 1938 expedition was, in theory, merely a reconnaissance. Houston suspected that was the real reason for Wiessner's decision to stay home. Privately, Houston hoped to steal a march on Wiessner, whom he did not much like, and actually reach the summit.[74]

Just twenty-four years old in the fall of 1937, beginning his third year at Columbia University's College of Physicians and Surgeons, Houston set about organizing the First American Karakoram Expedition along the lightweight and mobile lines he had learned from Washburn in Alaska and from Tilman in the Himalaya. In 1909, the Duke of the Abruzzi had been accompanied to K2 by seven professional guides from Courmayeur, plus a cartographer, a doctor, and the photographer Vittorio Sella. Houston set out to recruit a party of six, including himself.[75]

That fall, Houston reached out to several friends. Burdsall would come, and so would Bob Bates, whom Houston had climbed with on the 1933 Crillon expedition, and who had gone on to reach the summit of Lucania with Brad Washburn earlier that year. Houston hoped to bring along a number of their Harvard Mountaineering Club buddies, particularly Minya Konka and Nanda Devi veterans. Toward the end of November, he wrote to Bates to report on his progress. He wasn't having much luck rounding up the usual suspects, like Farnie Loomis, and was now ready to consider alternative candidates:

> Loomis recommends Paul Petzoldt from the Teton country and the West very strongly; do you know anything of him at all, and if so what do you think? If you don't know of him will you try to get some dope on him and let me know your feeling.[76]

Even though some of the worthies of the American Alpine Club frankly doubted whether "this Wyoming packer and guide" would fit in socially with the others and not disgrace himself in the company of

their British hosts, Petzoldt passed muster; the Harvard mountaineers—
Loomis, Emmons, and Moore—as it turned out, all had other commit-
ments and declined. Bill House, Yale Mountaineering Club alumnus and
Wiessner's partner on Mount Waddington in 1936, signed on. The five
of them (Houston, Burdsall, Bates, Petzoldt, House) were a small but
very strong and experienced party. The addition of Captain Norman
Streatfeild, who would join them when they reached India, made six.
They were, Houston would write, a "small party of friends."[77]

In mid-April 1938, all the Americans but Houston sailed for London
(he would follow, once he completed third-year medical exams). They
gathered up preordered equipment and then crossed the channel to
Paris. There, Petzoldt would later say, he made a shocking discovery.
Houston, sharing the disdain of the eastern climbing establishment for
ironmongery, had skimped on climbing hardware. "We hardly had a piton
or carabiner," Petzoldt recalled. "And hell, you could look at K2. That's
rock! And there's places on it, if you fell you'd go down 10,000 feet before
you'd land."[78] According to his subsequent account, Petzoldt snuck out
to a local climbing shop and bought fifty pairs of carabiners and pitons,
secreting them among the rest of the expedition supplies.

Houston and Petzoldt certainly had different attitudes about climbing
hardware, and things may have happened that way—except it is not clear
how Petzoldt would have come up with the considerable sum necessary
to buy the carabiners and pitons. His passage was being paid for through
the generosity of his friend Farnie Loomis, and he was traveling on a tight
budget. While a good story, a more likely scenario is that, noticing the
dearth of ironware, Petzoldt insisted to his better-heeled companions
that they needed to add to their supplies while they had the chance.[79]

In any case, from Marseilles the four Americans, plus their newly
acquired climbing gear, sailed to India. On May 8, they rendezvoused in
Rawalpindi with Streatfeild and the team of six Sherpas he had recruited
for the expedition. Houston arrived the following day, having caught
up with them thanks to the innovation of airline travel from London to
Karachi.[80]

The challenge that lay ahead dwarfed their previous experiences in

Alaska and Asia. Just getting from Karachi to their base camp below K2 required over a month of hard traveling through an increasingly wild and barren landscape—at first by truck, but soon by horse and on foot: Karachi to Srinagar, Srinagar to Skardu, Skardu to Askole, the last human habitation, where Petzoldt came down with a high fever and was nursed back to health by medical student Houston.

They were following in the footsteps of the Workmans, who had made the same journey in 1899 to Askole and a little farther to the Biafo Glacier. It was hard, dry country most of the way, followed by a stunning icy mountainscape, known to them from the classic panoramic photographs shot by Vittorio Sella on the Duke of the Abruzzi's 1909 approach march, including peaks with names far more lyrical than the prosaic K2: Muztagh Tower, Gasherbrum, Masherbrum, Chogolisa. Houston and a revived Petzoldt caught up with their compatriots on the Baltoro Glacier, finally coming to the huge icy amphitheater known as Concordia, the confluence of the Savoia and Godwin-Austen Glaciers below K2. From there they swung north onto the Godwin-Austen Glacier and the approach to K2, where they established base camp. They were already at an altitude higher than any summit in the United States outside of the Alaska Territory, and they still had 12,000 vertical feet to climb.[81]

K2 is a quadrangular pyramid, with four main buttress ridges. The Duke of the Abruzzi had attempted two of these in 1909: the northwest and the southeast. The duke had gotten highest on the southeast ridge (which the Houston party dubbed "Abruzzi Ridge," the name it has been known by ever since; as they ascended it they came across bits of debris left behind by the Italians nearly three decades earlier), reaching an altitude of 20,000 feet. But the Americans decided to try the northwest ridge first—and were turned back by slopes of impossibly steep and crevassed ice. Over the next several weeks they probed Abruzzi Ridge and the northeast ridge, favoring first one and then the other, and even returning to the northwest ridge for another look, all the while using up precious time and supplies. The climbers began to think they had underestimated the mountain. In a letter home to his parents, written on June 27, Houston worried that "we have a very weak party for so big a job."[82]

With morale at a dangerous low, the Americans debated their options at a "council of war." Houston leaned toward an attempt on the northeast ridge, but Petzoldt and House, the two strongest rock-climbers, were interested in another attempt on the Abruzzi route. Houston deferred to their judgment. And for the next month they worked their way up the ridge, putting in new camps every thousand feet or so. The rock-climbers were often in the lead. Even Houston had to admit that Petzoldt's pitons, however acquired, were proving their worth. Above Camp 3, at 20,700 feet, Petzoldt surmounted a vertical pinnacle by way of an overhanging crack, thereafter known as Petzoldt's Gendarme. Above Camp 4, at 21,500 feet, the climbers were stymied by a 150-foot rock buttress, until House led the way up a chimney that became one of the most famous features of that route on K2 and, inevitably, came to be known as House's Chimney.

By July 18, Houston and Petzoldt were approaching the famous Black Pyramid that caps Abruzzi Ridge. "This was to be the crux of the climb," Houston later wrote, "for, ever since our first examination of it, we felt that the last thousand feet leading onto the great snow shoulder was by far the most difficult and inaccessible stretch of all." On July 19, thanks in part to the Petzoldt pitons, the two men shook hands on the 25,000-foot snowfields of K2's southeast shoulder. They were standing 5,000 feet higher than the Duke of the Abruzzi had twenty-nine years before them. But the summit was still more than 3,000 feet above them.[83]

If they turned back at that point, they could still take satisfaction in having accomplished their stated objective: a reconnaissance to find a suitable route for the Wiessner-led expedition the following summer. But that night they held another council of war and decided that after ferrying supplies to a still higher camp, somewhere above 25,300 feet or so, Bates, House, and Sherpa Pasang Kikuli would descend to a lower camp while Houston and Petzoldt would spend the night, rise early, and see how far up the mountain they could go. Houston was more cautious than Petzoldt as to their prospects to achieve much more than a still-higher reconnaissance—but he wasn't ruling out reaching the summit either.

Charlie Houston at the high point of the 1938 K2 expedition.

And then something unexpected happened—one of those little things that can mean the difference between success and failure, and even life and death, in mountaineering. As Houston and Petzoldt settled into their high camp on the evening of July 20, prior to the next day's climbing, Petzoldt prepared to light their stove to melt snow. But he discovered that they had not carried any matches with them. Without matches they would have no water, and without water they could not climb. Houston scrounged nine fugitive matches of dubious quality from his pockets, and with the third one he managed to light the stove. Three more matches failed the next day before they could brew their morning tea. It would have to be their last day of climbing. Petzoldt was still going strong, but Houston was suffering from the effects of altitude, forced to a gasping rest every five or six steps. Finally, at 26,000 feet, at the base of the summit cone, he could go no farther. Petzoldt carried on a short way up the gulley that led to the summit but then reluctantly gave up. "We weren't turned back by bad weather," he later reflected bitterly. "We made up our mind not to climb the mountain."[84]

Houston saw it differently:

Bound by the standards and practice of that time, and very tired from five hard weeks of exploration and load-carrying, we were right to turn back. Others, years later, pushed the envelope further; some did great and heroic deeds, others died, needlessly, victims to ambition and the mind-numbing effects of great altitude. We lived to climb again, for many years. In true mountaineering, the summit is not everything.[85]

There still remained the possibility that another party, this time with matches, could make a bid for the summit, but the weather thickened, and they were tired, and so by July 25, all the climbers had descended to base camp, and soon after they set off for home.[86]

As usual, on returning from a Himalayan expedition, the first thing the climbers who had cut their teeth climbing in Alaska would do was write to their mentor Brad Washburn. "K2 is a magnificent but dangerous mt.," Bates wrote to Washburn on September 22, 1938, heading home on board the ocean liner *Bremen*:

I think we had more than our share of good breaks on it, but if we had not been forced to spend half our time in reconnaissance we probably would have climbed it. Bill House & I established Charley & Paul Petzoldt at Camp VII at 24,500 & from there they reached 26,000 next day. We didn't have enough food to take the chance of going on so we had to go back. Bad weather was coming in & a storm would probably have marooned us for there was very difficult rock work below. However we found the route that eventually will be used to climb the mt. The 2 routes we had considered most likely when we left New York turned out to be impossible.

Our crowd was a strong one, Petzoldt being the best man in the party (this strictly between you & me). It was a more dangerous mt. than most of the others considered it—at least that is my opinion—

but I believe our route may safely be followed to the top if adequate precautions are made.[87]

As it turned out, Bates and Houston were not yet done with that magnificent and dangerous mountain.

K2, 1939

If Fritz Wiessner, rather than Charlie Houston, had reached 26,000 feet on K2 in 1938 in the company of Paul Petzoldt, it is certain that the two men would have made a bid for the summit—and entirely possible that they would have achieved it. Many years later, in an interview with a climbing magazine, Wiessner stated flatly in regards to his own expedition to the mountain in 1939: "If I had had Petzoldt on our trip there would have been little doubt as to the outcome."[88]

Wiessner was a bolder and stronger climber than Houston, and not bound by the American standards and practice of the era. And if he could have reassembled the 1938 Houston team for his 1939 expedition, it also seems likely he would have reached K2's summit. But instead, he led a far weaker team. A number of the country's most experienced mountaineers refused to sign on to Wiessner's party, including Bill House, who had made the first ascent of British Columbia's Waddington with Wiessner in 1936, and on K2 had done the critical work of putting a route through his eponymous chimney.[89] Regardless of the comparative climbing abilities of the two men, other American climbers preferred Houston's relaxed and democratic leadership; Wiessner's style was well known for being domineering and autocratic (although off the mountain he was courteous and even generous in personal relations).

Wiessner's team consisted of six Americans, himself included (his citizenship papers arrived shortly before the expedition's departure), and a British liaison officer, Lieutenant George "Joe" Trench. Trench, in turn, recruited nine Sherpas for the expedition, five of whom had been with Houston on K2 the previous year, including the expedition sirdar (Sherpa leader), Pasang Kikuli.

The American climbing contingent included Chappel Cranmer, a Colorado-born Dartmouth undergraduate who had climbed with Wiessner in the Canadian Rockies in 1938; George Sheldon, another Dartmouth undergraduate with some limited experience in the Tetons; Tony Cromwell, a middle-aged New Yorker with a lengthy climbing résumé but no intent of going high on the mountain; and Jack Durrance, founder of the Dartmouth Mountaineering Club, who, with Paul Petzoldt and Petzoldt's brother Eldon, had put the first route up the north face of the Tetons in 1936 (distinct from the North Ridge route that Underhill and Fryxell had established five years earlier). Apart from Wiessner, Durrance was the strongest climber in the group. Finally, there was Dudley Francis Wolfe, myopic, middle-aged, and ungraceful. Wiessner would later say, a little oddly, of Wolfe's inclusion on the expedition: "He was not an elegant climber, but on the big peaks it isn't really necessary to have top-notch technicians unless you expect some difficult stuff."[90] K2, of course, abounded in "difficult stuff."

Wolfe had a taste for outdoor adventure but no particular aptitude for climbing; he was invited along largely because of a family fortune that helped subsidize the expedition. If he had not been involved in an attempted first ascent of the world's second-highest mountain, it would not be completely inaccurate to think of him as the first client to pay for the privilege of being led up a Himalayan peak. Some evidence suggests that that is precisely how he thought of himself. Wolfe's family worried that he was unqualified for the risky venture. To reassure his older brother Clifford, he described his relationship with the expedition's leader as akin to that he had enjoyed with European guides in the Swiss Alps:

> On this expedition there will be no professional guides, but Wiessner is as good as the best guides and will have the complete planning of the climb. As he nearly reached the top of Nanga Parbat and has had much other experience, I feel that he will be most conservative.[91]

The 1939 K2 expedition was the weakest Himalayan expedition ever sponsored by the American Alpine Club. Wiessner was taking a gaggle of the too young, the too old, and the too inexperienced to the world's second-highest mountain. The strengths of the leader, and the near miss on K2 the previous year by the Houston expedition, may have blinded the club to the expedition's shortcomings.[92]

The Second American Karakoram Expedition set out in the spring of 1939, retracing the route of its predecessor and arriving at base camp on May 31. "Will this be the crowning achievement of my climbing career?" Wiessner asked himself in his diary.[93]

He set off the following day with Tony Cromwell and Sherpa sirdar Pasang Kikuli to take a look at the northeast ridge (en route to India, Wiessner had stopped off in Genoa, where he had met Vittorio Sella, who, drawing on thirty-year-old memories, had recommended the northeast ridge).[94] While they were away, things began going wrong in base camp. Chappel Cranmer fell ill, vomiting and defecating uncontrollably, and coughing up pints of frothy liquid from his lungs, with Jack Durrance, who had aspirations to be a physician, doing what he could to save him. The crisis passed, but a convalescent Cranmer, whom Wiessner regarded as his "best man," would do no more climbing.[95]

On June 5, having satisfied himself that Houston had been right about Abruzzi Ridge, Wiessner led his climbers up the route—more than three weeks earlier in the year than the Houston party had begun its own attempt, which could have proved a tremendous advantage. For a little over two weeks, things went reasonably well, but then a blizzard pinned the party down in their tents for eight straight days. By the time the storm lifted, George Sheldon, who had been stuck at the highest camp throughout, was suffering from frostbitten feet, so he could no longer climb. A third of the expedition was incapacitated, and they had yet to reach the Houston party's high point.

Among the remaining American climbers, surprisingly, Wiessner chose Wolfe as his climbing partner. "Partner" is perhaps the wrong word; as Wolfe had suggested in the letter to his brother, theirs was more akin to the relationship of a client to a guide. Wiessner, as usual, insisted on leading every pitch. On July 1, Wolfe followed Wiessner's lead through House's Chimney to Camp 5. Wolfe remained at the camp while Wiessner and Pasang Kikuli climbed to 23,400 feet, just below the Black Pyramid, to establish Camp 6. As Sheldon described their strategy in a subsequent article for the *Saturday Evening Post*:

> Our plan was to establish a series of camps up to within striking distance of the summit. Each of those camps would be stocked with tents, sleeping bags, petrol, and a two week supply of food, in case a storm should maroon a party. The camps were to be near enough together to permit constant contact.[96]

However, unlike most Himalayan siege operations, on Everest, K2, and elsewhere, Wiessner never surrendered the lead. That meant he rarely descended from the highest camp on the mountain. As expedition leader, he lost touch with the state of the other climbers' health and morale. "Constant contact" was the last thing that characterized this expedition's progress.

On July 9, Wiessner made one of his rare descents to lower camps. He left Wolfe sitting at Camp 5, where he had now been for over a week. Arriving at Camp 2, Wiessner was visibly annoyed at finding Durrance and Cromwell doing nothing. So he spurred them and the expedition Sherpas up the mountain, ferrying supplies that he had assumed were already in place in the higher camps.

For every step forward, there was another step back. Having reached Camp 4 with a load of supplies, Cromwell decided he had gone high enough on the mountain, and he descended to base camp, never to return. The American climbing contingent was now reduced to half strength, with only Durrance, Wiessner, and Wolfe remaining.

Durrance and Wiessner climbed to Camp 5, where they re-joined Dudley Wolfe. The three Americans now moved up together to Camp 6. Durrance clearly saw Wolfe's limitations and rightly feared for his welfare. "It is unfair to take a man along . . . just because he was able to finance the undertaking," he confided to his diary, "and also dangerous if conditions hit him just right when he is dependent on his own resources."[97] Suffering from altitude sickness, as well as disenchantment, Durrance descended again on July 13. Wiessner, Wolfe, and three Sherpas kept heading upward.

What followed was a breakdown in communication among the remaining climbers, plus a series of disastrous decisions. Tony Cromwell, deputy leader, already preparing his own departure for home, inexplicably sent word up to Durrance at Camp 2 to have the Sherpas strip tents and sleeping bags from Camps 2, 3, and 4. Despite his unease with the order, with climbers still high on the mountain, Durrance complied. Meanwhile, having dragged Wolfe up to Camp 8 at 25,300 feet for no good reason beyond, perhaps, feeling an obligation to give his wealthy client an even higher perch, Wiessner left him there when Wolfe proved incapable of following any farther. Wiessner pushed ahead with Sherpa Pasang Lama to get into position for a summit bid. Wolfe, the weakest of them all, was the only American to remain high on the mountainside, without a single chance to rest at a lower camp, for what had now been nearly three weeks.

From Camp 9, Wiessner considered the options above. To the right, a gulley (the conventional route today) curved beneath an icy cliff and led to the summit. It looked like the easier route, but Wiessner worried about the ice towers above collapsing (as they would in a famous 2008 climbing disaster). Instead, he chose a route up the rocks to the left, a slower but possibly safer alternative. On the morning of July 19, accompanied by Pasang Lama, he made his bid for what, if he had managed to pull it off, would have been the greatest achievement in mountaineering history. The only problem was that they did not leave their high camp until 9:00 a.m.

They climbed well and steadily together, but nine hours later, at 6:00 p.m., they were still 800 feet, possibly three or four hours below the summit. They stood higher than any men had ever stood before, except on Everest. Climbing in darkness was rarely undertaken in the early decades of Himalayan mountaineering, but Wiessner was confident that he and Pasang Lama could safely reach the summit and descend after dark. "I had been counting for an hour on an all-night climb," he recalled in a subsequent article for the *American Alpine Journal*,

> as we were both in excellent condition, the weather safe, and the nights light at that altitude. From this point on, the going was clearly easier and there would be many resting places along the S[outh] ridge.[98]

But Pasang Lama would go no farther, declaring, "No Sahib, tomorrow." Wiessner considered going on by himself but, concerned for Pasang Lama's safety, gave in. He still hoped to make another attempt after a day of rest. That attempt would be complicated by the loss of their crampons; they had been strapped to Pasang Lama's rucksack, became tangled in the rope when he was rappelling down from an overhanging rock, and were lost when he freed the rope.[99]

Unknown to the summit team, a much greater threat to their success, and even their survival, was in the making. On July 20, while Wiessner and Pasang Lama rested, one of the Sherpas climbed up from below to check on the occupants of Camp 8 (where Dudley Wolfe lay sleeping). The Sherpa stopped a few hundred feet short of the tent and called out, but he got no response from Wolfe. Not bothering to climb the remaining distance to check the tent, he decided that all three climbers above him must surely have died in an avalanche or some other disaster in the five days since they had last been seen. He knew that the sahibs below had ordered the lower camps stripped of gear already. So, on the way down to base camp, he and two other Sherpas stationed at Camp 7 decided that the proper thing to do was to strip the upper camps of sleeping bags, mattresses, and food as well. The three unaccounted-for climbers were certainly not going to need them, since they were supposedly dead.

On July 21, Wiessner and Pasang Lama made their second and final attempt to reach the summit, this time via the snow gulley, and again they fell short, largely because of the missing crampons. Wiessner still had not given up, but in order to make another attempt they would need additional supplies, so the next day they descended to Camp 8. There they found Wolfe, but not the expected supplies.

There was nothing to do but for the three of them to descend to the next camp, which was hopefully well stocked. During the descent to Camp 7, Wolfe, never very graceful and now weakened from his prolonged sojourn at high altitude, tripped and nearly pulled all three of them off the mountain before Wiessner managed to arrest their fall with his ice ax. When they got to Camp 7, all they found was an empty tent—no Sherpas, no other climbers, no food. Wolfe decided he was too weak to go any farther, and Wiessner agreed that he should stay behind with their single remaining sleeping bag, while the two stronger climbers went for help, which surely would be found at the next camp down the mountain.

But no help, no supplies, and no other people were to be found at any of the abandoned camps below. Finally, on July 24, Wiessner and Pasang Lama staggered into base camp, much to the astonishment of the remaining expedition members. A furious Wiessner accused the other Americans of sabotage and attempted murder. In the first half of the twentieth century, this was surely the expedition that had degenerated the furthest from the ideal of a brotherhood of the rope.

In the days that followed, Durrance and a party of Sherpas attempted to rescue Wolfe, while an exhausted Wiessner recuperated in base camp. One of the Sherpas became ill, and Durrance brought him back down the mountain. Finally, on July 29, three Sherpas reached Wolfe's camp and found him listless, disoriented, and covered in urine and excrement. They gave him tea and did what they could to clean him up, but he refused to descend. They went back to Camp 6, promising to return the next day. Then the weather turned bad, and they could not return on July 30.

On August 1, despite the continuing storm, Sherpas Pasang Kikuli, Pinsoo, and Kitar, set out for Camp 7, determined either to drag Wolfe down the mountain or to have him write a note to Wiessner explaining his refusal to descend. The remaining Sherpa at Camp 6, Tsering, expected to see them later that day. They never came back. Nor, of course, did Wolfe, who by that point had been above 21,500 feet for forty days, through both his own choices and the decisions of the man he thought of as a cautious guide, Fritz Wiessner. Tsering descended to base camp on August 2, bearing the bad news.

Wiessner made one last attempt to rescue the climbers above (or at least learn their fate), but heavy snow and his own continued exhaustion stymied him. The remnants of the Second American Karakoram Expedition limped away from base camp on August 9. On August 20, from Skardu, Wiessner telegraphed the bad news to Wolfe's ex-wife, Alice:

DUDLEY WITH THREE SHERPAS LOST VICINITY CAMP SEVEN ACCIDENT CAUSE UNKNOWN AS SEVERE CONDITIONS PRE-VENTED RECOVERY OF BODIES THIS SEASON STOP DEEPEST SORROW FELT BY ALL AIRMAILED COMPLETE REPORTS TODAY STOP.[100]

These were the first deaths on an American expedition to the Himalaya.

Wiessner and Cranmer wrote the usual expedition report for the *American Alpine Journal*.[101] Ordinarily, that would be the end of the story, but not this time. Although Fritz Wiessner had made many friends in the American mountaineering community in his first decade in the United States, the news from K2 was so appalling that few could be heard speaking in his defense (Robert Underhill was one of the exceptions; he blamed Jack Durrance for the disaster). Previous controversies had centered on disputed claims of first ascents or the heights of mountains climbed. This one was about life and death. It did not help that Germany had just plunged Europe into war for the second time in a generation, and natural-ized citizen or not, Wiessner's autocratic style of leadership was seen to embody the faults of his homeland.[102]

Wolfe's brother Clifford hired a lawyer to investigate. The lawyer interviewed Durrance, who said that the cause for the disaster lay in Wiessner's decision to take on Dudley Wolfe as a quasi-client, rather than expecting him to be a genuine expedition member:

I think Dudley's ambition got away with him. I don't think he should have attempted to climb it. He was always guided. He never guided a rope himself. He was always taken up—and Wiessner did it. I think it was a frightful mistake.[103]

No one was more appalled than Charlie Houston. Three years earlier he had decided that Wiessner was too Germanic to accompany a British-American expedition to the Himalaya. He had been insulted when Wiessner failed to consult him before leaving for K2, as if his experience in 1938 and opinion counted for nothing. And there was also the fact that Pasang Kikuli, who now lay dead somewhere high on K2, having given his life to rescue a sahib, had been with Houston on Nanda Devi in 1936 and K2 in 1938, and the two had become good friends.

When the American Alpine Club set up a committee of inquiry under the chairmanship of Walter Wood to look into the tragedy, Houston declined an invitation to join. The committee, which included Joel Ellis Fisher, Bill House, Terris Moore, and Bestor Robinson, generally shared Houston's critical views of Wiessner's conduct on the mountain, although its final report diplomatically faulted the "human administration" of the expedition, rather than Wiessner by name. Wiessner correctly read that as a rebuke and resigned from the AAC at the end of 1940. Meanwhile, he was visited by agents of the Federal Bureau of Investigation, supposedly for harboring pro-Nazi views—a visit apparently prompted by enemies in the AAC.[104]

When the Council of the American Alpine Club met on May 18, 1940, to discuss the committee of inquiry's report on the K2 disaster, the newspaper headlines chronicled the German advance on Paris, the British retreat to Dunkirk, and British prime minister Winston Churchill's recent defiance of the Nazis in his "blood, sweat, and tears" speech. By that point, the question of who was responsible for Dudley Wolfe's death seemed trivial in comparison. After a brief discussion of the report, it was put aside, and the AAC voted to send a message of sympathy to the Alpine Club in London, a city that would soon come under air attack. Mountaineers everywhere were turning their attention to the greater hazards of war.[105]

THE SECOND WORLD WAR AND AMERICAN MOUNTAINEERING

Among the casualties of the German blitzkrieg in the spring of 1940 was Major Norman Streatfeild of the Bengal Mountain Artillery, serving with the British Expeditionary Force in France in 1940, killed at Dunkirk. Two years earlier he had served as the liaison officer to the American K2 expedition. The *Alpine Journal* in London asked Charlie Houston to write an obituary, which he did, and he noted in passing: "In America at peace are many whose hearts are with their friends abroad."[106] By 1941, when the obituary appeared, the American Alpine Club had donated two ambulances to the British war effort. Isolationism was not a popular sentiment in the traditionally Anglophile circles of American mountaineering.[107]

In the waning months of American neutrality in the fall of 1941, James Ramsey Ullman published a book entitled *High Conquest: The Story of Mountaineering*. His was the first attempt at a comprehensive history of the subject by an American author (although oddly including little about American mountaineering outside of Alaska). Ullman himself had climbed the Matterhorn as a Princeton undergraduate in the 1920s, but he was by no means an accomplished mountaineer (he was accepted as a member of the American Alpine Club largely on the basis of his publications). He was, however, a good storyteller and, above all, a mountaineering romantic. "The history of mountaineering," he wrote in his introduction, "is not merely a story of the conquest of mountains, but of the conquest of fear. It is not merely the record of stirring deeds, but of a great adventure of the human spirit."[108]

The book became a surprise best seller, given how few Americans actually climbed mountains in those prewar years. As a review in the *American Alpine Journal* noted: "Mountaineering in the United States is in the development stage; there can be little doubt that the wide circulation of Mr. Ullman's book will speed the process."[109]

In fact, for a whole generation of boys coming of age during the Second World War and its immediate aftermath, *High Conquest* proved the standard introductory text to the sport, offering an idealized vision of the fellowship and sense of individual achievement that those who climbed could attain. Future Yosemite climber Royal Robbins read it at age fifteen:

> I first came upon the book . . . in the Los Angeles Public Library searching the shelves for books on mountain climbing. I had been introduced to the sport/craft/way of life on a Boy Scout trip to the High Sierra. I was quite taken by climbing and wanted to learn more about it. Ullman's book intrigued, so I checked it out, took it home, and got lost in it. It's basically a history of mountaineering, but its most salient point is that the "high conquest" of the title is not truly getting to the top of the highest peaks; it's the conquest of those weak and timid parts of ourselves we don't want running the show. . . . I know I had my share, and the idea of using mountain climbing to rise above them was very appealing.[110]

Ullman viewed the history of mountaineering in part through the prism of recent international developments. British climbers in his book were invariably noble, plucky, and brave; their German counterparts, fanatics. Looking back at the Himalayan expeditions of the 1930s, Ullman saw the present world conflict foreshadowed on the slopes of Nanga Parbat, littered as it was with the dead of unsuccessful German efforts, such as the 1934 expedition that had cost the lives of ten men:

> The Germans were engaged in all-or-nothing assaults. They were after victory, and nothing else mattered. And while feeling sorrow for the brave individuals who lost their lives, one cannot but feel that collectively they met the fate that they deserved. Blind, mindless force is no more the key to the conquest of a great mountain than to the conquest of the world.[111]

To most Americans, mountaineering had always seemed an eccentric avocation without any particularly useful application. But World War II would begin to change that attitude. Mountaineering skills would be a grim necessity in places where Americans would soon see combat.

Climbing in the Swiss Alps in 1939, in the last days of peace, Bob Bates and Ad Carter had seen Swiss mountain troops on maneuvers and had been impressed by their prowess. The Germans understood the value of such units, and the Wehrmacht included a dozen specially trained mountain divisions. Bates and Carter lobbied both US secretary of war Henry Stimson (an enthusiastic climber and honorary member of the American Alpine Club), and US Army chief of staff George C. Marshall on the need for mountain troops. Bates and Carter's efforts, and those of others, including Brad Washburn and Charles Minot Dole (president of the National Ski Patrol), paid off with the creation of the Eighty-Seventh Mountain Infantry Battalion shortly before Pearl Harbor. That battalion, later expanded to regimental strength, became the core of what in 1943 was renamed the Tenth Mountain Division.

By 1942–43, mountain division recruits, including many members of the Sierra Club and other mountaineering organizations, were training at Camp Hale, near Leadville, Colorado, at 9,000 feet in the Rockies.[112] Among their number was Paul Petzoldt, who arrived at the camp in 1943 as an army private and was promptly set to work scrubbing floors. On his second day there, a medical officer recognized him, promoted him to sergeant, put him in charge of three squads, and gave him a task more suited to his talents: devising rescue techniques to bring wounded soldiers down from mountains.[113] Joe Stettner also served as an instructor at Camp Hale, along with what he called the "international brigade," composed of émigré and refugee Germans, Swiss, Austrians, Swedes, Italians, and Norwegians.[114]

All those hours the Sierra Club's Rock Climbing Section had spent practicing on the Cragmont and Tahquitz cliffs now paid off in an unexpected way. In 1943, Dave Brower and Raffi Bedayn were sent to train soldiers in assault climbing at Seneca Rocks, which rises above the Potomac River in West Virginia. Some of the pitons the trainees pounded into the steep faces of the formation are still being found by local climbers, with one section known as the "Face of a Thousand Pitons." The RCS was on the march.[115]

Not every American mountaineer who put on a uniform in those years served with the Tenth Mountain Division. Charlie Houston, posted as a naval flight surgeon in Pensacola, Florida, helped train pilots to recognize the symptoms of oxygen deprivation (vital knowledge to the survival of airmen as well as mountaineers). Farnie Loomis, Houston's expedition mate on Nanda Devi, served with the American intelligence agency (the Office of Strategic Services) behind Japanese lines in China. The Sierra Club's Dick Leonard tested climbing ropes for the army early in the war, and later he served behind enemy lines in Burma, winning a Bronze Star.[116]

Some who were too old to enlist found other ways to serve. The army needed an instructional manual for its new mountain troops, so Kenneth Henderson wrote one, entitled *Handbook of American Mountaineering* and published in 1942 by the American Alpine Club. The first such work by an American author, it replaced Geoffrey Winthrop Young's *Mountain Craft* as the go-to instructional book for aspiring mountaineers in the United States in the years following the war. It incorporated the advances in climbing made by Sierra Club climbers in the 1930s, including the dynamic belay technique.[117]

Veterans of Alaskan and Himalayan mountaineering expeditions played an important role in equipping the mountain troops. Starting in 1941, Brad Washburn, Bob Bates, Bill House, and Terris Moore served as civilian advisers to the War Department to oversee the development of cold-weather clothing and equipment. Following Pearl Harbor, Bates enlisted in the army and served in the Quartermaster Corps, ending the war with the rank of lieutenant colonel.[118]

In the summer of 1942, Bates, Washburn, Moore, and other climbers were directed to spend a month on Mount McKinley testing cold-weather gear for the US Army. Whether the army came up with the idea of sending them to the mountain on its own, or was persuaded by its climber-consultants to do so, was a matter of dispute among the participants in later years.[119] In any case, at a time when most civilian travel was circumscribed and little climbing was going on in Alaska or anywhere else, they were not unhappy to receive the assignment.

They set up camp at an altitude of 18,000 feet on the Harper Glacier, and evaluated everything from sleeping bags to lip balm. When Washburn and Einar Nilsson (a Swedish-born electrical engineer and Sierra Club member) climbed above Denali Pass to retrieve some supplies that had been dropped by parachute and gone astray, Washburn looked to his west. There, he looked carefully at the mountain's West Buttress and was inspired to write in his expedition diary, "I'm sure the mountain will be climbed this way some day."[120]

At the end of their assignment, on July 22, Washburn, Bates, Moore, and Nilsson were given permission to take a day off and make the third ascent of Denali—the first time it had been climbed in a decade. Three more climbers followed them up the mountain the next day for the fourth ascent. On a subsequent visit to Washington, DC, Washburn had an audience in the White House with President Franklin D. Roosevelt and presented him with a rock from Denali's summit.[121]

Some of the innovations introduced during wartime by the army Quartermaster Corps would have long-range implications for postwar mountaineering. Army scientists and mountaineers experimented with a new synthetic fiber known as nylon, deciding it would be ideal for the production of climbing rope for mountain troops, less likely to break or rot, stronger when wet or knotted than the traditional hemp ropes. And, because of the stretch and flexibility of nylon rope, less likely to break the ribs of a soldier tied onto the rope, in the event of a fall. Bates tested one of the new ropes in 1942 by tying off one end in his Washington office and rappelling out the window, to the surprise of the secretaries on lower floors, who saw him bouncing down the side of the building past their windows.[122]

Another innovation of lasting significance was a new kind of outdoor footwear. In 1939, Italian climber Vitale Bramani developed a cleated rubber soul for climbing boots that he called, after himself, Vibram. The new soles gripped better on slippery surfaces than the traditional

Tenth Mountain Division soldiers, members of the Eighty-Sixth Regiment, Company F, pause on Riva Ridge in Italy, in February 1945.

hobnailed boots, and in addition had no metal inserts to conduct cold to the climber's foot inside. Bates and Carter had seen Swiss troops using the boots in 1939, and Carter tracked down a pair owned by a New Hampshire climber. By 1943, soldiers in the Tenth Mountain Division were being issued knockoff copies of Bramani's boots (although, in a typical wartime snafu, the boots were not shipped overseas in 1944 when the division was deployed). American soldiers were also equipped with newly designed ice axes, pitons, piton hammers, tents, and sleeping bags.[123]

Allied armies landed on the Italian mainland in September 1943, and for the next year, until the capture of Rome at the start of June 1944, they struggled against fierce German defenses strung along the country's rugged interior hills, like Monte Cassino. More mountains loomed to the north. Army planners decided that was where the Tenth Mountain Division could do the most good. At the end of 1944 and the beginning of 1945, the division shipped out for the Italian front.

In one of the most famous of the unit's subsequent battles, the capture of Mount Belvedere in the beginning of March 1945, Joe Stettner's brother and climbing partner, Private First Class Paul Stettner, won a Silver Star for gallantry. Andreas Hennig, who had climbed the north wall of Mount Shuksan in 1939 with Otto Trott, received a Bronze Star for rescuing a wounded comrade while under heavy fire. And Captain Raffi Bedayn won a Bronze Star for leading a reconnaissance mission behind enemy lines. The Stettners, Hennig, and Bedayn survived the war, but many of their comrades did not. In heavy fighting in the winter and spring of 1945 in the north Apennine Mountains and the Po valley, nearly a quarter of the men in the division were killed or wounded. Theirs was truly a brotherhood of the rope.[124]

Some mountaineers, among them the Sierra Club's rock-climbing elite, enjoyed the luxury of alpine climbing while not under fire, courtesy of the Tenth Mountain Division. Raffi Bedayn attempted the Matterhorn from the Italian side, but he didn't make it to the summit, because of bad weather. He did summit Mont Blanc, making the 11,000-foot ascent from Courmayeur in a single day. His friend David Brower had an even better summer in 1945. Yosemite climbing partner Morgan Harris (on the faculty of the University of California at Berkeley as professor of zoology at the time) wrote Brower in August 1945 to thank him for his "good letter about the climbing in Europe," an excursion apparently including a stint in the French Alps:

> I'm glad you got the well-earned chance to see a little of that famous country as long as you had to be over there. From your description of the Charmoz Grepon traverse, it apparently lives up to the boast. The familiar pitches sound even more intriguing when related from first-hand experience. It will be interesting to get your impressions of the Alps as compared to Western mountains.[125]

With the war over, the soldier-climbers came home and returned to civilian pursuits—including climbing. The greatest generation of veterans would lead the major mountaineering organizations for the next three decades, a time of enormous increase in the popularity of climbing.

Before being deployed to Burma, Major Richard Leonard met a Washington, DC, climber and research engineer named Arnold Wexler. Wexler was employed by the National Bureau of Standards to test ropes for the army at the rock cliffs of Carderock, Maryland. Wexler, Leonard, and scientist and climber Sterling Hendricks (who had been on Denali with Brad Washburn in 1942), experimented with the dynamic belay theory, using ropes to toss and catch a 150-pound dummy known as "Oscar." Drawing upon the prewar experiments at Cragmont in Berkeley, and the wartime experiments at Carderock, Leonard and Wexler collaborated in 1946 on an article for the *Sierra Club Bulletin* intended to instruct climbers in proper belay procedures.[126]

The resulting article, reprinted as a pamphlet the following year, proved very influential with the next generation. It was a highly technical, even scholarly work, illustrated with charts and graphs and festooned with footnotes, with its main point the importance of employing a dynamic rather than a static belay in the event of a leader fall, reducing the "kinetic energy" of a sharp, sudden check.[127]

The wartime development and postwar availability of the nylon rope, with its improved strength and natural tendency to stretch when pulled taut (say, by a falling body), would soon make both the hemp rope and the dynamic belay obsolete. What remained relevant in the Leonard-Wexler article was the philosophy it embodied. They repudiated once and for all the conservative Geoffrey Winthrop Young doctrine that the "leader must not fall" and called for a "new approach":

The fatalistic doctrine that "a fall from above cannot be held" was unacceptable; it was not logical to tie the members of a party together with a climbing rope unless each knew, from experience, the most effective means of using that rope in any fall, a leader's included.[128]

Climbing was thus a partnership, not a hierarchy—a point of view that opened up a vast new realm of possibilities. A lead climber was a better climber and could be a bolder climber with the knowledge that a skilled and watchful belayer stood below him. Thus protected, he could extend himself and take risks that would have seemed unimaginable to earlier generations. The leader could fall, recover, and lead again. This was an optimistic and idealistic way of thinking about the possibilities of climbing, repudiating a "fatalistic" belief in limits, and fully consistent with the way Americans were feeling about themselves, their society, and their future in the aftermath of victory in the Second World War. Thanks both to new techniques and new attitudes, a dazzling and daring period was about to open for climbers in the United States.

CHAPTER SIX

RUCKSACK REVOLUTION, 1945-1963

There are no rappel points, Jim, absolutely no rappel points. There's nothing to secure a rope to. So it's up and over for us today.

—WILLI UNSOELD, SPEAKING VIA WALKIE-TALKIE
FROM HIGH ON THE WEST RIDGE OF MOUNT
EVEREST TO JIM WHITTAKER AT BASE CAMP,
AFTERNOON OF MAY 22, 1963

More than just a climbing area, it is a way of life.

—YVON CHOUINARD, "MODERN YOSEMITE
CLIMBING," *AMERICAN ALPINE JOURNAL*, 1963

To be committed in the common sense of the term suggests dedication. In the language of climbing, "committed" takes on additional meaning. It refers to a route up a mountain or a move on a rock face from which there is no retreat; a safe descent being impossible, "up and over" becomes the only option. To be committed that way is to accept risk; as Charlie Houston put it, climbers seek "the thrill of danger—but danger controlled by skill."[1]

In the second half of the twentieth century, American climbers were more committed than ever, in both senses of the term. For increasing numbers of Americans, climbing became a way of life—not without risk, but rich in satisfaction.

The notion of the brotherhood of the rope, strengthened by war-time celebration of self-sacrifice and collective endeavor, lived on in climbing circles in the decade or so following the Second World War. That spirit was particularly evident in the Himalayan mountaineering expeditions undertaken between 1953 and 1963. At the same time, a new spirit of competitiveness, bordering on a kind of hyperindividual-ism, was visible in the late 1950s and early 1960s in rock-climbing centers like Yosemite Valley. Both impulses, however contradictory, were examples of commitment deeply rooted in the larger American culture.

Nineteen sixty-three proved a high point in climbing achievement, and also a turning point in the history of American climbing. In the years that followed, climbing became a mass-participation activity. But what American climbing gained in popularity after 1963, it lost in cohesion and community.

COMING HOME

With the end of the war, the veterans returned from Europe and the Pacific. Climbers among them were eager to get back to the hills, fol-lowing a long absence (the last Sierra Club RCS excursion to Yosemite took place over Labor Day weekend 1942). Wartime gasoline rationing (4 gallons a week for most civilian vehicles) came to an end in August 1945; the first civilian cars manufactured since 1942 rolled off assem-bly lines in Detroit in October 1945. The roads to Yosemite—as well as Conway, New Hampshire; Jackson, Wyoming; and Government Camp, Oregon—were soon crowded. The university climbing clubs revived, and new ones started, their ranks filled in those first postwar years with veterans pursuing higher degrees on the GI Bill (the Stanford Alpine Club was founded in 1946 by three veterans—Al Baxter, Fritz Lippmann, and Larry Taylor; Taylor, the club's first president and a veteran of the 101st Airborne Division, came up with the SAC motto: "No Guts, No Glory").[2]

The regional outdoors clubs, back in business after the wartime hiatus, resumed their summer encampments. In the summer of 1946, eighty members of the Seattle Mountaineers, joined by twenty Mazamas, three Sierrans, and three Appies, headed for Mount Rainier. Sierran Louise Werner reported on the mass climb that was the traditional culminating moment of such gatherings. One feature of such climbs, both before and after the war, was the close collaboration between the clubs and the rule-enforcing park authorities:

> On the day the climbers leave camp, they are served a special hot meal at noon and pack enough squirrel food (dried fruit, nuts, rye crisp, cheese, sandwiches and candy), for a snack that night and two meals the next day. The Park Ranger is on hand to check equipment which must include: nailed boots, ice-axe, crampons, ropes, extra woolen wraps, flash-light, first aid, dark glasses, face grease, wool mittens, water- and wind-resistant parka and hood, sleeping bag and food.[3]

If there was much that was familiar in such rituals, there was also something new. That first summer after the war, much of the equipment that was being inspected by park rangers and employed on Rainier and other peaks was made in America. Sporthaus Schuster in Munich had survived the war but no longer enjoyed its internationally commanding role in the mountain gear market. In the United States, the "Age of Army Surplus" arrived.

A young Tenth Mountain Division veteran, Dick Emerson, wrote fellow veteran Dave Brower in March 1946 with a business proposition:

> There is something I would like your opinion on. If I could purchase a supply of ropes, pitons, piton hammers, snap links [carabiners], Bramoni sol[e]d mountain boots, etc., do you think there might be enough people willing to buy to make it worth while? Maybe

advertising to mountain clubs in the country. I have been told that all this equipment is being stored at the war[e]house in Ogden [Utah]. They are starting to sell much of their equipment now, but I don't know how soon the mountain stuff will be released. I can get my permits to buy it now and be all ready to grab it when it comes. What do you think? Would the Sier[r]a Club Rock Section be interested in some nylon ropes?[4]

Brower had no doubt there would be eager customers for Emerson's army surplus goods among Sierra Club members and others, writing back the very day he received the letter. "If you can get nylons [ropes], double time up there. Watch out for the pitons (as if you wouldn't)."[5]

An outdoor equipment and clothing retail infrastructure, more enduring than the ubiquitous postwar army surplus outlets, began to take form in those same years, catering to an expanding customer base with specialized tastes and disposable income. A Seattle-based cooperative, Recreational Equipment Cooperative (later changing its name to Recreational Equipment Incorporated, or REI), founded in 1938 with a few dozen members eager to acquire the latest European mountaineering gear, opened a retail outlet at 523 Pike Street in downtown Seattle in 1944. The cooperative launched its first mail-order catalogue (eight pages long) in 1948.

Another Seattle sporting goods operation, Eddie Bauer, had vastly expanded during the war through the sale of cold-weather gear (including sleeping bags and newly designed quilted down jackets) to the military. It now made its products available to civilian outdoors enthusiasts. When Charlie Houston returned to K2 in 1953 in a new attempt to reach its summit, all members were equipped in Bauer down jackets.[6]

A Tenth Mountain Division veteran named Gerry Cunningham opened a mountain equipment business in Utica, New York, in 1945, with a mail-order catalogue of climbing gear featuring rucksacks and climbing packs of his own design. The following year he relocated to Colorado, where Gerry Mountaineering became an institution, opening its first retail outlet in Boulder in 1958, and branching out into clothing, climbing gear, and tents (Edmund Hillary and Tenzing Norgay slept in a two-man Gerry tent the night before they reached the summit of Mount Everest in 1953).[7]

Before the war, climbing apparel was generally chosen for functionality, but it was by no means uniform (Kenneth Henderson, Robert Underhill's climbing partner, famously tackled difficult rock routes attired in business suit, necktie, fedora, and a pair of leather golf shoes). There was also a vogue in club circles for dressing like extras in the Shirley Temple musical *Heidi*: patterned sweaters, knickers, and kneesocks.

After the war, a new sartorial standard emerged, starting with the ubiquitous felt wool alpine hats of the era, adorned with club pins and badges. Many dressed in drab army surplus for their mountain outings, but rolled denim and flannel outfits were also common. Mountainclimbers could buy Vibram-soled army surplus climbing boots for five dollars a pair, which soon replaced the traditional hobnailed boots.

Only in rock-climbing footwear did the old reliance on foreign sources persist. Rock-climbers generally wore American-made sneakers, but some acquired stiffer-soled suede leather *Kletterschuhe* or rubber-soled canvas climbing shoes called "PAs" (for their designer, French climber Pierre Allain), both imported from Europe.

CHANGING OF THE GUARD

Despite Dave Brower's desire to secure a nylon rope and a collection of pitons from Dick Emerson, his own climbing days were drawing to a close, as were those of a number of leading figures in the prewar Rock Climbing Section of the Sierra Club. In the 1930s, Brower made sixteen first ascents in Yosemite Valley; no one matched that record until the late 1950s. But he racked up no more first ascents after the war, because his interests shifted to environmental activism.

Brower's personal trajectory reflected that of the Sierra Club organizationally, as it grew over the next several decades from a regional outdoor recreation group to the nation's preeminent voice for wilderness preservation. In 1950 the Sierra Club had just under seven thousand members, organized into six regional clubs in California. That year, a group of expatriate Californians in New York established an "Atlantic chapter" of the club. Twenty years later there were tens of thousands of members in chapters across the country.[8]

Brower had much to do with the Sierra Club's phenomenal postwar growth. In 1946 he chaired the club's editorial board, and in 1952 he was appointed its first executive director. Other RCS veterans joined him in leadership positions. Bestor Robinson, conqueror of Higher Cathedral Spire in 1934, was elected Sierra Club president in 1946, succeeded (after a few years' gap) by Dick Leonard, coconqueror of the spire, in 1953. The third man on that famous climb, Jules Eichorn, was elected to the club's board of directors in 1961.

As Yosemite climbing historian Joseph Taylor notes, in the late 1940s and early 1950s, the "'old guard' of RCS" became "the 'Young Turks' of the SC board."[9] (That didn't mean harmony always prevailed. In 1969, Dick Leonard spearheaded the organizational revolt that led to the ejection of his old climbing partner, Dave Brower, as the club's executive director, in a confrontation over policy and personality differences.)[10]

ARMCHAIR MOUNTAINEERING IN POSTWAR POPULAR CULTURE

In the immediate postwar era, mountaineering remained a sport practiced by a select few, if not quite as few as before the war. But popular interest in mountaineering, at least as measured by the sale of mountaineering books, grew more quickly than the ranks of climbers. The term "armchair mountaineer," of early-twentieth-century coinage in Britain, appeared for the first time in American publications.[11]

In 1945, James Ramsey Ullman, author of *High Conquest*, published his second best-selling mountaineering book, this time a novel entitled *The White Tower*, about the wartime climb of a Swiss peak by a downed American pilot and a German officer on leave. It sold a half million copies, mostly to readers who had never climbed a mountain. Experienced climbers tended to be a little sniffy about the novel, since Ullman's command of mountain terminology, such as "bergschrund," proved spotty. Whatever its deficiencies in that regard, *The White Tower* nudged some readers, like California's Warren Harding, into the climbing life.[12]

Noting the success of Ullman's novel, *Life* magazine ran its first ever cover story about mountaineering in December 1945, including a six-page photo essay entitled "'The White Tower's' Author Shows How to Master a Strenuous Sport," with Ullman posing on Mount Washington's Tuckerman Ravine.[13]

Another milestone in armchair mountaineering came with the publication of the first American edition of Maurice Herzog's *Annapurna* in early 1953, the French climber's best-selling book about the first ascent of an 8,000-meter peak in the Himalaya. *Annapurna* was the first account of a mountaineering expedition to win a wide readership in the United States, and it was reviewed favorably by Ullman in the *New York Times*.[14]

Ullman frequently received letters from his armchair-mountaineering fans. One such came from Alfred B. Fitt of Grosse Pointe, Michigan, in 1953. "Some months ago," Fitt wrote,

> my wife and I read "Annapurna." That started us on a binge of reading about high climbers, and one of the books we ran across was yours about the Mt. Everest expeditions. We got to know the North Col, the first and second steps, the slabs below the ridge; we agonized and theorized over Mallory and Irvine and the ice axe found in 1933 (neither of us think they made it to the top), and in general we got about as excited about the world's highest mountain as it is possible for people who will never see the Himalayas.[15]

Fitt signed off with an interesting question: "What is there about mountain climbing that grips even a suburban couple in their 30's ensconced in the middle west of the United States?"

The Fitts' self-identification as a "suburban couple" placed them at the forefront of the postwar American social transformation. Hailed as the fulfillment of the American dream, combining, as widely supposed, the independence of home ownership with the pastoral values of small-town life close to nature, the new suburban frontier would, in time, breed its own malaise—in particular, a sense of being cut off from real life.

What was it about mountain-climbing that gripped Mr. and Mrs. Fitt, as well as increasing numbers of Americans, in the years that followed? The authenticity of the experience (whether assimilated directly or vicariously), the element of risk and the unpredictable, the mastery of technique, the sense of commitment to the endeavor—all surely factor into the answer.

JOHN SALATHÉ AND THE REINVENTION OF YOSEMITE CLIMBING

Why, Yosemite climber and historian Steve Roper asked himself some years later, "did we spend so much time in the Valley?" The answer, he suggested, was "rebellion":

> Many of us regarded the 1950s and 1960s as a time when the world—and especially our country—had lost its way. We saw materialism and complacence during the Eisenhower years. . . . Perhaps we stayed close to the cliffs because we didn't want to join mainstream society. We Valley cragrats of the sixties were mostly college dropouts going nowhere, fast. . . . These same rebellious eccentrics, however, were the most gifted rockclimbers in the world.[16]

But before Roper's generation came to dominate the climbing scene in Yosemite, another gifted eccentric blazed the path for them. His name was John Salathé.

In the fall of 1945, Fritz Lippmann and Robin Hansen, both of them Sierra Club RCS members and Army Air Force veterans, had recently returned to the Bay Area. On an RCS outing to Eagle's Nest on Hunter's Hill in the Bay Area, they were joined by a forty-six-year-old novice climber from nearby San Mateo. Lippmann and Hansen roped the newcomer, John Salathé, between them, so that they could keep an eye on him and provide a belay as necessary. Hansen recounted what happened next:

> The most difficult pitch of the Eagle's Nest is a traverse secured by pitons 100 feet above the base of the rock. . . . I led the pitch and John was out of sight to both of us. After securing my belay position I called for John to climb and emphasized that he should "climb freely." This was our way of saying that neither the rope nor the pitons should be used for assistance. I felt no activity on the rope for two or three minutes, and suddenly John appeared around the corner *unroped*! He thought I had meant to climb free of the rope. Height had no meaning to John and to him fear was a stranger.[17]

John Salathé spent the first thirty years of his life in a center of alpine activity—from which he remained aloof. He was born near Basel, Switzerland, in 1899. A practical man, he was not interested in mountains, but instead was interested in iron and steel. He became a blacksmith. In 1929 he emigrated to the United States, settling in San Mateo, California, where he opened a blacksmith shop, the Peninsula Wrought Iron Works. Then a personal crisis arose. At the end of World War II, beset by health and marital problems, and undergoing what seems to have been a religious revelation, Salathé decided that an outdoor activity (plus a fruit diet) was the key to restoring his physical, mental, and spiritual well-being. And that led him to the newly revived Rock Climbing Section of the Sierra Club.

The climbing blacksmith soon graduated from the middle of the rope to leading climbs in Yosemite, such as Higher Cathedral Spire. On one of those climbs, on a route that others had pioneered, Salathé was dissatisfied with the soft-iron pitons he carried for protection. The European-style pitons then in general use had been designed for climbing on limestone, the kind of rock predominating in the eastern Alps. When hammered into a limestone crack, a soft-iron piton would, as designed, warp to fill in the irregularities in limestone cracks. Once in place, it would usually be left behind because, bent out of shape, it could not be reused. That meant, for a multipitch rock wall, starting off carrying a large number of pitons. Worse, hammered into the hard granite of Yosemite cracks, soft-iron pitons would often buckle before they could be securely placed—a characteristic that made them both wasteful and dangerous.

Spying a blade of grass growing out of a tiny crack in the Yosemite granite, Salathé had a revelation of immense practical significance: inside the crack, he realized, there was room to hold a piton securely, if only he had a piton capable of withstanding a hammer's blow without bending. That meant creating a piton forged from hard steel. After it was driven deep into a crack, the piton's holding power came from retaining its shape and pressing against the fissure's side, spring-like, rather than buckling to fill the available space.

Harder pitons had the added advantage that they could be retrieved by the second climber on the rope, who would clean the pitch and pass them back to the lead climber. That meant climbers needed to carry fewer pitons as they made their way up a multipitch rock face, while making more extensive use of the few they carried. And, since the emerging climbing ethics of the 1950s and thereafter favored leaving a route as close as possible to its original condition, being able to remove pitons served that end as well.

Salathé fashioned his new piton out of high-strength carbon steel alloy (in some versions of the story, taken from the rear axle of a Model A Ford). Over the next decade his pitons, which came in a variety of sizes all marked with a "P" (for Peninsula Wrought Iron Works), became highly coveted among Sierra Club climbers. Making use of his new pitons, in the course of the next four years Salathé made a contribution to American climbing technique every bit as consequential as those achieved in the prewar years by Robert Underhill and Fritz Wiessner.[18]

Three of Salathé's Yosemite climbs stand out: the first ascent of the southwest face of Half Dome in 1946, the first true ascent of Lost Arrow Spire in 1947, and the first ascent of the north face of Sentinel Rock in 1950. Thereafter, Salathé drifted away from climbing and ever deeper into mysticism, though he remained a respected elder in Yosemite climbing circles well into the 1960s.

Taken together, Salathé's three great climbs ushered in what came to be called the "golden age of Yosemite climbing," from the late 1940s to the early 1970s.[19] They were all examples of what was starting to be called "big-wall climbing"—exposed multipitch climbs of rock faces a thousand feet high or more, and, at least at first, taking more than a single day to accomplish.[20] To succeed on a big wall, as Salathé recognized, would require a far greater reliance on hammering in pitons, or drilling holes for expansion bolts, not just for protection but for direct aid—in marked contrast to techniques that prewar Sierra Club climbers, as innovative as they were, had been prepared to accept as proper and ethical.[21]

Salathé's hard steel pitons had their first serious test on the southwest face of Yosemite's Half Dome. Half Dome had known its first ascent in 1875 when George C. Anderson drilled and hammered his way up the formation's northeast shoulder. But no new routes had been put up by climbers in the seven decades that followed, although Dick Leonard had twice attempted the southwest face before the war without success.

Salathé and frequent climbing partner Anton (Ax) Nelson spent two days in November 1946 hammering a route up a crack on the unscaled face, involving 900 feet of roped climbing all told, placing 150 pitons for direct aid and protection, and spending a night on a ledge below the summit—the first such bivouac on a very technical route, and one without good ledges, in Yosemite. It was a relatively easy climb, compared to what was to come, but still a remarkable achievement, not least because of Salathé's age and the fact that he had been climbing for little over a year.[22]

Lost Arrow Spire is a rock pillar adjacent to Upper Yosemite Fall, detaching from the canyon wall below the rim surrounding Yosemite Valley. The spire tops out at a height of 6,930 feet, roughly the same height as the rim but separated from it by a 125-foot-wide chasm. Dick Leonard and Dave Brower, pushing the standard of the possible, had made the first attempt to climb it in 1937, ascending from the base. On a subsequent attempt in 1941, Brower looked at the summit of the pillar, which is all of

6 feet square, and considered that vertiginous platform "the one place I'd want most not to be."[23]

In August 1946, several months before his ascent of Half Dome, Salathé went to look at Lost Arrow Spire and perhaps do a little exploring of the climbing possibilities. He had planned to meet two friends on the canyon rim across from the spire, but they failed to show up. Undaunted, he rappelled down the 250 feet from the rim to the notch where the spire detaches from the wall. From there he began to work his way out onto a ledge that led to the east side of the spire, protected by a rope tied to a boulder in the notch—an act of radical unorthodoxy in California climbing circles, since neither solo climbing nor self-belay were on the Sierra Club's list of safe-climbing rules.

Salathé's climbing partner Anton Nelson likened Salathé's action to "stepping out of a window from the hundredth floor of the Empire State Building onto a window ledge."[24] The valley floor was 1,400 feet below Salathé's exposed perch, a sheer drop should anything go wrong. He worked his way up two crack systems on the pillar's outer face, until he reached a ledge (thereafter Salathé Ledge) 75 feet above the notch. But by then it was late afternoon, and after building a rock cairn to mark his high point, he turned back.[25]

Salathé returned the following week, this time with a partner, John Thune, with whom he gained another 80 feet up the spire, leaving 50 more feet to go. But the cracks ran out, and without them Salathé's pitons were useless.

Before Salathé could return, four Bay Area acquaintances—Fritz Lippmann, Robin Hansen, Jack Arnold, and Anton Nelson—decided they would make their own attempt on Lost Arrow Spire. Up on the canyon rim, where they stood facing the spire, they fixed the end of a light, weighted rope, and then spent the better part of a day trying to throw it over the Lost Arrow summit so that its other end would dangle down to Salathé Ledge. After repeated misses, they finally succeeded.

The next morning, Nelson and Arnold set out from the notch, hoping to reach the rope above them. With only soft-iron pitons, their progress was slow, and it wasn't until the second day, September 2, Labor Day, that they reached the ledge and the rope dangling from the summit. With that in hand, and with the aid of their compatriots on the canyon rim, they could pull another fixed rope, this one heavier and nylon, over the summit and down to the ledge. And then, using Prusik knots, now part of the standard repertoire of Yosemite climbers, they worked their way up the rope to the summit, with Arnold the first to stand on top at 4:00 p.m. Rather than returning the way they came, they made a spectacular Tyrolean traverse (crossing the abyss between rim and spire on a fixed rope, gripped with hands and feet).[26]

Nelson evoked the band-of-brothers spirit of wartime America in explaining the motives driving the conquerors of Lost Arrow Spire: "The three days of unforgettable adventure have forged a comradeship like that of a bomber crew coming through the perils of war."[27] Perhaps in making that comparison, Nelson was thinking of Fritz Lippmann, who had piloted bombers during the war, and Robin Hansen, who had piloted a P-38 fighter. Combat experience might have produced a greater acceptance of risk among the climbing veterans than had been the case with the prewar Sierrans.[28]

"We Climbed the Impossible Peak," the headline proclaimed above Lippmann's subsequent account of the climb in the *Saturday Evening Post*, the point being that there no longer was such a thing as an impossible peak.[29] However, whether the Lost Arrow effort amounted to a legitimate first ascent or was just a clever rope stunt remained a matter of dispute in climbing circles.[30]

What is more commonly accepted as the legitimate first ascent of Lost Arrow Spire took place a year later, in September 1947. Salathé was back, this time accompanied by Anton Nelson, his partner on Half Dome, and one of the four who had been on top of the spire the year before. The two men climbed from the spire's base up the 1,200-foot Lost Arrow chimney, reaching the notch after four days of effort, carrying a minimum of food (mostly dried fruit, Salathé's preferred diet in any case) and only enough water for each to drink about a quart a day until they reached the notch, where more water was lowered to them from supporters above on the rim. (Today, the recommendation is that climbers on big-wall climbs in

Yosemite carry a daily ration of at least a gallon of water per climber, or over 8 pounds of water per climber, per day.)[31]

No prewar Yosemite climb had ever lasted more than a single day. This kind of multiday rock-climbing, continuing without a break, dependent on what two men could haul up with them for supplies, required a willingness to suffer discomfort, as well as a high level of technical proficiency. As Nelson wrote in his account for the *Sierra Club Bulletin*: "Bivouacking on the chockstones, with our feet dangling, our backs aching where they were being nudged by granite knobs, and our shoulders tugging at their anchors, we got little sleep. . . . Food, sleep, and water can be dispensed with to a degree not appreciated until one is in a position where little can be had."[32]

They persevered, reaching the Salathé Ledge on the fifth day, and continuing above that to the last 50 feet where the cracks ran out. It took eight expansion bolts to surmount the last section and reach the summit, parched but fulfilled. They had completed the hardest rock climb achieved to that date in the United States.[33]

Salathé's third and last great climb came in 1950, although it was undertaken at another climber's initiative. Allen Steck decided he wanted to attempt Sentinel Rock, a 7,038-foot peak across the valley floor from Yosemite Falls. Steck was part of the new generation of RCS climbers, a protégé of David Brower and Dick Leonard. He joined the group while attending UC Berkeley on the GI Bill, after navy service in World War II. (In later life he would be coeditor of *Ascent* magazine, coauthor of *Fifty Classic Climbs in North America*, as well as cofounder of the trekking company Mountain Travel, today Mountain Travel Sobek).[34]

From the valley floor, a likely route ran up Sentinel Rock along a crack system beside a buttress that reached two-thirds of the way up the cliff. Beyond that, however, was a headwall without visible cracks, and above that a dark and inscrutable chimney leading to the summit. Steck had made several unsuccessful attempts on Sentinel Rock in the late 1940s. In May 1950, two other climbers—Bill Long and Phil Bettler—reached the top of the Flying Buttress (as it was called), but were stymied by the headwall.

Steck was scheduled to leave in midsummer for an expedition to Mount Waddington, and he feared that the prize would be snatched before his return. So with the July Fourth holiday coming up, and in the absence of any of his usual climbing partners, the twenty-four-year-old Steck called fifty-one-year-old Salathé, who readily agreed to join him in tackling the Sentinel.

The two climbers may have been separated by decades in age, but they worked together as an effective team—Steck the better free climber of the two; Salathé, the better aid climber. There was plenty of both free and aid climbing on the route. Two days brought them to the top of the buttress. Another hard day's work led them across the headwall and into the chimney. It was hot and they were thirsty; they carried only 2 gallons of water, and as they rationed their supply out over the days, they lost interest in the food they were carrying, most of which they abandoned en route.

The interior of the chimney now revealed a new obstacle, sufficiently daunting that there would have been no disgrace if they had turned back then and there. The chimney was sealed at the top by an overhanging rock; they were in a climbing cul-de-sac. But the next day, Salathé's brilliant placement of his superior pitons solved the problem, enabling him to reach the edge of the overhang and surmount it. The way to the summit was open, although they would not reach it until noon of the fifth day of their ascent.

"Ordeal by Piton," Steck famously called it in an article for *Appalachia* magazine. The "supreme climax" of the climb for him, he reported, came not atop the Sentinel, but later that day when he jumped, fully clothed, into a pool of water at the foot of a small waterfall. Salathé and Steck established a new model for big-wall climbing in Yosemite.[35] More than just a report on a difficult climb, "Ordeal by Piton" was a manifesto for direct-aid climbing:

Many have questioned the quality of this sort of achievement, deploring the use of pitons, tension traverses, and expansion bolts, but the record speaks for itself. This is a technical age and climbers will continue in the future to look for new routes. There is nothing more satisfying than being a pioneer.[36]

Others would soon follow in the path that Steck and Salathé had pioneered.

WASHBURN RETURNS TO DENALI

While John Salathé and his climbing partners were reinventing Yosemite climbing, Brad Washburn was turning to unfinished business in Alaska: finding a way to the summit of Denali via its West Buttress.

He would get his first postwar chance to return to the mountain, though not to its western approach, thanks to James Ramsey Ullman and *The White Tower*. RKO Pictures optioned Ullman's novel when it became a best seller in 1945, eventually releasing it as a feature film in 1950.[37] As a prerelease publicity stunt, someone at the studio came up with the idea of sponsoring an expedition to climb Mount Everest. Cameramen could accompany the climbers to the summit, and the resulting documentary would make a great lead-in, the publicist figured, to the eventual release of *The White Tower*.

Brad Washburn was approached and asked if he would like to lead the effort. He pointed out that neither Tibet nor Nepal was allowing expeditions to Everest, but he suggested a Denali expedition as an alternative. The studio agreed and, in the words of Washburn's biographer, David Roberts, "the most extravagant boondoggle of Brad's mountaineering career" was launched.[38]

And so, in late March 1947, Washburn, accompanied by a crew of climbers who included wife Barbara, set off for Denali, to climb the mountain by the now-traditional northeast route of Muldrow Glacier to Karstens Ridge to Harper Glacier. The strong team of climbers included George Browne, son of Denali pioneer Belmore Browne. With the studio paying the bills, Washburn and his compatriots were kept well supplied by airplanes landing on the Muldrow, and a dog team that ferried sleds to an altitude of 10,000 feet. They were thus possibly the only Denali climbers ever to enjoy frozen strawberries and fresh peaches for dessert.

On June 6 they reached the summit. The following day they returned to climb the North Summit, the first time since the Sourdough Expedition of 1910 that anyone had stood there. Operation White Tower, as the expedition was dubbed by the studio's publicity department, thus accomplished the first dual summit ascent of Denali, while Barbara Washburn became the first woman ever to reach (or for that matter attempt) either peak. As for her husband, he became the first person to climb the mountain twice. In terms of the future of Alaskan climbing, the most important result of Operation White Tower was that Washburn got another look at the West Buttress. He made up his mind that, in the event of a return trip, that would be the route he would take to the summit.[39]

Washburn was not the only climber interested in putting up a route from the west on Denali. Henry Buchtel, a Denver urologist and president of the Colorado Mountain Club, took the initiative in the fall of 1950 in organizing an expedition to attempt the West Buttress the following year. Buchtel's first recruit was a precocious eighteen-year-old undergraduate from the University of Cincinnati named Barry Bishop, who had spent childhood summers in Estes Park with his family, joining the Colorado Mountain Club by the age of ten, where he had been tutored in mountaineering skills by veterans of the Tenth Mountain Division.[40] Buchtel and Bishop were joined by three Denver climbers: John Ambler, Melvin Griffiths, and Jerry More.

As a courtesy to the climber whose name had so often been linked with Denali in the past, Buchtel wrote to Washburn to let him know his plans. Washburn wrote back and essentially invited himself along on the expedition. Buchtel graciously consented, and Washburn, along with Bill Hackett and Jim Gale, both of whom had reached the summit of Denali in 1947, were added to the expedition roster. The celebrity from Boston, of course, was soon in effective command. The expedition would be sponsored jointly by the Boston Museum of Science, the University of Denver, and the University of Alaska.[41]

In mid-June 1951, Washburn, Gale, Buchtel, and Hackett were flown in to Kahiltna Glacier, west of the mountain, by Terris Moore, veteran of Mount Fairweather and Minya Konka. Since his climbing days, Moore had become president of the University of Alaska and also a skilled pilot. Moore had designed a hydraulic ski wheel for his Piper 125 Super Cub, a two-seat monoplane favored by bush pilots, allowing for takeoffs and landings from either runway or glacier.

On June 20, encamped at 7,650 feet on the upper Kahiltna Glacier, Washburn wrote exultantly in his journal:

> This camp & these landings mark the first time in history that anyone has ever set foot in this stupendous amphitheatre of the upper Kahiltna & seen the terrific 10,000-foot western cliffs of [Denali] at close hand. And they are some sight, towering 13,000 feet above this camp in only 6 miles to our northeast. To the west towers 17,000-foot Mt. Foraker & to the southeast is the fantastic icy spire of Mt. Hunter (14,500 ft. high).[42]

In decades to come, Kahiltna Glacier became the staging area for many of the most daring climbs in the region, including ascents of Mounts Foraker and Hunter.[43]

Washburn's team began survey work for a project to map the mountain, in the course of which they made the first ascent of 12,411-foot Kahiltna Dome west of Denali. They also gathered supplies air-dropped to them by an air force C-47. The rest of the team approached the mountain in more traditional fashion, with a packtrain of horses carrying their supplies via the Peters Glacier. En route, Moore and Bishop made the first ascent of 10,571-foot Peters Dome, northwest of Denali. The overland party crossed Kahiltna Pass, the col connecting Kahiltna and Peters Glaciers, on June 30, joining Washburn's team at base camp, at 10,000 feet, at the head of the Kahiltna Glacier.[44]

Three days later, Bishop wrote home to his parents in Cincinnati from base camp, outlining the plan for the ascent of the mountain, and conveying his excitement at the prospects that lay before him:

> The route to the top of Mt. McKinley looks good. We will occupy a camp at 13,000 feet at base of buttress as soon as possible. An

emergency igloo at 14,000 feet in that little cirque will be built. Another camp at 17,000 feet on top of West Buttress will follow. Then Denali Pass and the top! . . .

As for me, my lips, tongue, ears and nose are sunburned. I have lost no weight, I guess, but I have gotten solid. I never have worked physically so hard continuously in my life . . .

The silence up here is ethereal—broken only by the boom of avalanches. It's wonderful. The party as a whole can't be beaten, and I am having a wonderful time with them and am learning a great deal—a lot that can't be learned except by living with other men.[45]

Washburn, Hackett, and Gale took the lead in pushing the route, establishing their first camp at 13,000 feet, on a shoulder where the glacier ran into the West Buttress. They called it Windy Corner, for reasons easily imaginable. Two additional camps went in, at 15,500 feet and at 17,200 feet (at the latter camp they built an igloo, which they found snugger than any tent). From there, on July 10, Washburn, Gale, and Hackett set off for the summit, which they reached at 5:30 that afternoon.

Apart from altitude, the route involved "no great difficulties," as Washburn explained to readers in *American Alpine Journal*, and included some distinct advantages over the previous path to the summit, including a more direct exposure to the sun. "And last but not least," he concluded, "the prevailing westerly winds are always behind your back as you climb instead of cutting squarely into your face."[46] With this climb, Washburn became the first to reach Denali's summit three times.[47]

They stayed forty-five minutes before descending. "We hated to leave," Washburn reported:

The view was marvelous: Mount Hayes, the Coast Range, Mount Marcus Baker, Mount Spurr, Mount Foraker—all cloudless; Lake Minchumina like a jewel on the plains; the hills beyond Anchorage and the grey haze over Cook Inlet; the deep green lowlands of the Clearwater; Wonder Lake; the Tokositna; the Yentna and the Skwentna; then those endless lowlands stretching off to the westward, river after river sparkling in the sun and twisting and winding off into the distance.[48]

Over the next few days, the rest of the expedition summited and returned safely. The West Buttress route thereafter became the standard route on Denali. In the 1950s, a few climbers would climb that route each year. By the early twenty-first century, that number had grown to five hundred or more climbers annually.[49]

RETURN TO THE HIMALAYA, 1950–1960

With the end of the Second World War, Himalayan mountaineers hoped to return to the region. Brad Washburn's protégés Charlie Houston and Bob Bates had both served in the military during the war, and upon discharge they immediately began planning a new expedition to K2. But turmoil in India and Pakistan following independence and partition put the mountains off-limits in the late 1940s.

Another event with profound implications for Himalayan mountaineering was the Communist triumph in China in 1949, followed by the seizure of Tibet the next year. No more Western expeditions could approach Mount Everest from the north. However, fearing it might share Tibet's fate, the "hermit kingdom" of Nepal threw open its borders in 1950 to foreigners for the first time, which is how Maurice Herzog's expedition found itself climbing the central Nepalese peak of Annapurna in June of that year.

Four months later, in November, another foreign expedition crossed into Nepal, this one consisting mostly of Americans and headed for Mount Everest, intent on the first reconnaissance of Mount Everest from the south. Charlie Houston, veteran of Nanda Devi in 1936 and K2 in 1938, was its leader; and Bill Tilman, who had reached the summit of Nanda Devi in 1936, was a last-minute recruit.[50]

The party's five members were the first westerners ever to explore the Solu-Khumbu region of Nepal, home of the Sherpa people, and the gateway to the southern side of Everest. They visited Namche Bazaar, the largest community in the region, and Tengboche Monastery. While their companions remained behind as guests at Tengboche, Houston and Tilman continued alone up the Khumbu Glacier to the very foot of Everest.

Tilman knew from the British Everest expeditions of the 1930s that the approach to the mountain from the north was relatively easy; serious climbing difficulties started higher on the mountain, above the North Col. From the south, in contrast, as Tilman and Houston immediately understood, the approach itself was fraught with danger. As the Khumbu Glacier descended southward off the mountain, it was forced through a narrow chute between Everest and neighboring Nuptse, resulting in a gigantic chaotic icefall.

Tilman and Houston were appalled at the prospect of climbers threading a route upward through that jumbled mass of ice towers, blocks, debris, and crevasses to reach the enclosed valley of the Western Cwm that lay 2,000 feet above. Standing at the foot of the Khumbu Icefall, Houston concluded that while it probably "could be forced," it certainly did not offer mountaineers "a very attractive route of access" to Everest.[51]

Houston and Tilman had time for only a two-day reconnaissance. Before they departed, they wanted to see what lay beyond the icefall. And so, on November 18, their last day below the mountain, the two men started up 18,450-foot Kala Pattar, a peak offering a view across the Khumbu Glacier of the Everest-Lhotse-Nuptse massif. Tilman, who had spent the previous few months tramping around the Annapurna region, reaching a height of over 22,000 feet, was well acclimated, but Houston, who only three weeks earlier had left New York, was not. As a result, with Houston lagging, they halted about 300 vertical feet below Kala Pattar's summit.

They could see a terribly steep ridge dropping from the summit, which they surmised must end up on the South Col. They could not see the col itself, because it was blocked from view by a shoulder of Nuptse, as was the lower face of Lhotse. The ridge that they could see leading to the summit did not seem promising.

Their limited view led them to a misconception. The ridge visible

Houston-Tilman Everest reconnaissance party, 1950. From left to right: Anderson Bakewell, Oscar Houston, Betsy Cowles, Bill Tilman, and Charlie Houston.

to them from Kala Pattar was not linked to the South Col at all. It was Everest's Southwest Ridge, which connected to a buttress (later named the South Pillar) that fell steeply and directly to the Western Cwm. What they could not see from where they stood was that farther to the east lay another ridge, Everest's Southeast Ridge, the ridge that actually connected to the South Col, and one that was, at least relatively, less steep and forbidding. Had they been able to climb the additional 300 feet to Kala Pattar's summit, they would have found a broader vista opening up to them, in which the true nature of the route to Everest's summit would have been apparent.[52]

In a report featured on the front page of the *New York Times*, Houston and Tilman concluded that climbing Everest from its Nepalese side "may well be impossible." They "could see no practicable climbing route."[53]

They were certainly right about the dangers of the Khumbu Icefall, which claimed many lives in the decades to come. But they were quickly proved wrong about the lack of a practicable climbing route to the summit. A British reconnaissance in 1951 identified the Southeast Ridge as the likely route to the summit, and a Swiss expedition in 1952 followed it to within a few hundred vertical feet of that goal. And on May 29, 1953, on a subsequent British expedition, New Zealander Edmund Hillary and Sherpa Tenzing Norgay surveyed the world from the vantage point of the top of the world's highest mountain.[54]

By the time Tenzing and Hillary reached Everest's summit, another Charlie Houston–led expedition was en route to the Himalaya, this time heading for Pakistan rather than Nepal. Its goal was K2.[55]

Official permission for the expedition, which Houston and Robert Bates had sought ever since 1946, was long in coming from the government of Pakistan. It did not arrive until 1952, too late to launch an expedition that year. So the expedition was put off until the following year. Houston and Bates used the interval to interview forty candidates before they decided on the five who would join them, all of whom were younger climbers just beginning to make names for themselves: George Bell, Bob Craig, Art Gilkey, Dee Molenaar, and Pete Schoening.

Despite their youth, they were a strong group: Dee Molenaar had been in the party that made the second ascent of Mount Saint Elias in Alaska in 1946, Bob Craig had made first ascents in the Alaska Coast Range in 1946 and had climbed Denali with Brad Washburn in 1947, George Bell had organized the expedition that made the first ascent of 21,769-foot Yerupajá in Peru in 1950, and Pete Schoening had led a group from the Seattle Mountaineers to make the first ascent of 14,070-foot Mount Augusta, in the Saint Elias Mountains on the border of Alaska and the Canadian Yukon in 1952. Art Gilkey, a PhD candidate in geology at Columbia University, had worked as a guide in the Tetons and had been on mountaineering expeditions in Alaska. None had previous Himalayan experience.[56]

Apart from climbing credentials, Houston and Bates looked for people who could get along; what they didn't want, they later wrote, was "the brilliant climber who thinks only in terms of personal success" (a swipe at Fritz Wiessner).[57] British army captain Tony Streather served as expedition transportation officer, but he functioned on the mountain as part of the climbing team. The expedition was larger than the 1938 party but considerably smaller than the one assembled to climb Everest that year, which numbered fourteen British and Commonwealth members (including a reporter and film cameraman) and thirty-six Sherpas.

Sherpas, as Buddhists, were not allowed in newly independent and Muslim Pakistan in 1953, so the Americans would rely on local and less skilled Hunza tribesmen, who would carry supplies up to only about 20,000 feet on K2. And unlike the Everest party (and indeed most expeditions to 8,000-meter peaks in the 1950s and 1960s), the Americans carried no bottled oxygen with them. Houston's expeditionary ideal, showing the continuing influence of Bill Tilman, was to keep things simple. And nonhierarchical. Their Pakistani liaison officer, Colonel Mohammad Ata-Ullah, noted that Houston was "determined never to be anything more than the first among equals."[58]

News of the British (or New Zealand–Sherpa) triumph on Everest reached the Americans in Pakistan. Houston wrote to his father from a campsite en route to K2: "I think we are secretly a little disappointed to have the British make Everest before we could make our peak." Still, he reported, "We have high hopes and a good party."[59]

Their hopes seemed vindicated by their initial progress. On June 19 they established base camp at 16,250 feet. By early July they had passed through the obstacle of House's Chimney, well remembered from 1938, and established Camp 5 at 22,000 feet. In a letter written on July 18, intended for friends and supporters back in the United States, Houston predicted a summit bid sometime between August 1 and 3.

On July 31, Schoening and Gilkey led the way to what was intended as the expedition's next-to-last campsite, Camp 8, at 25,300 feet, about 500 feet above the top of the Black Pyramid, a pyramid-shaped rock buttress that required careful maneuvering on its steep icy cliffs. They were soon joined at their high camp by the other five American climbers, plus Tony Streather. They hoped for two consecutive days of good weather—one to put in an additional camp at about 27,000 feet, and the next for the summit bid. Three days of consecutive good weather would allow two parties to reach the summit.

But the good weather was at an end. Snow began to fall on August 1 and continued until August 7. Had the climbers retreated to a lower camp at the start of the storm, they might have weathered it in relative comfort and avoided the physical deterioration of a prolonged stay at high altitude. But in 1953, even experienced mountaineers had yet to understand some of the basics of altitude sickness. As Molenaar recalled: "We thought that by [staying] up we were acclimatizing," when in fact he and his companions were "getting weaker and not thinking as clearly as we should."[60]

On August 7 the weather improved slightly. Leaving his tent to stretch his legs, Gilkey immediately collapsed. Houston was horrified to discover that Gilkey was suffering from thrombophlebitis, a clotting of the veins in his left leg, potentially fatal. Gilkey would have to be evacuated to base camp, 9,000 feet below. That meant descending technically challenging obstacles like the Black Pyramid and House's Chimney with an incapacitated man in tow. Houston kept his worries to himself, but he believed the effort was doomed. Still, they had to try. They set out at 10:00 that morning, Gilkey wrapped in his sleeping bag and the remains of a wrecked tent, with ropes attached to lower and slide him down. But the two feet of powder snow they encountered below their camp was unstable, and they were forced to retreat, lest they trigger an avalanche.

For three days they waited in vain for improved conditions. Houston could hear in Gilkey's cough that blood clots were settling in his lungs. He began to wonder whether any of the party would get off the mountain alive. Finally, on the morning of August 10, Houston decided they could wait no longer. Gilkey was again wrapped in tent and sleeping bag and alternately towed and lowered down the mountain by his comrades. Progress was slow, and they triggered a mini-avalanche that nearly carried away Craig and Gilkey. By midafternoon it was clear to the retreating climbers that they had no chance of reaching Camp 6 at 23,300 feet that day. They would need to traverse to their left across an icy slope to reach the tiny platform that was Camp 7, a thousand feet higher.

At about 3:00 p.m. the climbers were arrayed across the slope to the west of Camp 7, with Gilkey belayed from above by Schoening. Another rope ran from Gilkey to Molenaar. They had just succeeded in lowering

Gilkey over the edge of a rock cliff when Bell lost his footing. That set up a chain reaction of falling men. Bell was roped to Streather, who was pulled off his feet. Streather's rope became entangled with a rope linking Houston and Bates to Gilkey (and above to Schoening). The four falling men snagged the rope linking Molenaar and Gilkey. Molenaar started sliding. Craig was the only expedition member who was not roped to others, and it seemed for a moment that all seven of his companions—Bell, Streather, Houston, Bates, Molenaar, Gilkey, and Schoening—would momentarily be pulled off into space, tumbling thousands of feet to the Godwin-Austen Glacier below.

What happened next earned Schoening's ice ax an honored place in the American Alpine Club's museum. Before the calamity began, Schoening had taken the precaution of jamming the ax into the snow behind a small boulder, wrapping the rope that attached him to Gilkey around it, and then around his waist. When the others began to fall, he instantly put all his weight on the ax. The nylon rope stretched and tightened—but it held. Schoening saved the lives of six men, and likely his own, in the instinctive act thereafter known in mountaineering circles as "The Belay."

They were not out of danger. There were cracked ribs, gashed legs, frozen hands (Bell lost his mittens in the fall). Houston suffered a concussion. They needed to take shelter and, gathering their wits and scattered equipment, edged their way over to the Camp 7 site to set up the two tents they had brought with them from Camp 8. For the moment, they left Gilkey wrapped in his sleeping bag, anchored to the slope in a gulley about 150 feet west of the campsite.

They managed to set up their tents. But when Bates, Craig, and Streather returned to check on their injured teammate, they saw to their horror that the gulley was empty. Gilkey, ropes, and ice-ax anchors had all apparently been swept away by avalanche (unless, as some believed, Gilkey had released himself in an act of self-sacrifice, knowing he could not be saved and was only putting the others' lives at risk).

It took five more days for the battered survivors to reach base camp. After they had time to recover, they built a 10-foot-high cairn to honor the twenty-seven-year-old Gilkey's memory. It still stands and has accumulated a large collection of plaques and tin plates stamped with the names of other climbers who have since died on K2.

Although the group failed to reach the summit, the attempt to save Gilkey's life, and the struggle for survival that followed, distinguished the 1953 K2 expedition. Charlie Houston summed up the highest ideals of the midcentury American expeditionary culture when he said of his K2 comrades, "We entered the mountain as strangers, but we left as brothers."[61]

Two other significant American expeditions were undertaken in the Himalaya over the next few years, both organized by Nick Clinch, a recent graduate of Stanford Law School, where he had been a member of the Stanford Alpine Club. The first, launched in 1958, tackled 26,469-foot (or 8,068-meter) Gasherbrum I, better known as Hidden Peak, in the Karakoram range. It is the eleventh-highest mountain in the world and was one of three mountains over 8,000 meters still unclimbed that year.

Clinch recruited Andy Kauffman, past president of the Harvard Mountaineering Club, and a foreign service officer stationed at the American embassy in Paris, for the expedition. Another recruit was K2 veteran Pete Schoening. They were joined by Tom McCormick, Bob Swift, Tom Nevison, Gil Roberts, and Dick Irvin, drawn mostly from the Stanford Alpine Club and the Sierra Club Rock Climbing Section. Two Pakistani climbers also joined the expedition.

They established base camp on June 6 at 17,000 feet on the Abruzzi Glacier, to the southwest of the mountain. They chose a route up a ridgeline that they called the Roch Arête, named for French climber André Roch, who had attempted the mountain by that route in 1934 (it is now known as the IHE Ridge, or International Himalayan Expedition Ridge). Using supplementary oxygen (the first American expedition to the Himalaya to do so), they made swift progress up a long but not technically challenging route.

By July 4, their high camp at 23,500 feet was in place, and at 3:00 the next morning, the summit team of Kauffman and Schoening set off. Ten hours of plodding brought them to the top, where, for the traditional victory photo, they displayed the flags of Switzerland, Britain, France, Pakistan, and the United Nations, as well as the Stars and Stripes, to emphasize that Himalayan mountaineering was an international enterprise to which many nations had contributed. An 8,000-meter peak had been climbed for the first time by Americans, in record time, in exemplary style, and safely.[62]

Not that anyone in the United States seemed to care. Americans were paying increasing attention to mountaineering exploits but curiously seemed more interested in the efforts of foreigners than those of their own mountaineers. Maurice Herzog's *Annapurna* had been a best seller, Edmund Hillary and Tenzing Norgay's ascent of Everest had made the cover of *Life* magazine, but if Herzog, Hillary, and Tenzing were now well-known names, most Americans would have been hard-pressed to name a single leading US mountaineer such as Houston, Clinch, or Schoening. Press coverage of the ascent of Hidden Peak was limited in the *New York Times* to a couple of wire service stories on an inside page—the first understating the height of the mountain by 2,000 feet, and neither noting that this was the first (and, as it turned out, only) 8,000-meter peak whose first ascent was accomplished by an American team.[63]

Clinch's second expedition to the Karakoram was an attempt on unclimbed 25,659-foot Masherbrum, whose summit fell just below the 8,000 meters that defined the world's highest mountains but was actually a more difficult and dangerous peak than Gasherbrum I. Willi Unsoeld, a Teton guide and philosophy professor, and George Bell (another K2 veteran) achieved Masherbrum's first ascent on July 6, 1960, followed two days later by Clinch and Pakistani climber Jawad Akhter Khan. Again, few Americans noticed or cared. The *New York Times* confined its coverage to a single three-paragraph wire story on page sixty, noting in passing that a "Dr. William E. Sunsoeld [*sic*] of Corvallis, Oregon, was in the first party to reach the top."[64]

FRED BECKEY, "NOT AN EXPEDITION MAN"

No American mountaineer spent as many years climbing, or made as many first ascents, as Wolfgang Paul Heinrich Beckey, better known as

Fred Beckey, or just "Beckey"—the latter spoken by those who knew him in tones of either (sometimes both) admiration and exasperation. Like the Sierra's Norman Clyde, who in a long climbing career also put up an impressive number of first ascents, Beckey was a lone wolf: although he sometimes climbed with others, including some leading American and European mountaineers, he neither developed nor sought lasting climbing partners. Unlike Clyde, who rarely ventured from the Sierra, Beckey, in addition to dominating climbing in his home base of the North Cascades, made his mark in many other remote and challenging mountain environments of North America and elsewhere in the world.[65]

Beckey made an additional contribution to American mountaineering as the author of a collection of classic guidebooks. *A Climber's Guide to the Cascade and Olympic Mountains of Washington*, published in 1949 by the American Alpine Club, contributed to the popularity of mountaineering in the region and also helped the AAC recruit in the Pacific Northwest, previously a place where very few climbers had signed up as club members. In the 1970s Beckey reworked and expanded the original guidebook into a three-volume series, "each one," Northwest writer Timothy Egan noted in a portrait of Beckey, "revered by the cult of climbers who've followed his every handhold."[66]

Beckey was born in 1923 in Düsseldorf, Germany, and brought to the United States by his parents two years later. The family settled in Seattle, where his father practiced medicine. Fred began climbing as a teenager in Seattle in the 1930s with a Boy Scout troop, and later with the Mountaineers, instructed in mountaineering technique by Lloyd Anderson, founder of the REI coop. In 1939, at age fifteen, in company with Anderson and another climber, Beckey made the first of what eventually became hundreds of first ascents, in this case 7,296-foot Mount Despair in the North Cascades, which the cautious elders of the Mountaineers had written off as unclimbable.

The next year, at age sixteen, Beckey returned to the North Cascades, again accompanied by Anderson, as well as Beckey's younger brother Helmy and several others, and made the first ascent of 8,815-foot Forbidden Peak. Two years later the youthful Beckey brothers, climbing and skiing on their own, pulled off the second ascent of Mount Waddington, following the Wiessner-House route from 1935.[67]

Following stateside military service in the Second World War, Beckey attended the University of Washington, where he received a master's degree in business administration and found various forms of marginal employment that made it easy to take time off for climbing. Never marrying, he won a reputation in climbing circles not only for first ascents, but for his bedroom exploits. "Beware of Beckey," an admiring T-shirt warned, "He will steal your woman, steal your route."[68] He became legendary early in life, and anecdotes, reliable or not, were passed from climber to climber, among them the existence of a little black book that Beckey was supposed to carry, in which he ticked off one by one a long list of unclimbed routes still awaiting their first ascent (asked at age ninety if that was true, he denied it).[69]

In the later 1940s, Beckey began to expand his horizons beyond the North Cascades. Taking up a challenge that had defeated Fritz Wiessner, Beckey, along with Bob Craig and Cliff Schmidtke, made the first ascents in 1946 of 10,016-foot Kates Needle and 9,077-foot Devils Thumb, in the Sitkine Icecap region of the Alaska Coast Range on the border of Alaska and British Columbia.[70]

Too many first ascents followed to chronicle—in the North Cascades, Alaska, British Columbia, Wind Rivers, Tetons, and other ranges. In just two months of one particularly stellar year, Beckey pulled off a "triple crown of first ascents" in Alaska, including the first ascent of the Northwest Buttress of the North Summit of Denali, plus the first ascent of Alaska's 12,339-foot Mount Deborah and 14,573-foot Mount Hunter, the latter two completed in alpine style, one continuous push each time, in the company of German climber Henry Meybohm, and Austrian climber Heinrich Harrer (of Eiger and *Seven Years in Tibet* fame).[71]

Despite Beckey's growing celebrity and genuine achievements, a reputation for recklessness and being a bit of a curmudgeon would make him persona non grata in establishment mountaineering circles. He was the most talented climber ever to come out of the Seattle-based

Mountaineers, but the club turned down the chance to publish his 1949 climbing guide (though a quarter century later they were happy to bring out his three-volume guide to the Cascades).

Beckey was criticized for the loss of a partner who perished in a climbing accident in British Columbia in 1947, and again when another partner died in a 1952 ascent of 6,129-foot Mount Baring in the North Cascades. In 1955 he was invited on an international expedition to 27,940-foot Lhotse, organized by the Swiss-American climber Norman Dyhrenfurth. Dyhrenfurth was offered a $10,000 contribution toward the expenses of the expedition by Henry S. Hall, president of the American Alpine Club, if he included Beckey as a member. "Why is that so important?" Dyhrenfurth recalled asking Hall:

> And he said, "Well, he's such a good climber and he's never been invited on a major expedition. And I feel that he should be given the chance." I was happy to get the $10,000. But I regretted it later, because I was forced into taking somebody who is not an expedition man.[72]

On that expedition, Beckey descended from a high camp, leaving behind a snow-blind tentmate who was suffering from cerebral edema, whom other expedition members had to rescue. The exact circumstances of Beckey's actions remain obscure, and some felt he got a bad rap from Dyhrenfurth subsequently, but the fact remains that Beckey was never again invited on a high-profile expedition to the Himalaya or anywhere else.[73]

Beckey ignored his critics (and outlasted them as an active climber). In time, he became an institution in the climbing world, admired for his absolute commitment to mountaineering, and for his lack of interest in profiting off his fame, apart from the limited income he gained from writing books and giving talks. He never did product endorsements. The closest he came was in the form of a distinctly inside joke: agreeing to appear in a photograph in the 2004 catalogue of Patagonia outdoor clothing, looking like anything other than a climbing fashion model.

Corey Rich's photograph of Fred Beckey for
the 2004 Patagonia catalogue.

RUCKSACK REVOLUTION

In the course of the 1950s, a few hundred poets, novelists, artists, and their camp followers in places like Greenwich Village, San Francisco, Berkeley, and Venice, California, established a loose community of self-described outsiders. More important, they established the myth of the Beat generation. The Beats thought of themselves as a prophetic saving remnant of cultural rebels whose ideas and way of life represented a repudiation of materialism and conformism. They hewed to a vision of radical individualism, authenticity, and self-transformation.

In the decade that followed, tens of thousands of other young Americans would aspire to pursue their own version of the beatific way of life charted in such seminal works as Jack Kerouac's 1957 novel *On the Road.* Kerouac had admirers among the young climbers gathering in Yosemite

Valley in the 1950s. One of them, Royal Robbins, referred to *On the Road* as "sort of our bible at the time."[74]

Kerouac climbed his one and only serious mountain two years before the publication of his landmark novel. In October 1955, spurred on by his Berkeley-based friend, poet Gary Snyder, the two Beats journeyed to 12,285-foot Matterhorn Peak in the Sawtooth Range at the northern boundary of Yosemite National Park. Snyder was an experienced mountaineer who had joined the Mazamas climbing club as a teenager and climbed Mount Hood, Mount Adams, and Mount Saint Helens in his high school years.[75] No longer in his prime after years of hard living, Kerouac found Matterhorn Peak a challenge, quitting a hundred or so feet below the summit, while Snyder continued to the top.[76]

No matter. Kerouac may have missed the summit, but he gained some valuable material for his next novel, *The Dharma Bums*. "Dharma" has multiple meanings in Hinduism and Buddhism, among them "one's righteous duty" and "right way of living"—concerns that Kerouac wrestled with throughout his life, without ever quite resolving. His new novel met a mixed critical reception on publication in 1958 and never obtained the popularity of *On the Road* (although a number of Yosemite climbers were among its fans).

But the book did contain a prophecy, extraordinary both for the loopy brilliance of Kerouac's prose and the fact that within a few years' time something not far removed from what he foresaw actually came to pass. In words Kerouac gives to the character Japhy Ryder, a stand-in in the novel for Gary Snyder, Ryder predicts the coming of a "rucksack revolution":

> See the whole thing is a world full of rucksack wanderers, Dharma Bums refusing to subscribe to the general demand that they consume production and therefore have to work for the privilege of consuming, all that crap they didn't really want anyway such as refrigerators, TV sets, cars, at least new fancy cars . . . all of them imprisoned in a system of work, produce, consume, work, produce, consume, I see a vision of a great ruck-

sack revolution thousands or even millions of young Americans wandering around with rucksacks, going up to mountains to pray . . . .

. . . Why, do you realize the Jurassic pure granite of Sierra Nevada with the straggling high conifers of the last ice age and lakes we just saw is one of the greatest expressions on this earth, just think how truly great and wise America will be, with all this energy and exuberance and space focused into the Dharma.[77]

Kerouac was no geologist; the granite of the Sierra Nevada extends back further than the Jurassic to the Cretaceous.[78] And there is no record that he ever read the writings of John Muir. Snyder, however, had been a fan of Muir since his high school days in Seattle. In a collection of poems published in 1960, Snyder condensed and recast Muir's 1894 account of a moment of terror and transcendence on Mount Ritter in 1872 into a twenty-four-line free-verse poem that concluded:

I seemed suddenly to become possessed
Of a new sense. My trembling muscles
Became firm again, every rift and flaw in
The rock was seen as through a microscope,
My limbs moved with a positiveness and precision
With which I seemed to have
Nothing at all to do.[79]

In Snyder's reading, Muir had a Zen epiphany on Mount Ritter, in which he learned that by surrendering control, he would paradoxically regain control.[80]

In the rucksack revolution–*Dharma Bums* manifesto of 1958, Kerouac, channeling Snyder, channeling Muir, suggests the underlying continuities of the American love affair with mountains from the 1860s to the 1960s and beyond. Mountains are places of renewal and redemption, where Americans reconnect with the values of their forebears and determine whether they measure up to their exacting standards, spiritual and patriotic. "Had I been borne aloft upon wings," Muir wrote of his experience on Mount Ritter in 1872, "my deliverance could not have been more complete."[81] The "Jurassic pure granite of Sierra Nevada," Jack Kerouac wrote in 1958, was proof of "how truly great and wise America will be."[82] The rucksack revolution was about to begin.

YOSEMITE, 1953–1958

Yosemite's climbing history has a distinct generational cast. There was the Brower-Leonard generation of the 1930s, gone by the end of the Second World War, followed by the Salathé-Steck generation, gone in turn by the mid-1950s. A third generation began to find its way up the vertical-crack systems of the "Jurassic pure granite of Sierra Nevada" by the mid-1950s. Like their Beat contemporaries, those belonging to this newest generation of Yosemite climbers formed a loose community of self-described outsiders. And, like the Beats, they would establish their own myth—that of the free-living, risk-taking, committed Yosemite big-wall climber.

Their quest for self-transformation and authenticity, righteous duty and right way of living, bore considerable overlap with the Beats' beatific vision. "Climbing is an Art (or can be)," Yvon Chouinard wrote fellow Yosemite climber Steve Roper in the summer of 1964. "Therefore it is love (or can be). It is possible for climbing to be the highest form of art attainable because you can *combine* oneness with the medium (the mother rock), loss of the narcissistic 'I,' and oneness with fellow man."[83]

Theirs was a powerful and prophetic vision, if not completely original (in addition to the Beats, there were echoes in it of Thoreau, and Muir, and even Charlie Houston, who spoke of mountaineering as a way to "strip off non-essentials, to come down to the core of life itself").[84] Like the Beats, the Yosemite big-wall climbers were destined to have an outsize impact on the imagination and aspirations of the coming generation.

The Sierrans of the 1930s had been educated urbanites, mostly from middle-class backgrounds, mostly from the Bay Area, who climbed on weekends. In their weekday lives in San Francisco and Berkeley, they held to the conventional norms of their upbringing and social position, including marriage, home ownership, and professional ambition. They were also organization builders, who poured their energies into the Sierra Club. They believed in the ideal of service, including military service, rushing to the colors in the crisis of the Second World War. They believed in cooperating with duly constituted authority, such as the National Park Service, helping the NPS to devise a registration system after World War II that was designed to screen out unqualified climbers from attempting Yosemite's walls.[85]

The climbers who followed from the mid-1950s through the 1960s represented something new. They put climbing at the center of their lives, at the expense and in place of conventional careers, community, and family life. There weren't many ways to make a living as a climber in that era, except as a professional guide in a few locations like the Tetons or Mount Rainier. The new Yosemite climbers weren't professionals in that sense, but the best of them were becoming, more or less, full-time climbers.

Most were Depression babies. Too young to have served in World War II, they came of age in the prosperity of postwar America but stood at odds with what they felt was its crass materialism and smug self-satisfaction. A number of them wound up serving in the military in the late 1950s and early 1960s, but only after exhausting all efforts to avoid the draft. Some, like Steve Roper, were from middle-class backgrounds (Roper's father was a chemist whose boss at Shell Oil was none other than 1930s Sierra Club/RCS stalwart Hervey Voge), but more commonly they were from working-class backgrounds.

Many were from southern California, rather than the Bay Area. They were often very bright but not, by and large, academically inclined. And whatever their pedigree and training, few seemed to harbor the middle-class aspirations of their Sierra Club predecessors. They also had little use for what they regarded as meddling authorities, whether from the National Park Service or the Sierra Club.

There were no budding Dave Browers in their ranks. Organizations didn't inspire their affections or loyalties. Their "club," as it took form in the later 1950s, required no dues but rather was measured by length of residence in a National Park Service campground located in the northern end of Yosemite Valley directly across the Merced River from Sentinel Rock, a dusty field dotted with pines and cedars and boulders officially known as Camp 4.[86]

In 1955, a climber named Mark Powell became the first long-term resident of Camp 4, moving in for the entire summer.[87] Over the next two summers of full-time climbing in the valley, he racked up an impressive list of first ascents—fifteen in all. He was known for using minimal aid in these attempts, which included a free climb of the Arrowhead Arête in October 1956 that secured his reputation as one of the boldest climbers of the new generation.[88]

Powell became a role model—as much for his lifestyle choices as for his climbing accomplishments. Over the next few years he was joined by a cohort of a half dozen or so like-minded, long-staying campers. By the early 1960s there would be dozens. At that moment, the height of the golden age of Yosemite climbing, climbers occupied perhaps a fifth of the fifty-odd campsites in Camp 4. The presence of nonclimbing tourists, with expensive tents, coolers, and gas stoves, reminded the climbers of an outside world and culture from which they felt they were refugees.

As the number of climbers grew in the early 1960s, and competition increased in the high tourist season for camping spaces, the rangers were under more pressure to actually enforce the rules. "We called ourselves the Valley Cong," one of the Camp 4 climbers, Yvon Chouinard, recalled. "We hid out from the rangers in nooks and crannies behind Camp 4 when we overstayed the two-week camping limit. We took special pride in the fact that climbing rocks and icefalls had no economic value in society. We were rebels from the consumer culture."[89]

Few Americans before the 1950s had climbed on a full-time basis. No one was paying Powell to do so. His choice to lead a hand-to-mouth existence in support of a full-time commitment to the climbing life became the hallmark of what came to be called "dirtbag climbers"—a name that, depending on point of view, could be an insult or an honorific.[90] The dirtbag climber lived to climb, scorned respectability, scrounged for meals, bathed infrequently.

The original dirtbag climber, it has been said, was Fred Beckey, but he was essentially a loner who moved around a lot, rarely staying in one place longer than it took to pull off a first ascent or two. The climbers of Yosemite stayed put long enough to form a kind of dirtbag community.[91]

Another characteristic of the dirtbag climber was that the species was largely male. The women who showed up in Camp 4 usually did so in the capacity of girlfriend—unlike the Sierra Club RCS in the 1930s, in which women were well integrated, and the Stanford Alpine Club, which in the course of the 1940s and 1950s produced some outstanding female climbers. There were few married Camp 4 climbers, and those who did attempt matrimony were soon divorced.[92]

Camp 4 was for men, a few of them straight arrows in outlook and behavior, but a larger contingent cultivating an air of the rowdy and the disreputable. Somehow, it all paid off in climbing accomplishments. Constant climbing through the warmer months in the valley meant that Camp 4 pioneers built the strength and skills to push rock-climbing to a new level, far above those of most of the "weekenders" from the Sierra Club and the university climbing clubs who they looked down upon—although in the mid-1950s some of the latter, like the SAC's Tom Frost, were every bit as competitive and skilled as the Camp 4 denizens.[93]

From the late 1940s through the mid-1960s, park rangers in Yosemite maintained a sign-out system, requiring climbing parties to be approved before heading to the cliffs. The RCS and SAC provided the Park Service with lists of members they regarded as "qualified leaders," and rangers would check the lists to make sure that parties of climbers were accompanied by one so designated. As Joseph Taylor notes in his history of valley climbing, the RCS thus "became the de facto gatekeeper to Yosemite."[94]

Most of the original Camp 4 climbers, in their younger pre-Yosemite days, had picked up the essentials of their craft in one Sierra Club chapter or another, and could thus pass as officially qualified climbers. Most, but not all. As with the two-week camping limit, the rules could be bent, and Camp 4 climbers who came from outside the club system climbed anyway, despite the lack of formal affiliation.[95]

If the golden age of Yosemite climbing began with John Salathé in the late 1940s, it was refined into its purest form in the late 1950s and early 1960s.[96] While scores of climbers made their own contribution to that moment, three of them—Warren Harding, Yvon Chouinard, and Royal Robbins—emerged as the era's representative figures.

Warren Harding was simultaneously the old man and the bad boy of the golden age. Born in 1924 in Oakland, California, he worked as a propeller mechanic in Sacramento during the war (a heart murmur kept him out of the military but didn't impinge on his later climbing exploits). After the war he supported himself as a surveyor with the California Department of Highways and was proud to carry a union card. He began climbing in the late 1940s, inspired by Ullman's *The White Tower*, tackling conventional routes on mountain peaks in the southern Sierra. Not until 1953, at age twenty-nine, did he finally find his way to Yosemite.

Within a year he was making first ascents in the valley, eventually adding up to more than two dozen all told. Like many climbers new to Yosemite, he also repeated the now-classic Salathé routes, including a second ascent of Lost Arrow Chimney, adding a variation near the top immortalized as the Harding Hole.

Short and wiry, known to friends as "Batso" for hanging on to sheer rock like a bat, Harding was ambitious and fearless. He was equally legendary for his lifestyle (the purple Jaguar that he raced between the Bay Area and Yosemite, the jugs of cheap red wine that he constantly swigged, the beautiful girlfriends who shared his tent). Steve Roper was a novice teenage climber when he first encountered Harding in Yosemite Valley in 1957. Harding struck an awed Roper as "a handsome, devilish fellow" far removed from the traditional-minded Sierra Club climbers that Roper had grown up around, "staid folks who would never have dreamed of wheeling up to a rock with a sports car and a jug and a flashy dame."[97]

No one would confuse Harding for a role model or mentor along the lines of a Robert Underhill or Brad Washburn. Nonetheless, he was responsible for pushing a number of aspiring Yosemite climbers to tackle some very hard climbs. He was not particular about his partners, casually picking them from among whoever was available in Camp 4. As Glen

Denny, who arrived at Camp 4, at age nineteen, in the summer of 1958 recalled:

> I was a rank beginner and Warren was introducing me to 5th class [protected] climbing. After I followed the first pitch he asked if I liked it. I said yes. Unfortunately, he suggested I take the next lead and offered me the sling of hardware. I had never placed a piton, but I didn't want to tell Warren because this seemed like my big chance. I struggled up the pitch, hammering in three pitons for protection. The first one seemed good, the next two didn't. On a delicate traverse my worn-out hiking boots slipped off the small holds and I plummeted toward the ground. On the way down I felt the first two pitons pull out. The last one held, and Warren stopped me a few feet above the ground.[98]

After that rough initiation, Denny became the unofficial photographer of record for Camp 4 and its resident climbers, as well as achieving a number of classic first ascents in Yosemite, and elsewhere in the world.[99]

Yvon Chouinard moved to southern California with his family at age seven. He was born in 1938 in Maine, the son of French Canadian immigrants, like his fellow New Englander Jack Kerouac. And, like Kerouac, he did not learn to speak English until he attended public school, in his case in Burbank, California, which gave him a sense, as he told an interviewer years later "of how Puerto Ricans and Chicanos feel about going to an English-speaking school."[100]

Chouinard's sense of outsider status was common to many leading climbers of the golden age in Yosemite. Before he became a climber, he developed a fascination for another outdoor avocation, falconry. Which, by an indirect route, led him to rock faces, because he would rappel down the cliffs where falcons made their nests to tag the chicks for a government study. After a while, instead of rappelling down, he began to climb up to the nests.

Chouinard took up with the Rock Climbing Section of the Los Angeles chapter of the Sierra Club, and went on its excursions to Tahquitz Rock

Glen Denny photograph of Chuck Pratt (left) and
Yvon Chouinard in Camp 4, 1969.

where, among others, he met Mark Powell, not yet in residence at Camp
4. And then he began going farther afield; at sixteen he soloed a new route
up the west face of 13,804-foot Gannett Peak, the highest mountain in
Wyoming. From there he moved on to the Tetons, where, over the next
several summers, he began to live the life of a dirtbag climber.

In the 1950s the Tetons developed its own version of Yosemite's
Camp 4, an abandoned Civilian Conservation Corps (CCC) camp at the
south end of Jenny Lake, popularly known as the "C-Camp." Chouinard
learned to eat squirrel meat, porcupine, and wild grouse on those summer
climbing trips. As another C-Camp veteran, John Gill, remembered:
Chouinard "was living on ten cents a day [while] I was luxuriating with
fifty cents a day."[101]

Chouinard decided at age eighteen to find a way to make a living related to his climbing interests. With money lent by his parents, he established a small business called Chouinard Equipment (which, a decade and a half later, spun off the outdoor clothing behemoth Patagonia). As he recalled of the humble origins of his company:

> In 1957, when I started my equipment business, Salathé had almost quit climbing, and his pitons were not available anyway. So I bought myself a little hand forge—a coal forge—and an anvil and some hammers and some tongs. I got some books and learned blacksmithing, and started making pitons out of chromolybdenum steel. All my machinery was portable, so I just loaded it all in my car and made the stuff wherever I was. I'd sell it directly to climbers.[102]

Chouinard's artisanal pitons were five times the cost of the European ones available at the time, but since they were made of hard steel and could be reused, they were the better bargain. Within a year he branched out to manufacturing aluminum carabiners, soon supplanting Raffi Bedayn as the supplier of choice for that item. Yosemite climbers were eager to purchase Chouinard equipment, and by the late 1950s, when he wasn't surfing or visiting other climbing centers, Yvon Chouinard was a regular at Camp 4.[103]

Royal Robbins was introduced to climbing in southern California by his scout troop in the late 1940s. Born in 1935, he grew up in Los Angeles as a loner, from a difficult family background, occasionally in trouble with the law, and a high school dropout by age sixteen. Climbing was his salvation, and he made it his cause. Inspired by Ullman's *High Conquest*, he found his way to the Sierra Club's Rock Climbing Section in 1950 and honed his skills at Tahquitz Rock, where, in 1954, he met Warren Harding. "I could see that Harding felt about climbing the way I did," Robbins recalled: "It wasn't a pastime, it was a lifetime."[104]

In the early 1950s, Robbins was mentored by southern California rock-climbing stalwarts John Mendenhall and Chuck Wilts.[105] Mendenhall and Wilts taught Robbins valuable lessons in rope and piton technique, but he soon found himself chafing at the conservative climbing style and techniques favored by the RCS leaders. "It was simply that we brought a different attitude to the game," he recalled. "We had faith in our equipment and we were up there willing to fall."[106] His elders, in turn, were appalled by his rashness. "He'll be a great climber," one observed sourly, "if he lives past 20."[107]

Still a teenager, Robbins had indeed established an impressive climbing record, including the first free ascent of a difficult corner route on Tahquitz called Open Book, along with climbing partner Don Wilson. In his first big-wall achievement, Robbins made the second ascent of Salathé and Steck's route on Yosemite's Sentinel Rock, along with Wilson and Jerry Gallwas. Planning on taking five days for the climb, the three young climbers blazed up the route in just two.[108]

The climb that marked the beginning of this latest golden age came in 1957, on the northwest face of Half Dome, among the best-known and most distinctive formations in the valley, presenting would-be climbers with the prospect of scaling nearly 2,000 feet of sheer, steep granite to reach the summit.

In John Muir's writings, Yosemite's pillars and domes took on living and endearing qualities, "dear friends" that "seemed to have warm blood gushing through their granite veins."[109] But then Muir never contemplated climbing the intimidating northwest face of his old friend "Tissiack" (the Indian name for Half Dome, meaning "cleft rock"). He reached the summit of Half Dome by the tamer cable route laid out in 1875 on the east slope.

For Camp 4 residents contemplating the next great problem in Yosemite climbing, thoughts of "warm blood gushing" on the great rock face were not so comforting; it would be their blood, not Tissiack's, if anything went wrong. There were only two routes to Half Dome's summit in the mid-1950s: the cable route and Salathé's 1946 route on the southwest face. The latter had represented a significant advance in climbing technique, the first demonstration of the utility of Salathé's hard alloy pitons, but the rounded southwest face involved less than half the 2,000-foot altitude gain of the sheer and vertical northwest face. A reconnaissance of the northwest face in 1954 had made it less than 200 feet up from the base, and an attempt by Royal Robbins, Warren Harding, Jerry Gallwas, and Don Wilson in 1955 stopped 1,500 feet short of the summit.

Robbins and Gallwas were back in June 1957, this time joined by Michael Sherrick; all three were southern Californians who had learned their rock-climbing on Tahquitz granite. Robbins and Harding had originally planned to join forces in a renewed assault on Half Dome, but for whatever reason, perhaps an emerging personal rivalry, that collaboration faltered. Harding, Mark Powell, and Bill Feuerer had separately planned their own attempt on Half Dome for that summer, but they were beaten to the punch by Robbins's party.[110]

It was not a climb to undertake lightly. "We feared the enormity of the wall," Robbins recalled. "We were awestruck by it—and we were very aware that no one had ever ventured a wall so steep and so vast."[111]

Robbins set the pace and, more important, the style for the climb. Style was a concept much on the minds of Yosemite climbers in the 1950s and 1960s. Getting to the top was a question subordinate to how one reached that goal. New techniques and equipment threatened to drain the adventure and uncertainty from climbing. To restore the challenge, Robbins determined that his party would attempt to make the climb in one nearly continuous push. They would use pitons and bolts (Gallwas forged some specially designed extra-wide chrome-molybdenum horizontal pitons for the wide cracks they had spotted from the ground), but only within limits; they had no intention of nailing their way up the face. Robbins wished make a statement about the ethics of big-wall climbing, what might be called an aesthetic of restraint.[112]

They set out on the afternoon of June 23, making 150 feet that day, placing a fixed rope to descend to the base to spend the night. On the morning of June 24, they returned to their high point from the previous day, with no intention of departing from their vertical perches again until they reached the summit. They made rapid progress up the section that Robbins and Gallwas were already familiar with from their 1955 attempt. For the next four days they worked their way up tiny crack systems and the occasional chimney, placing pitons and expansion bolts for protection and aid, catching what sleep they could while hunched up on small ledges.

Key to the climb was surmounting a large blank section about half-way up, which they encountered on the afternoon of the second day. Robbins spotted a chimney system to the right that bypassed the blank wall and that he hoped might provide access to the summit. But how to get there? Natural traverses are not a feature of Yosemite granite; routes tend to go up, rather than sideways. Robbins got across the blank space with a pendulum maneuver, swinging from his bolted pivot point far enough to grab a ledge on the other end, thereafter known as the Robbins Traverse. By June 26 they were three-quarters of the way to the summit, at 1,500 feet.

They sought to climb safely (they left a rope stretched across the Robbins Traverse in the event they would need to retreat) but were not averse to risk. They knew that if one of their party was injured, it might be difficult, if not impossible, to get him safely off the wall. So they were committed to getting up and over. At two points the climbers had to trust that flakes (semidetached rocks protruding from the rock wall) would hold their weight. Undercling Flake (named for the climbing technique Robbins used to work his way to its top) and Psych Flake (named for more obvious reasons) held for them, but in later years, both detached and fell to the base, fortunately in neither case with a climber clinging to them.[113]

As on so many Yosemite climbs over the preceding decade, heat and thirst were as much the climbers' adversaries as the unrelentingly steep rock face. By the fourth day they were suffering from lack of food, water, and sleep. Above them they could see an overhanging ceiling, dubbed the Visor, which they dreaded tackling. But, unexpectedly, on the fifth day they came upon a ledge (thereafter "Thank God Ledge") that led to a vertical crack, taking them to another ledge, around the overhang, and leaving two easy pitches to the summit. They stepped out on top of Half Dome shortly before sunset. They could now view Tissiack with the same detached benevolence that John Muir had decades before. Sherrick concluded his report for the *American Alpine Journal*:

Some have said that we did the "impossible," and it is unfortunate that for decades the word *impossible* has been such a common term in the mountaineers' vocabulary, being applied to that part of a mountain which presents an extreme in difficulty usually too demanding for the equipment and technique of the day. But improvements in technique and equipment just keep on happening.[114]

In the years that followed, when more than a dozen new routes were put up the northwest face (two by Robbins), the original route took on the humdrum name of the "Regular Northwest Face of Half Dome," commonly climbed in two days, sometimes in under two hours.[115]

The climb attracted little public attention, but other climbers knew what had been accomplished. Warren Harding was on the summit to greet Robbins and his comrades as they topped out, bringing them sandwiches and, even more welcome, a gallon of water (their own supply was down to a few ounces). It was a gracious gesture. It was also prelude to an attempt to solve whatever it was that Harding decided would be the next great problem in Yosemite climbing. "Warren was a serious competitor," Robbins remembered thinking, "and as I watched him start down the cables, I wondered what he would attempt next."[116]

For Harding, there was no doubt that the only prize left in the valley equivalent to Robbins's success on the northwest face of Half Dome was the first ascent of El Capitan.[117] Named by the Mariposa Battalion when they stumbled into Yosemite in 1851, the valley's preeminent granite monolith a century later had become known familiarly to local climbers as "El Cap." Nearly 2,900 feet high, its summit was reachable by trail from the valley rim, but it had never been climbed by its faces. Even in a region where glaciers had polished away most protuberances on rock walls, El Cap offered a particularly unpromising prospect to would-be climbers. Steve Roper once commented that "the cliff face looks scrubbed, as if cleansed daily by the gods."[118]

A few days after Robbins, Gallwas, and Sherrick's victory on Half Dome, the rival trio of Harding, Mark Powell, and Bill "Dolt" Feuerer studied El Capitan from the valley floor, lying on their backs and passing a pair of binoculars among themselves.[119] After considering various routes, they settled on one that ran up the south buttress where El Cap's two great rock faces, the southwest and the southeast, came together. In a few years that line came to be called the Nose.

There were, they could see, crack systems along the way, if by no means continuous—some to one side, some to the other side of the buttress. If they could be linked, by pendulum swing, or by bolting the blank spaces, they might provide a way to the top. And there were also some small ledges that potentially could be used for bivouacs. And the route just looked good to the three climbers. As Harding recalled: "We chose the Nose as much for its aesthetic appeal as for its practical features."[120]

But they knew they couldn't climb it in the continuous upward push that had characterized the great Yosemite climbs of the past decade, from the five days that Salathé and Steck had spent on the Sentinel in 1950 to the recent five-day ascent of Half Dome by Robbins, Gallwas, and Sherrick. Of necessity, they would need to apply and adapt some of the tactics of the great Himalayan expeditions to big-wall climbing. As Harding recorded:

> We agreed unanimously that the only feasible plan of attack would be to establish a succession of camps up the face, linking them with fixed ropes. Supplies would be hauled up from the ground as needed. . . . Our technique was similar to that used in ascending high mountains, with prusiking and rappelling gear replacing ice axe and crampons as aids for climbing, and winch and hauling lines instead of Sherpas.[121]

The fixed lines they placed and left on El Cap's granite rib served a dual function: a way to move supplies up the route, and a way to move climbers off the route (both for rest and refitting below or, in the event of mishap, rescue). They expected to make no more than 100–200 feet a day, which, given the 2,900 feet in elevation they needed to gain, meant that the climb would take weeks, not days.

Since the 1930s, climbs on Yosemite Valley walls had attracted spectators—but usually only a few close friends and fellow climbers. First ascents were written up—but usually only in the pages of the *Sierra Club*

Bulletin. This time, because of the duration of the climb, the permanently dangling fixed ropes, and the physical and symbolic prominence of El Capitan, Harding and his party were going to attract the attention of nonclimbers visiting the valley, as well as the national media.

On July 4, 1957, Harding, Powell, and Feuerer began their climb. For the first three days they worked their way up toward a wide ledge they had spotted from below, dubbed Sickle Ledge, about 550 feet up the face. They used nylon ropes for climbing and, initially, as shuttle lines from their high point to the ground (the fixed lines were later replaced with manila rope). Each night they rappelled down to the valley floor. Once they reached Sickle Ledge, they ferried supplies up to establish a camp (the equivalent of Camp 1 in Himalayan terms). They spent the next four nights bivouacked on the ledge as they worked their way progressively higher on the stretch of wall above them, using direct aid for most of the climbing.

They reached another feature they had spotted from the ground, 300 or so feet of rock face lined by cracks too wide to hold conventional pitons. Here they protected themselves with an unusual piece of mountain gear: three 9-inch-long metal stove legs scrounged from a dump, each retrofitted with a hole and a ring to which a carabiner could be clipped.[122] They supplemented their pitons and stove legs by drilling holes for expansion bolts.

By their seventh day on the Nose, July 11, they were a third of the way up, over a thousand feet above the ground. But their stove leg pitons were bent out of shape and no longer of any use, and they retreated to the base of El Cap. There they discovered that the gawking crowds gathered to watch their progress from below were creating traffic jams on the valley floor. At the request of the park rangers, the climbers agreed to postpone the remainder of the climb until after Labor Day. They left their manila lines fixed in place.[123]

Before they could resume the climb, Powell had to drop out because of a climbing accident in September that left him with a dislocated ankle and a lifelong limp, although he returned for a brief stint on El Cap in the spring, and he continued to add to his list of first ascents into the 1960s.[124]

Harding recruited two others, Allen Steck and Wally Reed, to join the team. He also extended an invitation to Royal Robbins, but Robbins wasn't interested in an extended siege operation and declined. The turnover in personnel was one way in which siege climbing in Yosemite differed from its counterpart in the Himalaya. Before the El Cap ascent was over, eight climbers had taken part; Harding was the only one continuously involved.

They resumed the climb on Thanksgiving, with a turkey dinner hauled up to Sickle Ledge. The next four days of climbing brought them to 1,200 feet. After that they took a four-month winter break. One disadvantage of the prolonged siege was that the fixed manila ropes began to rot from exposure to sun, rain, and ice, requiring Harding and Feuerer to replace them in March with more durable and expensive nylon ropes. In another innovation, the climbers experimented with winching supplies up the route in the "Dolt Cart," a bicycle-wheel-mounted wagon that Feuerer had constructed over the winter (rather than the traditional and exhausting alternative of pulling up a rope tied to a bag of supplies), but the Dolt Cart displayed an unfortunate propensity to flip over.

There were additional changes in personnel as Powell re-joined the group and Steck dropped out, followed by Feuerer later that spring. When the summer of 1958 rolled around, they were again banned from climbing by ranger edict. Harding went off to try a new route on the east face of Washington Column, leaving El Cap unfinished but festooned with fixed ropes.[125]

The weekend after Labor Day 1958, Harding, with an entirely new team apart from Powell, resumed work on the Nose of El Cap.[126] Progress was slow. Harding rethought the upper route. Ropes had to be reset, supplies ferried, and Powell, still ailing, dropped out for the second and final time. By that point they had reached about 1,900 feet, which left another 1,000. Park rangers, who had come to regard Harding and his fellow climbers as a problem second only to the foraging bears, now gave them a final deadline: they had to be finished by Thanksgiving. (Harding wasn't overly concerned; after all, once they were on the wall, there was not much the NPS could do to get them off.)

The final push began on November 1, the party now consisting of

Harding, Rich Calderwood, Wayne Merry, and George Whitmore. Progress was slow, the exposure unsettling (Calderwood, just twenty-one years old and with a pregnant wife at home, soon bailed). The days were short, and toward the end they endured sleet and snowstorms. Still, by November 11 they were within 120 feet of the summit, where friends awaited, shouting down encouragement.

At dusk on the evening of November 11, Harding set off in the lead, and throughout the night he hammered his way up the remaining stretch of overhanging rock. And at 6:00 on the morning of November 12, fourteen hours and twenty-eight bolts later, he pulled himself up on the summit, his two companions following shortly thereafter. "Long, sustained, and flawless," as a recent guide to Yosemite big walls concluded, the Nose is probably "the best rock climb in the world; it is certainly the best known."[127]

There were banner headlines in the Bay Area newspapers, a *Life* magazine reporter took photos of the victorious climbers (though they were never used), and Harding published accounts in both the *American Alpine Journal* and the men's magazine *Argosy* (the latter in collaboration with Merry) about the climb. All told, Harding and his various companions had spent forty-five days on the climb over a year and a half. Harding estimated that he had placed 675 pitons and 125 expansion bolts, 90 percent of which were for direct aid.[128]

Both the extent of the rock-engineering and the resulting publicity proved controversial. Conrad Wirth, director of the National Park Service, grumbled about "stunt" climbers "hoping to be able to commercialize on what they accomplish," and some Yosemite climbers agreed.[129] Because Harding was first over the top and alone was involved from start to finish, it was remembered as his climb, although he had traded off leads with Powell in the early days and with Merry in the concluding push. He also won an unshakable reputation as a showboat, even though he had not pursued the publicity that the climb attracted, whereas previous climbers, from Dave Brower on Shiprock to Charlie Houston and Bob Bates on K2, had sold stories to popular magazines about their experiences.

THE GUNKS

Developments in the climbing culture of Yosemite had parallels elsewhere in the United States: in the Jenny Lake climbing camp in the Tetons; in Eldorado Canyon south of Boulder, Colorado; and in New York's Shawangunks. The latter is a high ridgeline 10 miles in length, rising west of the Hudson River near the college town of New Paltz, and running in a southwest–northeast direction.

The Gunks, as they came to be known in the 1950s, lie 90 miles north of New York City and, with the opening of the New York State Thruway in the mid-1950s, were an easy drive for city climbers. They are sometimes referred to as Yosemite East, although bearing little physical resemblance to their California counterpart. The Gunks feature cliffs a few hundred feet high rather than the 2,000- to 3,000-foot faces of Yosemite, marked by horizontal- rather than vertical-crack systems.[130] But if there was no need for the multiday big-wall epics of Yosemite, the Shawangunk cliffs are still steep, frequently overhung near the top, technically challenging, and sometimes fatal to those who climb them.[131]

The Gunks, which were on private land at the time (now a mixture of private and public lands), were discovered as a climbing site by Fritz Wiessner in 1935, and Wiessner and his fellow immigrant Hans Kraus put up most of the original and most daring routes.[132] (Kraus, born in Trieste, came of age and was educated as a doctor in Vienna. He fled Austria following the Nazi seizure of power in that country in 1938, settling in New York. Apart from his climbing achievements, he was a pioneer in sports medicine and is best remembered for having consulted with John F. Kennedy in the White House about the president's perennial back problems.)[133]

Where Wiessner and Kraus pioneered, others followed, many of them members of the New York City chapter of the Appalachian Mountain Club. Like the Sierrans in Yosemite, the New York Appies came to regard the Gunks with proprietary affection, and they sought to maintain control over who climbed there and how they climbed. And, as in Yosemite Valley, in the course of the 1950s that attitude led to generational conflict.[134]

Among the leading figures in the Gunks in the 1950s, and by the early 1960s among the best climbers in the Northeast, was James P. McCarthy, who made his first visit to the cliffs in 1951 as an inexperienced member of the newly founded Princeton Mountaineering Club. Wiessner by this point had moved to Stowe, Vermont, leaving Kraus as the main influence over younger Gunk climbers like McCarthy. Under Kraus's tutelage, McCarthy began putting up tough new routes of his own, and free-climbing many routes that had previously required direct aid.[135]

In 1958, McCarthy was featured on the cover of *Sports Illustrated* (the magazine's first ever climbing cover) putting up a route known as "Foops" on an impossible-looking overhang in the Shawangunks. As the magazine explained to readers more accustomed to reading about team sports:

> This overhang presents the sort of problem any advanced climber might face on any number of imposing mountains around the world. This particular overhang, however, is merely an unusually tough formation McCarthy found in the old, worn-down Shawangunk Mountains near his home. McCarthy spends many weekends in this area hunting out interesting problems that help keep him fit for the tougher tests he gets during the summers climbing the Dolomites, the French Alps and the Rockies. "Any hard climb anywhere," McCarthy points out, "is preparation, and even in such small mountains it is an end in itself, enjoyable for its own sake."[136]

In a few years McCarthy would be putting up new big-wall routes in Canada, in the company of Yosemite veterans like Royal Robbins, Layton Kor, and Dick McCracken, and a few years after that he would be setting a new standard in eastern ice-climbing in the company of Yvon Chouinard. But in some ways, McCarthy's career as a climber followed an older model, very different from the Yosemite style. He was not an Appie (a genteel weekend climber), but he was also not a dirtbag climber in the emerging Yosemite model. A successful professional lawyer in New York City, McCarthy was also much more organizationally minded than the

Camp 4 crew, eventually serving as president of the American Alpine Club.[137]

In the first decade or so of climbing in the Shawangunks, a Saturday might see a dozen climbers making their way up the cliffs. By the time McCarthy appeared on the *Sports Illustrated* cover, those numbers had grown to a couple of hundred weekend visitors, including members of the Canadian Alpine Club, along with various university mountaineering clubs. But the Appies still held sway, and they assumed, as the Sierra Club had in Yosemite, that they should set the rules governing who climbed and how.

The AMC maintained a registration system for climbers, assigned them to rope teams for designated routes, and determined the qualifications of prospective climb leaders. A "Safety Code" distributed by the AMC to would-be Gunks climbers in the 1950s proclaimed: "Climb only with a recognized mountaineering organization of conservative tradition."[138] But the self-satisfied conservative tradition of the Appies was about to be challenged.

It first was questioned from within the AMC itself, by a group of young turks tired of being told by their elders what they could or could not climb, reinforced in their defiance by the small circle of climbers around Hans Kraus, who knew themselves to be far superior climbers to the Appie leaders and disliked all the red tape. The dissidents were, however, a kind of loyal opposition, socially and culturally still much a part of the AMC establishment.[139]

The roughnecks who began to show up in the later 1950s did not share such allegiance to the AMC. In 1957, a local carpenter named Dave Craft came to the Gunks for the first time and, under AMC tutelage, learned to climb. The following year, two undergraduate members of the outing club at the City College of New York—Roman Sadowy and Claude Suhl—arrived on the scene and also learned to climb with the AMC. Others who did not fit the traditional Appie model soon followed. Art Gran, although an Appie himself, was growing disillusioned with the AMC's elaborate training program and rules. He started climbing on his own off-season, when most Appies weren't around, and formed a close relationship with the newcomers from City College and other outsiders, who for a while were known as "Art's boys." As Gran recalled:

> When we climbed together, we did not do so as part of the AMC trip; this more or less started the growth of the independent movement, and it soon mushroomed to gigantic proportions.[140]

The "independent movement" could be distinguished by climbing style (much more daring than Appie orthodoxy allowed), social origins (working-class rather than middle-class professional), and dress (early beatnik versus the Appie preference for twee alpine accessories like patterned sweaters). The Appies couldn't stand the independents and labeled them "vulgar." Unperturbed, the reprobate independents started calling themselves "Vulgarians." They had youth, and soon numbers, on their side, outnumbering the Appies by the early 1960s. The premier chroniclers of New England and New York mountaineering, Guy and Laura Waterman, noted:

> The Vulgarians worked hard at becoming one of the more colorful circles that ever whirled through the northeastern climbing orbit. Brash, boisterous, and ever eager to shock, they exalted bad manners to the level of an art form. They held wild parties . . . , climbed nude . . . , invaded Appie campgrounds with their all-night orgies [and] urinated off the roof on Appies as they emerged from a local restaurant. They also did superb climbing.[141]

By the early 1960s, the AMC's credibility and authority as gatekeepers to the Gunks had been demolished, along with any attempt to regulate who climbed there or how—part of the national trend in which the premier outdoors clubs steadily lost their influence over the future of American climbing.

THE YOSEMITE WAY OF LIFE, 1959—1963

In September 1961, Royal Robbins, Tom Frost, and Chuck Pratt put up the second route on El Capitan (the first being Warren Harding's epic 1957–58 ascent of the "Nose"). The new route ran up the southwest face, also known as the Salathé Wall. Robbins, Frost, and Pratt fixed ropes on the lower 800 feet of the route, returned to the ground to ferry more supplies to their high point (siege style), but climbed the last 2,000 feet alpine style in one continuous six-day push.

The total climb took nine and a half days spread out over two weeks in September. They used pitons for protection and direct aid, but, as Robbins preferred, placed a minimum of bolts, thirteen in total, and all on the lower, fixed-rope portion of the climb. It was, in the opinion of Camp 4 regulars like Steve Roper and Yvon Chouinard, among the greatest rock climbs ever done. The *American Alpine Journal* devoted four sentences to it.[142]

In the 1950s and early 1960s, the American Alpine Club counted few adherents among Yosemite climbers (or younger rock-climbers in general, and particularly younger climbers in the western states). "We were used to being ignored by the American Alpine Club," Royal Robbins recalled in the early 1970s. "It didn't bother us. I was once asked to join but I didn't see the point of it."[143]

Before the term "generation gap" became popular, AAC leaders were becoming aware of the split between young climbers and their elders. In February 1961, Nick Clinch, recently returned from leading the first ascent of Masherbrum in the Himalaya, and an AAC officer, wrote to club president Bob Bates to report on a meeting he had attended at the University of Colorado in Boulder:

The talk centered around the American Alpine Club. . . . The young climbers seem to feel that a large number of AAC members are antagonistic to the type of climbing that they do. I explained that the club was composed of many different types of mountaineers but that we did not disapprove of difficult rock climbing—most of the club members did rock climbing of a high standard for their day. However, rock climbing was not an end in itself. This has always been the main breach between the AAC and younger climbers.[144]

Within a few years of the Salathé Wall ascent, the AAC started making a determined effort to reach out to younger climbers in Yosemite and elsewhere. One reflection of the change could be seen in 1963 in the *American Alpine Journal*, which ran four articles about Yosemite climbing in a single issue. Of the four, the one that drew the most notice was by Yvon Chouinard, entitled "Modern Yosemite Climbing." Chouinard began with a bold assertion:

> Yosemite climbing is the least known and understood and yet one of the most important schools of rock climbing in the world today. Its philosophies, equipment and techniques have been developed almost independently of the rest of the climbing world. In the short period of thirty years, it has achieved a standard of safety, difficulty and technique comparable to the best European schools.[145]

In the pages that followed, Chouinard offered a highly technical account of what made climbing Yosemite's vertical granite crack systems unique, in terms of both the evolution of technique and ethics. But he also talked more generally about the community of climbers that had gathered in the valley. Toward the end he described the "strange, passionate love" that he felt for climbing in Yosemite, and concluded: "More than just a climbing area, it is a way of life."

The half decade between Harding's ascent of the Nose and the appearance of Chouinard's article had been crowded and intense years for the Camp 4 regulars, full of achievements—and controversies. To mention just a few highlights:

In April 1960, Yvon Chouinard and Tom Frost tried out a new climbing device that Chouinard had just invented and given the whimsical name "Realized Ultimate Reality Piton," or RURP, a razor blade–sized, wedge-shaped piton that proved capable of holding the weight of a climber when inserted into a hairline crack on an otherwise smooth granite face. They used the RURPs in making the first ascent of the southwest side of Kat Pinnacle, a steep, blank pillar just outside the valley. Every move up the pinnacle required direct aid and, until the invention of the RURP, would have been impossible to contemplate without drilling bolts into the rock.[146]

In September 1960, Robbins, Chuck Pratt, Joe Fitchen, and Tom Frost repeated the Nose route on El Capitan in seven days—three days faster than planned, and weeks faster than the first ascent. Even more important, they used no fixed ropes, but climbed alpine style.[147] This was a committing climb; no umbilical cord linked them to the ground.

The climb deepened the Robbins-Harding rivalry and sealed the fate of fixed-rope siege climbing in the valley (which even Harding soon abandoned). As Robbins wrote a few years later in the pages of the *American Alpine Journal*: "Siege climbing makes success certain, thus depriving alpinism of one of its most important elements: adventure. What fun is there in a game when the odds are a hundred to one in your favor?"[148] However, there is no doubt that the Robbins party benefited from the bolts that Harding had fixed on the route in his original siege of 1957–58.[149]

In March 1961, Chouinard published an opinion piece in the influential climbing magazine *Summit*, attacking the use of bolts in climbing. "The main objection to bolts," he wrote,

> is that they permanently mar the beauty of the rock. Bolts also enable inexperienced and unqualified persons to climb difficult routes with comparative ease. Bolts are often a means for making up for inexperience and inadequacies, and I like to think that not every route is for every climber.[150]

The bolt controversy spread from the pages of *Summit* to the walls of Yosemite, where critics of bolting began "chopping" (removing) bolts they considered unnecessary for either protection or direct aid.[151]

In October 1961, immediately following the Robbins-Frost-Pratt ascent of the Salathé Wall, Harding, Glen Denny, and Al Macdonald

Glen Denny's photo of Warren Harding on the first ascent of the west face of the Leaning Tower.

climbed the severely overhanging west face of the Leaning Tower in Yosemite in an eighteen-day siege effort in which, demonstrating what Harding thought of Chouinard's *Summit* manifesto, he placed more than a hundred bolts. Harding would not be intimidated by the self-righteous critics whom he later dismissed as "Valley Christians."[152]

Two years later, in October 1963, Chouinard, in his first attempt on El Capitan, joined three veteran El Cap climbers—Frost, Pratt, and Robbins—to attempt a first ascent of the monolith's southeast face, the greatest unclimbed rock wall remaining in the valley, also known as the North America Wall (so named for a patch of black diorite in its center, surrounded by white granite, with a vague resemblance to a map of North America).

For six days they climbed in brutal heat; then it began to rain; then it began to snow. Ice water ran down their arms and legs as they hammered

Glen Denny photograph of Royal Robbins (left) and Tom Frost on the North America Wall of El Capitan.

in their pitons and drilled holes for a minimum number of bolts (thirty-eight). Finally, on the last day, the sun came out again. Under a deep-blue sky they admired the view from their bivouac ledge. It was Halloween day. Six hours later they had, as Robbins recorded, "overcome the last problems and shook hands on top, happy as pagans."[153]

The happy pagans were beginning to bring Yosemite-style technique to other walls. At the conclusion of his *American Alpine Journal* article on modern Yosemite climbing, Chouinard predicted that Yosemite would prove to be the training ground for a "new generation of super alpinists who will venture forth to the high mountains of the world to do the most esthetic and difficult walls on the face of the earth."[154]

By the time Chouinard's article appeared, Yosemite climbers had already established an impressive record of first ascents outside the valley. Don Wilson, Mark Powell, and Jerry Gallwas explored the possibilities for climbing sandstone needles in the American Southwest, achieving a first ascent in September 1956 of Cleopatra's Needle, in the Valley of Thundering Water, New Mexico. Wilson, Powell, and Gallwas were joined by "Dolt" Feuerer in the first ascent of the Totem Pole in Arizona's Monument Valley in June 1957.[155]

In August 1960, David Rearick and Bob Kamps made the first ascent of the Diamond, the sheer and distinctively shaped upper half of the nearly 2,000-foot east face of Colorado's Longs Peak. Previously, climbs on the route had been banned, but the National Park Service gave Rearick and Kamps permission to try it. Following a Yosemite-like vertical-crack system through the middle of the Diamond, they took three days to reach the summit.

Unlike Yosemite, the climb combined high exposure with high altitude, with the last 250 feet to the summit over 14,000 feet. The lifting of the ban on attempts on the Diamond proved a significant victory for American mountaineers; thereafter, there were few Park Service edicts against climbing on particular mountains or routes, except to protect endangered species or archaeological sites.[156]

Venturing farther afield, Royal Robbins and Gary Hemming put up the American Direct route on the west face of the Petit Dru (part of the Mont Blanc massif in Chamonix, France) in 1962, the most difficult route yet on a rock formation where the cream of European alpinists, including Walter Bonatti, had preceded them. Robbins was back in 1965 with John Harlin to put up another route on the Petit Dru's west face, the American Direttissima. (The following year Harlin, who in 1962 had been the first American to climb the North Face of the Eiger, died in an attempt to put up a direct route in winter on the same face.)[157]

And in 1963, Robbins, Layton Kor, Jim McCarthy, and Dick McCracken headed to the Canadian backcountry to make the first ascent of the southeast face of 8,563-foot Mount Proboscis in the Logan Mountains of the Northwest Territories.[158]

By 1963, Yosemite's place in the firmament of world-class climbing was well established. Camp 4 would pass into legend. As Steve Roper recalled of the golden age: "Chouinard's statement about Valley climbing being 'a way of life' struck many of us as an absolute truth." As he observed:

> By 1963 people such as Robbins, Chouinard, [Chuck] Pratt, [Eric] Beck, and myself had lived in the Valley for months at a time. We felt as if we truly belonged in the Valley; it was our spiritual home. Away from the cities and responsibilities, we lived simply, feeling at peace with ourselves and the world. . . . Humbled often by the walls, we had to look deeply into ourselves to find out what made us tick.[159]

AMERICANS ON EVEREST

Nineteen sixty-three was, perhaps, the greatest year in the history of American climbing, and Yosemite was only part of the story. The other great events were taking place 7,500 or so miles to the west, on the slopes of the world's highest mountain. If Yosemite epitomized the competitive individualism coming to the fore in big-wall climbing, the American expedition to Everest was perhaps the last golden moment of the spirit of the brotherhood of the rope.

In a prospectus written in the summer of 1960 for the American Mount Everest Expedition (or AMEE), Norman Dyhrenfurth used a justification for climbing the mountain considerably more contemporary in its concerns than the old Mallory chestnut, "because it's there." Noting Chinese claims to have reached the summit of Everest that spring, Dyhrenfurth suggested that Americans needed to prove that they, too, were up to the challenge of ascending the world's highest mountain. "Most mountaineers of the Free World agree that the struggle for the Himalaya should remain a purely idealistic, non-political pursuit. And yet there can be no doubt that the ascent of [Everest] by an American team would go a long way toward winning new friends in many places."[160]

Just who these foreign friends were who were so eager to see an American team raise the Stars and Stripes atop Everest was left vague in the prospectus. But it was a brilliant and well-timed marketing ploy. Dyhrenfurth, son of well-known Swiss mountaineer and geologist Günther Dyhrenfurth, emigrated to the United States shortly before World War II. Following military service, he embarked on a successful career as a documentary filmmaker. He retained close ties with the European climbing community, serving as photographer on the 1952 Swiss Everest expedition, and leading an unsuccessful attempt to climb Everest's neighbor, Lhotse, in 1955, as well as taking part in several other Himalayan expeditions.

He passionately wanted to return to Everest, this time with an American team. The problem was raising the money to do it—several hundred thousand dollars' worth. When he mentioned the project to Nick Clinch, organizer of the successful Hidden Peak and Masherbrum expeditions, Clinch told him flatly, "You'll never get that kind of money in this country. . . . Nobody gives that much of a damn about mountains or mountaineering."[161]

What people in the United States (and in the US government) did care about in the early 1960s was the Cold War, and the competition with the Soviet Union for international status. That competition took many forms, including an arms race and a space race. Dyhrenfurth made the unlikely, if effective, pitch that putting an American on top of Everest, as a later AMEE press release promised, would prove "a feather in our cap, a booster to our prestige, a refutation beyond argument of our detractors' taunt that we are a nation gone soft and gutless."[162]

This was not the way John Muir or, for that matter, Charlie Houston would have sold an expedition. But it was language that the new president of the United States, John F. Kennedy, could appreciate. And eventually, through various schemes to carry out government-subsidized scientific and social scientific research, a significant number of federal dollars flowed into AMEE's coffers. The National Geographic Society also signed on as a sponsor. And there were book, and film, and *Life* magazine deals.[163]

Dyhrenfurth assembled the largest and most elaborately organized expedition in American mountaineering history, twenty members strong. He personally would function as both expedition leader and filmmaker.

He sought out the country's strongest climbers to join him in Nepal, as long as they were what he thought of as "expedition men" (Fred Beckey would not be invited).[164]

Thirteen of the twenty members of the expedition were from the western United States, by either origin or adoption, by now the norm on American Himalayan expeditions. Nine had worked as professional guides in the Tetons or Cascades. Several were connected with the retail end of mountaineering. And Dyhrenfurth was positioning himself as a professional organizer of expeditions. The old "amateur" ideal of the gentleman climber was giving way to a new professionalism. This expedition, much more than those of the past, consisted of men whose lives and careers had been shaped by their involvement with mountaineering.

Two and a half years after going public with the idea of an American Mount Everest Expedition, in January 1963, Dyhrenfurth and an advance guard of climbers flew to Kathmandu. Others followed, and on February 20 a long line consisting of nine hundred porters, thirty-odd high-altitude Sherpas, and twenty members of AMEE set off from Kathmandu en route to Everest. Official expedition historian James Ramsey Ullman had to turn back almost immediately because of health problems, so he served instead in AMEE's press headquarters in Kathmandu.

On the approach march, the climbers debated strategy. Dyhrenfurth's number one priority was getting a climber with an American flag on the summit, and that meant following the by now "standard route" that the British had climbed in 1953 and the Swiss had followed on their own successful expedition in 1956: up the Khumbu Icefall to the Western Cwm, from there up Lhotse Face to the South Col, and then up the southeastern ridge to the summit. But with twenty climbers involved, other goals could be pursued.

One option was for a "grand slam" of gaining the summit of not only Everest, but also its two immediate neighbors, Lhotse and Nuptse. Tom Hornbein, Willi Unsoeld, Dick Emerson, and a few others were in favor of another option: putting a totally new route up to the summit of Everest via the West Ridge, the dividing line between Nepal and China. Dyhrenfurth tentatively agreed, provided the Southeast Ridge remained the priority, but in the ensuing weeks there would be a constant struggle between the West Ridgers and their rivals for resources—especially for the labor power of the expedition's Sherpas to carry supplies.

Base camp was established on March 21, at 17,800 feet, below the Khumbu Icefall. Two days later a work party was in the icefall finding a route through its jumbled mass of ice towers and crevasses, when one of the towers collapsed, killing Jake Breitenbach, a twenty-seven-year-old Dartmouth alum and Teton guide from Jackson Hole, Wyoming. His body could not be recovered but would emerge seven years later at the base of the icefall.[165]

Breitenbach was well liked, and his death shook the expedition. Nonetheless, work was soon resumed on the icefall route. By March 30, Camp 1 had been placed on the Western Cwm. Hornbein, Unsoeld, and others moved onto terrain that no human being had ever before stood on as they worked their way up to the mountain's West Shoulder, beneath the West Ridge. But in mid-April, Dyhrenfurth called a temporary end to their exploration, concentrating all resources on moving up the Southeast Ridge.

And so it was that on the morning of May 1, a full month before the 1953 British expedition had been in its highest camp, Jim Whittaker and Sherpa Nawang Gombu set off for the summit, which they reached at 1:00 p.m. Whittaker planted an American flag on a 4-foot aluminum stake on the summit, and with that gesture Dyhrenfurth's expedition had achieved its official and minimal goal. President Kennedy hailed the achievement of "our gallant countrymen," not yet informed that one of them was not from the United States.

If Whittaker and Gombu's ascent had marked the end of the American Mount Everest Expedition, it would have been an event that pleased the public but left many of the climbers dissatisfied. But now AMEE would truly make mountaineering history, by launching an assault on two separate routes on the same day, with climbers from the Southeast Ridge and climbers from the West Ridge rendezvousing at the summit and then descending together to the South Col. As Barry Bishop explained in a letter home to Arnold Wexler on May 9: "Lute Jerstad & I have the nod &

we'll move up the 11th for an 'all or nothing' try on the 18th. Plans call for Unsoeld & Hornbein to try for the top the same day—via the W. Ridge. Talk about a long shot!"[166]

There were delays: high winds the night of May 16 played havoc with the tents on the West Ridge. But finally, on May 21, four Americans bedded down for the night in two assault camps on opposite sides of Everest.

Hornbein and Unsoeld awoke at 4:00 a.m. on May 22 and set out at 7:00 a.m. They took nothing with them but oxygen, a little food, their personal effects, and a walkie-talkie. They would not be returning the same way. They made their way up a couloir (thereafter the Hornbein Couloir) through the stretch of rotten rock known as the Yellow Band, laboriously cutting steps. Near the top of the couloir they came to a

Willi Unsoeld (left) and Tom Hornbein reconnoiter the West Ridge of Everest, April 1963. Photograph by Barry Bishop.

60-foot cliff. Hornbein took the lead and led to within 8 feet of the top when, exhausted, he had to drop back down beside Unsoeld.

Protected by the piton Hornbein had placed at his high point, and cranking his oxygen up full blast, Unsoeld surmounted the obstacle—the hardest climbing they would do that day. He then belayed Hornbein to the top. It was from that position that they radioed Jim Whittaker at base camp to say that they were committed to the route. They could not return the way they had come. To survive to climb another day, they would have to reach the summit and then traverse the mountain.

At 6:15 p.m., just over eleven hours after setting out, they looked up and could see the flag that Whittaker and Gombu had left on the summit three weeks before. They walked together to the top, arms linked. "Now some people have suggested it was to avoid the argument as to who got there first," Unsoeld would later tell audiences at the slide shows he did about the climb, "but there are other reasons to link arms with your buddy."[167]

Jerstad and Bishop were not waiting for them; they had arrived nearly three hours earlier on their own successful summit day. So after a short

Lute Jerstad approaches the summit of Everest, with Jim Whittaker's flag still flying, May 22, 1963. Photograph by Barry Bishop.

time at the top, Hornbein and Unsoeld set off down the Southeast Ridge following their comrades' footsteps. By 7:30 it was too dark to see even their own feet, let alone the tracks left by Bishop and Jerstad. But calling out in the darkness, they were answered by the two men ahead of them. The four rendezvoused at about 9:30 p.m., all close to exhaustion, Bishop in a very bad way. Hornbein, who still had a little oxygen left in his tank, gave it to Bishop. They continued down in the darkness, but by midnight they decided it was too dangerous to continue. So they sat on a rock outcrop and waited for daylight.

Their open bivouac that night, at over 28,000 feet, was the highest ever attempted. They were blessed with a rare windless night. All their oxygen had now run out; whether from the effects of exhaustion or hypoxia, they were not thinking as clearly as they needed to. Of the four men, only Hornbein thought to take his crampons off to avoid conducting cold to his feet. It did not occur to him to suggest to the others that they do the same. At one point Unsoeld offered to warm Hornbein's feet against his stomach, and Hornbein took him up on it. But when Hornbein, in turn, offered to warm his companion's feet, Unsoeld declined. His feet, he said, were feeling fine. That's because they were frozen, and he could feel nothing.

The next morning they made it safely down toward Camp 6 above the South Col and met their anxious expedition mates, Dave Dingman and Sherpa Girmi Dorje. Unsoeld and Bishop, with the worst cases of frostbite, were evacuated by helicopter to a Kathmandu hospital. Bishop lost all his toes; Unsoeld, all but one.

President Kennedy sent another congratulatory telegram, and in July, back in the United States, there was a Rose Garden ceremony at the White House, with the president presenting medals to all expedition members. The expedition put American mountaineering in the national and international spotlight, with subsequent stories in *Life* magazine and *National Geographic* magazine, an expedition history by James Ramsey Ullman, a lavishly illustrated big-format Sierra Club book by Tom Hornbein about the West Ridge climb, and an hour-long National Geographic Society documentary that earned the highest ratings up to that time for televised documentaries.

No one, not even the British, who had invented the sport of alpinism, could look down on American mountaineering after the Everest triumph. Bill Tilman, reviewing James Ramsey Ullman's book about AMEE for the *Alpine Journal*, declared that the West Ridge climb lifted the American Everest expedition "to a plane level with that of the first ascent of the mountain in 1953."[168]

Many young Americans, exposed to the barrage of Everest publicity, decided that they wanted to become mountaineers too. In one measure of the newfound popularity of climbing (or at least dressing like a climber), Jim Whittaker's employer, Recreational Equipment Incorporated (REI), increased its membership from 50,000 in 1965 to 250,000 in 1972. A rival retail chain, Eastern Mountain Sports, was

Young hut crew members packing supplies to the AMC's Lakes of the Clouds hut on Mount Washington, 1969.

established in 1967, and local retail distributors sprang up in many cities. In another such measure, Sierra Club membership grew from 29,000 members in 1965 to 100,000 in 1970. Many more came to climbing outside the traditional club framework. The rucksack revolution was on.[169]

EPILOGUE

1964-2015

In December 1964, Royal Robbins was invited to give a slide presentation on Yosemite climbing at the annual dinner of the American Alpine Club, held that year in Boston. The invitation was part of the club's ongoing campaign to broaden its appeal to both younger and western US climbers. John Harlin was also invited, to talk about his 1962 ascent of the Eigerwand, the North Face of the Eiger. Robbins recalled that the mood of the meeting was "euphoria" because the recent string of successes "on the Eiger, in Yosemite, and on Everest gave one the feeling of witnessing a renaissance in American climbing."[1]

Climbing had finally become a mass participation activity in the United States. Thousands of novice climbers were initiated into the mysteries of rope craft, rappelling, protection, and direct aid, relying for guidance sometimes on outdoors clubs, as in the past, but also on newly published how-to books, or newly established climbing schools and programs.[2]

Climbing became more diverse—if not racially (it remained, as it had always been, almost exclusively white), certainly in terms of gender. By the 1980s, young women climbers like Yosemite's Lynn Hill were emerging as equal contenders for the top ranks of American climbing.[3]

Almost all the regional outdoors clubs gained members in the 1960s and in succeeding decades, but at the same time they lost much of their previous influence over the development of American climbing. The new generation of climbers was, by and large, like the Camp 4 regulars in the 1950s, not organizationally minded. In the course of the 1960s, the spectacle of the mass climb sponsored by the Mazamas and similar groups came to be derided by younger climbers, and that tradition was eventually abandoned by the clubs themselves.[4]

In the 1970s, the major climbing clubs, one by one, dropped formal membership qualifications. Potential recruits no longer needed to be nominated by existing members to join, or to submit a long climbing résumé (or, as had been the case for some people in the past, worry about being of the wrong religion or race).[5]

What the clubs gained in size and diversity, they lost in intimacy and involvement. To be a Sierra Club member in the 1930s meant to be part of an active community of outdoor enthusiasts, many known to one another and based in local chapters. To be a Sierra Club member at the end of the twentieth century meant sending in a yearly dues check to the club's national headquarters, receiving a monthly issue of *Sierra* magazine in return, and perhaps buying a copy of a glossy wilderness photo calendar on the eve of the new year. The club outings continued (in smaller groups) but became more a commercial than a communal enterprise. A survey of Sierra Club members in the late 1980s revealed that a mere 13 percent of members had attended a single club meeting.[6]

As American climbing expanded in the later decades of the twentieth century, it formed too many stories to be captured in a single narrative. The era of the all-around climber was drawing to a close. New specialties, like frozen-waterfall climbing, competitive sport climbing, and gym climbing emerged (the first indoor climbing wall opened in Seattle in 1987). By the start of the twenty-first century, there was even a niche specialty called "deep-water soloing," which involved free-climbing on sea cliffs, with the only protection being a wet landing in the waters below, if a climber fell.[7]

As climbing fragmented, techniques and ethics diverged. In the late 1960s and early 1970s, many rock-climbers, led by Yvon Chouinard and Royal Robbins, came to embrace an ethic of "clean climbing," abandoning the use of pitons and expansion bolts for the nonscarring alternative of "chocks" (hexagonal devices attached to slings that could be wedged into cracks for protection and direct aid).[8] But with the rise of sport climbing in the 1980s and 1990s, the pendulum, at least for some, swung back to fixed bolts.

Sport climbing put an emphasis on speed and gymnastic ability as climbers, on both rock faces and indoor climbing walls, raced up a prepared route that featured permanent anchors bolted into the climbing surface. "Trad" (or traditional) climbers and sport climbers often found themselves waging turf battles over the appropriate use of this or that rock face.

Traditional climbers found the sport-climbing technique of "hang-dogging" (hanging on a rope to practice a move on a difficult pitch) objectionable. More objectionable still, to traditionalist sensibilities, was the willingness of some sport climbers to physically groom routes, either by "chipping" holds to make them easier to grasp, or by gluing holds to attach them more securely. At a debate over evolving climbing ethics at the annual meeting of the American Alpine Club in 1986, some of the "trads" in the audience, dubbed "rock police" by sport climbers, came adorned in T-shirts reading "SPORT CLIMBING IS NEITHER."[9]

The era of Robert Underhill and Brad Washburn, the paternal authorities looked to for guidance on all questions alpinist, was over. The leading climbers of the later twentieth century inspired admiration, even adulation, but rarely played any direct role as mentors to coming generations. For one thing, they were too busy. Almost without exception, the climbers who were on the cutting edge of the sport at the start of the twenty-first century (when, perhaps for the first time, it was truly appropriate to speak of climbing as a sport) were professionals, with corporate sponsors from the ever-expanding outdoor retail industry, like Yvon Chouinard's Patagonia clothing line. They trained and climbed year-round, honing their specialties, to the benefit of their own celebrity career and their sponsors' marketing stratagems. Patagonia's "ambassadors," as the company preferred to call them, included in 2015 such climbing stars as Lynn Hill and Tommy Caldwell.[10]

Sponsorship was not restricted to big-wall climbing in the United States. Himalayan mountaineers sought and attracted financial backers. They were also in demand as motivational speakers at corporate events.[11] The era of the brotherhood of the rope in expeditionary climbing was also coming to an end. In the 1970s a series of acrimonious expeditions, to Everest, K2, and Nanda Devi, recounted by disgruntled participants in tell-all accounts, revealed the spread of Yosemite-style competitiveness to that region.[12] On Everest, the rise of commercial guided climbing provided a new form of employment for Himalayan climbers but also led to bottlenecks on the Southeast Ridge, and to ensuing climbing disasters, most famously in 1996, as chronicled by Jon Krakauer in *Into Thin Air*.[13]

Yet for all the changes, some things remained the same. Americans still believed in the therapeutic effects of pursuing the strenuous life on mountainous terrain. Memoirist Cheryl Strayed's millions-selling book *Wild* (published in 2012 and released in 2014 as a feature film starring Reese Witherspoon), was the story of a young woman who overcame grief, addiction, a wrecked marriage, and an aimless existence by heading out to the mountains on a solitary wilderness trek, finding redemption somewhere between the Sierra and the Cascades (or, as the subtitle summarized her experience, traveling "from lost to found on the Pacific Crest Trail"). In what was described as the "Wild Effect," the number of through hikers on the Pacific Crest Trail jumped the year after Strayed's book appeared.[14] John Muir would have approved; so might Teddy Roosevelt (if he could have overlooked the fact that Strayed was a woman).

We attach our dreams to mountains. Mountains, we hope, will bring us strength, purpose, unity, salvation. We go to the mountains on a quest that, at various times and places, has been national, spiritual, personal, or some combination of all three. "I keep a mountain anchored off eastward a little way," Henry David Thoreau wrote in a letter to a correspondent in 1857, "which I ascend in my dreams both awake and asleep." He could see this phantom mountain as clearly as the real mountains he climbed, comparing it to Wachusett, the Massachusetts peak he had described in his first published travel essay fifteen years earlier. "I keep this mountain to ride instead of a horse," he concluded.[15] A little over a century later, approaching a much larger mountain than Thoreau's Wachusett, Tom Hornbein found himself wondering, before Everest, "if I had not come a long way only to find that what I really sought was something I had left behind."[16]

American climbing has a long history, and an acute historical memory. Climbers have always been deeply interested in their predecessors and the routes they established on rock faces and snowy ridgelines—even as successive generations constantly reinvent climbing techniques and ethics. The mountains will be with us forever. What Americans choose to do on those mountains and to think of and hope for atop them in years to come is impossible to predict, except that it will surely involve a blending of tradition and innovation.

NOTES

PREFACE AND ACKNOWLEDGMENTS

1. Outdoor Foundation, *Outdoor Participation Rate: 2014*, 40, http://www.outdoor foundation.org/pdf/ResearchParticipation2014.pdf.

CHAPTER ONE: PIONEERS, 1642–1842

1. For primary sources documenting Darby Field's climb, see Richard S. Dunn, James Savage, and Laetitia Yeandle, eds., *The Journal of John Winthrop, 1630–1649* (Cambridge, MA: Harvard University Press, 1996), 393–94, 417; and David Mazel, *Pioneering Ascents: The Origins of Climbing in America, 1642–1873* (Harrisburg, PA: Stackpole Books, 1991), 12–15.
2. Quoted in Allen Bent and Charles Fay, "Earliest American Mountaineering," in *A Century of American Alpinism*, ed. William Putnam (Boulder, CO: American Alpine Club, 2002), 7.
3. For the history and worldview of the Pigwacket, see Christopher Johnson, *This Grand & Magnificent Place: The Wilderness Heritage of the White Mountains* (Durham: University of New Hampshire Press, 2006), 10–13.
4. For a description of Mount Washington and its surroundings, see Stephen D. Smith and Mike Dickerman, *The 4000-Footers of the White Mountains*, 2nd ed. (Littleton, NH: Bondcliff Books, 2008), 136–41. For a description of the White Mountains and their geological origins, see Randall H. Bennett, *The White Mountains: Alps of New England* (Charleston, SC: Arcadia, 2003), 10–15. The exact route by which Field climbed the mountain remains in dispute; it may have been from the east via present-day Boott Spur, or, alternately, from the southwest over the southern Presidentials—Mounts Eisenhower, Franklin, and Monroe—then up to the summit from Lakes of the Clouds (roughly the route of the present-day Crawford Path). See Smith and Dickerman, *4000-Footers*, 143; Bennett, *White Mountains*, 28; and Laura Waterman and Guy Waterman,

Forest and Crag: A History of Hiking, Trail Blazing and Adventure in the Northeast Mountains (Boston: Appalachian Mountain Club, 1989), 9–12.

5. Russell M. Lawson, *Passaconaway's Realm: Captain John Evans and the Exploration of Mount Washington* (Hanover, NH: University Press of New England, 2002), 3–4.

6. Englishman John Josselyn made several lengthy trips to New England between the 1630s and the 1670s, and in a 1672 account of his journeys published in London, he described New Hampshire's mountains as being "known by the name of *White Mountains*, upon which lieth Snow all the year." Josselyn, *New England's Rarities* (Boston: William Veazie, 1865), 36; Paul J. Lindholt, ed., *John Josselyn, Colonial Traveller: A Critical Edition of Two Voyages to New England* (Hanover, NH: University Press of New England, 1988), xxi, xxx; Roderick Frazier Nash, *Wilderness and the American Mind*, 4th ed. (New Haven, CT: Yale University Press, 2001), 53; Thomas Starr King, *The White Hills: Their Legends, Landscape and Poetry* (Boston: Crosby and Nichols, 1862), 35, 37–39.

7. David S. Walls, "On the Naming of Appalachia," in *An Appalachian Symposium: Essays Written in Honor of Cratis D. Williams*, ed. J. W. Williamson (Boone, NC: Appalachian State University Press, 1977), 56–59.

8. Anthony Huxley, ed., *Standard Encyclopedia of the World's Mountains* (New York: G. P. Putnam's Sons, 1962), 79, 85; François Furstenberg, "The Significance of the Trans-Appalachian Frontier in Atlantic History," *American Historical Review* 113 (June 2008): 647; "Geologic Provinces of the United States: Appalachian Highlands Province," U.S. Geological Survey, http://geomaps.wr.usgs.gov/parks/province/appalach.html, accessed June 12, 2015. I am grateful to Todd Rayne, Barbara Tewksbury, and Dave Bailey of the Hamilton College Department of Geosciences for their contribution to my understanding of the complex geological history of the Appalachians.

9. Dunn, Savage, and Yeandle, *Journal of John Winthrop*, 394.

10. Ibid., 417.

11. Accounts of Darby Field's ascent (which do not agree on all essentials) include Waterman and Waterman, *Forest and Crag*, 7–14; Bennett, *White Mountains*, 27–29; and Lawson, *Passaconaway's Realm*, 8–15.

12. For climbing in the White Mountains between 1642 and 1784, see Pavel Cenkl, *This Vast Book of Nature: Writing the Landscape of New Hampshire's White Mountains, 1784–1911* (Iowa City: University of Iowa Press, 2006), 2–4.

13. Martin Luther, *The Creation: A Commentary on the First Five Chapters of the Book of Genesis* (n.p.: BiblioLife, 2009), 273; Marjorie Hope Nicolson, *Mountain Gloom and Mountain Glory: The Development of the Aesthetics of the Infinite* (Ithaca, NY: Cornell University Press, 1959), 78–95, 100–4. Thomas Burnet's *The Sacred Theory of the Earth*, published in 1681, presented a scriptural/scientific explanation of the impact of the flood on the earth's surface, leaving "a World lying in its Rubbish." Quoted in Robert Macfarlane, *Mountains of the Mind* (New York: Pantheon Books, 2003), 27.

14. On European attitudes toward mountains in the premodern era, see Fergus Fleming, *Killing Dragons: The Conquest of the Alps* (New York: Atlantic Monthly Press, 2000), 1–10; Jeremy Bernstein, *Ascent: Of the Invention of Mountain Climbing*

and Its Practice (Lincoln: University of Nebraska Press, 1979), 20. For discussions of Puritan beliefs, see Nicolson, *Mountain Gloom and Mountain Glory*, 43–44; and Johnson, *This Grand & Magnificent Place*, 14–25.

15. The 3,560-foot Mount Snowdon in Wales, nearly 3,000 feet below the level of Mount Washington, and well known to Britons since Roman times, had its first ascent only in 1639, three years before Field's climb. Frederick L. Wolfe, *High Summits: 370 Famous Peak First Ascents* (Englewood, CO: Hugo House, 2013), 224, 227.

16. William Bradford, *History of Plymouth Plantation* (Boston: Wright and Palmer, 1900), 95.

17. Quoted in Alan Heimert, "Puritanism, the Wilderness, and the Frontier," *New England Quarterly* 26 (September 1953): 372.

18. Charles Shain and Samuella Shain, eds., *The Maine Reader: The Down East Experience from 1614 to the Present* (Jaffrey, NH: David R. Godine, 1997), 27; John Neff, *Katahdin, an Historic Journey: Legends, Exploration, and Preservation of Maine's Highest Peak* (Boston: Appalachian Mountain Club, 2006), 6–10; John Giles, *Memoirs of Odd Adventures, Strange Deliverances, Etc., in the Captivity of John Giles* (Cincinnati, OH: Spiller and Gates, 1869), 46–47. Giles's captivity narrative, originally printed in Boston in 1736, provides the first published reference to Katahdin. Also see Waterman and Waterman, *Forest and Crag*, 3.

19. Belden Lane, "Jonathan Edwards on Beauty, Desire, and the Sensory World," *Theological Studies* 65 (2004): 51. For a discussion of Edwards's attitudes toward the natural world, see Perry Miller, "From Edwards to Emerson," in *Errand into the Wilderness* (New York: Harper, 1964), 184–203.

20. Jonathan Edwards, *The Works of Jonathan Edwards*, vol. 17, *Sermons and Discourses, 1730–1733*, 433, WJE Online, http://edwards.yale.edu.

21. Clarence Walworth Alvord and Lee Bidgood, *The First Explorations of the Trans-Allegheny Region by the Virginians, 1650–1674* (Cleveland, OH: Arthur H. Clark, 1912), 209–26; R. P. Stephen Davis Jr., "The Travels of James Needham and Gabriel Arthur through Virginia, North Carolina, and Beyond, 1673–74," *Southern Indian Studies* 39 (1990): 31–55; Richard B. Drake, *A History of Appalachia* (Lexington: University of Kentucky Press, 2001), 27–28.

22. Lynda McDaniel, *High Road Guide to the North Carolina Mountains* (Atlanta: Longstreet, 1998), 3; Nevin M. Fenneman, *Physiography of the Eastern United States* (New York: McGraw-Hill, 1938), 163–65; Huxley, *Standard Encyclopedia*, 96.

23. Thomas Jefferson, *Notes on the State of Virginia* (New York: Norton, 1972), 20.

24. Quoted in Carl Becker, *Beginnings of the American People*, vol. 1 (Boston: Houghton Mifflin, 1915), 30–31.

25. John Lederer, *The Discoveries of John Lederer*, ed. William P. Cumming (Charlottesville: University of Virginia Press, 1958), 18–19; Alvord and Bidgood, *First Explorations*, 63–69; "John Lederer," Virginia Places, http://www.virginiaplaces .org/settleland/lederer.html, accessed June 12, 2015. Also see the facsimile edition, *The Discoveries of John Lederer* (Ann Arbor, MI: University Microfilms, 1966).

26. Lederer, *Discoveries of John Lederer*, 36; "Physiographic Regions of Virginia," Vir-

ginia Places, http://www.virginiaplaces.org/regions/physio.html, accessed June 12, 2015.

27. Lederer, *Discoveries of John Lederer*, 89.

28. Alexander Spotswood, governor of Virginia, led an expedition of wealthy Virginians, dubbed the "Knights of the Golden Horseshoe," into the Shenandoah Valley in 1716, through the gap in the Blue Ridge created by the James River, opening the region to land speculations and settlement. On the journey, the group climbed to the top of a peak they called Mount George (probably 2,224-foot High Top), where they "drank King George's Health." Lewis Preston Summers, *History of Southwestern Virginia, 1746–1786* (Johnson City, TN: Overmountain Press, 1989), 17, 38–39; Drake, *History of Appalachia*, 33; William H. Goetzmann and Glyndwr Williams, *The Atlas of North American Exploration: From the Norse Voyages to the Race to the Pole* (Norman: University of Oklahoma Press, 1992), 82.

29. Walter Klinefelter, *Lewis Evans and His Maps* (Philadelphia: American Philosophical Society, 1971), 21; Henry Savage, *Discovering America, 1700–1875* (New York: Harper & Row, 1979), 58.

30. Quoted in Philip Gibson Terrie Jr., "The Adirondacks, from Dismal Wilderness to Forever Wild: A Case Study of American Attitudes toward Wilderness" (PhD diss., George Washington University, 1979), 17.

31. W. J. Eccles, *The Canadian Frontier, 1534–1760* (Albuquerque: University of New Mexico Press, 1974), 149; David Lavender, *The Rockies* (Lincoln: University of Nebraska Press, 2003), 32–34; Donald Jackson, *Thomas Jefferson and the Rocky Mountains* (Norman: University of Oklahoma Press, 2002), 3; Walter R. Borneman and Lyndon J. Lampert, *A Climbing Guide to Colorado's Fourteeners* (Boulder, CO: Pruett, 1998), 10–11; J. N. Bowman and R. F. Heizer, *Anza and the Northwest Frontier of New Spain* (Los Angeles: Southwest Museum, 1967), 45.

32. The best overview of the history of the last French and Indian War is provided in Fred Anderson, *Crucible of War: The Seven Years' War and the Fate of Empire in British North America, 1754–1766* (New York: Vintage, 2001). For skirmishing in the region of the White Mountains in the various wars between the French and British, see Bennett, *White Mountains*, 33–38.

33. Colin Calloway, *The Scratch of a Pen: 1763 and the Transformation of North America* (New York: Oxford University Press, 2006), 92–99.

34. John Mack Faragher, *Daniel Boone: The Life and Legend of an American Pioneer* (New York: Henry Holt, 1992), 126–27.

35. Bennett, *White Mountains*, 41–43.

36. George Washington to the President of Congress, June 17, 1783, in *Writings of Washington*, vol. 27, http://www.archive.org/stream/writingsofgeorge27wash/writingsofgeorge27wash_djvu.txt.

37. Thomas Jefferson to Benjamin Rush, January 16, 1811, in *The Works of Thomas Jefferson*, vol. 11, *Correspondence and Papers 1808–1816*, http://oll.libertyfund.org/?option=com_staticxt&staticfile=show.php%3Ftitle=807&chapter=88070&layout=html#a_2004793.

38. Quoted in James D. Drake, *The Nation's Nature: How Continental Presumptions Gave Rise to the United States of America* (Chancellorsville: University of Vir-

ginia Press, 2011), 24. Also see Drake, *History of Appalachia*, 19–24; Norman K. Risjord, *Jefferson's America, 1760–1815* (Madison, WI: Madison House, 1991), 195; and William H. Goetzmann, *New Lands, New Men: America and the Second Great Age of Discovery* (New York: Viking, 1986), 110–12.

39. Pamela Regis, *Describing Early America: Bartram, Jefferson, Crèvecoeur, and the Rhetoric of Natural History* (Dekalb: Northern Illinois University Press, 1992), xi, 5–6.

40. William Bartram, *Travels and Other Writings*, ed. Thomas Slaughter (New York: Library of America, 1996), 275–81; Gail Fishman, *Journeys through Paradise: Pioneering Naturalists in the Southeast* (Gainesville: University Press of Florida, 2000), 34–41; Savage, *Discovering America*, 68; Regis, *Describing Early America*, 43; Nash, *Wilderness and the American Mind*, 54.

41. Quoted in James P. Ronda, *Jefferson's West: A Journey with Lewis and Clark* ([Charlottesville, VA]: Thomas Jefferson Foundation, 2000), 19.

42. Jefferson would undertake one expedition in the name of science, botanizing with James Madison on a 1791 tour that took them to the eastern edge of the Adirondacks in New York, and down the Connecticut River valley in Vermont. Jackson, *Thomas Jefferson and the Rocky Mountains*, 68–69.

43. That suggestion, offered in the original version of *Notes*, was cut by Jefferson in later editions. Pioneering Scottish geologist James Hutton would offer a similar explanation for the seashell phenomenon in his three-volume *Theory of the Earth*, which was published several years *after* the publication of Jefferson's *Notes*. Macfarlane, *Mountains of the Mind*, 34.

44. Thomas Jefferson, *Notes on the State of Virginia* (Chapel Hill: University of North Carolina Press, 1955), 19.

45. Jackson, *Thomas Jefferson and the Rocky Mountains*, 37.

46. Waterman and Waterman, *Forest and Crag*, 27. The account that follows draws upon their book, 21–27, and the map on p. 42. Also see Johnson, *This Grand & Magnificent Place*, 26–31.

47. William Parker Cutler and Julia Perkins Cutler, eds., *Life, Journals and Correspondence of Rev. Manasseh Cutler, LL.D.*, vol. 2 (Cincinnati, OH: Robert Clarke, 1888), 221. Cutler returned to the mountain in 1804 with the respected scientists Nathaniel Bowditch and William D. Peck, and after further barometric efforts came up with a new, if still inaccurate, estimate of the height of the summit: 7,055 feet. Bennett, *White Mountains*, 46–47.

48. Jeremy Belknap, *Journal of a Tour to the White Mountains in July, 1784* (Boston: Massachusetts Historical Society, 1876), 16. For Belknap and Cutler's role in the naming of Mount Washington, see Lawrence Martin, "Who Named Mount Washington?" *Geographical Review* 28 (April 1938): 303–5.

49. Timothy Dwight, *Travels in New-England and New-York*, vol. 2 (New Haven, CT: T. Dwight, 1821), 261. For Dwight's climbs in New England and the Catskills, see Waterman and Waterman, *Forest and Crag*, 57, 71.

50. Quoted in Nicolson, *Mountain Gloom and Mountain Glory*, 305.

51. Ibid., 271–303.

52. Edmund Burke, *A Philosophical Enquiry into the Origin of Our Ideas of the Sublime and Beautiful* (London: Dodsley, 1764), 57.

53. Macfarlane, *Mountains of the Mind*, 74–81. A related aesthetic category, the "picturesque," emerged in the later decades of the eighteenth century, celebrating the pleasures that came from observing the rough and irregular features of nature. Nash, *Wilderness and the American Mind*, 46.

54. Percy Bysshe Shelley, "Mount Blanc: Lines Written in the Vale of Chamouni," in *Shelley*, ed. William Meredith (New York: Dell, 1962), 37. Shelley remained a favorite of mountaineers for more than a century; on ship, en route to his third and final Mount Everest expedition in 1924, George Leigh-Mallory read André Maurois's biography of the poet; confined to their tents by a storm at Camp 3, just below Everest's North Col, Mallory and his tentmates read aloud Shelley's "Mount Blanc." Macfarlane, *Mountains of the Mind*, 261, 265.

55. For background on the American sense of the sublime, see Richard H. Gassan, *The Birth of American Tourism: New York, the Hudson Valley, and American Culture 1790–1830* (Amherst: University of Massachusetts Press, 2008), 52–57; Waterman and Waterman, *Forest and Crag*, 69–77.

56. John R. Fitzmier, *New England's Moral Legislator: Timothy Dwight, 1752–1817* (Bloomington: Indiana University Press, 1998), 3, 52, 145; Risjord, *Jefferson's America*, 197. For Thoreau and Dwight, see J. Parker Huber, ed., *Elevating Ourselves: Thoreau on Mountains* (Boston: Houghton Mifflin, 1999), 6.

57. Timothy Dwight, *The Conquest of Canaan: A Poem in Eleven Books* (Hartford, CT: Elisha Babcock, 1785), 253.

58. During the French Revolution, as Peter Hansen notes, mountains took on a similar symbolic role as representative of national purpose. The district of Savoy, in which Mont Blanc lies, was incorporated into the revolutionary French state in 1792, and models of large white mountains, crowned by a temple of reason, were often incorporated into revolutionary festivals. On the other hand, Mont Blanc also took on symbolic importance for royalist exiles, who fled through Savoy to refuge in Italy. And within a few years, mountains lost favor as revolutionary symbols, their very height being taken as an affront to notions of republican equality. Peter H. Hansen, *The Summits of Modern Man: Mountaineering after the Enlightenment* (Cambridge, MA: Harvard University Press, 2013), 60–89.

59. Quoted in Jackson, *Thomas Jefferson and the Rocky Mountains*, 8.

60. Ibid., 74–78.

61. Broughton Bluff, a steep basaltic crag in Troutdale, Oregon, east of Portland, is thought to mark the farthest point of Lieutenant Broughton's expedition up the Columbia. The westernmost edge of the Columbia River Gorge, the bluff is a popular rock-climbing destination.

62. Alexander Mackenzie, *Voyages from Montreal, on the River St. Laurence, through the Continent of North America, to the Frozen and Pacific Oceans; in the Years 1789 and 1793* (London: R. Noble, 1801), 411; Barry M. Gough, *Distant Dominion: Britain and the Northwest Coast of North America, 1579–1809* (Vancouver: University of British Columbia Press, 1980), 138–39.

63. Nevin M. Fenneman, *Physiography of the Western United States* (New York: McGraw-Hill, 1931), 92–132, 150–224; Howard Palmer, "The Rocky Mountains of the United States," *American Alpine Journal* 1 (1931): 360–67.

64. For the background of the members of the Corps of Discovery, see Charles

G. Clarke, *The Men of the Lewis and Clark Expedition* (Lincoln: University of Nebraska Press, 2002). This account of the Lewis and Clark expedition's encounter with the Rockies is based upon the expedition journals, plus Stephen E. Ambrose, *Undaunted Courage: Meriwether Lewis, Thomas Jefferson, and the Opening of the American West* (New York: Simon and Schuster, 1996), 251–301; James P. Ronda, *Lewis and Clark among the Indians* (Lincoln: University of Nebraska Press, 1998), 133–62; Paul Russell Cutright, *Lewis and Clark: Pioneering Naturalists* (Lincoln: University of Nebraska Press, 2003), 185–213; and Maurice Isserman, *Across America: The Lewis & Clark Expedition* (New York: Facts on File, 2005), 102–17.

65. Gary E. Moulton, ed., *The Lewis and Clark Journals: An American Epic of Discovery* (Lincoln: University of Nebraska Press, 2003), 174.

66. Ibid., 206.

67. Ibid., 209.

68. Ibid., 212.

69. Ibid., 294.

70. John Allen, "The Maps of the Lewis and Clark Expedition," in *Mapping the West: America's Westward Movement, 1524–1890*, ed. Paul E. Cohen (New York: Rizzoli, 2002), 92–94.

71. The account of Pike's expedition that follows is drawn from W. Eugene Hollon, *The Lost Pathfinder: Zebulon Montgomery Pike* (Norman: University of Oklahoma Press, 1949), 101–57; William M. Bueler, *Roof of the Rockies: A History of Colorado Mountaineering* (Golden: Colorado Mountain Club Press, 2000), 10–15; William H. Goetzmann, *Army Exploration in the American West, 1803–1863* (New Haven, CT: Yale University Press, 1959), 36–38; Matthew L. Harris and Jay H. Buckley, *Zebulon Pike, Thomas Jefferson, and the Opening of the American West* (Norman: University of Oklahoma Press, 2012); and Maurice Isserman, *Exploring North America, 1800–1900* (New York: Facts on File, 2005), 30–35.

72. Donald Jackson, ed., *The Journals of Zebulon Montgomery Pike*, vol. 1 (Norman: University of Oklahoma Press, 1966), 345.

73. Borneman and Lampert, *Climbing Guide to Colorado's Fourteeners*, 2. The Colorado Front Range is bounded to the south by the Arkansas River and to the north by the Cache la Poudre River. Fenneman, *Physiography of the Western United States*, 98.

74. Jackson, *Journals of Zebulon Montgomery Pike*, 1:350–52; Fred Beckey, *Mountains of North America* (San Francisco: Sierra Club Books, 1982), 74–75. For the various candidates put forward over the years for the peak that Pike and his companions scaled, see Bueler, *Roof of the Rockies*, 10–13.

75. I'm grateful to Walter R. Borneman for helping me plot Pike's route and that of other visitors to South Park. Trout Creek Pass had an earlier-documented crossing, by a Spanish expedition led by Juan Bautista de Anza in 1779, traveling in the opposite direction from Pike. Pike also passed near present-day Fairplay, Colorado, the town that is the model for the community portrayed in the television series *South Park*. Howard Ensign Evans notes that Pike's party may have been preceded into South Park the previous year by a Kentucky-born American trader based in Santa Fe named James Purcell, who later told Pike he had visited the

region with a party of Kiowa Indians. Evans, *The Natural History of the Long Expedition to the Rocky Mountains, 1819–1820* (New York: Oxford University Press, 1997), 4–6.

76. Jay H. Buckley offers a more positive account of the expedition in his essay "Pike as a Forgotten and Misunderstood Explorer," in Harris and Buckley, *Zebulon Pike*, 21–59.

77. The account of the Long expedition that follows draws upon Evans, *Natural History of the Long Expedition*, 141–49; Bueler, *Roof of the Rockies*, 15–19; Goetzmann, *Army Exploration*, 40–44; and Isserman, *Exploring North America*, 81–85.

78. According to a treaty that the United States negotiated with Spain in 1819, the Red and the Arkansas Rivers were now recognized by both countries as the official dividing line between the heretofore vaguely defined boundaries of the United States' Louisiana Territory and Spanish-owned lands to the south.

79. Maxine Benson, ed., *From Pittsburgh to the Rocky Mountains* (Golden, CO: Fulcrum, 1988), 157.

80. Ibid., 193.

81. James's record would stand until 1854, when California's 14,179-foot Mount Shasta had its first recorded ascent. The qualification "highest ascent *yet recorded*" is essential, because archaeological evidence suggests that western Native Americans, unlike their eastern counterparts, did climb mountains, and even very high ones. It is thought that Indians reached the summit of Longs Peak (14,259 feet) and Blanca Peak (14,338 feet) in Colorado, as well as Middle Teton (12,804 feet) and possibly Grand Teton (13,775 feet) in Wyoming, long before those mountains were climbed by white Americans. Bueler, *Roof of the Rockies*, 3; Leigh N. Ortenburger and Reynold G. Jackson, *A Climber's Guide to the Teton Range*, 3rd ed. (Seattle: Mountaineers, 1996), 152.

82. Benson, *From Pittsburgh*, 224.

83. Lavender, *Rockies*, 75. James did leave his name on another high place: a 13,294-foot peak west of Denver was named James Peak.

84. In 1832, US Army major B. L. E. Bonneville headed west to explore the Rockies. Under his orders, fur trapper Joseph Walker led an exploring party west from Salt Lake to California, crossing from the east via the Carson River and Stanislaus River route in 1833, and returning farther south, through what became known as Walker Pass, 5,250 feet in elevation. In between, some of Walker's party caught a glimpse of, without entering, the Yosemite Valley. Bonneville did not accompany the expedition. He was on leave from the army, without official orders, and traveling at his own expense. Goetzmann, *Army Exploration*, 52; James G. Moore, *Exploring the Highest Sierra* (Stanford, CA: Stanford University Press, 2000), 22–23; Francis P. Farquhar, *History of the Sierra Nevada* (Berkeley: University of California Press, 1965), 32–38. Bonneville did make a notable climb of his own in 1833, a first ascent of a Wind River Range mountain, probably 13,804-foot Gannett Peak.

85. There may be one exception to the rule that mountain men were uninterested in reaching mountain summits. According to a thirdhand account published in 1873, a mountain man by the name of "Michaud" (possibly Michaud LeClaire of

the Hudson's Bay Company) claimed to have attempted to reach the summit of Grand Teton thirty years earlier, in 1843. Ortenburger and Jackson, *Climber's Guide to the Teton Range*, 152.

86. The account of the mountain men that follows draws upon Robert M. Utley, *A Life Wild and Perilous: Mountain Men and the Paths to the Pacific* (New York: Henry Holt, 1997), 11–22, 39–67, 83–102; Richard Edward Oglesby, *Manuel Lisa and the Opening of the Missouri Fur Trade* (Norman: University of Oklahoma Press, 1963), 35–98; William H. Goetzmann, *Exploration and Empire: The Explorer and the Scientist in the Winning of the American West* (New York: Knopf, 1966), 17–35, 105–80; Barton H. Barbour, *Jedediah Smith: No Ordinary Mountain Man* (Norman: University of Oklahoma Press, 2009), 31–156; Goetzmann, *New Lands, New Men*, 125–49; Gary Ferguson, *The Great Divide: A Biography of the Rocky Mountains* (Woodstock, VT: Countryman Press, 2006), 58–97; and Isserman, *Exploring North America*, 37–61.

87. Washington Irving, *Astoria, or Anecdotes of an Enterprise beyond the Rocky Mountains* (Philadelphia: Carey, Lea, and Blanchard, 1836), 2. For another example, see Washington Irving, *The Adventures of Captain Bonneville* (Philadelphia, 1837). The genre of mountain-men tales had an enduring appeal that survived the disappearance of the men themselves by the 1850s; for later examples, see Dewitt C. Peters, *The Story of Kit Carson's Life and Adventures* (Hartford, CT: Dustin, Gilman, 1875).

88. Colter's exact route has been the subject of much debate. For a detailed examination of the questions involved, see Burton Harris, *John Colter: His Years in the Rockies* (New York: Scribner, 1952), 73–114; and Merrill J. Mattes, *Colter's Hell & Jackson's Hole: The Fur Trapper's Exploration of the Yellowstone and Grand Teton Region* (n.p.: Yellowstone Library and Museum Association, 1962), especially pp. 13–15, 19–21. Also see Robert B. Betts, *Along the Ramparts of the Tetons: The Saga of Jackson Hole, Wyoming* (Boulder: Colorado Associated University Press, 1978), 31–49.

89. Betts, *Along the Ramparts of the Tetons*, 64.

90. For Smith's early life, see Dale L. Morgan, *Jedediah Smith* (New York: Bobbs Merrill, 1953), 23–26; and Barbour, *Jedediah Smith*, 14–30.

91. Quoted in Barbour, *Jedediah Smith*, 17.

92. Quoted in Dale L. Morgan, ed., *The West of William H. Ashley, 1822–1838* (Denver: Old West Publishing Company, 1964), 97.

93. Quoted in Barbour, *Jedediah Smith*, 57.

94. Jedediah Smith, *The Southwest Expedition of Jedediah S. Smith*, ed. George R. Brooks (Lincoln: University of Nebraska Press, 1989), 36–37.

95. Ibid., 149.

96. Although Smith's party made the first recorded crossing of the Sierra, others had preceded him but left no record. The Paiute Indians, who lived to the east of the Sierra Nevada, and the Monache Indians, who lived to the west of the range, crossed mountain passes, including the 11,800-foot Kearsage Pass, to trade with each other. Moore, *Exploring the Highest Sierra*, 13, 22. Also see Farquhar, *History of the Sierra Nevada*, 23–26.

97. Barbour, *Jedediah Smith*, 11.

98. Francis Parkman, *The Oregon Trail*, ed. E. N. Feltskog (Madison: University of Wisconsin Press, 1969), 148.

99. Washington Irving, *The Sketch Book*, ed. Elmer E. Wentworth (Boston: Allyn & Bacon, 1895), 38.

100. Pierre M. Irving, ed., *Life and Letters of Washington Irving*, vol. 1 (New York: Putnam, 1862), 42.

101. Bruce C. Wadsworth, *Guide to Catskill Trails* ([Lake George, NY]: Adirondack Mountain Club, 1994), 2–5; Edward G. Henry, *Catskill Trails: A Ranger's Guide to the High Peaks*, bk. 1 (Hensonville, NY: Black Dome Press, 2000), 23–33; Fenneman, *Physiography of the Eastern United States*, 319–23.

102. James Fenimore Cooper, *The Leatherstocking Tales*, vol. 1, *The Pioneers* (New York: Library of America, 1985), 295. Cooper lived in Paris from 1826 to 1833, visiting the Swiss Alps as a tourist, but not as a climber. Putnam, *Century of American Alpinism*, 40; Wayne Franklin, *James Fenimore Cooper: The Early Years* (New Haven, CT: Yale University Press, 2007), 341.

103. David Stradling, *Making Mountains: New York City and the Catskills* (Seattle: University of Washington Press, 2007), 79–84; David Schuyler, *Sanctified Landscape: Writers, Artists, and the Hudson River Valley, 1820–1909* (Ithaca, NY: Cornell University Press, 2012), 8–27.

104. Stradling, *Making Mountains*, 59–72; Schuyler, *Sanctified Landscape*, 28–46.

105. The links that connect Cooper's and Irving's writings, Cole's paintings, the tourist industry, and American nationalism are suggested in Franklin, *James Fenimore Cooper*, 432–33; and Gassan, *Birth of American Tourism*, 3–4. Also see Kenneth Myers, *The Catskills: Painters, Writers, and Tourists in the Mountains, 1820–1895* (Yonkers, NY: Hudson River Museum of Westchester, 1988), 19–20; and Eric Hirsch, "Landscape: Between Place and Space," in *The Anthropology of Landscape: Perspectives on Place and Space*, eds. Eric Hirsch and Michael O'Hanlon (New York: Oxford University Press, 1995), 2.

106. Thomas Cole, "Essay on American Scenery," *American Monthly Magazine* 1 (January 1836), https://www.csun.edu/~ta3584/Cole.htm; Nash, *Wilderness and the American Mind*, 80–81.

107. Beckey, *Mountains of North America*, 40–41.

108. Lucy Crawford, *The History of the White Mountains*, 3rd ed. (Portland, ME: Thurston, 1886), 47.

109. For a discussion of the importance of Lucy Crawford's history, see Cenkl, *This Vast Book of Nature*, 3–51.

110. Barbara Novak, *Nature and Culture: American Landscape and Painting, 1825–1875* (New York: Oxford University Press, 1980), 4–9; Earl A. Powell, *Thomas Cole* (New York: Abrams, 1990), 35; John F. Sears, *Sacred Places: American Tourist Attractions in the Nineteenth Century* (New York: Oxford University Press, 1989), 49–71.

111. At first, four additional Adirondack peaks were measured at over 4,000 feet, but they actually fall a little short of that height. They are still included on the list of peaks known as the "46-ers"—and climbing all forty-six originally thought to be 4,000 feet or higher brings the honorific of being a "Forty-Sixer." For a complete

list, see Adirondack Forty-Sixers, "The Peaks!" http://adk46er.org/peaks.html, accessed June 12, 2015.

112. Jerry Jenkins, *The Adirondack Atlas: A Geographic Portrait of the Adirondack Park* (Syracuse, NY: Syracuse University Press, 2004), 10–12; Paul Schneider, *The Adirondacks: A History of America's First Wilderness* (New York: Henry Holt, 1997), 129–130; Stephen B. Sulavik, *Adirondack: Of Indians and Mountains, 1535–1838* (Fleischmanns, NY: Purple Mountain Press, 2005), 69–70.

113. Sulavik, *Adirondack*, 36.

114. Waterman and Waterman, *Forest and Crag*, 65–67.

115. Quoted in Sulavik, *Adirondack*, 93. Also see Waterman and Waterman, *Forest and Crag*, 101–7.

116. Waterman and Waterman, *Forest and Crag*, 110–11.

117. Quoted in Novak, *Nature and Culture*, 15.

118. Frémont's name is sometimes rendered accentless; other times, given an accent. For the sake of consistency, it is spelled throughout this account as Frémont.

119. The account of Frémont's 1842 Wind River expedition is drawn from Tom Chaffin, *Pathfinder: John Charles Frémont and the Course of American Empire* (New York: Hill and Wang, 2002), 117–46; David Roberts, *A Newer World: Kit Carson, John C. Frémont, and the Claiming of the American West* (New York: Touchstone, 2000), 26–49; and Isserman, *Exploring North America*, 86–90.

120. Andrew Menard, *Sight Unseen: How Frémont's First Expedition Changed the American Landscape* (Lincoln: University of Nebraska Press, 2012), 126–27.

121. John C. Frémont, *Narrative of the Exploring Expedition to the Rocky Mountains in the Year 1842 and to Oregon and North California in the Years 1843–44* (New York: Appleton, 1846), 46. Planting the national flag on the summit of a mountain upon its first ascent would later become a ritual of mountaineering (especially in the Himalaya). But relatively few nineteenth-century climbers, in the United States or elsewhere, bothered with carrying a flag to the summit or, if they did, attached much significance to the act. As Andrew Menard notes, in 1820 Stephen Long "had also carried a flag when he climbed what is now known as Pike's Peak, but he never made patriotism an issue." Menard, *Sight Unseen*, 142.

122. Menard, *Sight Unseen*, xxviii–xxix.

123. Frémont, *Narrative of the Exploring Expedition*, 46.

124. Ibid.

CHAPTER TWO: HARDY MOUNTAIN PLANTS, 1842–1865

1. For the significance of this early essay in Thoreau's development as a writer, see Robert D. Richardson Jr., *Henry Thoreau: A Life of the Mind* (Berkeley: University of California Press, 1986), 119–20.

2. Henry David Thoreau, "A Walk to Wachusett," in *Thoreau in the Mountains* (New York: Farrar, Strauss, Giroux, 1982), 4–6, 23–24, 37; Walter Harding, *The Days of Henry Thoreau* (New York: Knopf, 1965), 132.

3. Thoreau, "Walk to Wachusett," 41.

4. Ibid., 27; Lauriat Lane Jr., "Mountain Gloom and Yankee Poetry: Thoreau, Emerson, Frost," *Dalhousie Review* 55 (Winter 1975–76): 618.

5. Henry David Thoreau, *Walden* (Princeton, NJ: Princeton University Press, 1989), 321. For Thoreau's interest in the history of exploration, see Richardson, *Henry Thoreau*, 13.

6. For an overview of the movement, see Philip Gura, *American Transcendentalism: A History* (New York: Hill and Wang, 2007).

7. Kant wasn't a mountain-climber, but the German romantic painter Caspar David Friedrich, influenced by Kant, provided an endlessly reproduced image of alpine inspiration in his 1818 painting *Wanderer above the Sea of Fog*, depicting a lone climber in the Elbe Sandstone Mountains of Saxony in south-eastern Germany. For a discussion of the painting's significance, see Michael Gorra, *The Bells in Their Silence* (Princeton, NJ: Princeton University Press, 2004), xi–xii.

8. Quoted in Laura Dassow Walls, *Seeing New Worlds: Henry David Thoreau and Nineteenth-Century Natural Science* (Madison: University of Wisconsin Press, 1995), 3. On Immanuel Kant, see Laura Dassow Walls, *The Passage to Cosmos: Alexander von Humboldt and the Shaping of America* (Chicago: University of Chicago Press, 2009), 32–33.

9. Ralph Waldo Emerson, "Nature," in *Emerson's Nature—Origin, Growth, Meaning*, eds. Merton M. Sealts Jr. and Alfred R. Ferguson (New York: Dodd, Mead, 1969), 30–31, 33.

10. Gura, *American Transcendentalism*, 94–95, 102–3; Richardson, *Henry Thoreau*, 21.

11. Robert D. Richardson Jr., *Emerson: The Mind on Fire* (Berkeley: University of California Press, 1995), 123, 134–35.

12. Laura Waterman and Guy Waterman, *Forest and Crag: A History of Hiking, Trail Blazing and Adventure in the Northeast Mountains* (Boston: Appalachian Mountain Club, 1989), 73.

13. Craig Brandon, *Monadnock: More than a Mountain* (Keene, NH: Surrey Cottage Books, 2007), 21.

14. Ralph Waldo Emerson, *Emerson, Collected Poems and Translations* (New York: Library of America, 1994), 56. Also see Gay Wilson Allen, *Waldo Emerson: A Biography* (New York: Viking, 1981), 486–87.

15. Thomas Star King, *The White Hills: Their Legends, Landscape and Poetry* (Boston: Crosby and Nichols, 1862), 327.

16. J. Parker Huber, ed., *Elevating Ourselves: Thoreau on Mountains* (Boston: Houghton Mifflin, 1999), 3.

17. Henry David Thoreau, *A Week on the Concord and Merrimack Rivers* (Princeton, NJ: Princeton University Press, 1980), 314; Harding, *Days of Henry Thoreau*, 90–93.

18. Quoted in Linck C. Johnson, "Historical Introduction," in Thoreau, *Week on the Concord*, 449.

19. J. Parker Huber, *The Wildest Country: A Guide to Thoreau's Maine* (Boston: Appalachian Mountain Club, 1981), 145; Waterman and Waterman, *Forest and Crag*, 73–74.

20. John Neff, *Katahdin, an Historic Journey: Legends, Exploration, and Preserva-*

tion of Maine's Highest Peak (Boston: Appalachian Mountain Club, 2006), xxiii.

21. Ibid., 21. Also see Waterman and Waterman, *Forest and Crag*, 50–51.

22. For the pre-Thoreau climbing history of the mountain, see Waterman and Waterman, *Forest and Crag*, 50–56, 93–97.

23. While Thoreau's route cannot be traced with absolute certainty, he approached the mountain from the south, following a compass line to the northeast, toward the mountain's South Peak, on a line 2 miles to the east of the present-day Abol Trail. Following the Abol streambed and then turning away from it, he climbed to the west of Abol and Rum Mountains.

24. For accounts of Thoreau's climb, see Harding, *Days of Henry Thoreau*, 210; Neff, *Katahdin*, 233–38; Huber, *Wildest Country*, 141–57; Thoreau, *Thoreau in the Mountains*, 85–161; and Richardson, *Henry Thoreau*, 179–82.

25. Thoreau, *Thoreau in the Mountains*, 144.

26. "Unhandselled" is an archaic phrase meaning "untouched" or "untamed." Thoreau, *Thoreau in the Mountains*, 149; James McIntosh, *Thoreau as Romantic Naturalist: His Shifting Stance towards Nature* (Ithaca, NY: Cornell University Press, 1974), 204–5.

27. The Rockies are longer than the Sierra Nevada, but not in a single continuous line of mountains. James G. Moore, *Exploring the Highest Sierra* (Stanford, CA: Stanford University Press, 2000), 1–9; Francis P. Farquhar, *History of the Sierra Nevada* (Berkeley: University of California Press, 1965), 1–2; George Wuerthner, *Yosemite: A Visitor's Companion* (Mechanicsburg, PA: Stackpole Books, 1994), 5, 50–76.

28. Stephen Porcella and Cameron M. Burns, *Climbing California's Fourteeners: The Route Guide to the Fifteen Highest Peaks* (Seattle: Mountaineers, 1998), 1; Farquhar, *History of the Sierra Nevada*, 14–15.

29. Fred Beckey, *Mountains of North America* (San Francisco: Sierra Club Books, 1982), 169.

30. The account that follows of Frémont's 1843–44 expedition is drawn from William H. Goetzmann, *Army Exploration in the American West, 1803–1863* (New Haven, CT: Yale University Press, 1959), 85–101; David Roberts, *A Newer World: Kit Carson, John C. Frémont, and the Claiming of the American West* (New York: Touchstone, 2000), 128–40; Tom Chaffin, *Pathfinder: John Charles Frémont and the Course of American Empire* (New York: Hill and Wang, 2002), 173–238; and Maurice Isserman, *Exploring North America, 1800–1900* (New York: Facts on File, 2005), 98–102.

31. John C. Frémont, *The Exploring Expedition to the Rocky Mountains, Oregon and California* (New York: Miller, Orton & Mulligan, 1856), 334.

32. Quoted in Roberts, *Newer World*, 134.

33. Frémont, *Exploring Expedition*, 358–59.

34. Quoted in Chaffin, *Pathfinder*, 243.

35. The account of Frémont's 1845–46 expedition is drawn from Goetzmann, *Army Exploration*, 116–22; Roberts, *Newer World*, 141–80; Chaffin, *Pathfinder*, 267–350; and Isserman, *Exploring North America*, 102–9.

36. Robert W. Cherny, Richard Griswold del Castillo, and Gretchen Lemke-Santangelo, *Competing Visions: A History of California* (Boston: Houghton Mifflin, 2005), 98.

37. Quoted in Kevin Starr, *Americans and the California Dream, 1850–1915* (New York: Oxford University Press, 1973), 21.

38. Quoted in John Hope Franklin, *A Southern Odyssey: Travelers in the Antebellum North* (Baton Rouge: Louisiana State University Press, 1976), 117. Myers became the best-known southern travel writer of the era, with the publication of his *Sketches on a Tour through the Northern and Eastern States, the Canadas, and Nova Scotia* (Harrisonburg, VA: Wartmann and Brothers, 1849).

39. Quoted in David Mazel, *Pioneering Ascents: The Origins of Climbing in America, 1642–1873* (Harrisburg, PA: Stackpole Books, 1991), 104.

40. "Elisha Mitchell, 19 Aug. 1793–27 June 1857," Documenting the American South, http://docsouth.unc.edu/browse/bios/pn0001194_bio.html, accessed June 23, 2015; William Putnam, ed., *A Century of American Alpinism* (Boulder, CO: American Alpine Club, 2002), 9. Two earlier deaths of mountain-climbers in the United States were recorded, both on Mount Washington: Frederick Strickland, an Englishman, in 1849; and Lizzie Bourne, in 1855. Waterman and Waterman, *Forest and Crag*, 274; Christopher Johnson, *This Grand & Magnificent Place: The Wilderness Heritage of the White Mountains* (Durham: University of New Hampshire Press, 2006), 158–59.

41. "The Re-interment," in *A Memoir of the Rev. Elisha Mitchell, D.D.* (Chapel Hill, NC: Henderson, 1858), 44.

42. Lynda McDaniel, *High Road Guide to the North Carolina Mountains* (Atlanta: Longstreet, 1998), 89.

43. Stephen L. Harris, *Fire Mountains of the West: The Cascade and Mono Lake Volcanoes* (Missoula, MT: Mountain Press, 1988), 201–28.

44. Fred Beckey, *Cascade Alpine Guide: Climbing and High Routes*, vol. 1, *Columbia River to Stevens Pass* (Seattle: Mountaineers, 1973), 3, 8–9, 11; Harris, *Fire Mountains of the West*, 5, 15–19; Dwight R. Crandell, *The Geologic Story of Mount Rainier*, Geological Survey Bulletin 1292 (Washington, DC: US Government Printing Office, 1969), 3–12.

45. California's two principal Cascade peaks, 14,179-foot Mount Shasta and 10,457-foot Mount Lassen, also known as Lassen Peak, were climbed in the 1850s as well.

46. Thomas J. Dryer, "Editorial Correspondence / Camp, 40 Miles North Vancouver / August 19th, 1853," *Oregonian*, September 3, 1853. The two additional mountains would have been Mount Adams in Washington and Mount Jefferson in Oregon.

47. Beckey, *Cascade Alpine Guide*, 1:55–56. George H. Himes, "First Climbers of Mount Adams," *Steel Points* 1, no. 3 (April 1907): 134–35.

48. Harris, *Fire Mountains of the West*, 172.

49. Joel Palmer, *Journal of Travels over the Rocky Mountains to the Mouth of the Columbia River*, in Reuben Gold Thwaites, *Early Western Travels, 1748–1846*, vol. 30 (Cleveland, OH: Arthur H. Clark, 1906), 133–34; Jack Grauer, *Mount Hood: A Complete History*, 7th ed. (Vancouver, WA: Jack Grauer, 2007), 10–14; John Bell, *On Mount Hood: A Biography of Oregon's Perilous Peak* (Seattle: Sasquatch Books, 2011), 107–11; Malcolm Clark Jr., *Eden Seekers, The Settlement of Oregon,*

1818–1862 (Boston: Houghton Mifflin, 1981), 181; Nicholas A. Dodge, *A Climbing Guide to Oregon* (Beaverton, OR: Touchstone Press, 1975), 45. The glacier that Palmer is thought to have descended was named for him in 1924.

50. Grauer, *Mount Hood*, 248; Bell, *On Mount Hood*, 112–15.

51. Peter H. Hansen, *The Summits of Modern Man: Mountaineering after the Enlightenment* (Cambridge, MA: Harvard University Press, 2013), 184.

52. Grauer, *Mount Hood*, 248.

53. *Oregonian*, August 15, 1857, reprinted in Grauer, *Mount Hood*, 251. Also see Bell, *On Mount Hood*, 114.

54. Quoted in Paul E. Cohen, *Mapping the West: America's Westward Movement 1524–1890* (New York: Rizzoli, 2002), 157. Also see Malcolm J. Rohrbough, *Days of Gold: The California Gold Rush and the American Nation* (Berkeley: University of California Press, 1997), 55–71.

55. Quoted in Farquhar, *History of the Sierra Nevada*, 72. Also see Gary Arce, *Defying Gravity: High Adventure on Yosemite's Walls* (Berkeley, CA: Wilderness Press, 1996), 2–3; Wuerthner, *Yosemite*, 20; William H. Goetzmann, *Exploration and Empire: The Explorer and the Scientist in the Winning of the American West* (New York: Knopf, 1966), 368–69.

56. David Robertson, *West of Eden: A History of the Art and Literature of Yosemite* ([Yosemite National Park, CA]: Yosemite Natural History Association, 1984), 4–6. Also see James Mason Hutchings, *In the Heart of the Sierras* (Oakland, CA: Pacific Press, 1888); John F. Sears, *Sacred Places: American Tourist Attractions in the Nineteenth Century* (New York: Oxford University Press, 1989), 124–27.

57. Quoted in Starr, *Americans and the California Dream*, 101. King's Yosemite dispatches were reprinted in John A. Hussey, ed., *A Vacation among the Sierras: Yosemite in 1860* (San Francisco: Book Club of California, 1962). Also see Farquhar, *History of the Sierra Nevada*, 122, 127; Wuerthner, *Yosemite*, 20–23.

58. From the *Boston Transcript*, November 1860, reprinted in Charles W. Wendte, *Thomas Starr King: Patriot and Preacher* (Boston: Beacon Press, 1921), 145.

59. Quoted in Glenna Matthews, *The Golden State in the Civil War: Thomas Starr King, the Republican Party, and the Birth of Modern California* (New York: Cambridge University Press, 2012), 139; King's role in shaping eastern perceptions of Yosemite is discussed on pp. 131–54.

60. Ralph H. Anderson, "Carleton E. Watkins, Pioneer Photographer of the Pacific Coast," *Yosemite Nature Notes* 32 (April 1953): 34; Nancy K. Anderson and Linda S. Ferber, *Albert Bierstadt: Art & Enterprise* (New York: Hudson Hills Press, 1990), 78–84; Robertson, *West of Eden*, 21–26, 55–74.

61. Marjorie Hope Nicolson, *Mountain Gloom and Mountain Glory: The Development of the Aesthetics of the Infinite* (Ithaca, NY: Cornell University Press, 1959), 159.

62. Quoted in George P. Merrill, *The First One Hundred Years of American Geology* (New Haven, CT: Yale University Press, 1924), 123.

63. For a discussion of Hutton's significance in geological thought, see Robert Macfarlane, *Mountains of the Mind* (New York: Pantheon Books, 2003), 32–36, 59, 62.

64. Ibid., 35, 48–49.

65. Sir Charles Lyell, *A Second Visit to the United States of North America*, vol. 1

(London: John Murray, 1850), 84. Also see Charles Lyell, *Travels in North America in the Years 1841–2* (New York: Wiley and Putnam, 1845).

66. Walt Unsworth, *Hold the Heights: The Foundations of Mountaineering* (Seattle: Mountaineers, 1994), 53, 56.

67. Quoted in Edward Lurie, *Louis Agassiz: A Life in Science* (Chicago: University of Chicago Press, 1960), 98. Also see Louis Menand, *The Metaphysical Club: A Story of Ideas in America* (New York: Farrar, Strauss and Giroux, 2001), 106–7; Macfarlane, *Mountains of the Mind*, 124–26.

68. Thoreau, however, was skeptical of Agassiz's ice-age hypothesis. Gary M. Fleeger and Jon D. Inners, "Henry David Thoreau and His Mentors of the 'Diluvial' Landscape of New England" (paper presented at the Geological Society of America annual meeting, October 22, 2006), 34. I am grateful to Jon D. Inners for providing me a copy of this paper. Also see Merrill, *First One Hundred Years*, 615–42; and Lurie, *Louis Agassiz*, 116, 122–65.

69. Menand, *Metaphysical Club*, 98–99.

70. "The Philosophers' Camp at Follensby Pond," Adirondack Museum, http://www.adkmuseum.org/about_us/adirondack_journal/?id=129, accessed June 23, 2015.

71. Henry David Thoreau, *Walden* (New York: Thomas Y. Crowell, 1910), 67, 120, 152.

72. Henry David Thoreau, "Walking," *Atlantic Monthly* 9 (June 1862): 657.

73. Ibid., 664–65; Harding, *Days of Henry Thoreau*, 286; McIntosh, *Thoreau as Romantic Naturalist*, 283–88.

74. Roderick Frazier Nash, *Wilderness in the American Mind*, 4th ed. (New Haven, CT: Yale University Press, 2001), 84–86.

75. Michael L. Smith, *Pacific Visions: California Scientists and the Environment, 1850–1915* (New Haven, CT: Yale University Press, 1987), 28–33; Goetzmann, *Exploration and Empire*, 355.

76. Diehl's account of his solo ascent of Shasta was reprinted in James M. Hutchings's *Scenes of Wonder and Curiosity in California* (1862), http://www.yosemite.ca.us/library/scenes_of_wonder_and_curiosity/mount_shasta.html. Also see Charles L. Stewart, "Early Ascents of Mount Shasta," *Sierra Club Bulletin* 19, no. 3 (June 1934): 58–70; and Darla Greb Mazariegos, *Mount Shasta* (Charleston, SC: Arcadia, 2007), 41. For a description of Pearce's original route, still the most popular way to climb the mountain, see Andy Selters and Michael Zanger, *The Mt. Shasta Book* (Berkeley, CA: Wilderness Press, 1989), 44–49.

77. William H. Brewer, *Up and Down in California in 1860–1864* (Berkeley: University of California Press, 1949), 309, 318, 324; Chris Jones, *Climbing in North America* (Seattle: Mountaineers, 1997), 31–32; Putnam, *Century of American Alpinism*, 17–18; Thurman Wilkins, *Clarence King: A Biography* (Albuquerque: University of New Mexico Press, 1988), 143–44.

78. Arce, *Defying Gravity*, 5. The first ascent of Mount Hoffman is sometimes mistakenly attributed to John Muir, who climbed it in 1869.

79. Brewer, *Up and Down in California*, 408–9; Arce, *Defying Gravity*, 5–6.

80. Robert Wilson, *The Explorer King: Adventure, Science and the Great Diamond Hoax—Clarence King in the Old West* (New York: Scribner, 2006), 45–46;

Goetzmann, *Exploration and Empire*, 370; Moore, *Exploring the Highest Sierra*, 40, 42.

81. Farquhar, *History of the Sierra Nevada*, 131–33; Arce, *Defying Gravity*, 6.

82. Wilson, *Explorer King*, 45–46; Goetzmann, *Exploration and Empire*, 370; Moore, *Exploring the Highest Sierra*, 40, 42.

83. James G. Moore, *King of the 40th Parallel: Discovery in the American West* (Stanford, CA: Stanford University Press, 2006), 25; Wilson, *Explorer King*, 53–56; Wilkins, *Clarence King*, 30–42.

84. Quoted in Moore, *King of the 40th Parallel*, 58; Goetzmann, *Exploration and Empire*, 371. Mount Lassen was first ascended by a group of prospectors in 1851.

85. Brewer, *Up and Down in California*, 524; Moore, *Exploring the Highest Sierra*, 49, 51.

86. Chris Jones suggests that King was in "large measure inspired to climb" by Tyndall's memoir, *Hours of Exercise in the Alps*. But Tyndall's book wasn't published until 1871. As Jones also suggests, however, the book may have served as literary inspiration for Clarence King's own 1872 memoir, *Mountaineering in the Sierra Nevada*. Jones, *Climbing in North America*, 33.

87. Brewer, *Up and Down in California*, 525; Wilkins, *Clarence King*, 65.

88. Clarence King, *Mountaineering in the Sierra Nevada* (Lincoln: University of Nebraska Press, 1997), 75. The account of the ascent of Mount Tyndall that follows is drawn from King, *Mountaineering in the Sierra Nevada*, 69–94; Brewer, *Up and Down in California*, 521–27; Farquhar, *History of the Sierra Nevada*, 146–54; Moore, *Exploring the Highest Sierra*, 51–57; Wilkins, *Clarence King*, 65–67; and Moore, *King of the 40th Parallel*, 78–92.

89. King, *Mountaineering in the Sierra Nevada*, 71.

90. Ibid., 74.

91. Farquhar, *History of the Sierra Nevada*, 145.

92. Royal Robbins, *Fail Falling* (Ojai, CA: Pink Moment Press, 2010), 19.

93. King, *Mountaineering in the Sierra Nevada*, 86.

94. Ibid., 94.

95. Porcella and Burns rate Mount Tyndall as a Yosemite Decimal System Class 3 climb, involving steep scrambling and dangerous exposure, but not true rock-climbing. *Climbing California's Fourteeners*, 129.

96. Quoted in Farquhar, *History of the Sierra Nevada*, 147.

97. Porcella and Burns, *Climbing California's Fourteeners*, 14.

98. Elizabeth Stevenson, *Park Maker: A Life of Frederick Law Olmsted* (New York: Macmillan, 1977), 260; Goetzmann, *Exploration and Empire*, 370.

99. Wilkins, *Clarence King*, 75.

100. My argument here follows that made by Simon Schama in *Landscape and Memory* (New York: Vintage Books, 1996), 191.

101. Quoted in Jen A. Huntley, *The Making of Yosemite: James Mason Hutchings and the Origins of America's Most Popular National Park* (Lawrence: University of Kansas Press, 2011), 111.

102. Quoted in Wilkins, *Clarence King*, 80.

CHAPTER THREE: GOOD TIDINGS, STRENUOUS LIFE,
1865-1903

1. Katharine Lee Bates, quoted in Lynn Sherr, *America the Beautiful: The Stirring True Story behind Our Nation's Favorite Song* (New York: Public Affairs, 2001), 34. This account of Bates's ascent of Pikes Peak is drawn from Sherr, *America the Beautiful*, 9–34. Also see Dorothy Whittemore Bates Burgess, *Dream and Deed: The Story of Katharine Lee Bates* (Norman: University of Oklahoma Press, 1952); and James D. Drake, *The Nation's Nature: How Continental Presumptions Gave Rise to the United States of America* (Chancellorsville: University of Virginia Press, 2011), 320–21.

2. For the evolution of Bates's poem into the musical version, see Sherr, *America the Beautiful*, 39–61.

3. For a discussion of the ways in which Americans in the decades leading up to and following the Civil War came to imbue natural features of the landscape with both national and divine significance, see John F. Sears, *Sacred Places: American Tourist Attractions in the Nineteenth Century* (New York: Oxford University Press, 1989), especially pp. 4–7.

4. Quoted in George S. Merriam, *The Life and Times of Samuel Bowles*, vol. 2 (New York: Century, 1885), 4. For Bowles's tour of Switzerland, see pp. 364–85 in volume 1 of the same work.

5. Charles Parry made a number of first ascents in the Colorado Rockies, including 13,294-foot James Peak, 13,223-foot Mount Audubon, 13,122-foot Mount Flora, 13,370-foot Mount Guyot, and 13,391-foot Parry Peak, the latter named in his honor. William M. Bueler, *Roof of the Rockies: A History of Colorado Mountaineering* (Golden: Colorado Mountain Club Press, 2000), 27–28.

6. Samuel Bowles, *Our New West* (Hartford, CT: Hartford Publishing, 1869), 132; Walter R. Borneman and Lyndon J. Lampert, *A Climbing Guide to Colorado's Fourteeners* (Boulder, CO: Pruett, 1998), 62–64.

7. William Henry Jackson, *Time Exposure: The Autobiography of William Henry Jackson* (Albuquerque: University of New Mexico Press, 1986), 216–18; Aaron Sachs, *The Humboldt Current: Nineteenth-Century Exploration and the Roots of American Environmentalism* (New York: Viking, 2006), 219; Gary Ferguson, *The Great Divide: A Biography of the Rocky Mountains* (Woodstock, VT: Countryman Press, 2006), 159. The year 1876 was also when Colorado achieved statehood, winning it the nickname the "Centennial State." In 1951 the US Postal Service issued a commemorative stamp marking the seventy-fifth anniversary of Colorado statehood, featuring the Mount of the Holy Cross.

8. Thurman Wilkins, *Thomas Moran: Artist of the Mountains*, 2nd ed. (Norman: University of Oklahoma Press, 1998), 136–50; Borneman and Lampert, *Climbing Guide to Colorado's Fourteeners*, 64; Ferguson, *Great Divide*, 158–59; Bueler, *Roof of the Rockies*, 37. For a detailed account of the discovery of the Mount of the Holy Cross and its artistic legacy, see Emily Ballew Neff, *The Modern West: American Landscapes 1890–1950* (New Haven, CT: Yale University Press, 2006), 12–21. The Mount of the Holy Cross was declared a national monument by President Herbert Hoover in 1929, though in the decades that followed, erosion obscured the

image of the cross. It continued to attract pilgrims well into the twentieth century. Thomas M. Jenkins, "The Cross of Snow," *Summit*, December 1976, 18–22, 44.

9. Editorial, *New York Times*, September 18, 1871.

10. James G. Moore, *King of the 40th Parallel: Discovery in the American West* (Stanford, CA: Stanford University Press, 2006), 138–40.

11. Thurman Wilkins, *Clarence King: A Biography* (Albuquerque: University of New Mexico Press, 1988), 99–102.

12. Good overviews of the history of the Great Surveys include Richard A. Bartlett, *Great Surveys of the American West* (Norman: University of Oklahoma Press, 1962); William H. Goetzmann, *Exploration and Empire: The Explorer and the Scientist in the Winning of the American West* (New York: Knopf, 1966), 430–576; William H. Goetzmann, *New Lands, New Men: America and the Second Great Age of Discovery* (New York: Viking, 1986), 401–12; and Thomas G. Manning, *Government in Science: The US Geological Survey, 1867–1894* (Lexington: University of Kentucky Press, 1967), 1–29.

13. James D. Horan, *Timothy O'Sullivan: America's Forgotten Photographer* (New York: Bonanza Books, 1966), 151–73; Weston J. Naef and James N. Wood, *Era of Exploration: The Rise of Landscape Photography in the American West, 1860–1885* (Buffalo, NY: Albright-Knox Art Gallery, 1975), 131–32; Moore, *King of the 40th Parallel*, 194–97; Martha A. Sandweiss, *Print the Legend: Photography and the American West* (New Haven, CT: Yale University Press, 2002), 78–80, 181–83.

14. Clarence King, *Mountaineering in the Sierra Nevada* (Lincoln: University of Nebraska Press, 1997), 319.

15. For King's route, see Andy Selters and Michael Zanger, *The Mt. Shasta Book* (Berkeley, CA: Wilderness Press, 1989), 55–56.

16. Clarence King, "On the Discovery of Actual Glaciers in the Mountains of the Pacific Slope," *American Journal of Sciences and Arts*, 3rd ser., 1 (March 1871): 159; King, *Mountaineering in the Sierra Nevada*, 242–43. In the same article, King reported on the "discovery" of glaciers on Mount Hood and Mount Rainier by other parties working under the auspices of his fortieth-parallel survey. Also see Wilkins, *Clarence King*, 139–44; Moore, *King of the 40th Parallel*, 202–7.

17. King, *Mountaineering in the Sierra Nevada*, 287; Moore, *King of the 40th Parallel*, 215–16.

18. King, *Mountaineering in the Sierra Nevada*, 287.

19. King had been puzzled that the barometric measurements he made atop what he believed was Mount Whitney were hundreds of feet below the level of the actual mountain, but he persuaded himself that some sort of freak atmospheric condition had been at work. Wilkins, *Clarence King*, 154.

20. Quoted in Robert Wilson, *The Explorer King: Adventure, Science and the Great Diamond Hoax—Clarence King in the Old West* (New York: Scribner, 2006), 230. Also see Moore, *King of the 40th Parallel*, 257–60; Wilkins, *Clarence King*, 154; and Stephen Porcella and Cameron M. Burns, *Climbing California's Fourteeners: The Route Guide to the Fifteen Highest Peaks* (Seattle: Mountaineers, 1998), 35–37, 56. King subsequently added a coda to his chapter on his "Mount Whitney" ascent, admitting his error.

21. Dayton Duncan and Ken Burns, *The National Parks: America's Best Idea* (New York: Knopf, 2009), 30–35.

22. Robert B. Betts, *Along the Ramparts of the Tetons: The Saga of Jackson Hole, Wyoming* (Boulder: Colorado Associated University Press, 1978), 4, 119–21; Fred Beckey, *Mountains of North America* (San Francisco: Sierra Club Books, 1982), 102.

23. In 1898, a party from the Rocky Mountain Club of Denver, led by Wyoming surveyor and civil engineer William Owen, and including Franklin Spalding (the Episcopal bishop of Utah) along with two others (Frank Peterson and John Shive), reached the summit of Grand Teton. Owen announced that their effort constituted the true first ascent. The controversy continued over the next century. Orrin H. Bonney and Lorraine G. Bonney, *The Grand Controversy: The Pioneer Climbs in the Teton Range and the Controversial First Ascent of the Grand Teton* (New York: AAC Press, 1992), 34–35, 102–24; Leigh Ortenburger and Reynold G. Jackson offer the judicious opinion that the Owen-Spalding party made "the first *certain* ascent of the Grand Teton." Ortenburger and Jackson, *A Climber's Guide to the Teton Range*, 3rd ed. (Seattle: Mountaineers, 1996), 152.

24. The best account of Powell's life is Donald Worster, *A River Running West: The Life of John Wesley Powell* (New York: Oxford University Press, 2001). But also see the classic work by Wallace Stegner: *Beyond the Hundredth Meridian: John Wesley Powell and the Second Opening of the West* (Boston: Houghton Mifflin, 1954).

25. Native Americans, perhaps from the Ute or Arapaho tribe, had probably climbed high or to the summit of the mountain by this time. Dougald MacDonald, *Longs Peak: The Story of Colorado's Favorite Fourteener* (Englewood, CO: Westcliffe, 2004), 41–44.

26. Mike Anton, "William Byers Brought Denver Its First Newspaper and Raised a City to Read It," *Rocky Mountain News*, May 2, 1999, http://m.rockymountainnews.com/news/1999/may/02/william-byers-brought-denver-its-first-newspaper-a.

27. Quoted in Phyllis J. Perry, *It Happened in Rocky Mountain National Park* (Guilford, CT: TwoDot, 2008), 5.

28. Quoted in MacDonald, *Longs Peak*, 49.

29. Quoted in C. W. Buchholtz, *Rocky Mountain National Park: A History* (Boulder: University Press of Colorado, 1987), 155.

30. Worster, *River Running West*, 60–61.

31. Quoted in Bueler, *Roof of the Rockies*, 31. Also see MacDonald, *Longs Peak*, 50–55; Perry, *It Happened*, 1–7; L. W. Keplinger, "First Ascent of Longs Peak," *Trail* 7, no. 8 (January 1914): 13–15; and William N. Byers, "First Ascent of Long's Peak," *Trail* (October 1914): 21–23.

32. John Wesley Powell, *Exploration of the Colorado River of the West and Its Tributaries* (Washington, DC: Government Printing Office, 1875).

33. MacDonald, *Longs Peak*, 48.

34. "The Valley of Sixt," *Saturday Review of Politics, Literature, Science and Art* 10 (September 22, 1860): 367.

35. For the "eighth" designation, see J. Monroe Thorington, "The First American Ascent of Mont Blanc," *American Alpine Journal* 1 (1931): 327; and Henry F.

Montaignier, "Narratives of an Ascent of Mont Blanc," *Alpine Journal* 33 (1921): 14. Other accounts call it the thirteenth. Frederick L. Wolfe, *High Summits: 370 Famous Peak First Ascents* (Englewood, CO: Hugo House, 2013), 235.

36. William Howard, *Narrative of a Journey to the Summit of Mount Blanc* (Baltimore: Fielding Lucas Jr., 1821), http://www.gutenberg.org/files/32823/32823-h/32823 -h.htm; J. Monroe Thorington, "Early American Ascents in the Alps," in *A Century of American Alpinism*, ed. William Putnam (Boulder, CO: American Alpine Club, 2002), 44. Not until 1854 did another American, Dr. Israel Tisdale Talbot, reach the summit of Mont Blanc, although there had been several failed attempts in the interim. For a reprint of Talbot's original account, see "The Second American Ascent of Mont Blanc," *American Alpine Journal* 3 (1937): 66–85.

37. Roger Frison-Roche and Sylvain Jouty, *A History of Mountain Climbing* (New York: Flammarion, 1996), 62–81; Chris Bonington, *The Climbers: A History of Mountaineering* (London: Hodder and Stoughton, 1992), 33–38, 56–57; Mike C. Parsons and Mary B. Rose, *Invisible on Everest: Innovations and the Gear Makers* (Philadelphia: Northern Liberties Press, 2003), 46–47.

38. Peter H. Hansen, "British Mountaineering, 1850–1914" (PhD diss., Harvard University, 1991), 115. Also see Fergus Fleming, *Killing Dragons: The Conquest of the Alps* (New York: Atlantic Monthly Press, 2000), 162–73.

39. Mark Twain, *A Tramp Abroad* (New York: Modern Library, 2010), 157. Harriet Beecher Stowe described her visit to Chamonix in *Sunny Memories of Foreign Lands*, vol. 2 (Boston: Phillips, Sampson, 1854), 216. Also see "A Survey of American Ascents in the Alps in the Nineteenth Century," *American Alpine Journal* 2 (1935): 360.

40. Thorington, "Early American Ascents," 43.

41. Quoted in J. Monroe Thorington, "American Entries in the Travellers' Book of the Grands Mulets, 1861–75," *American Alpine Journal* 8, no. 2 (1952): 295.

42. Quoted in Simon Schama, *Landscape and Memory* (New York: Vintage Books, 1996), 504.

43. Quoted in J. Monroe Thorington, "James Kent Stone and the Alps," *Alpine Journal* 72 (November 1967): 276–77.

44. In addition to Thorington, "James Kent Stone and the Alps," see A. L. Mumm, *The Alpine Club Register, 1857–1863* (London: Alpine Club, 1923), 313–14. I am grateful to Peter Hansen for drawing my attention to Stone.

45. Ronald W. Clark, *The Victorian Mountaineers* (London: Batsford, 1953), 181; Bill Birkett and Bill Peascod, *Women Climbing: 200 Years of Achievement* (Seattle: Mountaineers, 1990), 23.

46. Rebecca A. Brown, *Women on High: Pioneers of Mountaineering* (Boston: Appalachian Mountain Club, 2002), 59–76.

47. Ronald W. Clark, *An Eccentric in the Alps: The Story of W. A. B. Coolidge, the Great Victorian Mountaineer* (London: Museum Press, 1959), 24–39, 76–79. Among other works, Coolidge was the author of *The Alps in Nature and History* (New York: Dutton, 1908).

48. F. H. Chapin, "The Ascent of Long's Peak," *Appalachia* 5, no. 2 (June 1888): 119. Chapin's *Mountaineering in Colorado—The Peaks about Estes Park* (Boston: Appalachian Mountain Club, 1889) soon sold out its first edition and was

reprinted three more times in the 1890s. For an overview of Chapin's life, see James H. Pickering's foreword to the 1987 Bison Book edition of *Mountaineering in Colorado* (Lincoln: University of Nebraska Press), vii–xxxv.

49. Edward Whymper, "Scrambles among the Alps in the Years 1860–69, Chapter 5," *Lippincott's Magazine* 8 (November 1871): 425–40; Whymper, *Scrambles among the Alps* (Cleveland, OH: Burrows, 1872). I am grateful to Greg Glade for the information about the American editions of *Scrambles*. For Whymper's influence on coming generations of climbers, see Ian Smith, *Shadow of the Matterhorn: The Life of Edward Whymper* (Hildersley, UK: Carreg, 2011), 165; and Clark, *Victorian Mountaineers*, 137–38.

50. Edward Whymper, *Scrambles among the Alps in the Years 1860–1869* (New York: Thomas Nelson and Sons, 1871), 369. Also see Smith, *Shadow of the Matterhorn*, 165.

51. C. T. Dent, "Snow Craft," in *Mountaineering*, Badminton Library of Sports and Pastimes (London: Longmans, Green, 1892), 184. The following year, a rival guide was published by another member of the Alpine Club, Claude Wilson: *Mountaineering* (London: George Bell & Sons, 1893).

52. Clark, *Victorian Mountaineers*, 63; John Middendorf, "The Mechanical Advantage: Tools for the Wild Vertical," in *Ascent: The Climbing Experience in World and Image*, eds. Allen Steck, Steve Roper, and Davis Harris (Golden, CO: American Alpine Club, 1999), 149–50; Parsons and Rose, *Invisible on Everest*, 53–54.

53. William H. Pickering, *Guide to the Mt. Washington Range* (Boston: Williams, 1882), 9.

54. Lieutenant A. Kautz, "First Attempted Ascent, 1857," in *Mount Rainier: A Record of Exploration*, ed. Edmond S. Meany (New York: Macmillan, 1916), 74–75. Kautz's account originally appeared in the *Overland Monthly* in May 1875.

55. Fred Beckey, *Range of Glaciers: The Exploration and Survey of the North Cascade Range* (Portland: Oregon Historical Society Press, 2003), 298–302; Fred Beckey, *Fred Beckey's 100 Favorite North American Climbs* (Ventura, CA: Patagonia Books, 2011), 4. Also see Aubrey L. Haines, *Mountain Fever: Historic Conquests of Rainier* (Seattle: University of Washington Press, 1999), 20–28.

56. For the first ascent of Mount Baker, see Edmund Thomas Coleman, "Mountaineering on the Pacific," *Harper's New Monthly Magazine*, November 1869, 793–817; Beckey, *Range of Glaciers*, 291–98; Beckey, *Fred Beckey's 100 Favorite*, 24. Coleman Glacier on Mount Baker is named for its British conqueror. Coleman carried an ice ax on that climb, perhaps the first time one was ever employed in American mountaineering. Wolfe, *High Summits*, 426.

57. General Hazard Stevens, "First Successful Ascent, 1870," in *Mount Rainier: A Record of Exploration*, ed. Edmond S. Meany (New York: Macmillan, 1916), 98–99.

58. On the question of who was to blame for Coleman's departure, see Beckey, *Range of Glaciers*, 304–5.

59. Ibid., 303–9; also see Haines, *Mountain Fever*, 30–51.

60. In 1888, Van Trump would guide to the summit a party that included John Muir. For Muir's account of that climb, see John Muir, *Steep Trails* (Boston: Houghton Mifflin, 1918), 261–70.

61. "Up the Mountain High: P. B. Van Trump Relates Anecdotes of Ascents of Mount Tacoma [Rainier]," *Tacoma Daily Ledger*, April 16, 1893.

62. King, *Mountaineering in the Sierra Nevada*, 88.

63. Quoted in Roger Patillo, *The Canadian Rockies: Pioneers, Legends, and True Tales* (Aldergrove, CA: Amberlea Press, 2005), 120.

64. John Muir, "The Story of My Boyhood and Youth," in *Nature Writings* (New York: Library of America, 1997), 7. Terry Gifford, introduction to *John Muir: The Eight Wilderness Discovery Books* (Seattle: Mountaineers, 1992), 17. The best work on Muir's life is Donald Worster, *A Passion for Nature: The Life of John Muir* (New York: Oxford University Press, 2008).

65. Roderick Nash commented, "Muir had the good fortune to live at a time when he could reap the honors that belatedly came to Thoreau's ideas." Nash, "The American Cult of the Primitive," *American Quarterly* 18 (Autumn 1966): 531.

66. For Muir's early life, see John Muir, "Story of My Boyhood," 7–146; and Worster, *Passion for Nature*, 1–148. Muir described his journey from Indiana to Florida in John Muir, *A Thousand Mile Walk to the Gulf* (Boston: Houghton Mifflin, 1916).

67. John Muir, "My First Summer in the Sierra," in *Nature Writings* (New York: Library of America, 1997), 219.

68. Worster, *Passion for Nature*, 160.

69. Quoted in ibid., 194.

70. Quoted in ibid., 195.

71. Ibid.; "Clarence King (1842–1901)," Mount Shasta Companion, 2001, http://www.siskiyous.edu/shasta/env/king/index.htm; James G. Moore, *Exploring the Highest Sierra* (Stanford, CA: Stanford University Press, 2000), 70–71.

72. Worster, *Passion for Nature*, 211–15.

73. Muir, *Nature Writings*, 788.

74. James Brannon, "Radical Transcendentalism: Emerson, Muir and the Experience of Nature" (reprinted from *John Muir Newsletter* 16, no. 1 [Winter 2005/2006]), Sierra Club, http://www.sierraclub.org/john_muir_exhibit/john_muir_newsletter/radical_transcendentalism.aspx.

75. Quoted in Richard M. Leonard, "Piton Technique on the Cathedral Spires," *Appalachia* 20 (December 1934): 177.

76. Steve Roper and Allen Steck, *Fifty Classic Climbs of North America* (San Francisco: Sierra Club Books, 1979), 255; Fred Knapp, "The History of American Rock Climbing," *Rock & Ice*, no. 79 (May–June 1997): 45–46. A more legitimate example of a nineteenth-century climber anticipating later aid techniques is presented by Stanford University art professor Bolton Brown, who made the solo first ascent of 12,867-foot Mount Clarence King in the Sierra in August 1896. Coming to a crack he was unable to surmount, he tied knots in the rope he was carrying, threw them into the crack above his head, and pulled tight until they lodged. Then he pulled himself up the rope to the knot and repeated the process. Knapp, "History of American Rock Climbing," 46.

77. Pat Ament, *Wizards of Rock: A History of Free Climbing in America* (Berkeley: Wilderness Press, 2002), 7–8.

78. Muir, *Nature Writings*, 354–55; Worster, *Passion for Nature*, 182–83; Kevin Starr,

Americans and the California Dream, 1850–1915 (New York: Oxford University Press, 1973), 187–89.

79. John Muir, *Mountaineering Essays*, ed. Richard F. Fleck (Salt Lake City: Peregrine Smith Books, 1984), 86.

80. Muir, *Nature Writings*, 647; Worster, *Passion for Nature*, 184–85; John Muir, "Shasta in Winter," *Daily Evening Bulletin*, December 21, 1874; Don Cochran, "John Muir in Siskiyou County," *Siskiyou Pioneer* 1 (1949): 1–7.

81. Quoted in Worster, *Passion for Nature*, 205. As Robert Pogue Harrison noted in a review of Worster's biography, "There is no more quintessential image of Muir than that." Harrison, "The Ecstasy of John Muir," *New York Review of Books*, March 12, 2009, 22.

82. Charles E. Fay, "Mountain Climbing as an Organized Sport," *Outlook* 71 (June 7, 1902): 377.

83. Robert H. Wiebe, *The Search for Order: 1877–1920* (New York: Hill and Wang, 1967), 111–32.

84. Stephen Hardy, *How Boston Played: Sports, Recreation, and Community 1865–1915* (Boston: Northeastern University Press, 1982), 4–9; Howard P. Chudacoff, *The Age of the Bachelor: Creating an American Subculture* (Princeton, NJ: Princeton University Press, 1999), 155.

85. For a local and short-lived group, the Alpine Club of Williamstown spawned an extensive literature. See, for example, Samuel H. Scudder, "The Alpine Club of Williamstown, Mass.," *Appalachia* 4, no. 1 (December 1884): 45–54; Christopher Johnson, "Mountaineering Pioneers of the Berkshires: The Alpine Club of Williamstown," *Appalachia* 61 (Winter/Spring 2010): 81; Christopher Johnson, *This Grand & Magnificent Place: The Wilderness Heritage of the White Mountains* (Durham: University of New Hampshire Press, 2006), 148–50; Laura Waterman and Guy Waterman, *Forest and Crag: A History of Hiking, Trail Blazing and Adventure in the Northeast Mountains* (Boston: Appalachian Mountain Club, 1989), 183–85; Susan R. Schrepfer, *Nature's Altars: Mountains, Gender and American Environmentalism* (Lawrence: University Press of Kansas, 2005), 69; and Matthew S. Willen, "Composing Mountaineering: The Personal Narrative and the Production of Knowledge in the Alpine Club of London and the Appalachian Mountain Club, 1858–1900" (PhD diss., University of Pittsburgh, 1995), 201.

86. John M. Gould, *How to Camp Out* (New York: Scribner, 1877), 12; Johnson, *This Grand & Magnificent Place*, 150–51, 160.

87. "Constitution," *Appalachia* 1 (June 1876): 3, 58–59; E. C. Pickering, "The Annual Address of the President," *Appalachia* 1 (March 1877), 62–70.

88. Pickering traced his origins to John Pickering of Salem in 1634; Scudder, to John Scudder of Cape Cod in 1635. Solon I. Bailey, *Biographical Memoir of Edward Charles Pickering, 1846–1919* (Washington, DC: National Academy of Sciences, 1932); Alfred Goldsborough Mayor, *Samuel Hubbard Scudder, 1837–1911* (Washington, DC: National Academy of Sciences, 1919); Willen, "Composing Mountaineering," 205; "Constitution," *Appalachia*, 3.

89. Jill Cotter, "Our History," August Camp, http://www.augustcamp.org/ourhistory .html, accessed June 23, 2015; Elizabeth Roberts, "August Camp Reviewed,"

Appalachia 24 (June 1942): 75–86; Fay, "Mountain Climbing as an Organized Sport," 380.

90. Emily A. Thackeray, "The Fair Mountaineers," *White Mountain Echo*, August 3, 1889.

91. Chris Stewart and Mike Torrey, eds., *A Century of Hospitality in High Places: The Appalachian Mountain Club Hut System, 1888–1988* (Boston: Appalachian Mountain Club, 1988), 1–5; Mark Chalafour, "125 Years in the White Mountains," *AMC Outdoors*, May/June 2013, 26–33; Michael Matza, "Hiking Club's 'Huts' Draw Fire: Critics Say Rustic Lodges Degrade the Appalachian Wilderness," *Philadelphia Inquirer*, July 1, 1996, http://articles.philly.com/1996-07-01/news/25619494_1_hut-system-amc-white-mountain-national-forest. I am grateful to Becky Fullerton, AMC librarian, for drawing my attention to the "Appalachian Motel Club" controversy.

92. Pickering, foreword to *Mountaineering in Colorado*, xviii.

93. Phil Dowling, *The Mountaineers: Famous Climbers in Canada* (Edmonton, AB: Hurtig. 1979), 14; John Ritchie, "In Memoriam," *Appalachia* 18 (June 1931), 303–5; Howard W. Vernon, "Charles E. Fay," *American Alpine Journal* 1, no. 3 (1931): 373–76; William Howell Reed, "Charles Ernest Fay: 1846–1931," *Tuftonian* 5, no. 3 (1946): 160.

94. Pickering, foreword to *Mountaineering in Colorado*, xx–xxi. For Chapin's account of the ascent of Ypsilon Mountain, see Chapin, *Mountaineering in Colorado*, 119–35.

95. On Fay's relations with Whymper, see Smith, *Shadow of the Matterhorn*, 264–67. Vittorio Sella became a corresponding member of the AMC in 1891, and in 1893 the club arranged for an exhibition of his photos of the Alps and the Caucasus at the Boston Art Club gallery. "Proceedings of the Club," *Appalachia* 6, no. 3 (July 1891): 269; Charles E. Fay, "The Sella Exhibition," *Appalachia* 7, no. 3 (March 1894): 229–38.

96. Charles E. Fay, "President's Address," *Appalachia* 2, no. 1 (June 1879): 11; Johnson, *This Grand & Magnificent Place*, 154.

97. Howard Palmer and J. Monroe Thorington, *A Climber's Guide to the Rocky Mountains of Canada*, 3rd ed. (New York: American Alpine Club, 1940), vii–viii.

98. Allen H. Bent, "Early American Mountaineers," *Appalachia* 13, no. 1 (June 1917) f: 59; Arthur Oliver Wheeler, *The Selkirk Range*, vol. 1 (Ottawa: Government Printing Bureau, 1905), 267; Pierre Berton, *The National Dream: The Great Railway, 1871–1881* (Toronto: McClelland and Stewart, 1970), 164; William Putnam, *A Climber's Guide to the Interior Ranges of British Columbia*, 5th ed. (New York: American Alpine Club, 1971), 117; William Putnam, *The Great Glacier and Its House: The Story of the First Center of Alpinism in North America, 1885–1925* (New York: American Alpine Club, 1982), 17–20.

99. Putnam, *Great Glacier and Its House*, 40–47; R. W. Sandford, *The Canadian Alps: The History of Mountaineering in Canada*, vol. 1 (Banff, AB: Altitude Publishing, 1990), 97; Joe Bensen, *Souvenirs from High Places: A History of Mountaineering Photography* (Seattle: Mountaineers, 1998), 64. Of course, as Howard Palmer and J. Monroe Thorington pointed out in their 1921 climbing guide to the Canadian Rockies, the analogy to Switzerland could be overemphasized. "Along the rail-

roads alone are there places that can be regarded as climbing centers. Depart from these but a little and a pack train must be employed, so that far more time will be spent in travel than in actual climbing." Palmer and Thorington, *A Climber's Guide to the Rocky Mountains of Canada* (New York: American Alpine Club, 1921), vii.

100. Charles E. Fay, "Up to the Crags of Sir Donald," *Appalachia* 10, no. 2 (1893): 157–64; Charles E. Fay, "The First Ascent of Mount Victoria," *Appalachia* 9, no. 1 (May 1899): 1–10; Fay, "Mountain Climbing as an Organized Sport," 378; Chic Scott, *Pushing the Limits: The Story of Canadian Mountaineering* (Calgary, AB: Rocky Mountain Books, 2000), 42–43; Putnam, *Great Glacier and Its House*, 71–72.

101. H. P. Nichols, "Back Ranges of the Selkirks," *Appalachia* 7 (December 1893): 101–2. Also see Wheeler, *Selkirk Range*, 1:295–96. Reverend Nichols was an influential member of the AMC, although never an officer of the club. He would go on to become a founding member of the American Alpine Club, and he served as its president from 1923 to 1925. In 1906 he wrote to President Theodore Roosevelt, informing the president that he had been given honorary membership in the AAC, and recalling their meeting "between the Jungfrau and the Matterhorn" in 1881. Harry Pierce Nichols to Theodore Roosevelt, February 27, 1906, American Alpine Club Library archives, Golden, CO. Also see "Dr. Harry Pierce Nichols," *Appalachia* 23 (June 1941): 390–91; and "Harry Pierce Nichols," *American Alpine Journal* 4 (1941): 278–81.

102. Putnam, *Great Glacier and Its House*, 101; Patillo, *Canadian Rockies*, 109–12; Sandford, *Canadian Alps*, 102.

103. Quoted in Patillo, *Canadian Rockies*, 114. Also see Yandell Henderson, "The Summer of 1894 around Lake Louise," *Canadian Alpine Journal*, 1933, 133–51.

104. Walter D. Wilcox, *The Rockies of Canada* (New York: G. P. Putnam's Sons, 1916), 41–42.

105. Samuel E. S. Allen, "Ascent of Mount Temple, Canadian Rockies," *Appalachia* 7 (June 1895): 281–87; Patillo, *Canadian Rockies*, 115–22; Scott, *Pushing the Limits*, 44–45.

106. For Abbot's European experience, see Philip Stanley Abbot, "An Ascent of the Weisshorn," *Appalachia* 7, no. 2 (December 1893): 109–23.

107. Philip S. Abbot, "The First Ascent of Mount Hector, Canadian Rockies," *Appalachia* 8, no. 1 (January 1896): 1.

108. Charles S. Thompson, "Mt. Castor and the Asulkan Ridge," *Appalachia* 8, no. 1 (January 1896): 22; Wheeler, *Selkirk Range*, 305–6.

109. Sandford, *Canadian Alps*, 113–14; Scott, *Pushing the Limits*, 46.

110. As a warm-up for Lefroy, Abbot, Thompson, and Little made the first ascent of 10,397-foot Rogers Peak. "Exploration," *Appalachia* 8, no. 3 (July 1897): 277.

111. There was still considerable confusion in the 1890s about the identity and naming of the mountains around Banff. Carol Ann Sokoloff sorts out the confusion of Green, Victoria, and Lefroy in *Eternal Lake O'Hara* (Victoria, BC: Ekstasis Editions, 1993), 23.

112. Charles E. Fay, "The Casualty on Mount Lefroy," in *Philip Stanley Abbot: Addresses at a Memorial Meeting of the Appalachian Mountain Club, October 21, 1896* (Boston: Appalachian Mountain Club, 1896), 9.

113. Fay, "Casualty on Mount Lefroy," 9.

114. Ron Dart, "A Death in Canada, 1896," *Appalachia* 61 (Summer–Fall 2010): 48–56. Also see Beckey, *Fred Beckey's 100 Favorite*, 93–94; Scott, *Pushing the Limits*, 46–47; and Dowling, *Mountaineers*, 20–22.

115. The col between Mounts Lefroy and Green/Victoria would be renamed Abbot's Pass, and a hut built there in Abbot's memory. Dart, "Death in Canada," 53.

116. Walt Unsworth, Chris Jones, Fred Beckey, and Chic Scott all described Abbot as the first to die in a mountaineering accident in North America: Unsworth, *Hold the Heights: The Foundations of Mountaineering* (Seattle: Mountaineers, 1994), 204; Jones, *Climbing in North America* (Seattle: Mountaineers, 1997), 47; Beckey, *Fred Beckey's 100 Favorite*, 93; Scott, *Pushing the Limits*, 47. As recounted in Chapter 2, at least three other climbers died in the United States before the Civil War: two on Mount Washington (Frederick Strickland in 1851, and Lizzie Bourne in 1855), and one on Mount Mitchell (Elisha Mitchell in 1857). And in 1884, Carrie J. Welton died on Longs Peak following a successful summit attempt. Buchholtz, *Rocky Mountain National Park*, 101.

117. "Fell 1,000 Feet over a Cliff," *New York Times*, August 6, 1896. Fay and Charles Thompson returned to Lefroy the following summer, joined at Fay's invitation by leading British climbers and Alpine Club members, including Norman Collie, who the previous year had made the first serious, although unsuccessful, attempt to climb an 8,000-meter peak, Nanga Parbat on the western flank of the Himalaya. They completed the first ascent of Mount Lefroy on August 3, 1897, a year to the day after Abbot's death. Two days later, Fay, Collie, and several others made the first ascent of Lefroy's neighbor, 11,365-foot Mount Victoria. As a result of this trip, Norman Collie fell in love with the Canadian Rockies, returning many times and making many first ascents, although he graciously conceded that "Americans from the States were the first who began serious mountaineering in this district." Quoted in Unsworth, *Hold the Heights*, 202. Also see Scott, *Pushing the Limits*, 47; and Sandford, *Canadian Alps*, 127–32.

118. Fay, "Casualty on Mount Lefroy," 19. Also see Sandford, *Canadian Alps*, 125–27.

119. Muir, *Steep Trails*, 261–70.

120. John Bell, *On Mount Hood: A Biography of Oregon's Perilous Peak* (Seattle: Sasquatch Books, 2011), 117.

121. Quoted in Erik Weiselberg, "He All but Made the Mountains: William Gladstone Steel, Mountain Climbing, and the Establishment of Crater Lake National Park," *Oregon Historical Quarterly* 103 (Spring 2002): 53–54.

122. Ibid., 71.

123. The *New York Times* report, adding 1,500 feet to the height of the mountain, describing it as "12,720 feet high," also reported that Steel's exploit represented "the first time that a human being has spent a night on the summit of the mountain," although in fact he was about 1,500 vertical feet short of the summit. "Mount Hood Illuminated: An Oregon City's Celebration of the Fourth," *New York Times*, July 6, 1887; "Red Fire on the Mountain: Historic Pyrotechnics on Mount Hood," *Oregonian*, July 3, 2010; J. M. Baltimore, "Illumination of Mount Hood," *Frank Leslie's Illustrated Newspaper*, July 30, 1887, 381, 387; Erik Weiselberg, "Ascendancy of the Mazamas: Environment, Identity and Mountain

Climbing in Oregon, 1870 to 1930" (PhD diss., University of Oregon, 1999), 31–39; Bell, *On Mount Hood*, 122; Weiselberg, "He All but Made the Mountains," 61–62; "Illuminating Mount Hood," *WyEast Blog*, July 7, 2010, http://wyeastblog .org/2010/07/07/illuminating-mount-hood.

124. W. G. Steel, *The Mountains of Oregon*, souvenir ed. (Portland, OR, 1892), frontis-piece.

125. "A Visit to Mount Hood: Mr. Steel's Recent Exploration," *Oregonian*, December 4, 1892.

126. Stephen R. Mark, "Seventeen Years to Success: John Muir, William Gladstone Steel, and the Creation of Yosemite and Crater Lake National Parks," Sierra Club, http://www.sierraclub.org/john_muir_exhibit/life/17_years_to_success_s_ mark.aspx, accessed June 23, 2015.

127. John D. Scott, *We Climb High: A Chronology of the Mazamas, 1894–1964* (Port-land, OR: Mazamas, 1969), 1; William G. Steel, "Preliminary History of the Mazamas," *Mazama* 1 (May 1896): 13; Miss E. Fay Fuller, "Historian's Report for 1894," *Mazama* 1 (May 1896), 12–18; Weiselberg, "Ascendancy of the Mazamas," 125–26, 134.

128. "American Mountaineering This Summer," *Land and Water*, August 1897.

129. Michael P. Cohen, *History of the Sierra Club, 1892–1970* (San Francisco: Sierra Club Books, 1988), 5–8; Roderick Frazier Nash, *Wilderness and the American Mind*, 4th ed. (New Haven, CT: Yale University Press, 2001), 131; Worster, *Passion for Nature*, 310–21; John Muir, "Treasures of the Yosemite," *Century Magazine* 40 (August 1890): 483; John Muir, "Features of the Proposed Yosemite National Park," *Century Magazine* 40 (September 1890): 667.

130. Cohen, *History of the Sierra Club*, 8–10; Worster, *Passion for Nature*, 315, 328–30.

131. Cohen, *History of the Sierra Club*, 11. Kevin Starr notes that "very wealthy" Cali-fornians were noticeably absent from the ranks of the club. "Railroad kings, real estate developers, timber barons, and the like . . . were naturally hostile to the conservationist core of the Sierra Club ideology." Starr, *Americans and the Cali-fornia Dream*, 190.

132. "Announcement, Fifth Annual Outing of the Sierra Club, Mount Rainier Para-dise Park, July–August 1905," Sierra Club Scrapbook, BANC MSS 71/103c, vol. 3, Bancroft Library, University of California, Berkeley.

133. Susan Schrepfer notes that the admiration between the Sierra Club and Whym-per was mutual: when his portrait was damaged in the 1906 San Francisco earth-quake, Whymper saw to its replacement. Schrepfer, *Nature's Altars*, 24. On David Starr Jordan, see Starr, *Americans and the California Dream*, 307–12.

134. Cohen, *History of the Sierra Club*, 18; Worster, *Passion for Nature*, 329.

135. John Muir, *Our National Parks* (Boston: Houghton Mifflin, 1901), 56.

136. "Build, therefore, your own world," Emerson wrote in *Nature*. "As fast as you con-form your life to the pure idea in your mind, that will unfold its great proportions. A correspondent revolution in things will attend the influx of the spirit. . . . As when the summer comes from the south; the snow-banks melt, and the face of the earth becomes green before it, so shall the advancing spirit create its orna-ments along its path, and carry with it the beauty it visits, and the song which enchants it; it shall draw beautiful faces, warm hearts, wise discourse, and heroic

acts, around its way, until evil is no more seen." Ralph Waldo Emerson, *The Complete Works of Ralph Waldo Emerson*, vol. 1 (Boston: Houghton Mifflin, 1903), 76.

137. Thomas Jefferson, "First Inaugural Address," March 4, 1801, http://avalon.law
.yale.edu/19th_century/jefinau1.asp.

138. John Mack Faragher, ed., *Rereading Frederick Jackson Turner* (New York: Henry Holt, 1994), 2–3, 59–60.

139. For Turner's New England ancestry, see Ray Allen Billington, *Frederick Jackson Turner: Historian, Scholar, Teacher* (New York: Oxford University Press, 1973), 3.

140. Frank Branch Riley, "This Is the Life," *Mazama* 4, no. 3 (December 1914): 29–30. Of course, for all its celebration of social equality, the listing of professions likely to be found at a Mazamas encampment was equally revealing of the social exclusiveness of the club's membership.

141. The best overview of this decade in American life in the 1890s is provided by John Higham, "The Reorientation of American Culture in the 1890s," in *The Origins of Modern Consciousness*, ed. John Weiss (Detroit: Wayne State University Press, 1965), 25–48. Also see Michael S. Kimmel, "The Contemporary 'Crisis' of Masculinity in Historical Perspective," in *The Making of Masculinities: The New Men's Studies*, ed. Harry Brod (Boston: Allen & Unwin, 1987), 139–40.

142. George M. Beard, *American Nervousness; Its Causes and Consequences*, reprint ed. (New York: Arno Press, 1972), 7–8.

143. Gail Bederman, *Manliness & Civilization: A Cultural History of Gender and Race in the United States, 1880–1917* (Chicago: University of Chicago Press, 1995), 99–100.

144. Muir, *Our National Parks*, 1.

145. As historian Roderick Nash noted in his classic study of wilderness and the American mind: "At the end of the nineteenth century, cities were regarded with the hostility once reserved for wild forests." Nash, *Wilderness and the American Mind*, 143.

146. Quoted in John Neff, *Katahdin, an Historic Journey: Legends, Exploration, and Preservation of Maine's Highest Peak* (Boston: Appalachian Mountain Club, 2006), 58. For Roosevelt's formative years and influences, see Douglas Brinkley, *The Wilderness Warrior: Theodore Roosevelt and the Crusade for America* (New York: Harper Collins, 2009), 22–146; Kathleen Dalton, *Theodore Roosevelt: A Strenuous Life* (New York: Knopf, 2002), 15–76.

147. Quoted in Brinkley, *Wilderness Warrior*, 141. Also see Dalton, *Theodore Roosevelt*, 79.

148. Brinkley, *Wilderness Warrior*, 392–95.

149. Theodore Roosevelt, "The Strenuous Life," April 10, 1899, Voices of Democracy, http://voicesofdemocracy.umd.edu/roosevelt-strenuous-life-1899-speech-text; Brinkley, *Wilderness Warrior*, 349–50; Bederman, *Manliness & Civilization*, 192–96.

150. Fay, "Mountain Climbing as an Organized Sport," 384.

151. On Muir's and Roosevelt's differing environmental philosophies, see Robert W. Righter, *The Battle over Hetch Hetchy: America's Most Controversial Dam and the Birth of Modern Environmentalism* (New York: Oxford University Press, 2005).

152. Quoted in Worster, *Passion for Nature*, 366.

153. Quoted in Duncan and Burns, *National Parks*, 97.

154. "The President in The Yosemite Park," *New York Times*, May 16, 1903.

155. "The President Enjoys Yosemite Valley," *New York Times*, May 18, 1903.

CHAPTER FOUR: BROTHERHOOD OF THE ROPE, 1900–1946:
PART I

1. Quoted in Michael P. Cohen, *The History of the Sierra Club, 1892–1970* (San Francisco: Sierra Club Books, 1988), 104.

2. Robert L. M. Underhill, "On the Use and Management of the Rope in Rock Work," *Sierra Club Bulletin*, February 1931, 68.

3. Charles S. Houston and Robert M. Bates, *K2: The Savage Mountain* (Guilford, CT: Lyons Press, 2000), 24.

4. "American Alpine Club Founders," in *Constitution, By-Laws, List of Members* (n.p.: American Alpine Club Library, 1902), 9–16; Howard Palmer, "Early History of the American Alpine Club," *American Alpine Journal* 5 (1944): 163–96.

5. Palmer's own mountaineering experience included a first ascent of 11,545-foot Mount Sir Sandford, the highest peak in the Canadian Selkirks, in 1912. "American the First to Scale Ice Peak," *New York Times*, August 2, 1912; Howard Palmer, *Mountaineering and Exploration in the Selkirks: A Record of Pioneering Work among the Canadian Alps, 1908–1912* (New York: Putnam, 1914).

6. Howard Palmer to Henry S. Hall Jr., January 23, 1917, Henry Hall Correspondence, American Alpine Club Library, Golden, CO. Also see William Lowell Putnam, "Henry Snow Hall, 1895–1987," *American Alpine Journal* 29 (1987): 341–44.

7. The Henry S. Hall Jr. Library of the American Alpine Club in Golden, Colorado, is named in his memory.

8. William Lowell Putnam, "A Great Many Years" (speech, American Alpine Club Board Meeting, 2011), http://inclined.americanalpineclub.org/2012/05/a-great-many-years-honorary-president-william-lowell-putnam; "Who We Are," American Alpine Club, http://www.americanalpineclub.org/p/history-american-alpine-club, accessed July 7, 2015; Joan Firey, "The American Alpine Club," *Summit* 21 (March 1975): 10–11. The other practical activity of the club was the publication of a series of guidebooks, beginning with J. Monroe Thorington and Howard Palmer, *A Climber's Guide to the Rocky Mountains of Canada* (New York: Putnam, 1921).

9. For the first recorded use of "H'Appies," see *Appalachia Bulletin* 11 (September 1918): 174. I am grateful to Becky Fullerton of the AMC library for digging up that reference. The Rock Climbing Sections of the Sierra Club in southern and northern California added annual banquets to their activities in the late 1930s, but they were apparently far more informal affairs than the AAC gathering. See Joseph E. Taylor III, *Pilgrims of the Vertical: Yosemite Rock Climbers & Nature at Risk* (Cambridge, MA: Harvard University Press, 2010), 73.

10. William A. Brooks, "With Sierrans and Mazamas—July 1905," *Appalachia* 11, no. 2 (May 1906): 124. For more on the 1905 Mazama-sponsored outing to Mount Rainier, see C. E. Rusk, *Tales of a Western Mountaineer: A Record of Mountain*

Experiences on the Pacific Coast (Boston: Houghton Mifflin, 1924), 136–51, which described it as a "gathering of the mountain clans." On the social function of clubs, see Taylor, *Pilgrims of the Vertical*, 61–66.

11. *Bylaws and Register of the American Alpine Club* (New York: American Alpine Club, 1919), 42; Le Roy Jeffers, *The Call of the Mountains: Rambles among the Mountains and Canyons of the United States and Canada* (New York: Dodd, Mead, 1923), v–ix; *Bulletin of the Associated Mountaineering Clubs of North America*, May 1925. The federation disappeared within a few years, but most of the constituent clubs survived.

12. Laura Waterman and Guy Waterman, *Yankee Rock & Ice: A History of Climbing in the Northeastern United States* (Mechanicsburg, PA: Stackpole Books, 1993), 112–13.

13. "A Yankee Girl Climbs the Matterhorn," *New York Times*, August 26, 1895; Annie Smith Peck, "A Woman's Ascent of the Matterhorn," *McClure's Magazine* 7 (July 1896): 127–36.

14. William Siri, "Cordillera Blanca," *Sierra Club Bulletin* 38, no. 8 (October 1953): 3. For nineteenth-century and early- to mid-twentieth-century mountaineering by Americans in the region, see Evelio Echevarría, "Early American Ascents in the Andes, 1854–1950," *American Alpine Journal* 28 (1986): 111–16.

15. Annie Smith Peck, *High Mountain Climbing in Peru & Bolivia: In Search of the Apex of America* (London: Fisher Unwin, 1912), xi. The American edition was published under the title *A Search for the Apex of America*. For a study of Peck's feminism, see Hannah Scialdone-Kimberley, "Woman at the Top: Politics and Feminism in the Texts and Life of Annie Smith Peck" (PhD diss., Old Dominion University, 2012).

16. At a number of mountain summits in the Andes, evidence of human presence has been discovered, including the mummies of male and female Inca child sacrifices atop 22,110-foot Llullaillaco, on the Chilean-Argentine border. Kathy Sawyer, "Mummies of Inca Children Unearthed," *Washington Post*, April 7, 1999.

17. Rebecca A. Brown, *Women on High: Pioneers of Mountaineering* (Boston: Appalachian Mountain Club, 2002), 144–50; Elizabeth Fagg Olds, *Women of the Four Winds* (Boston: Houghton Mifflin, 1985), 17–47.

18. Brown, *Women on High*, 190–93.

19. The five books about the Himalaya by Fanny Bullock Workman and William Hunter Workman are *In the Ice World of Himalaya: Among the Peaks and Passes of Ladakh, Nubru, Suru, and Baltistan* (London: Fisher Unwin, 1900); *Ice-Bound Heights of the Mustagh: An Account of Two Seasons of Pioneer Exploration and High Climbing in the Baltistan Himalaya* (London: Constable, 1908); *Peaks and Glaciers of Nun Kun: A Record of Pioneer Exploration and Mountaineering in the Punjab Himalaya* (London: Constable, 1909); *The Call of the Snowy Hispar: A Narrative of Exploration and Mountaineering on the Northern Frontier of India* (London: Constable, 1910); and *Two Summers in the Ice-Wilds of Eastern Karakoram: The Exploration of Nineteen Hundred Square Miles of Mountain and Glacier* (London: Fisher Unwin, 1917).

20. For the early history of mountaineering in the Karakoram, see Maurice Isserman and Stewart Weaver, *Fallen Giants: A History of Himalayan Mountaineering*

from the Age of Empire to the Age of Extremes (New Haven, CT: Yale University Press, 2008), 34–50.

21. Brown, *Women on High*, 195.

22. Isserman and Weaver, *Fallen Giants*, 53.

23. Kenneth Mason, the author of the first authoritative history of Himalayan mountaineering, and an old India Survey hand, noted that the Workmans "lacked a sense of topography." Mason, *Abode of Snow: A History of Himalayan Mountaineering and Exploration* (New York: Dutton, 1955), 132; Isserman and Weaver, *Fallen Giants*, 52–53.

24. Workman and Workman, *Peaks and Glaciers of Nun Kun*, 88; Isserman and Weaver, *Fallen Giants*, 54–56. For Matthias Zurbriggen's extraordinary mountaineering exploits, see Matthias Zurbriggen and Mary Alice Vialls, *From the Alps to the Andes; Being the Autobiography of a Mountain Guide* (London: Unwin, 1899).

25. Scialdone-Kimberley, "Woman at the Top," 33.

26. Peck, *High Mountain Climbing in Peru and Bolivia*, 3.

27. Ibid., 344; Brown, *Women on High*, 182–83.

28. "Mrs. Peck's Story of Her Record Climb," *New York Times*, December 23, 1908. In 1883, English climber William Woodward Graham claimed to have reached the summit of 24,258-foot Kabru in the eastern Himalaya, but many of his contemporaries and some, if not all, historians have questioned that assertion. Another contender for the altitude record was Martin Conway, who in 1892 claimed to have reached 23,000 feet on Baltoro Kangri in the Karakoram, 800 vertical feet below the summit, although there is some doubt about that claim as well. Matthias Zurbriggen's 1897 ascent of 22,837-foot Aconcagua in the Andes is the highest undisputed ascent of a summit in the nineteenth century, surpassed in 1907 by Tom Longstaff's ascent of 23,360-foot Trisul. In 1909 the Duke of the Abruzzi reached 24,600 feet on Chogolisa in the Karakoram, 500 vertical feet short of the summit, setting an altitude (if not a summit) record that would last until the British Everest expeditions of the 1920s. Isserman and Weaver, *Fallen Giants*, 34, 44, 72, 77.

29. For Peck's original claim, see Annie Peck, "The Conquest of Huáscáran," *Bulletin of the American Geographical Society* 41 (June 1909): 355–65. For Bullock Workman's reply, see "Miss Peck and Mrs. Workman," *Scientific American* 102 (February 12 and 26, April 16, 1910). For good secondary accounts, see Luree Miller, *On Top of the World: Five Women Explorers in Tibet* (Seattle: Mountaineers, 1984), 122–24; and Olds, *Women of the Four Winds*, 57–60.

30. Quoted in Scialdone-Kimberley, "Woman at the Top," 93.

31. Brown, *Women on High*, 184.

32. "Miss Peck Goes Out to Climb the Heights," *New York Times*, June 3, 1911.

33. Howard Palmer, "Mountain Climbing" in *Handbook of Travel* (Cambridge, MA: Harvard University Press, 1918), 159.

34. Roger Frison-Roche and Sylvain Jouty, *A History of Mountain Climbing* (New York: Flammarion, 1996), 81–87; Isserman and Weaver, *Fallen Giants*, 132; Taylor, *Pilgrims of the Vertical*, 30–31. Welzenbach was a professional engineer and designed the first ice piton. For more on him, see Eric Roberts, *Welzenbach's*

Climbs: A Biographical Study and the Collected Writings of Willo Welzenbach (Seattle: Mountaineers, 1981).

35. For a discussion of the advantages of the running belay, see Royal Robbins, *Basic Rockcraft* (Glendale, CA: La Siesta Press, 1971), 28–29.

36. Middendorf, "Mechanical Advantage," 149–73; Doug Scott, *Big Wall Climbing* (New York: Oxford University Press, 1974), 20; Kerwin Lee Klein, "A Vertical World: The Eastern Alps and Modern Mountaineering," *Journal of Historical Sociology* 24 (December 2011), 535–36; Andrew Selters, *Ways to the Sky: A Historical Guide to North American Mountaineering* (Golden, CO: American Alpine Club, 2004), 88–89; Frison-Roche and Jouty, *History of Mountain Climbing*, 90–93; Bonington, *Climbers*, 71–76; Walt Unsworth, *Hold the Heights: The Foundations of Mountaineering* (Seattle: Mountaineers, 1994), 104; Mike C. Parsons and Mary B. Rose, *Invisible on Everest: Innovations and the Gear Makers* (Philadelphia: Northern Liberties Press, 2003), 137–38, 146–48. Two other important innovations in climbing gear were developed by British climber Oscar Eckenstein in these years. In 1908 he designed a ten-point crampon, offering greatly improved traction on snow or ice compared to the old four- or six-point crampons. And in 1910 he designed a 34-inch ice ax, considerably shorter and lighter weight than the ice axes that had been in use since the late nineteenth century—a design that became the standard for ice axes thereafter. David Dean, T. S. Blakeney, and D. F. O. Dangar, "Oscar Eckenstein, 1859–1921," *Alpine Journal* 65 (May 1960): 63–79; Bob Bridle, ed., *Mountaineers: Great Tales of Bravery and Conquest* (New York: DK, 2011), 196–97; Isserman and Weaver, *Fallen Giants*, 38.

37. Isserman and Weaver, *Fallen Giants*, 132.

38. Joe Bensen, *Souvenirs from High Places: A History of Mountaineering Photography* (Seattle: Mountaineers, 1998), 68, 76.

39. Geoffrey Winthrop Young, *Mountain Craft* (London: Methuen, 1920), 200–1; Allen Hankinson, *Geoffrey Winthrop Young: Poet, Educator, Mountaineer* (London: Hodder and Stoughton, 1995), 223–24.

40. The Seattle Mountaineers kept Young's *Mountain Craft* as required reading for their climbing courses until the mid-1950s. Steven M. Cox and Kris Fulsaas, eds., *Mountaineering: The Freedom of the Hills*, 7th ed. (Seattle: Mountaineers, 2003), 8.

41. Walter A. Wood, *A History of Mountaineering in the Saint Elias Mountains* (Scarborough, ON: Yukon Alpine Centennial Expedition, 1967), vii–viii, 1.

42. Michael Wood and Colby Coombs, *Alaska: A Climbing Guide* (Seattle: Mountaineers, 2001), 15–18.

43. "At the Foot of St. Elias," *New York Times*, July 16, 1886.

44. Francis E. Caldwell, *Land of the Ocean Mists: The Wild West Ocean Coast West of Glacier Bay* (Edmonds, WA: Alaska Northwest, 1986), 134. The duke's party did include a number of Americans, white and Indian, who served as packers and porters, but not as climbers. For a contemporary account of the duke's ascent, see Filippo De Filippi, *The Ascent of Mount St. Elias by H.R.H. Prince Luigi Amadeo di Savoia, Duke of the Abruzzi* (London: Constable, 1900). Also see Mirella Tenderini and Michael Shandrick, *The Duke of the Abruzzi: An Explorer's Life* (Seat-

tle: Mountaineers, 1997). The second ascent of Mount Saint Elias came in 1946, in a Harvard Mountaineering Club expedition that included mountaineering writer Dee Molenaar.

45. Quoted in Terris Moore, *Mt. McKinley: The Pioneer Climbs*, 2nd ed. (Seattle: Mountaineers, 1981), 1.

46. Eminent peaks being named for prominent living politicians from Ohio who would never see them was a theme in Alaskan topography; Mount Foraker was given the name of US senator J. B. Foraker by the lieutenant commanding an expedition exploring the Alaskan interior in 1899. Bradford Washburn and David Roberts, *Mount McKinley* (New York: Abrams, 1991), 25. On the renaming of Denali, see Reuters, "Mount McKinley to Be Renamed 'Denali'" *New York Times*, August 31, 2015, http://www.nytimes.com/video/multimedia/100000003883128/mount-mckinley-to-be-renamed-denali.html.

47. Alfred H. Brooks and D. L. Reaburn, "Plan for Climbing Mt. McKinley," *National Geographic Magazine* 14 (January 1903): 30–35. For Brooks's 1902 foray, see Jonathan Waterman, *High Alaska: A Historical Guide to Denali, Mount Foraker & Mount Hunter* (New York: American Alpine Club, 1996), 39; Moore, *Mt. McKinley*, 25–29.

48. Waterman, *High Alaska*, 39–40; Washburn and Roberts, *Mount McKinley*, 26–27.

49. Washburn and Roberts, *Mount McKinley*, 40–43.

50. For Browne's life and account of the climb, see Belmore Browne, *The Conquest of Mount McKinley*, 2nd ed. (Boston: Houghton Mifflin, 1956); and Robert H. Bates, *Mountain Man: The Story of Belmore Brown, Hunter, Explorer, Artist, Naturalist, and Preserver of Our Northern Wilderness* (Clinton, NJ: Amwell Press, 1988).

51. Quoted in Washburn and Roberts, *Mount McKinley*, 48.

52. The case against Cook's claims is exhaustively presented in Bradford Washburn and Peter Cherici, *The Dishonorable Dr. Cook: Debunking the Notorious McKinley Hoax* (Seattle: Mountaineers, 2001). Also see Browne, *Conquest of Mount McKinley*, 113–23.

53. Frederick A. Cook, "The Conquest of Mount McKinley," *Harper's Monthly Magazine* (May 1907): 825–37; Frederick A. Cook, *To the Top of the Continent: The First Ascent of Mount McKinley, 1903–1906* (New York: Doubleday, Page, 1908).

54. Frederick A. Cook, *My Attainment of the Pole: Being the Record of the Expedition That First Reached the Boreal Center* (New York: Polar Publishing, 1911); Moore, *Mt. McKinley*, 51–66; Robert M. Bryce, *Cook and Peary: The Polar Controversy Resolved* (Mechanicsburg, PA: Stackpole Books, 1997).

55. For the $500 figure, see, for example, Waterman, *High Alaska*, 42; Mick Conefrey and Tim Jordan, *Mountain Men: A History of the Remarkable Climbers and Determined Eccentrics Who First Scaled the World's Most Famous Peaks* (Cambridge, MA: Da Capo Press, 2001), 112. For $5,000, see Washburn and Roberts, *Mount McKinley*, 67.

56. Waterman, *High Alaska*, 43–44; Washburn and Roberts, *Mount McKinley*, 66–69; Moore, *Mt. McKinley*, 69–75.

57. Washburn and Roberts, *Mount McKinley*, 70–73; Moore, *Mt. McKinley*, 77–85.

58. Washburn and Roberts, *Mount McKinley*, 74–75; Moore, *Mt. McKinley*, 87–88.

59. Quoted in Moore, *Mt. McKinley*, 96.

60. Washburn and Roberts, *Mount McKinley*, 75–81.

61. Quoted in Moore, *Mt. McKinley*, 109.

62. Moore, *Mt. McKinley*, 108–9.

63. As Stuck wrote in his account of the expedition, his concern for the previous ten years had been with "the native people of Alaska, a gentle and kindly race, now threatened with a wanton and senseless extermination." Hudson Stuck, *The Ascent of Denali: A Narrative of the First Complete Ascent of the Highest Peak in North America* (New York: Charles Scribner's Sons, 1918), 187. Also see David Dean, *Breaking Trail: Hudson Stuck of Texas and Alaska* (Athens: Ohio University Press, 1988).

64. Stuck, *Ascent of Denali*, 123. The most complete life of Karstens is to be found in Tom Walker, *The Seventy Mile Kid: The Lost Legacy of Harry Karstens and the First Ascent of Mount McKinley* (Seattle: Mountaineers, 2013).

65. Moore, *Mt. McKinley*, 111.

66. Robert G. Tatum diary, March 15–July 8, 1913, 113–15. The original of the diary is deposited at the University of Tennessee, and is available online at http://dlc.lib.utk.edu/spc/view?docId=tei/0012_003086_000201_0000/0012_003086_000201_0000.xml.

67. Quoted in Moore, *Mt. McKinley*, 120. For an account of the climb emphasizing the important role of Harry Karstens in the party's success, see Walker, *Seventy Mile Kid*, 231–63.

68. Walker, *Seventy Mile Kid*, 285.

69. Alfred H. Brooks, "Mountain Exploration in Alaska," *Alpina Americana*, no. 3 (1914): 21.

70. Albert R. Ellingwood, "Technical Climbing in the Mountains of Colorado and Wyoming," *American Alpine Journal* 1 (1930): 140.

71. Chris Jones, *Climbing in North America* (Seattle: Mountaineers, 1997), 103. Founded in 1909, the Oxford University Mountaineering Club produced a host of distinguished alumni, from Andrew Irvine (a Merton student who perished with George Leigh-Mallory on Everest in 1924) to Stephen Venables, who climbed a new route on the Kangshung Face of Everest in 1988. Andrew Ross, "100 Years of the OUMC: A Brief and Personal History," *Alpine Journal* 114 (2009): 229–35.

72. Jeff Arnold has written the only full-scale biography of Ellingwood: *Albert Ellingwood: Scholar of Summits* (Pueblo, CO: My Friend the Printer, 2010). Also see "Albert R. Ellingwood," *American Alpine Journal* 2 (1935): 388–90; "Albert R. Ellingwood," *Trail and Timberline*, June 1934, 81, 85; and Beth Wald, "Albert Ellingwood," *Climbing*, no. 111 (December 1988): 97–98.

73. *Guide to Paths and Camps in the White Mountains, Part I* (Boston: Appalachian Mountain Club, 1907), 17. Laura and Guy Waterman suggest that it took a few years longer for AMCers to follow up on the suggestion. They write that "1916 merits immortality as the year when true rock climbing began in the Northeast," but even then only among a small circle of Boston enthusiasts. Waterman and Waterman, *Yankee Rock & Ice*, 16. Around the same time, John Case, future president of the American Alpine Club, began exploring the cliffs above Keene Valley in the Adirondacks, employing rope techniques he had learned in the Alps. Don Mellor, *American Rock: Region, Rock and Culture in American Climbing* (Woodstock, VT: Countryman Press, 2001), 25.

74. Opinion on this question varies. Fred Knapp says flatly that Ellington returned to Colorado with "nailed shoes, a hemp rope and pitons." Knapp, "The History of

American Rock Climbing," *Rock & Ice*, no. 79 (May–June 1997): 47. Biographer Jeff Arnold says more cautiously that he may have brought back some pitons. Arnold, *Albert Ellingwood*, 13.

75. Ellingwood, "Technical Climbing," 141 (emphasis in original). Ellingwood made exceptions for Longs Peak, Grand Teton, and a few others.

76. Jeff Achey, Dudley Chelton, and Bob Godfrey, *Climb! The History of Rock Climbing in Colorado* (Seattle: Mountaineers, 2002), 12–13; Mellor, *American Rock*, 25. In the early 1920s, Boulder climber Rudolph Johnston described the thrill of climbing the Flatirons, noting that he "always used a rope" in his climbs, "and it has been a lifesaver several times." But he reminded his readers of the leader-must-not-fall rule: "The first man up or the last man down gets no advantage of the rope." Rudolph Johnston, "Scaling the Flatirons," *Trail and Timberline*, March 1923, 4.

77. Wald, "Albert Ellingwood," 97–98; Arnold, *Albert Ellingwood*, 14.

78. Fred Beckey, *Fred Beckey's 100 Favorite North American Climbs* (Ventura, CA: Patagonia Books, 2011), 192. By 1925, Ellingwood had climbed all of Colorado's 14,000-foot peaks, only the third person to have done so. Carl Blaurock and Bill Evans preceded him. For an overview of Eleanor Davis's life and climbing career, see Janet Robertson, *The Magnificent Mountain Women: Adventures in the Colorado Rockies* (Lincoln: University of Nebraska Press, 2003), 30–36.

79. Albert L. Ellingwood, "First to Climb Lizard Head," *Outing* 79 (November 1921): 2.

80. Ibid., 55. Also see Pat Ament, *Wizards of Rock: A History of Free Climbing in America* (Berkeley: Wilderness Press, 2002), 17; Knapp, "History of American Rock Climbing," 48.

81. Arnold, *Albert Ellingwood*, 82–83; Fritiof Fryxell and Phil D. Smith, *Mountaineering in the Tetons: The Pioneer Period, 1898–1940* (Jackson, WY: Teton Bookshop, 1978), 27–28.

82. Quoted in Steve Roper and Allen Steck, *Fifty Classic Climbs of North America* (San Francisco: Sierra Club Books, 1979), 187.

83. Ibid., 187–89; Selters, *Ways to the Sky*, 86.

84. Ellingwood's favorite climbing partner, Eleanor Davis, by then known by her married name, Eleanor Davis Ehrman, died in 1993 at age 107. Robertson, *Magnificent Mountain Women*, 35–36.

85. Henry Ford, *My Life and Work* (Garden City, NY: Garden City Publishing, 1922), 73.

86. "The Mountaineer," *Boston Evening Transcript*, September 19, 1914.

87. John H. Williams, *Yosemite and Its High Sierra*, rev. ed. (San Francisco: Sierra Club, 1921), 57–58, 62, 64. "First Automobile Permit Issued 1100 Years Ago," National Park Service, August 23, 2013, http://www.nps.gov/yose/blogs/First-Automobile-Permit-Issued-100-Years-Ago_500611.htm.

88. Fritiof Fryxell, *The Teton Peaks and Their Ascents* (Grand Teton National Park: Crandall Studios, 1932), 3–5, 38; Fryxell and Smith, *Mountaineering in the Tetons*, 5; Leigh N. Ortenburger and Reynold G. Jackson, *A Climber's Guide to the Teton Range*, 3rd ed. (Seattle: Mountaineers, 1996), 14–15.

89. Allen Carpé, "The Mount Logan Adventure," *American Alpine Journal* 2 (1933): 74.

90. W. S. Ladd, "Allen Carpé, 1894–1932: In Memoriam," *American Alpine Journal* 1 (1932): 507–9; Geoff Radford, "Allen Carpé," *Climbing*, no. 111 (December 1988): 92–93; Fred Beckey, *Mount McKinley: Icy Crown of North America* (Seattle: Mountaineers, 1993), 129.

91. Firey, "American Alpine Club," 11.

92. Joe Josephson, "Mountain Profile: Mount Logan," *Alpinist*, no. 31 (Summer 2010): 38–39; Zachary Bass Robinson, "'Selected Alpine Climbs': The Struggle for Mountaineering in the Canadian Rockies, 1886–1961" (PhD diss., University of Alberta, 2007), 98.

93. Carpé, "Mount Logan Adventure," 74.

94. Ibid., 75.

95. Ibid., 69. Also see Josephson, "Mountain Profile: Mount Logan," 38–41; Jones, *Climbing in North America*, 86–90. The mixed Canadian-American makeup of the expedition led to differing emphases in the coverage that its triumph received north and south of the border. The *Toronto Daily Star* proclaimed in its headline, "Mt. Logan Has Been Climbed for the First Time: Party of Six Canadians Reported Back from Successful Climb, Americans Drop Out," while the *New York Times* declared, "Mt. Logan Scaled by Six Climbers: American in the Lead." Robinson, "'Selected Alpine Climbs,'" 116.

96. Roper and Steck, *Fifty Classic Climbs*, 9; Caldwell, *Land of the Ocean Mists*, 134. One unintended consequence of the effort was that it inspired a rival climber. In 1927 a seventeen-year-old prep school student named Bradford Washburn heard Carpé speak about his failed effort on the mountain at the annual meeting of the American Alpine Club in New York City. Inspired by what he heard, three years later Washburn made his own attempt to be the first up Fairweather—without success. It was the first of many expeditions that Washburn would lead in Alaska in years to come. Bradford Washburn and Lew Freedman, *Bradford Washburn: An Extraordinary Life* (Portland, OR: Westwinds Press, 2005), 45; Lew Freedman, ed., *Exploring the Unknown: Historic Diaries of Bradford Washburn's Alaska/Yukon Expeditions* (Kenmore, WA: Epicenter Press, 2001), 11.

97. Robert Moore, "Chimborazo, Bolivar's Tower of the Universe," *American Alpine Journal* 1 (1932): 93–105; Terris Moore, "Sangay Survived—The First Time," *Alpine Journal* 86 (1981): 28–31.

98. Geoffrey Hattersley-Smith, "Terris Moore," *Polar Record* 34 (April 1998): 149–51; Stuart Pregnall, "Terris Moore," *Climbing*, no. 111 (December 1988): 92.

99. Allen Carpé, "The Ascent of Mount Bona," *American Alpine Journal* 1 (1931): 245.

100. Roper and Steck, *Fifty Classic Climbs*, 12; William S. Ladd, "The Fairweather Climb," *American Alpine Journal* 1 (1932): 442–43.

101. Caldwell, *Land of the Ocean Mists*, 41.

102. Washburn and Freedman, *Bradford Washburn*, 48.

103. This was the Lindley-Liek expedition, led by Minnesota businessman Alfred Lindley and McKinley Park superintendent Harry Liek, with two others in the summit party. Washburn and Roberts, *Mount McKinley*, 102.

104. Henry B. deV. Schwab, "The Mount McKinley Disaster," *American Alpine Journal* 1 (1932): 511–14; Edward P. Beckwith, "The Mount McKinley Cosmic Ray Expedition 1932," *American Alpine Journal* 2 (1933): 45–68.

105. Bestor Robinson, "The First Ascent of the Higher Cathedral Spire," *Sierra Club Bulletin* 19 (June 1934): 34–37, reprinted in Galen A. Rowell, ed., *The Vertical World of Yosemite: Writings on Rock Climbing in Yosemite* (Berkeley, CA: Wilderness Press, 1974), 9–12. Also see Robert H. Bates, "Robert L. M. Underhill, 1889–1983," *Alpine Journal* 89 (1984): 266.

106. Miriam O'Brien Underhill, "Manless Alpine Climbing," *National Geographic Magazine* 66 (August 1934): 131–70; Laura Waterman, "The Chronicle of Miriam Underhill: New England's Greatest Woman Mountaineer," *New England Outdoors* 4 (November 1978): 41–47; "Miriam Underhill, 1899–1976," *Alpine Journal* 82 (1977): 272–73. Underhill helped introduce fellow New Englanders to alpine climbing, as climbing leader of a sixteen-member AMC expedition to Arolla, Valais, Switzerland, in 1927. "Excursion to Arolla, Valais, Switzerland, August 6–21, 1927," box 2002, Appalachian Mountain Club Library, Boston, MA. Also see Ed Webster, "Fritz Wiessner: A Man for All Mountains," in *Cloud Dancers: Portraits of North American Mountaineers*, ed. Jonathan Waterman (Golden, CO: American Alpine Club, 1993), 11.

107. Waterman and Waterman, *Yankee Rock & Ice*, 13–14.

108. Kenneth Henderson, "Some Rock Climbs in the White Mountains," *Appalachia* 67 (December 1929): 343–50. Also see Guy Waterman and Laura Waterman, "Kenneth Henderson," *Climbing*, no. 111 (December 1988): 101; "In Memoriam: Kenneth A. Henderson," *Appalachia* 53 (December 2001): 112–13; Stewart M. Green, *Rock Climbing New England* (Guilford, CT: Globe Pequot Press, 2001), 4.

109. Ellingwood, "Technical Climbing," 142; Fryxell and Smith, *Mountaineering in the Tetons*, 49–50; Kenneth A. Henderson, "The Grand Teton," *American Alpine Journal* 1 (1930): 138–39. Underhill and Henderson also made several first ascents in the Wind River Range that summer. Kenneth A. Henderson, "The Wind River Range in Wyoming," *American Alpine Journal* 1 (1930): 128–37.

110. Fritiof M. Fryxell, "The Ascent of Mount Owen," *American Alpine Journal* 1 (1931): 320–26; William Clack, "Ken Henderson (1906–2001)," http://www.atkinsopht.com/mtn/khendrem.htm, accessed July 7, 2015.

111. Bates, "Robert L. M. Underhill," 267; Robert L. M. Underhill, "An Attempt on Mt. Robson by the NW (Emperor Falls) Ridge," *Canadian Alpine Journal* 19 (1931): 66–68. Mount Robson, the highest of the Canadian Rockies, at 12,972 feet, had its first ascent, as well as first traverse, in 1913 by two American climbers (Albert MacCarthy and William Foster) and Austrian guide (Conrad Kain), part of an expedition organized by the Alpine Club of Canada.

112. Farquhar may have gotten the idea to solicit such an article by Underhill from a previous piece appearing in the AMC journal: Robert L. M. Underhill, "On Roping Down," *Appalachia* 17 (June 1928): 53–64.

113. Underhill, "On the Use and Management," 68.

114. Ibid.

115. Ibid., 67.

116. In his history of climbing in Yosemite, Joseph Taylor challenges the assumption

that Underhill single-handedly brought American rock-climbing up to European standards. Underhill, he notes, "was but one of many influences" introducing new techniques and equipment. While that is true, too many climbers at the time and since have spoken to Underhill's singular role in drawing attention to the new standards of rope craft to discount his importance. Taylor, *Pilgrims of the Vertical*, 15–16, 38–41.

117. Fryxell and Smith, *Mountaineering in the Tetons*, 54; Ortenburger and Jackson, *Climber's Guide to the Teton Range*, 15; Rebecca Woods, "Glenn Exum," *Climbing*, no. 111 (December 1988): 97. For Paul Petzoldt's arrival in the Tetons and early career as a Teton guide, see Raye C. Ringholz, *On Belay! The Life of Legendary Mountaineer Paul Petzoldt* (Seattle: Mountaineers, 1997), 33–46.

118. Fryxell and Smith, *Mountaineering in the Tetons*, 32–33.

119. Quoted in Jones, *Climbing in North America*, 119.

120. Fritiof M. Fryxell, "The Grand Teton by the North Face," *American Alpine Journal* 1 (1932): 467; Fryxell and Smith, *Mountaineering in the Tetons*, 58–61; Ortenburger and Jackson, *Climber's Guide to the Teton Range*, 15, 20–21; Selters, *Ways to the Sky*, 92–93. In Nick Clinch's opinion, "Underhill and Fryxell's climb of the North Ridge of the Grand Teton was the hardest climb yet done in the US. The Higher Spire in Yosemite was a lot more technical, but the total situation of the North Ridge makes it a much greater endeavor." Nick Clinch, e-mail to the author, July 25, 2010.

121. Quoted in Bill Oliver, "A Tribute to the Honorary Members of the Sierra Peaks Section, Past and Present," *Sierra Echo* 33 (November–December 1989): 9. According to Oliver, Farquhar overlooked a belayed roped climb the previous summer by Sierra Club member John Mendenhall on 11,818-foot Laurel Mountain. For Mendenhall's precedent, see John G. Ripley, "John Dale Mendenhall: 1911–1983," *American Alpine Journal* 26 (1984): 348.

122. Norman Clyde, *Close-ups of the High Sierra* (Glendale, CA: La Siesta Press, 1962), 67; Robin Ingraham, "Norman Clyde," *Climbing*, no. 111 (December 1988): 96; Moore, *Exploring the High Sierra*, 140–42.

123. Beckey, *Fred Beckey's 100 Favorite*, 217–18; Oliver, "Tribute to the Honorary Members," 10–12.

124. Robert L. M. Underhill, "Mount Whitney by the East Face," *Sierra Club Bulletin* 17 (February 1932): 58.

125. Roper and Steck, *Fifty Classic Climbs*, 279; Jones, *Climbing in North America*, 126–27.

126. Cohen, *History of the Sierra Club*, 67–71.

127. Richard M. Leonard, "Values to Be Derived from Local Rock-Climbing," *Sierra Club Bulletin* 19 (June 1934): 28–29.

128. For facsimiles of RCS minutes and correspondence from this period, see "RCS Articles and Letters from the Early Days," Yosemite Climbing Association, http://www.yosemiteclimbing.org/content/rcs-articles-and-letters-early-days, accessed July 7, 2015.

129. Royal Robbins, *Fail Falling* (Ojai, CA: Pink Moment Press, 2010), 10–11; Taylor, *Pilgrims of the Vertical*, 45–54.

130. "My father did not attend college. He did take some courses at Cal Berkeley in

the architectural department. He was self taught and had a successful construction business. His parents owned a small grocery store and there wasn't money
for college (5 children)." Kathy Bedayn (daughter of Raffi Bedayn), e-mail to the
author, May 18, 2014.

131. Richard M. Leonard, "Piton Technique on the Cathedral Spires," *Appalachia* 20
(December 1934): 179; Taylor, *Pilgrims of the Vertical*, 54; Selters, *Ways to the Sky*,
95.

132. William Alsup, *Missing in the Minarets: The Search for Walter A. Starr, Jr.* (San
Francisco: Yosemite Conservancy, 2005); Arce, *Defying Gravity*, 19.

133. Leo Maduschka, "Neuseitliche Felstechnik," 1931, translated and condensed
by E. A. Stewardson as "Modern Rock Technique," in *Mountaineering Journal*
1 (March–May 1933): 156–64. For the article's influence in the United States,
see Richard M. Leonard and Arnold Wexler, *Belaying the Leader* (San Francisco:
Sierra Club, 1947), 5. The *Mountaineering Journal*, published from 1932 through
1938, was unusual in the world of mountaineering publications because it was
not sponsored by a club. Bensen, *Souvenirs from High Places*, 83. For a basic illustrated description of the use of the Prusik knot, see Cox and Fulsaas, *Mountaineering*, 146–47; and Steve Roper, *Camp 4: Recollections of a Yosemite Rockclimber*
(Seattle: Mountaineers, 1994), 36.

134. "Sporthaus Schuster," Muenchen.de, http://www.muenchen.de/int/en/shopping/
typical-munich/sport-schuster.html, accessed July 7, 2015; Mike C. Parsons and
Mary B. Rose, *Invisible on Everest: Innovations and the Gear Makers* (Philadelphia: Northern Liberties Press, 2003), 141.

135. Roper, *Camp 4*, 21.

136. William Shand Jr., "Some Yosemite Rock-Climbs," *American Alpine Journal* 5
(1944): 203. For Shand's climbing career, see B. G. F. [Benjamin Greeley Ferris],
"William Shand, Jr., 1918–1946," *American Alpine Journal* 6 (1947): 423.

137. Roper, *Camp 4*, 11.

138. Leonard would return to Washington Column with Morgan Harris and Jack
Riegelhuth in 1935 and make the first ascent. Their route, called the Piton Traverse, proved the most popular single route in the valley in the 1930s, with fourteen ascents by 1939. Roper, *Camp 4*, 28.

139. Quoted in Roper, *Camp 4*, 192.

140. Selters, *Ways to the Sky*, 94.

141. Leonard, "Piton Technique," 178.

142. Robinson, "First Ascent of the Higher Cathedral Spire," 35. Joseph Taylor has an
interesting discussion of Yosemite climbing as "performance," in *Pilgrims of the
Vertical*, 71–72.

143. Robinson, "First Ascent," 37.

144. The *American Alpine Journal* noted that the Upper Cathedral Spire climb "marks
the first use of pitons to any extent in the Sierra Nevada." "Climbs and Expeditions," *American Alpine Journal* 2 (1935): 414. And the equipment used made
it into the headline of *Appalachia*'s account: Richard M. Leonard, "Piton Technique on the Cathedral Spires," *Appalachia* 20 (December 1934): 177–83. Also
see Roper, *Camp 4*, 22–25; Ament, *Wizards of Rock*, 29–30; Jones, *Climbing in
North America*, 128–30.

145. David R. Brower to Norman Clyde, October 31, 1935, Sierra Club Members Papers, carton 4:7, BANC MSS 79/9, Bancroft Library, University of California, Berkeley.
146. Robert Ormes, "A Piece of Bent Iron," *Saturday Evening Post* 111 (July 20, 1939): 13.
147. Robert Ormes to Dick Leonard, September 2, 1938, Sierra Club Members Papers, carton 82:27, BANC MSS 71/295c, Bancroft Library, University of California, Berkeley.
148. David Brower to Melvin Griffith, October 5, 1939, Sierra Club Members Papers, carton 82:27, BANC MSS 71/295c, Bancroft Library, University of California, Berkeley.
149. Fred Beckey, *Mountains of North America* (San Francisco: Sierra Club Books, 1982), 162.
150. Bestor Robinson, "Shiprock," *American Alpine Journal* 4 (1940): 56. On the ascent of Shiprock, also see David R. Brower, "It Couldn't Be Climbed," *Saturday Evening Post* 112 (February 3, 1940): 24–25, 72–79; David Brower, *For Earth's Sake: The Life and Times of David Brower* (Salt Lake City: Peregrine Smith Books, 1990), 65–80; Roper and Steck, *Fifty Classic Climbs*, 209–15; Beckey, *Mountains of North America*, 157–62.
151. Bensen, *Souvenirs from High Places*, 83.

CHAPTER FIVE: BROTHERHOOD OF THE ROPE, 1900–1946: PART II

1. Chris Jones, *Climbing in North America* (Seattle: Mountaineers, 1997), 105–7; John D. Gorby, *The Stettner Way: The Life and Climbs of Joe and Paul Stettner* (Golden: Colorado Mountain Club Press, 2003), 63–65; Jack Fralick, "The Stettner Way," *Climbing*, no. 169 (1997): 48; Fred Knapp, "The History of American Rock Climbing," *Rock & Ice*, no. 79 (May–June 1997): 49. The Stettners would go on to put up new routes on other mountains in the Colorado Rockies and the Tetons, and they were founding members of the Chicago Mountaineering Club in 1940.
2. Andrew Selters, *Ways to the Sky: A Historical Guide to North American Mountaineering* (Golden, CO: American Alpine Club, 2004), 98–100; "Wolf Bauer," *Northwest Mountaineering Journal*, http://www.alpenglow.org/nwmj/05/051_BauerBib.html, accessed July 7, 2015.
3. Otto T. Trott, *The Making of a Rescuer* (Victoria, BC: Trofford, 2008), 132–33; Jones, *Climbing in North America*, 145.
4. Lowell Skoog, "Dr. Trott's Mountain," in *Written in the Snows: Across Time on Skis in the Pacific Northwest* (Seattle, 2010), http://written-in-the-snows.net/ski-climbers6.html. In another notable first, Andy Hennig and Sigurd Hall made the first ski ascent of Mount Rainier in 1939. After the war and service in the Tenth Mountain Division, Hennig published the first guide in North America for high mountain ski touring: *Sun Valley Ski Guide* ([Omaha, NE]: Union Pacific Railroad, 1948).
5. The indispensable work on this topic is Dee Molenaar, *Mountains Don't Care, but We Do: An Early History of Mountain Rescue in the Pacific Northwest and*

the Founding of the Mountain Rescue Association (Seattle: Mountain Rescue Association, 2009). Also see Seattle Mountain Rescue, "History," http://seattlemountainrescue.org/about/history, accessed July 7, 2015.

6. Maurice Isserman and Stewart Weaver, *Fallen Giants: A History of Himalayan Mountaineering from the Age of Empire to the Age of Extremes* (New Haven, CT: Yale University Press, 2008), 354–55.

7. "Fritz Hermann Ernst Wiessner," Proposal, April 8, 1933, American Alpine Club Library, Golden, CO.

8. Laura Waterman and Guy Waterman, *Yankee Rock & Ice: A History of Climbing in the Northeastern United States* (Mechanicsburg, PA: Stackpole Books, 1993), 94–95; Mick Conefrey and Tim Jordan, *Mountain Men: A History of the Remarkable Climbers and Determined Eccentrics Who First Scaled the World's Most Famous Peaks* (Cambridge, MA: Da Capo Press, 2001), 160–63; Ed Webster, "A Man for all Mountains: The Life and Climbs of Fritz Wiessner," *Climbing*, December 1988, 102–8.

9. Fritz H. Wiessner, "Early Rock Climbing in the Shawangunks," *Appalachia* 33 (June 1960): 18.

10. Cliff Ranson, "Climbing in the Gunks," *National Geographic Adventure*, http://www.nationalgeographic.com/adventure/0509/sports/rock_climbing.html, accessed July 7, 2015.

11. Waterman and Waterman, *Yankee Rock & Ice*, 96. Also see Stewart M. Green, *Rock Climbing New England* (Guilford, CT: Globe Pequot Press, 2001), 97.

12. Ibid., 100–1.

13. Henry S. Hall Jr., "Reconnaissance in the Coast Range of British Columbia," *American Alpine Journal* 1 (1933): 88.

14. The Munday-Hall party did make the first ascent of 12,323-foot Mount Combatant in 1933, while failing to climb Waddington. Hall, "Reconnaissance in the Coast Range," 87; Hall, "Further Explorations and Ascents in the Coast Range of British Columbia," *American Alpine Journal* 2 (1934): 156–69; Hall, "The 1934 Attempts on Mt. Waddington," *American Alpine Journal* 2 (1935): 298–306; Barry Hagen, "Mount Waddington," *Ascent* 1 (May 1969): 20–28; Jones, *Climbing in North America*, 153–56; Andrew Selters, *Ways to the Sky: A Historical Guide to North American Mountaineering* (Golden, CO: American Alpine Club, 2004), 105–9.

15. Bestor Robinson, "Mount Waddington—1935," *Sierra Club Bulletin* 21 (February 1936): 11; Selters, *Ways to the Sky*, 123–24.

16. For House's background, education, and climbing career, see Laura Waterman and Guy Waterman, "William House," *Climbing*, no. 111 (December 1988): 90–91.

17. William P. House, "The Ascent of Mount Waddington," *American Alpine Journal* 3 (1937): 22.

18. Fritz H. Wiessner, "The First Ascent of Mt. Waddington," *Canadian Alpine Journal* 24 (1936): 12.

19. Ibid., 12.

20. Ibid., 13–17; Selters, *Ways to the Sky*, 124–26.

21. William P. House, "Devils Tower," *American Alpine Journal* 3 (1938): 136. For

Coveney, see Frank Cary, Percy Olton, and Fritz Wiessner, "Lawrence George Coveney, 1898–1981: In Memoriam," *American Alpine Journal* 24 (1982): 334–36.

22. Letter dated November 14, 1933, box 12000, folder 1: "Membership Correspondence, 1933–1941," Appalachian Mountain Club Library, Boston, MA.

23. "Youthful Mountain Climber Strangled," *Plattsburgh Daily Press*, April 4, 1939; Percy T. Olton Jr., "Deaths and Accidents," *Appalachia*, June 1939, 406–7.

24. Robert Underhill to "Dick" [Leonard], June 25, 1939, Sierra Club Members Papers, carton 81:1, BANC MSS 71/295c, Bancroft Library, University of California, Berkeley.

25. Steven Jervis, "The Shawangunks, Now and Then," *Appalachia* 62 (Summer/Fall 2011): 66–67.

26. In 1946, Underhill wrote to AAC president Henry S. Hall to complain about the manners and background of a fellow AAC member he had recently encountered in the White Mountains: "Have you the pleasure of a personal acquaintance with Mr. James Ramsey Ullman? Neither have I but Marion [Underhill's wife] and I have just spent a night at the Lakes of the Clouds hut where he was present with his two boys. Unless I miss my guess, he is a lowgrade New York Jew—at any rate his boys are beautifully Jewish and he is incontestably lowgrade. . . . The New York chapter of the AMC would never let such a mutt through their censors; can the A.A.C. be less choosey?" Robert Underhill to Henry S. Hall, June 24, 1946, Himalaya Library Archives, box K2, folder "1939 American Karakoram Expedition, K2," American Alpine Club Library, Golden CO; Isserman and Weaver, *Fallen Giants*, 234. Underhill had forgotten, or more likely didn't care, that the founder of the American Alpine Club, Angelo Heilprin, was of Jewish descent, his Polish-born father, Michael Heilprin, a noted Jewish biblical scholar. "Heilprin, Michael," JewishEncyclopedia, http://www.jewishencyclopedia.com/articles/7500-heilprin-michael, accessed July 7, 2015.

27. Richard Leonard, interview, Sierra Club Members Papers, carton 82:6, BANC MSS 71/295c, Bancroft Library, University of California, Berkeley. Interviewed in 1972, Leonard said that after the war, "Dave Brower and I and some of the younger [members of the Sierra Club governing board] got together and the board of directors unanimously objected to that racial prejudice and denounced it."

28. Charlie Houston to Brad Washburn, December 14, 1936, Bradford Washburn Collection, box 5, folder "Correspondence, Fall 1936, Part II," Howard Gotlieb Archival Research Center at Boston University. Bates and Houston were best known for leading pioneering expeditions to K2, in 1938 and 1953. Another Washburn protégé, H. Adams ("Ad") Carter, would also make his mark in Himalayan mountaineering, as part of expeditions to Nanda Devi in 1936 (with Houston) and again in 1976. As an expedition leader, he played an important role in introducing American climbers to the Peruvian Andes, leading fifteen expeditions all told to the region, and making a half dozen first ascents. Evelio Echevarría, "Early American Ascents in the Andes, 1854–1950," *American Alpine Journal* 28 (1986): 113–14.

29. For overviews of Washburn's life and mountaineering career, see Audrey Salkeld, "Skinning One Skunk at a Time: An Appreciation of the Work of Bradford Wash-

burn," *Mountain*, March/April 1989, 36–39; and Jonathan Waterman, "The Mission of Mr. McKinley, the Life Work of Bradford Washburn," *Rock & Ice*, January–February 1992, 24–27. Also see Jonathan Waterman, *In the Shadow of Denali: Life and Death on Alaska's Mount McKinley* (Guilford, CT: Lyons Press, 2010), 8–11.

30. Michael Sfraga, *Bradford Washburn: A Life of Exploration* (Corvallis: Oregon State University Press, 2004), 12. Washburn was elected a life member of the Massachusetts Society of Mayflower Descendants, in 1936. See George Ernest Bowman to Brad Washburn, October 9, 1936, Bradford Washburn Collection, box 5, folder "Correspondence, Fall 1936, Part I," Howard Gotlieb Archival Research Center at Boston University.

31. There would be two more books by Washburn on his youthful mountaineering adventures: *Bradford on Mount Washington* (1928) and *Bradford on Mount Fairweather* (1930). The three books were recently republished in a single volume: Bradford Washburn, *Washburn: Extraordinary Adventures of a Young Mountaineer* (Boston: Appalachian Mountain Club, 2004).

32. Washburn biographer David Roberts judges the ascent of the Aiguille Verte's north face "far and away the hardest alpine route yet pioneered by any American-born mountaineer anywhere in the world." David Roberts, *The Last of His Kind: The Life and Adventures of Bradford Washburn, America's Boldest Mountaineer* (New York: William Morrow, 2009), 8–25. The first to ascend the peak had been Edward Whymper in 1865, shortly before the Matterhorn ascent and tragedy.

33. Bradford Washburn, "Henry Bradford Washburn," *Alpinist*, March 1, 2004, http://www.alpinist.com/doc/ALP06/faces-washburn; also see Sfraga, *Bradford Washburn*, 25–26.

34. For Washburn's interest in the Himalaya and Alaska, see Roberts, *Last of His Kind*, 26–38; Bradford Washburn and Lew Freedman, *Bradford Washburn: An Extraordinary Life* (Portland, OR: Westwinds Press, 2005), 45–46. Michael Sfraga mentions two others who sparked Washburn's interest in southeastern Alaska: glaciologist William Field, who gave an illustrated lecture at Harvard in 1929 on his 1926 visit to Lituya Bay and Glacier Bay; and Bob Morgan, a friend of Washburn and veteran of the 1925 Mount Logan expedition. Sfraga, *Bradford Washburn*, 34–35.

35. David Roberts, foreword to *Washburn: Extraordinary Adventures of a Young Mountaineer*, by Bradford Washburn (Boston: Appalachian Mountain Club, 2004), xi.

36. H. Bradford Washburn Jr., "The Harvard Dartmouth Alaskan Expeditions, 1933–1934," *Geographical Journal* 87 (June 1936): 482; Roberts, *Last of His Kind*, 43–44; Sfraga, *Bradford Washburn*, 37–38.

37. Bradford Washburn, "The Conquest of Mount Crillon," *National Geographic Magazine* 67 (March 1935): 362. Many years later Washburn noted, "I learned from Fairweather . . . that Alaska's mountains were big and difficult and would take more experience and planning than I had." Washburn and Freedman, *Bradford Washburn*, 51.

38. Roberts, *Last of His Kind*, 49–51; Sfraga, *Bradford Washburn*, 39–40.

39. Quoted in Bernadette McDonald, *Brotherhood of the Rope: The Biography of Charlie Houston* (Seattle: Mountaineers, 2007), 31.

40. Ad Carter to Brad Washburn, September 25, 1936, Bradford Washburn Collection, box 4, folder "1936—Pt. 1," Howard Gotlieb Archival Research Center at Boston University; Charlie Houston to Brad Washburn, October 25, 1936, Bradford Washburn Collection, box 5, folder "Correspondence, Fall 1936, Part II," Howard Gotlieb Archival Research Center at Boston University.

41. Houston, Carter, and Child did pull off the first ascent of a subsidiary peak: 9,650-foot Mount Dagelet. Washburn and Houston remained friends, but the two never again climbed together.

42. William S. Child, "Crillon 1933," *American Alpine Journal* 2 (1934): 148–55; Washburn, "Conquest of Mount Crillon," 364–65; Roberts, *Last of His Kind*, 53–54; Sfraga, *Bradford Washburn*, 41–42; Washburn and Freedman, *Bradford Washburn*, 51–55.

43. Brad Washburn to his parents, August 24, 1933, Bradford Washburn Collection, box 2, folder "Washburn, B. Crillon Expedition; Letters, Telegrams Home, Summer 1933," Howard Gotlieb Archival Research Center at Boston University (emphasis in original).

44. Waterman and Waterman, *Yankee Rock & Ice*, 85–86; Selters, *Ways to the Sky*, 115.

45. Washburn, "Conquest of Mount Crillon," 367.

46. In making use of the large-format camera, Washburn was emulating one of his heroes, Vittorio Sella. Sfraga, *Bradford Washburn*, 48, 64.

47. Washburn, "Conquest of Mount Crillon," 400.

48. Brad Washburn to his parents, July 25, 1934, Bradford Washburn Collection, box 3, folder "Crillon Letters, 1934," Howard Gotlieb Archival Research Center at Boston University. Also see Sfraga, *Bradford Washburn*, 61–62.

49. Mary Desmond Rock, *Museum of Science, Boston: The Founding and Formative Years: The Washburn Era, 1939–1980* (Boston: Museum of Science, 1989). For the Mount Lucania climb, see Bradford Washburn, "The Ascent of Mount Lucania," *American Alpine Journal* 3 (1938): 119–26; and David Roberts, *Escape from Lucania: An Epic Story of Survival* (New York: Simon and Schuster, 2007). For some of Washburn's subsequent climbs in Alaska, see Bradford Washburn, "The Ascent of Mount Washburn," *American Alpine Journal* 4 (1941): 149–56; and Bradford Washburn, "The Ascent of Mount Hayes," *American Alpine Journal* 4 (1942): 323–34.

50. When Knowlton died in 1989, the *New York Times* obituary declared that she "became the first woman to climb as high as 20,000 feet in the Himalaya," having forgotten about Mrs. Workman. Glenn Fowler, "Elizabeth Knowlton Is Dead at 93: Pioneer of Himalayas in the 30's," *New York Times*, January 27, 1989, http://www.nytimes.com/1989/01/27/obituaries/elizabeth-knowlton-is-dead-at-93-pioneer-of-himalayas-in-the-30-s.html.

51. Elizabeth Knowlton, "Nanga Parbat, 1932," *American Alpine Journal* 2 (1933): 18–31; Fritz Wiessner, "Nanga Parbat in Retrospect," *American Alpine Journal* 2 (1933): 32–35; "Elbridge Rand Herron," *American Alpine Journal* 2 (1933): 110–

13; Isserman and Weaver, *Fallen Giants*, 148–55. For the disastrous 1934 Nanga Parbat expedition, see Isserman and Weaver, *Fallen Giants*, 172–79.

52. Richard L. Burdsall and Arthur B. Emmons, *Men against the Clouds: The Conquest of Minya Konka* (New York: Harper & Brothers, 1935), 6; "Minya Konka," *Harvard Mountaineering*, no. 4 (June 1936): 8.

53. Stuart Pregnall, "Terris Moore," *Climbing*, no. 111 (December 1988): 92; Isserman and Weaver, *Fallen Giants*, 191–92.

54. Burdsall and Emmons, *Men against the Clouds*, 8, 11.

55. Ibid., 175.

56. Ibid., 229.

57. Ibid., 149.

58. Ibid., 200.

59. Terris Moore, "The Minya Konka Climb," *American Alpine Journal* 2 (1933): 1–17.

60. "Foreword," *Harvard Mountaineering*, no. 4 (June 1936): 3.

61. Isserman and Weaver, *Fallen Giants*, 159.

62. Ibid., 165–71, 181–89.

63. Charles S. Houston, "Denali's Wife," *American Alpine Journal* 2 (1935): 285–97; Charles Houston, "Lofty Peaks of Mount Foraker Are Scaled for First Time by Man," *New York Times*, August 30, 1934; McDonald, *Brotherhood of the Rope*, 37–39.

64. Isserman and Weaver, *Fallen Giants*, 192.

65. See, for example, Isserman and Weaver, *Fallen Giants*, 192; and McDonald, *Brotherhood of the Rope*, 44.

66. Charles S. Houston to Henry S. Hall, n.d. [Spring 1936], Henry Hall Papers, folder "Houston, Charles S.," American Alpine Club Library, Golden, CO.

67. Isserman and Weaver, *Fallen Giants*, 192–93. Jim Perrin, *Shipton & Tilman: The Great Decade of Himalayan Exploration* (London: Hutchinson, 2013), 268–78, offers a compelling account of both the 1934 and 1936 Nanda Devi expeditions. But Perrin makes a few mistakes about the Americans in the latter expedition, oddly describing the four Harvard mountaineers as "frat boys," and saying that Loomis was "a distinguished Alaskan climber in his own right," which he was not (ibid., 270).

68. Houston to Hall, n.d. [Spring 1936].

69. Isserman and Weaver, *Fallen Giants*, 193; McDonald, *Brotherhood of the Rope*, 45–46; David Roberts, "Pioneers of Mountain Exploration: The Harvard Five," reprinted in *Cloud Dancers: Portraits of North American Mountaineers*, ed. Jonathan Waterman (Golden, CO: American Alpine Club, 1993), 30.

70. W. H. Tilman, *The Ascent of Nanda Devi* (Cambridge: Cambridge University Press, 1937), 198; Isserman and Weaver, *Fallen Giants*, 195–97; McDonald, *Brotherhood of the Rope*, 48–49; Charles S. Houston, "Nanda Devi," *American Alpine Journal* 3 (1937): 1–20.

71. Eric Shipton, "More Explorations Round Nanda Devi," *Alpine Journal* 90 (August 1937): 97–98; Isserman and Weaver, *Fallen Giants*, 191.

72. Carter to Washburn, September 25, 1936.

73. Houston to Washburn, October 25, 1936.

74. McDonald, *Brotherhood of the Rope*, 55; Isserman and Weaver, *Fallen Giants*, 207.

75. Isserman and Weaver, *Fallen Giants*, 207; Conefrey and Jordan, *Mountain Men*, 61–62.

76. Charlie Houston to Bob Bates, November 22, 1937, 1938 K2 Scrapbook, in Houston family possession.

77. Robert H. Bates and Charles S. Houston, *Five Miles High: The Story of an Attack on the Second Highest Mountain of the World* (New York: Dodd, Mead, 1939), 29; Isserman and Weaver, *Fallen Giants*, 207–8; McDonald, *Brotherhood of the Rope*, 56–57.

78. Raye C. Ringholz, *On Belay! The Life of Legendary Mountaineer Paul Petzoldt* (Seattle: Mountaineers, 1997), 89.

79. Isserman and Weaver, *Fallen Giants*, 208; McDonald, *Brotherhood of the Rope*, 56.

80. Isserman and Weaver, *Fallen Giants*, 208–9.

81. Ibid., 209–10.

82. Quoted in McDonald, *Brotherhood of the Rope*, 61. Also see William P. House, "K2—1938," *American Alpine Journal* 3 (1938): 244.

83. Isserman and Weaver, *Fallen Giants*, 213–14.

84. Ringholz, *On Belay!*, 111.

85. Charles Houston, "Heyday Climbs," in *Heroic Climbs*, ed. Chris Bonington and Audrey Salkeld (Seattle: Mountaineers, 1996), 159; Isserman and Weaver, 214–15. Also see House, "K2—1938," 229–54.

86. McDonald, *Brother of the Rope*, 62–63.

87. Bob Bates to Brad Washburn, September 22, 1938, on board the ocean liner *Bremen*, Bradford Washburn Collection, box 6, folder "September–Dec. 15, 1938," Howard Gotlieb Archival Research Center at Boston University.

88. David Dornan, "An Interview with Fritz Wiessner," *Ascent* 1 (May 1969): 18.

89. Among others who turned Wiessner down were Bestor Robinson of the Sierra Club; Alfred Lindley, who had made the second ascent of Denali in 1932; and Sterling Hendricks, who was part of a Brad Washburn expedition that made the third ascent of Denali in 1942. Isserman and Weaver, *Fallen Giants*, 215.

90. Dornan, "Interview with Fritz Wiessner," 18. Sources on Durrance's climbing career are relatively scarce, but see Reynold G. Jackson's capsule biography of him in "Park of the Matterhorns," Grand Teton Historic Resource Study, http://www.nps.gov/parkhistory/online_books/grte2/hrs16b.htm, accessed July 7, 2015.

91. Quoted in Conefrey and Jordan, *Mountain Men*, 166.

92. Isserman and Weaver, *Fallen Giants*, 215–16.

93. Quoted in Conefrey and Jordan, *Mountain Men*, 168.

94. George Sheldon, "Lost behind the Ranges," *Saturday Evening Post* 112 (March 1940): 123.

95. Conefrey and Jordan, *Mountain Men*, 172.

96. Sheldon, "Lost behind the Ranges," 123; Conefrey and Jordan, *Mountain Men*, 170.

97. Jack Durrance, K2 diary (typescript copy), Kauffman Collection, box 2, folder 2/8, American Alpine Club Library, Golden, CO; Isserman and Weaver, *Fallen Giants*, 218.

98. Chappel Cranmer and Fritz Wiessner, "The Second American Expedition to K2," *American Alpine Journal* 4 (1940): 16.

99. Conefrey and Jordan, *Mountain Men*, 177.

100. Quoted in ibid., 189.

101. Cranmer and Wiessner, "Second American Expedition to K2," 9–20.

102. Conefrey and Jordan, *Mountain Men*, 193–97.

103. Quoted in ibid., 195.

104. Ibid., 198. The controversy over who was to blame for the events of 1939 on K2 continued for decades afterward. As anti-Germanic sentiments cooled following the war, blame shifted from Wiessner to Jack Durrance (who probably was least responsible for the bad decisions made by the American climbers). The publication of Andrew J. Kauffman and William L. Putnam, *K2: The 1939 Tragedy* (Seattle: Mountaineers, 1992) shifted the blame back to Wiessner—also the position taken by Isserman and Weaver in their 2008 *Fallen Giants*. Mick Conefrey and Tim Jordan split the blame between Durrance and Wiessner in their 2001 *Mountain Men*. Doubtless, the controversy will continue.

105. Isserman and Weaver, *Fallen Giants*, 222.

106. Charles Houston, "Norman R. Streatfeild," *Alpine Journal* 53 (May 1941): 67.

107. "The Gift of an Ambulance," *Alpine Journal* 52 (May 1940): 298.

108. James Ramsey Ullman, *High Conquest: The Story of Mountaineering* (Philadelphia: Lippincott, 1941), 19.

109. "Book Reviews," *American Alpine Journal* 4 (1942): 484. Until Ullman came along, American authors writing about mountaineering appealed to a small circle of initiates. See, for example, the dry recital of facts in J. Monroe Thorington, *A Survey of Early American Ascents in the Alps* (New York: American Alpine Club, 1943).

110. Royal Robbins, "Inspirations, Part IV: High Conquest," *Alpinist*, April 2, 2008, http://www.alpinist.com/doc/web08s/wfeature-inspirations-high-conquest-robbins. Also see Royal Robbins, *To Be Brave* (Ojai, CA: Pink Moment Press, 2009), 41–43. Others who cited the influence of Ullman's book on their attraction to mountaineering include Tom Hornbein and Edmund Hillary; see Isserman and Weaver, *Fallen Giants*, 231, 476.

111. Ullman, *High Conquest*, 199. The 1937 German expedition to Nanga Parbat killed even more—sixteen in all—but since they died in an avalanche, it was hard to blame their deaths on ideological fanaticism. For a review of Ullman's book highlighting his argument about the suicidal efforts of the Germans on Nanga Parbat, see R. L. Duffus, "On Mountaineers and the Peaks They Have Climbed," *New York Times*, October 26, 1941.

112. Isserman and Weaver, *Fallen Giants*, 227–28; Gorby, *Stettner Way*, 121; Albert H. Jackman, "The Tenth Mountain Division," *American Alpine Journal* 6 (1946): 187–92; McKay Jenkins, *The Last Ridge: The Epic Story of the U.S. Army's 10th Mountain Division and the Assault on Hitler's Europe* (New York: Random House, 2003), 9–47; Peter Shelton, *Climb to Conquer: The Untold Story of World War II's 10th Mountain Division Ski Troops* (New York: Scribner, 2003), 7–26. Also see the folder "Efforts to Persuade the US Army to Establish Mountain Troops, 1940–1941," Bob Bates Papers, American Alpine Club Library, Golden, CO. About a thousand Sierra Club members served in the military during the war, as did more

than fifty of the 274 members of the American Alpine Club. "Proceedings of the Club," *American Alpine Journal* 5 (1943): 129, 132.

113. Ringholz, *On Belay!*, 154–55; Jenkins, *Last Ridge*, 81. While at Camp Hale, Petzoldt took part in a legendary four-day winter crossing on skis (the "Trooper Traverse") from Leadville to Aspen, Colorado, in a party of some thirty Tenth Mountain Division soldiers that included an up-and-coming Northwest climber named Fred Beckey. Lou Dawson, "Trooper Traverse—Leadville to Aspen on Skis—February 1944," *Backcountry Skiing Blog*, April 12, 2000, http://www .wildsnow.com/articles/trooper_traverse/trooper_trav_roster.html.

114. Gorby, *Stettner Way*, 113–14. Also see Fralick, "Stettner Way," 48.

115. Don Mellor, *American Rock: Region, Rock and Culture in American Climbing* (Woodstock, VT: Countryman Press, 2001), 98; Tom Gardner, "Raffi Bedayn: Rock Climber, Inventor, Advocate," *Yosemite Gazette*, http://legacy.yosemitegazette .com/index.php?option=com_content&view=article&id=47:raffi-bedayn&catid= 23:archives&Itemid=125, accessed July 7, 2015.

116. Charles Houston, *Going Higher: Oxygen, Man and Mountains*, 4th ed. (Seattle: Mountaineers, 1998), 17; Charles S. Houston, "William Farnsworth Loomis, 1914–1973," *American Alpine Journal* 19 (1974): 260; Jules M. Eichorn, "Richard Manning Leonard, 1908–1993: In Memoriam," *American Alpine Journal* 36 (1998): 322–23; Joseph E. Taylor III, *Pilgrims of the Vertical: Yosemite Rock Climbers & Nature at Risk* (Cambridge, MA: Harvard University Press, 2010), 100.

117. Kenneth A. Henderson, *Handbook of American Mountaineering* (New York: American Alpine Club, 1942). Royal Robbins was among the postwar climbers who taught themselves basic climbing technique from Henderson's handbook. Robbins, *To Be Brave*, 137–38. Another book used in training mountain troops was the *Manual of Ski Mountaineering*, edited by the Sierra Club's David Brower (Berkeley: University of California Press, 1942); 2nd rev. ed. (San Francisco: Sierra Club, 1961).

118. For Bates's wartime experiences, see his memoir: Robert H. Bates, *The Love of Mountains Is Best: Climbs and Travels from K2 to Kathmandu* (Portsmouth, NH: Peter E. Randall, 1994), 183–241.

119. Roberts, *Last of His Kind*, 206.

120. Washburn and Freedman, *Bradford Washburn*, 164.

121. Roberts, *Last of His Kind*, 210. For the Washburn-Roosevelt meeting, see Phillipa C. Burckett to Brad Washburn, March 10, 1943, Bradford Washburn Collection, box 7, folder "Correspondence, Nov. 1942–March 1943," Howard Gotlieb Archival Research Center at Boston University.

122. Isserman and Weaver, *Fallen Giants*, 228; Bates, *Love of Mountains Is Best*, 183–241; William P. House, "Mountain Equipment for the US Army," *American Alpine Journal* 6 (1946): 231; House, "Nylon Climbing Rope," *Appalachia* 13 (June 1947): 411–12; Washburn and Freedman, *Bradford Washburn*, 156–67; Taylor, *Pilgrims of the Vertical*, 95.

123. Isserman and Weaver, *Fallen Giants*, 229–30; Bates, *Love of Mountains Is Best*, 183–215; William P. House, "Surplus Army Outdoor Equipment," *Appalachia* 13 (June 1947): 411–12.

124. Isserman and Weaver, *Fallen Giants*, 227–28. On the combat history of the Tenth

Mountain Division, see Albert H. Jackman, "Tenth Mountain Division," 187–92; Hal Burton, *The Ski Troops* (New York: Simon and Schuster, 1971); Jenkins, *Last Ridge*; Shelton, *Climb to Conquer*; and the 1996 documentary *Fire on the Mountain*, by Beth Gage, directed by Beth Gage and George Gage (First Run Features, 1996). Also see the firsthand account by the Tenth Mountain Division veteran (and, later, president of the American Alpine Club) William Lowell Putnam: *Green Cognac: The Education of a Mountain Fighter* (New York: AAC Press, 1991).

125. Morgan Harris to David Brower, August 18, 1945, Sierra Club Members Papers, carton 5:16, BANC MSS 79/9c, Bancroft Library, University of California, Berkeley; David R. Brower, "Some GI Climbs in the Alps," *Sierra Club Bulletin* 20, no. 6 (December 1945): 79–85; David Brower, *For Earth's Sake: The Life and Times of David Brower* (Salt Lake City: Peregrine Smith Books, 1990), 115–22; Shelton, *Climb to Conquer*, 221–22. Brower may have learned about the Charmoz-Grépon Traverse, a difficult crossing of a rocky rampart in the Aiguilles de Chamonix first climbed in 1881 by a party including Alfred Mummery, from Brad Washburn, who had climbed it with a guide in 1927. Roberts, *Last of His Kind*, 22.

126. John Christian, "Arnold Wexler (1918–1997)," http://home.comcast.net/~gibell/cirque/awexler.html, accessed July 7, 2015; Eichorn, "Richard Manning Leonard," 322–23.

127. Richard M. Leonard and Arnold Wexler, *Belaying the Leader* (San Francisco: Sierra Club, 1947), 6–7.

128. Ibid., 7.

CHAPTER SIX: RUCKSACK REVOLUTION, 1945–1963

1. Charles S. Houston and Robert M. Bates, *K2: The Savage Mountain* (Guilford, CT: Lyons Press, 2000), 24.

2. John Rawlings, *The Stanford Alpine Club* (Stanford, CA: CSLI Publications, 1999), 1. Climbing clubs were also formed after the war for the first time at UC Berkeley, UCLA, and Caltech. Joseph E. Taylor III, *Pilgrims of the Vertical: Yosemite Rock Climbers & Nature at Risk* (Cambridge, MA: Harvard University Press, 2010), 97, 123–24.

3. Louise Werner, "The Mountain That Was God," [1947?], Sierra Club Records, carton 301:21, BANC MSS 71/103c, Bancroft Library, University of California, Berkeley.

4. Dick Emerson to David Brower, March 5, 1946, Sierra Club Members Papers, carton 4:27, BANC MSS 79/9c, Bancroft Library, University of California, Berkeley. Emerson would become a climbing ranger in Grand Teton National Park in the 1950s, where he made a first ascent of a route with a direct finish on the north face of Grand Teton with Leigh Ortenburger and Willi Unsoeld in 1953. He was also a member of the American Mount Everest Expedition in 1963. Reynold G. Jackson, "Park of the Matterhorns," Grand Teton Historic Resource Study, http://www.nps.gov/history/history/online_books/grte2/hrs16b.htm, accessed July 7, 2015; Fred Beckey, Mountains of North America (San Francisco: Sierra Club Books, 1982),100

5. David Brower to Dick Emerson, March 6, 1946, Sierra Club Members Papers,

carton 4:27, BANC MSS 79/9c, Bancroft Library, University of California, Berkeley. Also see William P. House, "Surplus Army Outdoor Equipment," *Appalachia* 13 (June 1947): 411–12. A lot of the army surplus gear was of mediocre quality, especially the surplus crampons. Stamped out of a flat sheet of steel, the crampons proved flimsy. The weight of the climber was enough to bend the points flat at inopportune moments—hence the derisive term for them, "folding crampons." I'm grateful to Tom Hornbein for this information; he still owns the pair of folding crampons he acquired after the war. Tom Hornbein, e-mail to the author, May 31, 2014. On army surplus equipment, also see Chris Jones, *Climbing in North America* (Seattle: Mountaineers, 1997), 175; and Pat Ament, *Wizards of Rock: A History of Free Climbing in America* (Berkeley: Wilderness Press, 2002), 42. Army surplus skis and ski boots originally intended for the Tenth Mountain Division were also being dumped on the civilian market right after the war, and they contributed to a boom in the ski industry, with many of the new ski resorts and ski schools popping up east and west run by Tenth Mountain veterans. See Peter Shelton, *Climb to Conquer: The Untold Story of World War II's 10th Mountain Division Ski Troops* (New York: Scribner, 2003), 233; and Peter W. Seibert, *Vail: Triumph of a Dream* (Boulder, CO: Mountain Sports Press, 2000), 55.

6. For REI, see REI, "1940s," http://reihistory.com/1940, accessed July 18, 2015. For Eddie Bauer, see Robert Spector, *The Legend of Eddie Bauer* (Lyme, CT: Greenwich Publishing Group, 1994), 21–41; and Mike C. Parsons and Mary B. Rose, *Invisible on Everest: Innovations and the Gear Makers* (Philadelphia: Northern Liberties Press, 2003), 109–10.

7. Gerry, "Our Heritage" (specifically "1945–46: First Gerry Catalog" [2nd time line mark], "1947: Carabiner Redesign" [3rd time line mark], and "1953: 1st Mount Everest Ascension" [5th time line mark]), http://gerryoutdoors.com/our-heritage .php#, accessed July 18, 2015; "Gerry of Colorado: Perhaps the Original Gear Pioneer," Oregon Photos, last revised March 6, 2015, http://www.oregonphotos.com/ Gerry1.html.

8. On the postwar growth of the Sierra Club membership, see "Sierra Club Membership as of November 1," Sierra Club Records, carton 310:15, BANC MSS 71/103c, Bancroft Library, University of California, Berkeley. On the formation of the Atlantic chapter of the Sierra Club, see Thomas H. Jukes questionnaire, Sierra Club Records, carton 82:13, BANC MSS 71/295c, Bancroft Library, University of California, Berkeley.

9. Joseph E. Taylor III, *Pilgrims of the Vertical: Yosemite Rock Climbers & Nature at Risk* (Cambridge, MA: Harvard University Press, 2010), 122.

10. On Brower's downfall in 1969, see Michael P. Cohen, *History of the Sierra Club, 1892–1970* (San Francisco: Sierra Club Books, 1988), 412–34; John McPhee, *Encounters with the Archdruid* (New York: Farrar, Strauss, and Giroux, 1971), 208–19.

11. The earliest recorded use of the term "armchair mountaineer" appears to be in a speech by Professor J. A. Ewings to the annual meeting of the London-based Climbers' Club in 1902. See the *Climbers Journal* 3–4 (1902): 195. The earliest use of the term in an American publication appears to be in a list of contributors to a

1942 issue of *Appalachia* magazine, in which Henry S. Hall is referred to as "far from being an armchair mountaineer." *Appalachia* 24 (December 1942): 146.

12. On Ullman's appeal to Harding, see Taylor, *Pilgrims of the Vertical*, 153. For a letter from an AAC member taking issue with Ullman's description of a bergschrund in the novel, see Henry A. Perkins to James Ramsey Ullman, May 12, 1946, James Ramsey Ullman Papers, box 71, folder 9, Department of Rare Books and Special Collections, Princeton University Library.

13. "'The White Tower's' Author Shows How to Master a Strenuous Sport," *Life*, December 31, 1945, 61–75. Also see Maurice Isserman and Stewart Weaver, *Fallen Giants: A History of Himalayan Mountaineering from the Age of Empire to the Age of Extremes* (New Haven, CT: Yale University Press, 2008), 232–33.

14. Reviewing *Annapurna* for the *New York Herald Tribune*, Ullman predicted it would become "one of the classics of climbing literature," which proved the case. James Ramsey Ullman, "Great Climb, Gallant Chronicle," *New York Herald Tribune*, January 18, 1953; Isserman and Weaver, *Fallen Giants*, 253.

15. Patricia Hewitt Fitt and Alfred B. Fitt to James Ramsey Ullman, June 1, 1953, James Ramsey Ullman Papers, box 80, folder 1, Department of Rare Books and Special Collection, Princeton University.

16. Steve Roper, *Camp 4: Recollections of a Yosemite Rockclimber* (Seattle: Mountaineers, 1994), 15.

17. Robin Hansen, "John Salathé, 1899–1993," *American Alpine Journal* 37 (1994): 321; Doug Scott, *Big Wall Climbing* (New York: Oxford University Press, 1974), 142.

18. Around the same time, Sierran Raffi Bedayn began manufacturing lightweight aluminum carabiners that would become standard equipment for American mountaineers over the next decade. For Bedayn carabiners, see William L. Putnam, "Raffi Bedayn, 1915–1982," *American Alpine Journal* 24 (1982): 336–37. For the significance of the new pitons, see Jones, *Climbing in North America*, 176; Taylor, *Pilgrims of the Vertical*, 125–26; Andrew Selters, *Ways to the Sky: A Historical Guide to North American Mountaineering* (Golden, CO: American Alpine Club, 2004), 143; Don Mellor, *American Rock: Region, Rock and Culture in American Climbing* (Woodstock, VT: Countryman Press, 2001), 29.

19. For the use of the term "golden age," see, for example, Roper, *Camp 4*, 11.

20. That definition is offered by Royal Robbins in *Advanced Rockcraft* (Glendale, CA: La Siesta Press, 1973), 55.

21. For an example of prewar ethics in conflict with the new climbing techniques, see Ansel Adams's declaration: "I abhor the drilling of expansion bolt holes in the pristine flanks of El Capitan and Half Dome; it is a desecration." Quoted in Cohen, *History of the Sierra Club*, 71; Roper, *Camp 4*, 32, 35.

22. Anton Nelson, "Half Dome, Southwest Face," *Sierra Club Bulletin* 31 (December 1946): 120–21; Taylor, *Pilgrims of the Vertical*, 128; Selters, *Ways to the Sky*, 143; Jones, *Climbing in North America*, 178; Roper, *Camp 4*, 40.

23. Quoted in Fritz Lippmann, "We Climbed the Impossible Peak," *Saturday Evening Post*, June 28, 1947, 21.

24. Anton Nelson, "Climbing the Lost Arrow," *Sierra Club Bulletin* 32 (May 1947): 2.

25. Steve Roper and Allen Steck, *Fifty Classic Climbs of North America* (San Fran-

cisco: Sierra Club Books, 1979), 237–38; Jones, *Climbing in North America*, 176–78.

26. Roper and Steck, *Fifty Classic Climbs*, 238–40.
27. Nelson, "Climbing the Lost Arrow," 10.
28. Taylor, *Pilgrims of the Vertical*, 100; Rawlings, *Stanford Alpine Club*, 1, 4. Wade Davis argues that combat experience in the First World War had a major impact on the postwar British Everest expeditions and the level of risk considered acceptable. Davis, *Into the Silence: The Great War, Mallory, and the Conquest of Everest* (New York: Knopf, 2011).
29. Lippmann, "We Climbed the Impossible Peak," 20.
30. Gary Arce, *Defying Gravity: High Adventure on Yosemite's Walls* (Berkeley, CA: Wilderness Press, 1996), 29.
31. Chris McNamara and Erik Sloan, *Yosemite Big Walls* (Mill Valley, CA: Supertopo, 2006), 202; Roper, *Camp 4*, 41.
32. Anton Nelson, "Five Days and Nights on the Lost Arrow, *Sierra Club Bulletin* 33 (March 1948): 108.
33. Nelson, "Five Days and Nights," 103–8; Roper and Steck, *Fifty Classic Climbs*, 240; Roper, *Camp 4*, 42; Jones, *Climbing in North America*, 179–80; Arce, *Defying Gravity*, 30–31.
34. Roper, *Camp 4*, 44–50; Woody [Bob Woodward], "Trailblazers: Allen Steck," August 25, 2014, http://outinunder.com/content/trailblazers-allen-steck.
35. Allen Steck, "Ordeal by Piton," *Sierra Club Bulletin* 36 (May 1951): 1–5; Roper and Steck, *Fifty Classic Climbs*, 243–46; Ament, *Wizards of Rock*, 56–57; Jones, *Climbing in North America*, 180–83; Arce, *Defying Gravity*, 31–32.
36. Steck, "Ordeal by Piton," 1.
37. The film version of Ullman's book was actually the second of his books to get the Hollywood treatment; 1947 had seen the release of a feature film entitled *High Conquest*, telling the fictional story of an American obsessed with climbing the Matterhorn. "The White Tower," AFI Catalog of Feature Films, http://www.afi.com/members/catalog/DetailView.aspx?s=&Movie=26568, accessed July 18, 2015.
38. David Roberts, *The Last of His Kind: The Life and Adventures of Bradford Washburn, America's Boldest Mountaineer* (New York: William Morrow, 2009), 227.
39. An eighteen-minute documentary of the climb, climaxing in a scene of triumphant climbers waving the Stars and Stripes atop Denali's summit, was released the following year. Bradford Washburn, "Operation White Tower," *American Alpine Journal* 7 (1948): 40–58; Roberts, *Last of His Kind*, 226–35; Bradford Washburn and Lew Freedman, *Bradford Washburn: An Extraordinary Life* (Portland, OR: Westwinds Press, 2005), 196–210.
40. Carl A. Blaurock, "Henry Augustus Buchtel III, 1906–1988," *American Alpine Journal* 31 (1989): 328–29; W. Andrew Marcus and Melvin G. Marcus, "Geographer, Explorer, Friend: The Worlds of Barry C. Bishop, 1932–1994," *Mountain Research and Development* 16 (August 1996): 193–98.
41. Bradford Washburn, "Mount McKinley: The West Buttress, 1951," *American Alpine Journal* 8 (1952): 212–16; Roberts, *Last of His Kind*, 236–37.
42. Brad Washburn, journal entry, June 20, 1951, Brad Washburn Collection, box

8, folder "Washburn—Personal," Howard Gotlieb Archival Research Center at Boston University.

43. The first ascent of 14,573-foot Mount Hunter was accomplished by Fred Beckey, Heinrich Harrer, and Henry Meybohm in 1954, via the west ridge. See Fred Beckey, "Mt. Deborah and Mt. Hunter: First Ascents," *American Alpine Journal* 9 (1955): 39–50. The first ascent of the south ridge, or Talkeetna Ridge, of 17,400-foot Mount Foraker was accomplished in 1968 by Alex Bertulis, Warren Bleser, Hans Baer, and Peter Williamson. The mountain had its first ascent in 1934 by Charlie Houston, T. Graham Brown, and Chychele Waterston. See Warren Bleser and Alex Bertulis, "Mount Foraker's South Ridge," *American Alpine Journal* 16 (1969): 289–94.

44. Jonathan Waterman, *High Alaska: A Historical Guide to Denali, Mount Foraker & Mount Hunter* (New York: American Alpine Club, 1996), 84.

45. Barry Bishop to Robert and Helen Bishop, July 2, 1951, Brad Washburn Collection, box 8, folder "Washburn—Personal," Howard Gotlieb Archival Research Center at Boston University.

46. Washburn, "Mount McKinley," 225.

47. Roberts, *Last of His Kind*, 239–40; Washburn and Freedman, *Bradford Washburn*, 227–34.

48. Washburn, "Mount McKinley," 223–24.

49. R. J. Secor, "Climbing Denali: The West Buttress Route," *Backpacker*, http://www.backpacker.com/may_2002_destinations_alaska_denali_west_buttress/destinations/4386, accessed July 18, 2015.

50. The other members of the party were Charlie Houston's father, Oscar, and family friends Betsy Cowles and Anderson Bakewell. The account of the 1950 Everest reconnaissance that follows is drawn from Isserman and Weaver, *Fallen Giants*, 255–64.

51. Charles Houston, "Towards Everest, 1950," *Himalayan Journal* 17 (1952): 14.

52. Sir Edmund Hillary later expressed surprise that "such experienced men" as Houston and Tilman, "should have made the mistake they did make on that trip." "Mountain Interview: Sir Edmund Hillary," *Mountain*, no. 45 (September/October 1975): 31.

53. Robert Trumbull, "U.S. Expedition Goes 18,000 Feet up Unexplored Side of Mt. Everest," *New York Times*, December 11, 1950. Houston offered an equally discouraging report in the *American Alpine Journal*, suggesting that the south side of the mountain did not offer "a reasonable route by which to climb Everest." See Charles S. Houston, "South Face of Mount Everest," *American Alpine Journal* 8 (1951): 18.

54. For a recent retelling of the final push to reach the summit of Everest, see Mick Conefrey, *Everest 1953: The Epic Story of the First Ascent* (Seattle: Mountaineers, 2014).

55. The account that follows is drawn from Isserman and Weaver, *Fallen Giants*, 305–14.

56. The account of the K2 expedition that follows draws upon Isserman and Weaver, *Fallen Giants*, 305–14; Bernadette McDonald, *Brotherhood of the Rope: The Biog-*

raphy of Charlie Houston (Seattle: Mountaineers, 2007), 119–40; and Houston and Bates, *K2: The Savage Mountain*.

57. Houston and Bates, *K2: The Savage Mountain*, 49.

58. Mohammad Ata-Ullah, *Citizen of Two Worlds* (New York: Harper, 1960), 235, 264.

59. Charles Houston to Oscar Houston, June 9, 1953, 1953 K2 Scrapbook, in Houston family possession.

60. "Material from Dee Molenaar about K2," Bob Bates Papers, box 83, folder "Efforts to Persuade the US Army to Establish Mountain Troops, 1940–1941," American Alpine Club Library, Golden, CO.

61. Houston and Bates, *K2: The Savage Mountain*, 269. For Gilkey's obituary, see Robert H. Bates, "Arthur K. Gilkey, 1926–1953," *American Alpine Journal* 9 (1954): 129.

62. This account of the Hidden Peak expedition is drawn from Isserman and Weaver, *Fallen Giants*, 336–40.

63. "Pakistan Peak Scaled: Eight Man US Team Climbs 24,470 Foot Mountain," *New York Times*, July 26, 1958; "Pakistan Peak Scaled: Gasherbrum I is Conquered by 2 of 8-Man US Team," *New York Times*, July 26, 1958. The *New York Times* obituary of Pete Schoening continued the neglect of this landmark in American mountaineering history, making no mention of his ascent of Hidden Peak: Douglas Martin, "Pete Schoening, 77, Legend of a Mountaineering Rescue," *New York Times*, September 27, 2004.

64. "Pakistan Peak Climbed," *New York Times*, August 21, 1960. This account of the Masherbrum expedition is based on Isserman and Weaver, *Fallen Giants*, 347.

65. Jon Krakauer, "Warning! Fred Beckey Is Still on the Loose!" *Outside* 17 (July 1992): 50; Harvey Manning, "America's Greatest Mountaineer: The Life and Legend of Fred (the Blankety-Blank) Beckey," *Backpacker* 6 (February 1978): 31.

66. Timothy Egan, *The Good Rain: Across Time and Terrain in the Pacific Northwest* (New York: Knopf, 1990), 73. For the guidebooks, see Fred Beckey, *A Climber's Guide to the Cascade and Olympic Mountains of Washington* (New York: American Alpine Club, 1949); Beckey, *Cascade Alpine Guide: Climbing and High Routes*, vol. 1, *Columbia River to Stevens Pass* (Seattle: Mountaineers, 1973); Beckey, *Cascade Alpine Guide: Climbing and High Routes*, vol. 2, *Stevens Pass to Rainy Pass* (Seattle: Mountaineers, 1973); and Beckey, *Cascade Alpine Guide: Climbing and High Routes*, vol. 3, *Rainy Pass to Fraser River* (Seattle: Mountaineers, 1981). In 1950, Joel Fisher, past president of the AAC wrote to congratulate the current president, Henry Hall, for the decision to publish Beckey's guidebook. The new publication "was paying dividends of nearly 10% on that investment the very first year," Fisher declared, as measured by new members signing up in the Northwest, "and that 10% may well prove to increase geometrically every year." Joel Fisher to Henry Hall, March 20, 1950, Henry Hall Papers, box 6, folder "Correspondence with Joel Fisher," American Alpine Club Library, Golden, CO. The bulk of AAC membership in the 1950s was still from the Northeast and Midwest. Beckey was an exception, having joined the AAC in 1944, according to club records.

67. Barry Blanchard, introduction to *Fred Beckey's 100 Favorite North American Climbs*, by Fred Beckey (Ventura, CA: Patagonia Books, 2011), xii–xiv; Lloyd

Anderson, "The Climb of Forbidden Peak," *Mountaineer* 33 (December 1940): 35; Jones, *Climbing in North America*, 145, 159–60; Roper and Steck, *Fifty Classic Climbs*, 113–17; Fred Beckey, "Climbing and Skiing in the Waddington Area," *American Alpine Journal* 5 (1943): 29–34.

68. "Outdoor Industry Inspiration Awards," *Topline Magazine*, January 31, 2013, http://www.toplinemagazine.com/2013/01/31/outdoor-industry-inspiration-award-honors-beckey.

69. Krakauer, "Warning!" 50; Amanda Fox, "Interviewing Fred Beckey at 90 Years Old," *Base Camp Blog, Climbing*, http://www.climbing.com/blog/interviewing-fred-beckey-at-90-years-old, accessed July 18, 2015.

70. "Awesome Peaks Scaled at Last!" *Seattle Times*, November 3, 1946; Jones, *Climbing in North America*, 218–19.

71. Beckey, "Mt. Deborah and Mt. Hunter," 39–50; Jones, *Climbing in North America*, 242; Blanchard, introduction to *Fred Beckey's 100 Favorite*, xiv–xv; Beckey, *Fred Beckey's 100 Favorite*, 48–50; Michael Brick, "At 85, More Peaks to Conquer and Adventures to Seek," *New York Times*, December 16, 2008.

72. Justin Nyberg, "Stoned," *Outside*, September 14, 2010, http://www.outsideonline.com/outdoor-adventure/athletes/Stoned.html. Also see G. O. Dyhrenfurth and Norman Dyhrenfurth, "Lhotse," *Mountain* 66 (March–April 1979): 40–41.

73. Brick, "At 85, More Peaks to Conquer"; Egan, *Good Rain*, 80; Blanchard, introduction to *Fred Beckey's 100 Favorite*, xix.

74. Royal Robbins, *The Golden Age*, My Life 3 (California: Royal Robbins Adventures, 2012), 18.

75. Timothy Gray, *Gary Snyder and the Pacific Rim: Creating Counter Cultural Community* (Iowa City: University of Iowa Press, 2006), 48.

76. Kerouac's Matterhorn Peak climb is discussed in John Suiter, *Poets on the Peaks: Gary Snyder, Philip Whalen & Jack Kerouac in the North Cascades* (Washington, DC: Counterpoint, 2002), 172–73.

77. Jack Kerouac, *The Dharma Bums* (New York: Viking, 1958), 97–98.

78. I'm grateful to my Hamilton College colleague, professor of geosciences Todd Rayne, for pointing out the Cretaceous origins of Yosemite granite and steering me to this source: N. K. Huber and J. A. Roller, "Bedrock Geology of the Yosemite Valley Area Yosemite National Park, California," Miscellaneous Geologic Investigations I-1639 (US Geological Survey, 1985).

79. Gary Snyder, *Myths & Texts* (New York: Corinth Books, 1960), 39.

80. This reading of Snyder's poem is suggested by Gray, *Gary Snyder and the Pacific Rim*, 89–90.

81. John Muir, *Nature Writings* (New York: Library of America, 1997), 354–55.

82. Kerouac, *Dharma Bums*, 98.

83. Yvon Chouinard to Steve Roper, January 16, 1964, Steve Roper Private Collection, reprinted in Taylor, *Pilgrims of the Vertical*, 145–46.

84. Houston and Bates, *K2: The Savage Mountain*, 24.

85. For the Stanford Alpine Club, see Rawlings, *Stanford Alpine Club*. Also see Taylor, *Pilgrims of the Vertical*, 118–19, 124–25. Fritz Lippmann, Nick Clinch, Gil Roberts, Irene Beardsley, John Harlin, Tom Frost, Leigh Ortenburger, Chuck Kroger, and Scott Davis were among the SAC's prominent alumni.

86. Yvon Chouinard proposed creating a "Yosemite Climbing Club" in 1960, specifying it would have "no officers, no constitution, or by-laws, and no dues," but even that anarchist ideal proved too bureaucratic for its intended members, and it died stillborn. Roper, *Camp 4*, 105–6. For descriptions of the Camp Four campsite, see Roper, *Camp 4*, 64; and Taylor, *Pilgrims of the Vertical*, 135.

87. Roper, in a rare factual error in *Camp 4*, puts Powell's arrival in residence at the campground in 1957, but Powell told historian Joseph Taylor that he arrived there two years earlier. Taylor, e-mail to the author, November 30, 2014; Roper, *Camp 4*, 83.

88. Roper, *Camp 4*, 59. Mark Powell's story began with an impressive act of self-transformation. On his first outing to Yosemite in 1954, overweight and a heavy smoker, he barely made it up Lower Cathedral Spire, being hauled to the top by partner Jerry Gallwas. Humiliated, Powell lost 40 pounds over the next year, and he went on to become a climbing star. Taylor, *Pilgrims of the Vertical*, 135; Scott, *Big Wall Climbing*, 145; Roper, *Camp 4*, 30–31, 58, 83, 92–93; Robbins, *Golden Age*, 81; Jones, *Climbing in North America*, 194; Arce, *Defying Gravity*, 40.

89. Yvon Chouinard, *Let My People Go Surfing: The Education of a Reluctant Businessman* (New York: Penguin Press, 2005), 18. On the hostilities between climbers and tourists, and the competition for campsites, see Roper, *Camp 4*, 145–46, 154.

90. The origins of the term "dirtbag climbers" remain a little obscure, although John Gill recalled already hearing it from one of the seminal figures of the golden age of Yosemite climbing, and at the very beginning of that era: "I can recall *Yvon Chouinard* talking about 'dirtbag climbers' in the late 1950s when we would meet in the Tetons during the summer." John Gill, comment in "Origin of 'Dirtbag Climber,'" November 8, 2014 (10:41 a.m.), Climber's Forum, Supertopo, http://www.supertopo.com/climbers-forum/2525001/origin-of-dirtbag-climber.

91. Taylor, *Pilgrims of the Vertical*, 134–35.

92. Roper, *Camp 4*, 158–59. Among the outstanding female alumnae of the Stanford Alpine Club was Irene Beardsley. With her husband, Leigh Ortenburger, she climbed extensively in the Tetons and Peru's Cordillera Blanca. In 1965 she and Sue Swedlund made the first female ascent of the north face of Grand Teton; and in 1978, as Irene Miller, she made the first female ascent of Annapurna I, along with Vera Komarkova. Rawlings, *Stanford Alpine Club*, 55–63; Arlene Blum, *Annapurna: A Woman's Place* (San Francisco: Sierra Club Books, 1980); Taylor, *Pilgrims of the Vertical*, 63–69, 124, 141–42.

93. Rawlings, *Stanford Alpine Club*, 123–29. For attitudes of Camp 4 regulars toward "weekenders," see Roper, *Camp 4*, 92–93.

94. Taylor, *Pilgrims of the Vertical*, 119.

95. Rawlings, *Stanford Alpine Club*, 156. Among the exceptions was Layton Kor, who came to Yosemite from Colorado, where in the late 1950s he had put up a string of stunning first ascents—in 1959 on the East Face of Longs Peak, and over the next several years in the emerging center of rock-climbing in Colorado, the sandstone Eldorado Canyon south of Boulder. His first big achievement in Yosemite came in 1963 when he and Steve Roper made the first ascent of the west buttress of El Capitan. Pat Ament, "Layton Kor, 1938–2013," *American Alpine Journal*

56 (2014): 381–82; Dougald MacDonald, "Layton Kor Is Dead," *Climbing*, http://
www.climbing.com/news/layton-kor-is-dead, accessed July 18, 2015. As Taylor
notes, similar arrangements between climbing clubs and the National Park Service could be found in other mountainous areas, with the Mountaineers the
gatekeepers to Mount Rainer, the Mazamas to Mount Hood, and the Colorado
Mountain Club to peaks in Rocky Mountain National Park. *Pilgrims of the Vertical*, 119.

96. Although Steve Roper applied the term "golden age" to Yosemite from the 1940s
to the 1970s, some historians of Yosemite climbing restrict it to the 1950s–1960s;
see, for example, Arce, *Defying Gravity*, 35–78.

97. Roper, *Camp 4*, 64–65. Also see Warren Harding, *Downward Bound: A Mad
Guide to Rock Climbing* (New York: Prentice Hall, 1975); Wolfgang Saxon,
"Warren Harding, 77, Early Rock Climber Who Became Legend," *New York Times*,
March 18, 2002; Taylor, *Pilgrims of the Vertical*, 153–54; Arce, *Defying Gravity*,
38–39; Burr Snider, "The Life of Warren 'Batso' Harding," http://www.climbing
.com/climber/the-life-of-warren-andquot-batsoandquot-harding, acccessed July
18, 2015.

98. Glen Denny, *Yosemite in the Sixties* (Santa Barbara, CA: Adler Books/Patagonia,
2007), 138.

99. Glen Denny, "Inspirations, Part VII; Glen Denny," *Alpinist*, September 17, 2008,
http://www.alpinist.com/doc/web08f/wfeature-inspirations-glen-denny.

100. Quoted in Jeremy Bernstein, "Yvon Chouinard: Ascending," in *Cloud Dancers:
Portraits of North American Mountaineers*, ed. Jonathan Waterman (Golden,
CO: American Alpine Club, 1993), 52.

101. John Gill, e-mail to the author, November 8, 2014. Gill was developing a specialty
in bouldering, and in 1958 he and Chouinard coauthored a lighthearted *Guide
to the Jenny Lake Boulders*. John Gill, "Jenny Lake Boulders," John Gill's Website,
http://www128.pair.com/r3d4k7/Bouldering_History3.2.html, accessed July 18,
2015. Also see John Gill, *The Origins of Bouldering: An Informal Survey of the
Sport from the Late 1800s to the 1960s and Beyond* (self-published, 2008). Among
other contributions to rock-climbing, Gill introduced the use of gymnastic chalk
in the sport in the late 1950s. Frederick L. Wolfe, *High Summits: 370 Famous
Peak First Ascents* (Englewood, CO: Hugo House, 2013), 479. For the history of
"C-Camp," see Jackson, "Park of the Matterhorns." For Chouinard's early life, see
Bernstein, "Yvon Chouinard," 52–56; the article originally appeared as Jeremy
Bernstein, "Ascending," *New Yorker*, January 31, 1977, 36–52. Also see Chouinard, *Let My People Go Surfing*, 7–15; and Verlyn Klinkenborg, "The Adventures
of a Renaissance Fun Hog," *Esquire*, January 1988, 92–98.

102. Quoted in Bernstein, "Yvon Chouinard," 57–58.

103. Ibid., 57–58; Chouinard, *Let My People Go Surfing*, 15–18; Taylor, *Pilgrims of the
Vertical*, 176–77.

104. Royal Robbins, *Fail Falling* (Ojai, CA: Pink Moment Press, 2010), 113; Taylor,
Pilgrims of the Vertical, 149–51.

105. Wilts shares credit with Robbins and Don Wilson for devising the Yosemite
Decimal System (YDS), a variation of the original Willo Welzenbach system
for measuring the difficulty of a climbing route. The Yosemite Decimal System

was originally called the "Sierra-Wilts Decimal System," until Wilts suggested another name. Wilts also developed a knife-blade piton, able to be inserted in the thinnest cracks. For his distinguished climbing career and achievements, see Ellen Beaumont Wilts, "Charles Wilts, 1920–1991," *American Alpine Journal* 34 (1992): 295. John Mendenhall was a stalwart member of the Southern California Rock Climbing Section of the Sierra Club, with many first ascents in the Sierra. John G. Ripley, "John Dale Mendenhall, 1911–1983," *American Alpine Journal* 26 (1984): 348.

106. Quoted in Arce, *Defying Gravity*, 37.

107. Robbins, *Fail Falling*, 15, 17, 67. Robbins writes that the RCS still clung to the notion that "the leader must not fall," which, in fact, they had long since repudiated. But it is true that by the early 1950s, the RCS was, in its own way, falling behind the cutting edge. For example, the RCS still regarded mastery of the dynamic belay as a crucial climbing skill. The method seemed archaic and irrelevant to younger climbers like Robbins, who realized that their new nylon ropes, now standard gear, "allowed the rope to stretch and absorb the force of a leader fall" without it (ibid., 179–82).

108. "Mountain Interview: Royal Robbins," *Mountain*, November 1971, 27; Royal Robbins, *To Be Brave* (Ojai, CA: Pink Moment Press, 2009), 164–66; Robbins, *Fail Falling*, 56–62, 77–91; Jones, *Climbing in North America*, 190; Taylor, *Pilgrims of the Vertical*, 151; Arce, *Defying Gravity*, 37; Beckey, *Fred Beckey's 100 Favorite*, 292–93.

109. John Muir, "A Geologist's Winter Walk," in *Steep Trails*, ed. William Frederic Badé (Boston: Houghton Mifflin, 1918), chap. 2, http://www.yosemite.ca.us/john_muir_writings/steep_trails/chapter_2.html.

110. Arce, *Defying Gravity*, 40.

111. Quoted in ibid., 41. Also see Steve Roper, foreword to *To Be Brave*, by Royal Robbins, x.

112. Joseph Taylor's account in *Pilgrims of the Vertical*, 152–53, 158, emphasizes the extent to which Robbins became "the sport's conscience" in terms of the style in which his team ascended Half Dome. In the end they placed 275 pitons and 20 expansion bolts. The latter were used, Robbins later wrote, "only where they seemed essential for progress or safety, and should be sufficient for parties making the climb in the future." Royal Robbins, "Half Dome—The Hard Way," *Sierra Club Bulletin* 42 (December 1957): 13. For Robbins's later reflections on the question of style in climbing, see his *Basic Rockcraft* (Glendale, CA: La Siesta Press, 1971), 62–65. For a classic discussion of the evolution of climbing style, see Lito Tejada-Flores, "Games Climbers Play," which originally appeared in *Ascent* magazine in 1967 and was reprinted in *The Games Climbers Play*, ed. Ken Wilson (London: Diadem Books, 1978), 19–26.

113. Robbins, "Half Dome—The Hard Way," 12–13. Rockfall is less of a problem at Yosemite than in many other climbing regions, but flakes loosened by climbers using them for protection have led to a number of deaths. For a recent example, see "Inadequate Protection," *Accidents in North American Mountaineering*, 2014, 38–40.

114. Michael Sherrick, "The Northwest Face of Half Dome," *Sierra Club Bulletin* 43

(November 1958): 19–23. The account of Half Dome's ascent draws upon Fred Knapp, "The Golden Age: The History of American Rock Climbing, Part II," *Rock & Ice*, no. 80 (July–August 1997): 74; Jones, *Climbing in North America*, 200; Scott, *Big Wall Climbing*, 145–46; McNamara and Sloan, *Yosemite Big Walls*, 158; Roper and Steck, *Fifty Classic Climbs*, 250–60; Arce, *Defying Gravity*, 41–43; and Roper, *Camp 4*, 59–62.

115. Roper and Steck, *Fifty Classic Climbs*, 259; McNamara and Sloan, *Yosemite Big Walls*, 160–62.

116. Robbins, *Fail Falling*, 170.

117. In 1952, Allen Steck, Bill Dunmire, Bill Long, and Will Siri climbed a subsidiary feature of El Capitan, its East Buttress, a significant rock-climbing achievement at the time, but not a big-wall ascent. As a result, El Capitan was still considered unconquered when Harding made his effort. Wolfe, *High Summits*, 476.

118. Roper, *Camp 4*, 63.

119. Bill Feuerer acquired the nickname "Dolt" from fellow residents of Camp 4 for the supposed deficiencies in his climbing style. According to Steve Roper, Feuerer, an engineer by training, "relished" the nickname and used it "as a trademark for the high quality equipment he later made." Roper, *Camp 4*, 59. But Feuerer's life was not a happy one. For his tragic end, see Don Lauria, "Dolt," *Yosemite Climbing Association*, http://www.yosemiteclimbing.org/content/dolt-don-lauria, accessed July 18, 2015.

120. Quoted in Roper, *Camp 4*, 67.

121. Warren J. Harding, "El Capitan," *American Alpine Journal* 11 (1959): 184–85. The account that follows is based on Harding's article, plus Roper and Steck, *Fifty Classic Climbs*, 261–67; Roper, *Camp 4*, 66–82; Taylor, *Pilgrims of the Vertical*, 154–58; Arce, *Defying Gravity*, 43–46; Jones, *Climbing in North America*, 251–56; Scott, *Big Wall Climbing*, 148–51; and McNamara and Sloan, *Yosemite Big Walls*, 76–77.

122. The stove legs inspired Chouinard's creation of new, wider-angled pitons, popularly called "bong bongs" because of the sound they made when hit with a piton hammer. Wolfe, *High Summits*, 480.

123. They were not idle in the intervening months. Powell, at the peak of his abilities, had a particularly impressive summer, establishing new routes on Pulpit Rock, Middle Cathedral Rock, Lower Watkins Pinnacle, Lower Cathedral Rock, North Dome, and Bridalveil East with a variety of partners, including, on some ascents, Harding and Feuerer. Roper, *Camp 4*, 84–85.

124. Steve Roper credits Powell with a total of twenty-one first ascents in the valley between 1955 and 1966, as well as two first free ascents. Roper, *Camp 4*, 87.

125. Harding would complete the Washington Column route the following summer, in partnership with Chuck Pratt and supported by Steve Roper and Glen Denny. Roper, *Camp 4*, 99–104.

126. Not everyone Harding asked to join the effort midway through agreed to do so. Robbins declined, as he recalled, "because it was his [Harding's] scene, and because I didn't want to do it that way [using siege tactics], even though I didn't think it could be done any other way." "Mountain Interview: Royal Robbins," 28.

127. McNamara and Sloan, *Yosemite Big Walls*, 76.

128. Harding, "El Capitan," 187.
129. Quoted in Roper, *Camp 4*, 82. Also see Taylor, *Pilgrims of the Vertical*, 157.
130. Cliff Ranson, "Climbing in the Gunks," *National Geographic Adventure*, http:// www.nationalgeographic.com/adventure/0509/sports/rock_climbing.html, accessed July 18, 2015.
131. Richard DuMais, "Shawangunks: The Northeast's Most Popular Crag," *Mountain*, no. 21 (May 1972): 23–26; Steven Jervis, "The Shawangunks, Now and Then," *Appalachia* 62 (Summer/Fall 2011): 60–72.
132. Art Gran, *A Climber's Guide to the Shawangunks* (New York: American Alpine Club, 1964), 14–16. Guy and Laura Waterman note that of the fifty-eight routes in place by 1950, Kraus put up twenty-six and Wiessner twenty-three; and on seven others they shared credit. Laura Waterman and Guy Waterman, *Yankee Rock & Ice: A History of Climbing in the Northeastern United States* (Mechanicsburg, PA: Stackpole Books, 1993), 121. Also see Susan Schwartz, *JFK's Secret Doctor: The Remarkable Life of Medical Pioneer and Legendary Rock Climber Hans Kraus* (New York: Skyhorse, 2012), 75; Alison Osius, "Hans Kraus," *Climbing*, no. 111 (December 1988): 98.
133. Osius, "Hans Kraus," 98.
134. Waterman and Waterman, *Yankee Rock & Ice*, 117–20; Jones, *Climbing in North America*, 201–2.
135. Waterman and Waterman, *Yankee Rock & Ice*, 172.
136. "One Man's Way to Reach the Summit," *Sports Illustrated*, October 20, 1958, 18.
137. Schwartz, *JFK's Secret Doctor*, 104, 152. For McCarthy's career, see "Honorary President Jim McCarthy," *The Climbing Blog*, American Alpine Club, April 10, 2014, inclined.americanalpineclub.org/2014/04/honorary-president-jim-mccarthy. For his association with the Yosemite climbers, see James P. McCarthy, "The Southeast Face of Proboscis: Technical Climbing in the Logan Mountains," *American Alpine Journal* 14, no. 1 (1964): 60–63. Another prominent Kraus protégé was Bonnie Prudden. She began climbing in the Gunks in the mid-1930s. Sidelined by a skiing accident that left her with a broken pelvis, she returned after the war and partnered with Hans Kraus, who traded leads with her. A fitness expert, she and Kraus collaborated on a study of fitness among American youth, and in the 1950s they persuaded the Eisenhower administration to establish the President's Council on Youth Fitness. Schwartz, *JFK's Secret Doctor*, 93.
138. Quoted in Waterman and Waterman, *Yankee Rock & Ice*, 139.
139. Gran, *Climber's Guide to the Shawangunks*, 17; Waterman and Waterman, *Yankee Rock & Ice*, 154–56.
140. "Art Gran," Vulgarian Chronicles: 1957–2010, http://www.vulgarianchronicles .net/vulgarianchronicles.net/Art_Gran.html, accessed July 18, 2015. Gran went on to author the first guidebook to climbing in the Gunks, notably published by the AAC rather than the AMC: *A Climber's Guide to the Shawangunks*.
141. Waterman and Waterman, *Yankee Rock & Ice*, 158. In a first for the *American Alpine Journal*, which was not ordinarily concerned with the manners of the climbers it described, Fritz Wiessner contributed an article to its pages that, in passing, attacked the "apparently unattached climbers" appearing in the Gunks "who have been guilty of loud and ungentlemanly behavior." Wiessner, "Early Rock Climb-

ing in the Shawangunks," *Appalachia* 33 (June 1960): 24. Also see "The Original Vulgarians," Vulgarian Chronicles: 1957–2010, http://www.vulgarianchronicles .net/vulgarianchronicles.net/Home.html, accessed July 18, 2015; Jones, *Climbing in North America*, 203–5; Mellor, *American Rock*, 81–83. At the start of the 1960s, some of the early Vulgarians, including Art Gran, Dave Craft, and Claude Suhl, made their way to Yosemite and told tales of their clashes with the Appies, reinforcing the Camp 4 residents' independently developed antisocial tendencies. Roper, *Camp 4*, 146.

142. Steve Roper, "El Capitan, Southwest Face," *American Alpine Journal* 13 (1962): 212; McNamara and Sloan, *Yosemite Big Walls*, 60; Arce, *Defying Gravity*, 51–54; Steve Roper, foreword to *To Be Brave*, xi; Roper, *Camp 4*, 124–25.

143. "Mountain Interview: Royal Robbins," 30.

144. Nick Clinch to Bob Bates, February 27, 1961, Robert Bates Papers, American Alpine Club Library, Golden, CO. That this was an ongoing concern of the AAC is shown by an internal memorandum written by George Bell, who, with Willi Unsoeld, had made the first ascent of Masherbrum in 1960, shortly after the annual meeting of the AAC Council held in New York City in December 1964. At that meeting, Bell noted, "It was generally agreed that the Club must make a continuing effort to represent and advance the responsible interests of the most active younger American climbers. Many of the most active younger climbers, who are currently pioneering ascents of a very high standard of difficulty, are not now members of the AAC, and indeed many are skeptical that the AAC has anything to offer them. This problem is of course a recurring one for any climbing group but one which calls for continuous efforts if a flow of hot young blood is to be maintained into the group." George Bell, memo to members of the Expeditions Committee, Re: AAC encouragement of expeditions in North America, n.d. [1965], Leigh Ortenburger Papers, box 30 M1503, series 9, folder "AAC Expedition Committee Correspondence, 1955–1962," Department of Special Collections, Stanford University.

145. Yvon Chouinard, "Modern Yosemite Climbing," *American Alpine Journal* 13 (1963): 319.

146. Yvon Chouinard, "West Face of Kat Pinnacle," *American Alpine Journal* 12 (1960): 369; Roper, *Camp 4*, 107–8; Taylor, *Pilgrims of the Vertical*, 157; Arce, *Defying Gravity*, 49. In a few years' time Chouinard and Frost went into partnership, and for a decade from the mid-1960s through the mid-1970s, Chouinard Equipment produced the world's most innovative climbing gear. Bernstein, "Yvon Chouinard," 46, 62–66; Chouinard, *Let My People Go Surfing*, 23–25, 30–31, 38.

147. "Yosemite, Other Yosemite Ascents," *American Alpine Journal* 12 (1961): 371.

148. Royal Robbins, "The North America Wall," *American Alpine Journal* 14 (1964): 331.

149. Robbins, *Golden Age*, 36–50; Roper, *Camp 4*, 116–17, 124–25. Chuck Pratt was a relative newcomer to the valley, making his first "first ascent" in the area (the north face of Fairview Dome in Tuolumne Meadows) in 1958 as a nineteen-year-old Berkeley student—a climb that earned a spot in Roper and Steck's *Fifty Classic Climbs*. Forty-seven more first ascents were to follow. Royal Robbins called Pratt "the best climber of our generation." His Yosemite first ascents included,

in addition to the Salathé Wall on El Cap in 1961, the North America Wall on El Cap in 1964 with Robbins, Frost, and Yvon Chouinard, and the south face of 8,500-foot Mount Watkins in 1964 with Chouinard and Warren Harding. After his Camp 4 days, Pratt went on to be a Teton guide. Robbins, "Charles Marshall Pratt, 1939–2000," *American Alpine Journal* 43 (2001): 460–64.

150. Yvon Chouinard, "Are Bolts Being Placed by Too Many Unqualified Climbers?" *Summit* 7 (March 1961): 10. Founded in 1955, *Summit* was the first and, for a long time, only climbing magazine in the United States that was not sponsored by a climbing club. Even more unusually, its founders and longtime editors were both women. Katie Ives, "The Sharp End: A House of Stone and Snow," *Alpinist*, no. 49 (Spring 2015): 13–14.

151. Roper, *Camp 4*, 120–21.

152. Allan Macdonald, "North America, United States, Washington, Sierra Nevada, Leaning Tower, West Face," *American Alpine Journal* 13 (1962): 211–12; Harding, *Downward Bound*, 117–21; Roper, *Camp 4*, 230. Despite the controversy over bolting, Harding and Chouinard, along with Chuck Pratt, would team up to make the first ascent of the imposing 2,000-foot south face of Mount Watkins in July 1964—one of the greatest climbs of Yosemite's golden age. The climb was a compromise between competing styles; they placed no fixed ropes, relied heavily on Chouinard's RURPs, but also drilled some bolts. Charles Pratt, "The South Face of Mount Watkins," *American Alpine Journal* 14 (1965): 339–46; Roper, *Camp 4*, 186–87.

153. Robbins, "North America Wall," 338.

154. Chouinard, "Modern Yosemite Climbing," 320.

155. Don Wilson, "Cleopatra's Needle," *Sierra Club Bulletin* 42 (June 1957): 63–64; Don Wilson, "The Totem Pole," *Sierra Club Bulletin* 43 (September 1958): 72.

156. David Rearick, "The First Ascent of the Diamond," *American Alpine Journal* 12 (1961): 297–301; Roper and Steck, *Fifty Classic Climbs*, 203–5; Jones, *Climbing in North America*, 214–15; Beckey, *Mountains of North America*, 82. Layton Kor and Royal Robbins climbed the route in a single day in 1963, and it has subsequently been climbed free. For conflicts over National Park Service regulations restricting climbing on Wyoming's Devils Tower National Monument, designed both to protect nesting birds and to respect Native American sacred rituals, see Tom Greaves, *Endangered Peoples of North America: Struggles to Survive and Thrive* (Westport, CT: Greenwood Press, 2001), 53.

157. John Harlin, "The Eigerwand," *American Alpine Journal* 13 (1963): 362–74; Rawlings, *Stanford Alpine Club*, 123–29; Roper, *Camp 4*, 154; Mirella Tenderini, *Gary Hemming: Beatnik of the Alps* (Glasgow, UK: Ernest Press, 1995), 80–81; Royal Robbins, "A New Route on the Petit Dru, West Face Direct," *American Alpine Journal* 13 (1963): 375; John Harlin, "Petit Dru, West Face Direttissima," *American Alpine Journal* 15 (1966): 81–89.

158. Arce, *Defying Gravity*, 58.

159. Roper, *Camp 4*, 168.

160. Norman Dyhrenfurth, "American Everest Expedition, 1961," typescript copy, n.d. [1960], James Ramsey Ullman Papers, box 92, folder 6, Department of Rare Books and Special Collections, Princeton University Library. The account of the 1963

American Everest expedition that follows is drawn from Isserman and Weaver, *Fallen Giants*, 354–75.

161. Quoted in Norman G. Dyhrenfurth, foreword to *Americans on Everest: The Official Account of the Ascent Led by Norman G. Dyhrenfurth*, by James Ramsey Ullman (Philadelphia: Lippincott, 1964), xx.

162. James Ramsey Ullman and Norman G. Dyhrenfurth, "Americans to Attempt Everest," *Summit* 7 (December 1961): 2.

163. In the end the expedition cost $400,000, the equivalent in 2014 of over $3 million.

164. Will Siri, leader of a 1954 Sierra Club expedition to Nepal's 27,838-foot Makalu, signed on as deputy leader. Willi Unsoeld, who had summited Masherbrum in 1960, would be climbing leader. Jim Whittaker, Rainier guide and REI's marketing director, became equipment coordinator. Tom Hornbein, a Colorado climber and another Masherbrum veteran, was given responsibility for oxygen equipment, and he designed a new and greatly improved breathing mask. Gil Roberts and Dave Dingman were expedition doctors. Barry Bishop of the National Geographic Society, who had summited Denali with Washburn in 1951 and gone on to make the first ascent of 22,493-foot Ama Dablam near Everest in 1961, was photographer; while Dan Doody would assist Dyhrenfurth as film cameraman. Dick Emerson (another Masherbrum veteran), Jim Lester, Maynard Miller, and Barry Prather were all part of the science and social science contingent (the latter added to attract government funding for research supposedly of benefit to the US space and defense effort). Jimmy Roberts, a retired British military attaché in Kathmandu became transport officer. Al Auten, Jake Breitenbach, Barry Corbet, Lute Jerstad, and Dick Pownall rounded out the team of climbers. Finally, James Ramsey Ullman planned to accompany the expedition as far as Everest base camp, as expedition publicist and historian. Dyhrenfurth had not forgotten or forgiven Fred Beckey for, in his eyes, having irresponsibly abandoned a sick tentmate at high altitude on the 1955 Lhotse expedition. Offended by his exclusion from consideration, Beckey went on a spree of racking up first ascents in North America, with thirty-three to his credit in 1962 alone. Krakauer, "Warning!" 52–53.

165. Four years earlier, Breitenbach had led a four-man party that put a new route up Denali via the South West Rib of the south face. The Denali climb won Breitenbach and fellow climbers Pete Sinclair, Bill Buckingham, and Barry Corbet (also part of the Everest team) a feature story in *Time*. "The Great One," *Time*, July 13, 1959, 29. Theirs was, at the time, the most difficult route yet established on the mountain.

166. Barry Bishop to Arnold Wexler, May 9, 1963, Bishop Papers, folder "MSS Bishop, Barry Corresp. w/ Arnold Wexler," American Alpine Club Library, Golden, CO.

167. Quoted in John Pielmeier, *Willi: An Evening of Wilderness and Spirit, Adapted from the Speeches of Willi Unsoeld* (Seattle: Rain City Projects, 1991), 24.

168. H. W. Tilman, review of *Americans on Everest*, by James Ramsey Ullman, *Alpine Journal* 71 (May 1966): 163–64. Ullman, *Americans on Everest*; Thomas F. Hornbein, *Everest: The West Ridge* (San Francisco: Sierra Club Books, 1965).

169. For REI and Sierra Club statistics, see Isserman and Weaver, *Fallen Giants*, 375, 519n. The availability and quality of climbing gear offered by the new mountaineering retail outlets increased dramatically; by decade's end, climbers were

equipped for the first time with specially designed helmets, harnesses, mechanical ascenders, belay devices, and an ever-expanding collection of protective devices designed to replace pitons and protect rock faces from scarring. For a description of the latest gear developments circa 1970, see Robbins, *Basic Rockcraft*, 11–18.

EPILOGUE: 1964–2015

1. "Mountain Interview: Royal Robbins," *Mountain*, November 1971, 30. Also see "Annual Meeting and Dinner," *American Alpine Journal* 14 (1965): 507–9.
2. Royal Robbins published two books in the early 1970s for novice climbers: *Basic Rockcraft* in 1971 and *Advanced Rockcraft* (Glendale, CA: La Siesta Press) in 1973. Another important source of climbing instruction was the Seattle Mountaineers' *Mountaineering: The Freedom of the Hills*, published first in 1960 and thereafter in many revised editions. Paul Petzoldt started the National Outdoor Leadership School (NOLS) in 1965, which taught tens of thousands of young Americans to climb. Henry Wood, "NOLS History," National Outdoor Leadership School, http://www.nols.edu/about/history/nols_history.shtml, accessed July 18, 2015.
3. Lynn Hill, *Climbing Free: My Life in the Vertical World* (New York: Norton, 2002). Also see Rachel da Silva, ed., *Leading Out: Women Climbers Reaching for the Top* (Berkeley, CA: Seal Press, 1992).
4. According to statistics gathered by the Seattle Mountaineers, in the 114 years between 1855, when the first attempt was made to climb Mount Rainier, and 1969, 14,797 climbers tried to reach the mountain's summit. After the club's founding in 1906 and down until the mid-1960s, it's likely that a majority of those climbers were members of the Mountaineers. In the eight years from 1970 to 1978, 26,332 climbers made the attempt on Rainier's increasingly crowded slopes—and it's equally likely that the majority of them were *not* members of the Mountaineers or any organized group. Wayne King, "Mountaineering Gains Popularity Despite Dangers," *New York Times*, June 29, 1981.
5. According to AMC library director Becky Fullerton, the AMC amended its club bylaws to do away with the nomination requirement in 1978. Fullerton, e-mail to the author, January 20, 2015.
6. "Bowling Alone with the Sierra Club," *Death of a Million Trees* (blog), December 27, 2011, http://milliontrees.me/2011/12/27/bowling-alone-with-the-sierra-club.
7. Chris Sharma, foreword to *Sport Climbing: From Top Rope to Redpoint, Techniques for Climbing Success*, by Andrew Bisharat (Seattle: Mountaineers, 2009), 12.
8. Chocks were also known as "nuts." Royal Robbins contributed an article to *Summit* magazine in 1967 that helped popularize their use in the United States. He extolled their versatility, and the speed and extra security they provided. And, he noted, "they do not change the nature of the route, as pitons often do, by weakening sections of rock and breaking off holds." Royal Robbins, "Nuts to You," *Summit* 13 (May 1967): 6. Also see Steven Schneider, *High Technology* (Chicago: Contemporary Books, 1980), 15–20. For subsequent changes in protective gear, see William Supple, "Rock Protection in the 1980s," *American Alpine Journal* 28 (1986): 117–19.

9. Hill, *Climbing Free*, 186–87; Bisharat, *Sport Climbing*, 34–36; Matt Samet, "Twenty-One Years of Sport Climbing in America," *Rock & Ice*, no. 133 (June 2004): 39.

10. Patagonia, "Company History," http://www.patagonia.com/us/patagonia.go?assetid =3351, accessed July 18, 2015; Patagonia, "Patagonia Ambassadors," http://www .patagonia.com/us/ambassadors, accessed July 18, 2015.

11. In 2015, Ed Viesturs, the first American to climb all fourteen 8,000-meter peaks, listed thirteen "sponsors," "partners," and "supporters" on his website. The website also noted that Viesturs was available to give talks at corporate events on such themes as "teamwork, goal setting, perseverance, risk management and inspirational entertainment in general." Ed Viesturs, "Sponsors," EdViesturs .com, http://www.edviesturs.com/sponsors, accessed July 18, 2015.

12. See, for example, Rick Ridgeway, *The Boldest Dream: The Story of Twelve Who Climbed Mount Everest* (New York: Harcourt, Brace, Jovanovich, 1979), 172.

13. Jon Krakauer, *Into Thin Air: A Personal Account of the Mount Everest Disaster* (New York: Random House, 1997).

14. Christopher Solomon, "The Call of the 'Wild' on the Pacific Crest Trail," *New York Times*, October 18, 2013, http://www.nytimes.com/2013/10/20/fashion/the -call-of-Cheryl-Strayeds-Wild-on-the-pacific-crest-trail.html?emc=eta1.

15. Henry David Thoreau to Harrison Blake, November 16, 1857, in *The Writings of Henry David Thoreau*, vol. 6 (Boston: Houghton Mifflin, 1906), 321.

16. Hornbein, *Everest: The West Ridge*, 45.

SELECTED BIBLIOGRAPHY

BOOKS

Achey, Jeff, Dudley Chelton, and Bob Godfrey. *Climb! The History of Rock Climbing in Colorado.* Seattle: Mountaineers, 2002.

Ament, Pat. *Wizards of Rock: A History of Free Climbing in America.* Berkeley, CA: Wilderness Press, 2002.

Arce, Gary. *Defying Gravity: High Adventure on Yosemite's Walls.* Berkeley, CA: Wilderness Press, 1996.

Arnold, Jeff. *Albert Ellingwood: Scholar of Summits.* Pueblo, CO: My Friend the Printer, 2010.

Bates, Robert H. *The Love of Mountains Is Best: Climbs and Travels from K2 to Kathmandu.* Portsmouth, NH: Peter E. Randall, 1994.

Bates, Robert H. *Mountain Man: The Story of Belmore Brown, Hunter, Explorer, Artist, Naturalist, and Preserver of Our Northern Wilderness.* Clinton, NJ: Amwell Press, 1988.

Bates, Robert H., and Charles S. Houston. *Five Miles High: The Story of an Attack on the Second Highest Mountain of the World.* New York: Dodd, Mead, 1939.

Beckey, Fred. *Mount McKinley: Icy Crown of North America.* Seattle: Mountaineers, 1999.

Beckey, Fred. *Mountains of North America.* San Francisco: Sierra Club Books, 1982.

Beckey, Fred. *Range of Glaciers: The Exploration and Survey of the Northern Cascade Range.* Portland, OR: Oregon Historical Society, 2003.

Belknap, Jeremy. *Journal of a Tour to the White Mountains in July, 1784.* Boston: Massachusetts Historical Society, 1876.

Bell, John. *On Mount Hood: A Biography of Oregon's Perilous Peak.* Seattle: Sasquatch Books, 2011.

Bensen, Joe. *Souvenirs from High Places: A History of Mountaineering Photography.* Seattle: Mountaineers, 1998.

Betts, Robert B. *Along the Ramparts of the Tetons: The Saga of Jackson Hole, Wyoming.* Boulder: Colorado Associated University Press, 1978.

Birkett, Bill, and Bill Peascod. *Women Climbing: 200 Years of Achievement.* Seattle: Mountaineers, 1990.

Bisharat, Andrew. *Sport Climbing: From Top Rope to Redpoint, Techniques for Climbing Success.* Seattle: Mountaineers, 2009.

Blum, Arlene. *Annapurna: A Woman's Place.* San Francisco: Sierra Club Books, 1980.

Blum, Arlene. *Breaking Trail: A Climbing Life.* New York: Scribner, 2005.

Borneman, Walter R., and Lyndon J. Lampert. *A Climbing Guide to Colorado's Fourteeners.* Boulder, CO: Pruett, 1998.

Brandon, Craig. *Monadnock: More than a Mountain.* Keene, NH: Surrey Cottage Books, 2007.

Brewer, William H. *Up and Down in California in 1860–1864.* Berkeley: University of California Press, 1949.

Brower, David. *For Earth's Sake: The Life and Times of David Brower.* Salt Lake City: Peregrine Smith Books, 1990.

Brown, Rebecca A. *Women on High: Pioneers of Mountaineering.* Boston: Appalachian Mountain Club, 2002.

Browne, Belmore. *The Conquest of Mount McKinley,* 2nd ed. Boston: Houghton Mifflin, 1956.

Bueller, William. *Roof of the Rockies: A History of Colorado Mountaineering,* 3rd ed. Golden: Colorado Mountain Club Press, 2000.

Burdsall, Richard L., and Arthur B. Emmons. *Men against the Clouds: The Conquest of Minya Konka.* New York: Harper & Brothers, 1935.

Cenkl, Pavel. *This Vast Book of Nature: Writing the Landscape of New Hampshire's White Mountains, 1784–1911.* Iowa City: University of Iowa Press, 2006.

Chaffin, Tom. *Pathfinder: John Charles Frémont and the Course of American Empire.* New York: Hill and Wang, 2002.

Chouinard, Yvon. *Let My People Go Surfing: The Education of a Reluctant Businessman.* New York: Penguin Press, 2005.

Clyde, Norman. *Close-ups of the High Sierra.* Glendale, CA: La Siesta Press, 1962.

Cohen, Michael P. *History of the Sierra Club, 1892–1970.* San Francisco: Sierra Club Books, 1988.

Conefrey, Mick, and Tim Jordan. *Mountain Men: A History of the Remarkable Climbers and Determined Eccentrics Who First Scaled the World's Most Famous Peaks.* Cambridge, MA: Da Capo Press, 2001.

Crawford, Lucy. *The History of the White Mountains,* 3rd ed. Portland, ME: Thurston, 1886.

Da Silva, Rachel. *Leading Out: Women Climbers Reaching for the Top.* Berkeley, CA: Seal Press, 1992.

Dean, David. *Breaking Trail: Hudson Stuck of Texas and Alaska.* Athens: Ohio University Press, 1988.

Denny, Glen. *Yosemite in the Sixties.* Santa Barbara, CA: Adler Books/Patagonia, 2007.

Evans, Howard Ensign. *The Natural History of the Long Expedition to the Rocky Mountains, 1819–1820.* New York: Oxford University Press, 1997.

Farquhar, Francis P. *First Ascents in the United States, 1642–1900*. New York: American Alpine Club, 1948.

Farquhar, Francis P. *History of the Sierra Nevada*. Berkeley: University of California Press, 1965.

Ferguson, Gary. *The Great Divide: A Biography of the Rocky Mountains*. Woodstock, VT: Countryman Press, 2006.

Fleming, Fergus. *Killing Dragons: The Conquest of the Alps*. New York: Atlantic Monthly Press, 2000.

Frémont, John C. *The Exploring Expedition to the Rocky Mountains, Oregon and California*. New York: Miller, Orton & Mulligan, 1856.

Frémont, John C. *Narrative of the Exploring Expedition to the Rocky Mountains in the Year 1842 and to Oregon and North California in the Years 1843–44*. New York: Appleton, 1846.

Fryxell, Fritiof. *Mountaineering in the Tetons: The Pioneer Period, 1898–1940*. Jackson, WY: Teton Bookshop, 1978.

Fryxell, Fritiof. *The Teton Peaks and Their Ascents*. Grand Teton National Park, WY: Crandall Studios, 1932.

Gassan, Richard H. *The Birth of American Tourism: New York, the Hudson Valley, and American Culture, 1790–1830*. Amherst: University of Massachusetts Press, 2008.

Goetzmann, William H. *Army Exploration in the American West, 1803–1863*. New Haven, CT: Yale University Press, 1959.

Goetzmann, William H. *Exploration and Empire: The Explorer and the Scientist in the Winning of the American West*. New York: Knopf, 1966.

Goetzmann, William H. *New Lands, New Men: America and the Second Great Age of Discovery*. New York: Viking, 1986.

Gorby, John D. *The Stettner Way: The Life and Climbs of Joe and Paul Stettner*. Golden: Colorado Mountain Club Press, 2003.

Grauer, Jack. *Mount Hood: A Complete History*, 7th ed. Vancouver, WA: Jack Grauer, 2007.

Hansen, Peter. *The Summits of Modern Man: Mountaineering after the Enlightenment*. Cambridge, MA: Harvard University Press, 2013.

Harding, Warren. *Downward Bound: A Mad Guide to Rock Climbing*. New York: Prentice Hall, 1975.

Harris, Matthew L., and Jay H. Buckley. *Zebulon Pike, Thomas Jefferson, and the Opening of the American West*. Norman: University of Oklahoma Press, 2012.

Hill, Lynn. *Climbing Free: My Life in the Vertical World*. New York: Norton, 2002.

Hollon, W. Eugene. *The Lost Pathfinder: Zebulon Montgomery Pike*. Norman: University of Oklahoma Press, 1949.

Hornbein, Thomas F. *Everest: The West Ridge*. San Francisco: Sierra Club Books, 1965.

Houston, Charles S., and Robert M. Bates. *K2: The Savage Mountain*. Guilford, CT: Lyons Press, 2000.

Huber, J. Parker, ed. *Elevating Ourselves: Thoreau on Mountains*. Boston: Houghton Mifflin, 1999.

Huntley, Jen A. *The Making of Yosemite: James Mason Hutchings and the Origins of America's Most Popular National Park*. Lawrence: University of Kansas Press, 2011.

Isserman, Maurice, and Stewart Weaver. *Fallen Giants: A History of Himalayan Mountaineering from the Age of Empire to the Age of Extremes.* New Haven, CT: Yale University Press, 2008.

Jackson, Donald. *Thomas Jefferson and the Rocky Mountains.* Norman: University of Oklahoma Press, 2002.

Jarvis, Kimberley A. *Franconia Notch and the Women Who Saved It.* Durham: University of New Hampshire Press, 2007.

Jenkins, McKay. *The Last Ridge: The Epic Story of the U.S. Army's 10th Mountain Division and the Assault on Hitler's Europe.* New York: Random House, 2003.

Johnson, Christopher. *This Grand & Magnificent Place: The Wilderness Heritage of the White Mountains.* Durham: University of New Hampshire Press, 2006.

Jones, Chris. *Climbing in North America.* Seattle: Mountaineers, 1997.

Jordan, Jennifer. *The Last Man on the Mountain: The Death of an American Adventurer on K2.* New York: Norton, 2010.

Jordan, Jennifer. *Savage Mountain: The True Stories of the First Five Women Who Climbed K2, the World's Most Feared Mountain.* New York: William Morrow, 2005.

Kauffman, Andrew J., and Wiliam L. Putnam. *K2: The 1939 Tragedy.* Seattle: Mountaineers, 1992.

King, Clarence. *Mountaineering in the Sierra Nevada.* Lincoln: University of Nebraska Press, 1997.

King, Thomas Starr. *The White Hills: Their Legends, Landscape and Poetry.* Boston: Crosby and Nichols, 1862.

Lavender, David. *The Rockies.* Lincoln: University of Nebraska Press, 2003.

Lawson, Russell M. *Passaconaway's Realm: Captain John Evans and the Exploration of Mount Washington.* Hanover, NH: University Press of New England, 2002.

MacDonald, Dougald. *Longs Peak: The Story of Colorado's Favorite Fourteener.* Englewood, CO: Westcliffe, 2004.

Mazel, David. *Pioneering Ascents: The Origins of Climbing in America, 1642–1873.* Harrisburg, PA: Stackpole Books, 1991.

McDonald, Bernadette. *Brotherhood of the Rope: The Biography of Charlie Houston.* Seattle: Mountaineers, 2007.

McFarlane, Robert. *Mountains of the Mind.* New York: Pantheon Books, 2003.

McNamara, Chris, and Erik Sloan. *Yosemite Big Walls.* Mill Valley, CA: Supertopo, 2006.

Menard, Andrew. *Sight Unseen: How Frémont's First Expedition Changed the American Landscape.* Lincoln: University of Nebraska Press, 2012.

Miller, Dorcas S. *Adventurous Women: The Inspiring Lives of Nine Early Outdoorswomen.* Boulder, CO: Pruett, 2000.

Molenaar, Dee. *Mountains Don't Care, but We Do: An Early History of Mountaineering Rescue in the Pacific Northwest and the Founding of the Mountain Rescue Association.* Seattle: Mountain Rescue Association, 2009.

Moore, James G. *Exploring the Highest Sierra.* Stanford, CA: Stanford University Press, 2000.

Moore, James G. *King of the 40th Parallel: Discovery in the American West.* Stanford, CA: Stanford University Press, 2006.

Moore, Terris. *Mount McKinley: The Pioneer Climbs*, 2nd ed. Seattle: Mountaineers, 1981.

Myers, Kenneth. *The Catskills: Painters, Writers, and Tourists in the Mountains, 1820–1895*. Yonkers, NY: Hudson River Museum of Westchester, 1988.

Nash, Roderick Frazier. *Wilderness and the American Mind*, 4th ed. New Haven, CT: Yale University Press, 2001.

Neff, John. *Katahdin, an Historic Journey: Legends, Exploration, and Preservation of Maine's Highest Peak*. Boston: Appalachian Mountain Club, 2006.

Nicolson, Marjorie Hope. *Mountain Gloom and Mountain Glory: The Development of the Aesthetics of the Infinite*. Ithaca, NY: Cornell University Press, 1959.

Olds, Elizabeth Fagg. *Women of the Four Winds*. Boston: Houghton Mifflin, 1985.

Ortenburger, Leigh N., and Reynold G. Jackson. *A Climber's Guide to the Teton Range*, 3rd ed. Seattle: Mountaineers, 1996.

Palmer, Howard. *Mountaineering and Exploration in the Selkirks: A Record of Pioneering Work among the Canadian Alps, 1908–1912*. New York: Putnam, 1914.

Patillo, Roger. *The Canadian Rockies: Pioneers, Legends, and True Tales*. Aldergrove, CA: Amberlea Press, 2005.

Peck, Annie Smith. *High Mountain Climbing in Peru and Bolivia: In Search of the Apex of America*. London: Fisher Unwin, 1912.

Perrin, Jim. *Shipton & Tilman: The Great Decade of Himalayan Exploration*. London: Hutchinson, 2013.

Porcella, Stephen, and Cameron M. Burns. *Climbing California's Fourteeners: The Route Guide to the Fifteen Highest Peaks*. Seattle: Mountaineers, 1998.

Putnam, William, ed. *A Century of American Alpinism*. Boulder, CO: American Alpine Club, 2002.

Putnam, William. *The Great Glacier and Its House: The Story of the First Center of Alpinism in North America, 1885–1925*. New York: American Alpine Club, 1982.

Putnam, William. *Green Cognac: The Education of a Mountain Fighter*. New York: AAC Press, 1991.

Rawlings, John. *The Stanford Alpine Club*. Stanford, CA: CSLI Publications, 1999.

Ringholz, Raye C. *On Belay! The Life of Legendary Mountaineer Paul Petzoldt*. Seattle: Mountaineers, 1997.

Robbins, Royal. *Fail Falling*. Ojai, CA: Pink Moment Press, 2010.

Robbins, Royal. *The Golden Age. My Life 3*. California: Royal Robbins Adventures. 2010.

Robbins, Royal. *To Be Brave*. Ojai, CA: Pink Moment Press, 2009.

Roberts, David. *Escape from Lucania: An Epic Story of Survival*. New York: Simon and Schuster, 2007.

Roberts, David. *The Last of His Kind: The Life and Adventures of Bradford Washburn, America's Boldest Mountaineer*. New York: William Morrow, 2009.

Roberts, David. *A Newer World: Kit Carson, John C. Frémont, and the Claiming of the American West*. New York: Touchstone, 2000.

Robertson, Janet. *The Magnificent Mountain Women: Adventures in the Colorado Rockies*. Lincoln: University of Nebraska Press, 2003.

Roper, Steve. *Camp 4: Recollections of a Yosemite Rockclimber*. Seattle: Mountaineers, 1994.

Roper, Steve, and Allen Steck. *Fifty Classic Climbs of North America*. San Francisco: Sierra Club Books, 1979.

Rowell, Galen A., ed. *The Vertical World of Yosemite: Writings on Rock Climbing in Yosemite*. Berkeley, CA: Wilderness Press, 1974.

Schneider, Paul. *The Adirondacks: A History of America's First Wilderness*. New York: Henry Holt, 1997.

Schrepfer, Susan R. *Nature's Altars: Mountains, Gender and American Environmentalism*. Lawrence: University Press of Kansas, 2005.

Schuyler, David. *Sanctified Landscape: Writers, Artists, and the Hudson River Valley, 1820–1909*. Ithaca, NY: Cornell University Press, 2012.

Schwartz, Susan. *JFK's Secret Doctor: The Remarkable Life of Medical Pioneer and Legendary Rock Climber Hans Kraus*. New York: Skyhorse, 2012.

Scott, Chic. *Pushing the Limits: The Story of Canadian Mountaineering*. Calgary, AB: Rocky Mountain Books, 2000.

Scott, Doug. *Big Wall Climbing*. New York: Oxford University Press, 1974.

Selters, Andrew. *Ways to the Sky: A Historical Guide to North American Mountaineering*. Golden, CO: American Alpine Club, 2004.

Sfraga, Michael. *Bradford Washburn: A Life of Exploration*. Corvallis: Oregon State University Press, 2004.

Shelton, Peter. *Climb to Conquer: The Untold Story of World War II's 10th Mountain Division Ski Troops*. New York: Scribner, 2003.

Sherwonit, Bill, ed. *Alaska Ascents: World Class Mountaineers Tell Their Stories*. Anchorage: Alaska Northwest Books, 1996.

Smith, Ian. *Shadow of the Matterhorn: The Life of Edward Whymper*. Hildersley, UK: Carregg, 2011.

Smith, Stephen D., and Mike Dickerman. *The 4000-Footers of the White Mountains*, 2nd ed. Littleton, NH: Bondcliff Books, 2008.

Stewart, Chris, and Mike Torrey, eds. *A Century of Hospitality in High Places: The Appalachian Mountain Club Hut System, 1888–1988*. Boston: Appalachian Mountain Club, 1988.

Stradling, David. *Making Mountains: New York City and the Catskills*. Seattle: University of Washington Press, 2007.

Stuck, Hudson. *The Ascent of Denali: A Narrative of the First Complete Ascent of the Highest Peak in North America*. New York: Charles Scribner's Sons, 1918.

Suiter, John. *Poets on the Peaks: Gary Snyder, Philip Whalen & Jack Kerouac in the North Cascades*. Washington, DC: Counterpoint, 2002.

Tabor, James M. *Forever on the Mountain: The Truth behind One of Mountaineering's Most Controversial and Mysterious Disasters*. New York: Norton, 2008.

Taylor, Joseph E. *Pilgrims of the Vertical: Yosemite Rock Climbers and Nature at Risk*. Cambridge, MA: Harvard University Press, 2010.

Tenderini, Mirella. *Gary Hemming: Beatnik of the Alps*. Glasgow, UK: Ernest Press, 1995.

Thompson, Simon. *Unjustifiable Risk? The Story of British Climbing*. Milnthorpe, UK: Cicerone, 2010.

Thoreau, Henry David. *Thoreau in the Mountains*. With commentary by William Howarth. New York: Farrar, Strauss, Giroux, 1982.

Thorington, J. Monroe. *A Survey of Early American Ascents in the Alps.* New York: American Alpine Club, 1943.

Tilman, H. W. *The Ascent of Nanda Devi.* Cambridge: Cambridge University Press, 1937.

Tilman, H. W. *Nepal Himalaya.* Cambridge: Cambridge University Press, 1952.

Ullman, James Ramsey. *Americans on Everest: The Official Account of the Ascent Led by Norman G. Dyhrenfurth.* Philadelphia: Lippincott, 1964.

Ullman, James Ramsey. *High Conquest: The Story of Mountaineering.* Philadelphia: Lippincott, 1941.

Underhill, Miriam. *Give Me the Hills.* London: Methuen, 1956.

Utley, Robert. *A Life Wild and Perilous: Mountain Men and the Paths to the Pacific.* New York: Holt, 1997.

Walker, Tom. *The Seventy Mile Kid: The Lost Legacy of Harry Karstens and the First Ascent of Mount McKinley.* Seattle: Mountaineers, 2013.

Washburn, Bradford, and Peter Cherici. *The Dishonorable Dr. Cook: Debunking the Notorious McKinley Hoax.* Seattle: Mountaineers, 2001.

Washburn, Bradford, and Lew Freedman. *Bradford Washburn: An Extraordinary Life.* Portland, OR: Westwinds Press, 2005.

Washburn, Bradford, and David Roberts. *Mount McKinley.* New York: Abrams, 1991.

Waterman, Jonathan, ed. *Cloud Dancers: Portraits of North American Mountaineers.* Golden, CO: American Alpine Club, 1993.

Waterman, Jonathan. *High Alaska: A Historical Guide to Denali, Mount Foraker & Mount Hunter.* New York: American Alpine Club, 1996.

Waterman, Jonathan. *In the Shadow of Denali: Life and Death on Alaska's Mount McKinley.* Guilford, CT: Lyons Press, 2010.

Waterman, Laura, and Guy Waterman. *Forest and Crag: A History of Hiking, Trail Blazing and Adventure in the Northeast Mountains.* Boston: Appalachian Mountain Club, 1989.

Waterman, Laura, and Guy Waterman. *Yankee Rock & Ice: A History of Climbing in the Northeastern United States.* Mechanicsburg, PA: Stackpole Books, 2002.

Whittaker, Jim. *A Life on the Edge: Memoirs of Everest and Beyond.* Seattle: Mountaineers, 2000.

Whittaker, Lou, and Andrea Gabbard. *Lou Whittaker: Memoirs of a Mountain Guide.* Seattle: Mountaineers, 1994.

Wilkins, Thurman. *Clarence King: A Biography.* Albuquerque: University of New Mexico Press, 1988.

Wilson, Ken, ed. *The Games Climbers Play.* London: Diadem Books, 1978.

Wolfe, Frederick L. *High Summits: 370 Famous Peak First Ascents.* Englewood, CO: Hugo House, 2013.

Wood, Michael, and Colby Coombs. *Alaska: A Climbing Guide.* Seattle: Mountaineers, 2001.

Woods, Walter A. *A History of Mountaineering in the Saint Elias Mountains.* Scarborough, ON: Yukon Alpine Centennial Expedition, 1967.

Worster, Donald. *A Passion for Nature: The Life of John Muir.* New York: Oxford University Press, 2008.

Worster, Donald. *A River Running West: The Life of John Wesley Powell.* New York: Oxford University Press, 2001.

DISSERTATIONS

Hansen, Peter H. "British Mountaineering, 1850–1914." PhD diss., Harvard University, 1991.

Robinson, Zachary Bass. "'Selected Alpine Climbs': The Struggle for Mountaineering in the Canadian Rockies, 1886–1961." PhD diss., University of Alberta, 2007.

Scialdone-Kimberley, Hannah. "Woman at the Top: Politics and Feminism in the Texts and Life of Annie Smith Peck." PhD diss., Old Dominion University, 2012.

Terrie, Philip Gibson, Jr. "The Adirondacks, from Dismal Wilderness to Forever Wild: A Case Study of American Attitudes toward Wilderness." PhD diss., George Washington University, 1979.

Weiselberg, Erik. "Ascendancy of the Mazamas: Environment, Identity and Mountain Climbing in Oregon, 1870 to 1930." PhD diss., University of Oregon, 1999.

Willen, Matthew S. "Composing Mountaineering: The Personal Narrative and the Production of Knowledge in the Alpine Club of London and the Appalachian Mountain Club, 1858–1900." PhD diss., University of Pittsburgh, 1995.

ILLUSTRATION CREDITS

113 John Wesley Powell: Reprinted with permission of Library of Congress, LC-USZ62-3862.

121 Teddy Roosevelt, 1881: Reprinted with permission of Library of Congress, LC-DIG-PPMS-CA-37586.

127 John Muir: Reprinted with permission of Library of Congress, LC-USZ62-52000.

136 Madison Spring Hut: Reprinted with permission of Appalachian Mountain Club.

140 Charles E. Fay and Canadian Alpine Club: Reprinted with permission of Appalachian Mountain Club.

143 Philip S. Abbot: Reprinted with permission of Appalachian Mountain Club.

149 Climber on Mount Hood: Reprinted with permission of Library of Congress, LC-USZ62-55746.

151 Sierra Club and AMC climb Mount Lyell: Reprinted with permission of Appalachian Mountain Club.

159 Teddy Roosevelt and John Muir: Reprinted with permission of Library of Congress, LC-DIG-PPMSCA-36413.

165 American Alpine Club dinner, 1909: Reprinted with permission of American Alpine Club.

167 Colorado Mountain Club at Mount Copeland: Reprinted with permission of American Alpine Club.

169 Annie Peck: Reprinted with permission of American Alpine Club.

174 Fanny Bullock Workman: Reprinted with permission of Library of Congress, LC-USZ62-108071.

188 Stuck party descending Denali: From Hudson Stuck's expedition account, *The Ascent of Denali* (1918).

193 Albert Ellingwood: Reprinted with permission of American Alpine Club.

195 Automobile passengers enjoying mountain scenery in New Hampshire: Reprinted with permission of Library of Congress, LC-D418-31544.

208 Palisades climbing school: From Glen Dawson Collection.

222 Fritz Wiessner, climbing on Crow's Nest Cliffs: Reprinted with permission of Appalachian Mountain Club.

249 Charlie Houston: Reprinted with permission of the Houston family.

265 Tenth Mountain Division: Reprinted with permission of Denver Public Library, Western History Collection, TMD 71.

290 Houston-Tilman Everest reconnaissance party: Reprinted with permission of American Alpine Club.

300 Fred Beckey: Reprinted with permission of Corey Rich.

309 Tom Frost and Yvon Chouinard: Reprinted with permission of Glen Denny.

326 Warren Harding, Leaning Tower: Reprinted with permission of Glen Denny.

327 Royal Robins and Tom Frost, El Capitan: Reprinted with permission of Glen Denny.

333 Willi Unsoeld and Tom Hornbein, West Ridge: Reprinted with permission of National Geographic Society.

334 Lute Jerstad approaches Everest summit: Reprinted with permission of National Geographic Society.

336 Hut crew members on Mount Washington: Reprinted with permission of Appalachian Mountain Club.

INDEX

Page numbers in *italics* refer to illustrations.